www.wadsworth.com

wadsworth.com is the World Wide Web site for Wadsworth and is your direct source to dozens of online resources.

At *wadsworth.com* you can find out about supplements, demonstration software, and student resources. You can also send email to many of our authors and preview new publications and exciting new technologies.

wadsworth.com
Changing the way the world learns®

A Research Primer for the Helping Professions

METHODS, STATISTICS, AND WRITING

ANDREW L. CHERRY, JR.
Barry University

Brooks/Cole
Thomson Learning™

Australia • Canada • Mexico • Singapore • Spain • United Kingdom • United States

Executive Editor: Lisa Gebo
Assistant Editor: Susan Wilson
Editorial Assistant: JoAnne von Zastrow
Marketing Manager: Caroline Concilla
Signing Representative: Miguel Ortiz
Project Editor: Matt Stevens
Print Buyer: Stacey Weinberger
Permissions Editor: Robert M. Kauser

Production Service: Forbes Mill Press
Text Designer: Adriane Bosworth
Copy Editor: Ardella Crawford
Cover Designer: Ross Carron
Cover Image: © PhotoDisc
Compositor: Forbes Mill Press
Printer: Custom Printing/Von Hoffmann Graphics

For permission to use material from this text, contact us by
    Web: www.thomsonrights.com
    Fax: 1-800-730-2215
    Phone: 1-800-730-2214

Library of Congress
Cataloging-in-Publication Data

Cherry, Andrew L.
    A research primer for the helping professions : methods, statistics, and writing / Andrew L. Cherry.
       p. cm.
    Includes bibliographical references and index.
    ISBN 0-534-35585-4 (acid-free paper)
    1. Social sciences--Research--Methodology. 2. Social service--Research--Methodology. 3. Qualitative research. 4. Statistical analysis. I. Title.

 H62.C374 1999
300'.7'2--dc21
                                    99-055701

For more information, contact
Wadsworth/Thomson Learning
10 Davis Drive
Belmont, CA 94002-3098
USA
www.wadsworth.com

International Headquarters
Thomson Learning
International Division
290 Harbor Drive, 2nd Floor
Stamford, CT 06902-7477
USA

UK/Europe/Middle East/South Africa
Thomson Learning
Berkshire House
168-173 High Holborn
London WC1V 7AA
United Kingdom

Asia
Thomson Learning
60 Albert Street, #15-01
Albert Complex
Singapore 189969

Canada
Nelson/Thomson Learning
1120 Birchmount Road
Toronto, Ontario M1K 5G4
Canada

 This book is printed on acid-free recycled paper.

Contents

Chapter 4

A Model for Conducting Qualitative (Naturalistic) Research in the Helping Professions: Five Phases of a Qualitative Study 48

Chapter 5

A Model for Conducting Quantitative (Statistical) Research in the Helping Professions: Nine (9) Phases of a Quantitative Study 76

Part Three

RESEARCH METHODS FOR HELPING PROFESSIONALS   97

Chapter 6

Single-Subject Research Designs   98

Chapter 7

Techniques for Collecting Your Quantitative (Statistical) Data   115

Chapter 8
The Questionnaire: Scales and Measures   *124*

Part Four

STATISTICS FOR HELPING PROFESSIONALS   133

Chapter 9   *134*
Variables, Data, and Data Organization   *134*

Chapter 10   *139*
The Normal Curve and Levels of Measurement   *139*

Chapter 14

Univariate, Bivariate, and Multivariate Analysis   *171*

Chapter 15

Frequency Distributions   *177*

Chapter 19

Correlation: Measure of Association   *217*

Chapter 20

Regression and Multiple Regression: Establishing Causation   235

Chapter 21

Analysis of Variance (ANOVA, MANOVA, ANCOVA, and MANCOVA): Group Comparisons   254

Chapter 22

Factor Analysis   266

Chapter 23

Discriminant Analysis   275

Chapter 24

Path Analysis   283

Chapter 25

Cluster Analysis   290

About the Author

Dr. Andrew L. Cherry, Jr., has been working in the helping professions since he received his BS degree from Troy State University, Troy, Alabama, in 1969. He received his Masters of Social Work from the University of Alabama and worked as a psychiatric social worker at Bryce Hospital, in Tuscaloosa, Alabama, for 10

years. He received his doctorate from the Columbia University School of Social Work, in New York City.

In addition to teaching research at the master and doctoral level and chairing dissertations at the Barry University School of Social Work, Professor Cherry conducts research and evaluations in the areas of homelessness, addiction, social services to children and families, and the influence of social bonds on human behavior.

Professor Cherry has authored numerous professional journal articles and conference presentations. He is also the author of *The Socialization Instinct: Individual, Family and Social Bonds* (1994) and the co-author of *Social Bonds and Teen Pregnancy* (1992), both published by Praeger Press. He is currently the series advisor for a set of 18 books entitled *A World View of Social Issues*, being published by Greenwood Press.

Dedication

I would like to dedicate this book to Mary, my wife, who read, and reread the manuscript of this book many times, and to the others who read the early versions of this book or parts of the book. No work of this nature is accomplished by one person or at one point in time. I also wish to thank Dr. Mike Connolly, Douglas Rugh, and those with whom I discussed this book when it was a figment of my imagination. Finally, this book is dedicated to the helping professionals whose work and success with their clients I hope will be improved as a result of this book.

Preface

Research and You as a Helping Professional

If you are to work and function effectively as a helping professional in the counseling, social work, and human service fields today, you need to have a basic understanding of the research methods and statistics that helping professionals use, especially those used to measure change. As helping professionals, we need the knowledge and skills in social research to assess, identify, develop, and test interventions to improve the services we offer clients. Managed care also demands that we document effectiveness and show quantitatively that the intervention benefited the client. This is important. Even without pressure from managed care organizations, however, ethical and competent professionals would continue to strive to provide the best available counseling, mental health, and substance abuse treatment services to their clients and the organizations that employ them. Nevertheless, to function as a helping professional, you will need the tools (social research knowledge and skills) to do the job and do it competently.

The helping professions are not the only professions or fields of study where research is considered as a professional tool. For example, in anthropology, education, psychology, sociology, and the allied health fields, developing a workable knowledge of research methods and statistics is an important part of the training and curricula. As a helping professional, you can better assess new information about your specialty if you have a basic understanding of research. In addition, you will better understand research needs in your field.

A helping professional who has no knowledge of social research methods is like a physician who has no knowledge of diagnostic procedures. Perhaps one could do well professionally without this knowledge, but those in both professions would be handicapped in their ability to understand and deal with new problems. As a professional in the human services, you will have more to contribute and will understand more about the people you work with if you possess a basic knowledge of research and apply these skills to your practice.

This book is designed to provide basic knowledge of research methods and statistics for students and professionals in the helping professions. This book is for you if you are—or plan to be—a counselor in the human services, a supervisor in a human service program, a new researcher (or undergraduate or graduate student) in the helping professions, an old researcher, a sporadic researcher, a consumer of human service research, a person who needs a basic reference on social science research, or a doctoral candidate in the helping professions who has completed, *All But the Dissertation* (ABD).

Students and practitioners in the helping professions need research texts that have to-the-point explanations of methods and statistics and that emphasize understanding through application. Research skills are necessary to the helping professional for three reasons:

1. Research methods and models are important tools available for validating our efforts and discoveries. They allow us to use theories and models to develop and extend our knowledge rather than relying on random trial and error.

2. Basic knowledge in research is needed to meet the *Standards of Practice* in the vast majority of professional accrediting and licensing organizations for the helping professions. These professional organizations expect members to use research results in their practice, and some expect members to participate in research.

3. All professional undergraduate and graduate courses of study in the helping professions require the student to take courses in research and statistics.

> This primer will make it easier for you to meet your educational and professional responsibilities and goals.

Acknowledgments

This Primer is the result of the classic struggle of the teacher and the student. The teacher tries to impart knowledge on a subject, and the student tries to understand the content and to differentiate between the teaching style and the important subject matter. I owe a great deal of thanks to my undergraduate, graduate, and doctoral students. The contents of this research primer were tested and validated by students in the classroom. They helped me identify the best approaches for teaching the concepts that are found in the following chapters.

I would like to thank the following reviewers whose suggestions were so valuable:

Ford Brooks, Shippensburg University
W. David Harrison, University of Alabama
Robert Hironimus-Wendt, Millikin University
Baila Miller, Case Western Reserve University
Lois Pierce, University of Missouri, St. Louis
Marshall Smith, Rochester Institute of Technology
Althea Truitt, Benedict College

Introduction

Why You Need This Research Primer

This primer will be a valuable reference book when you need to review or learn about a research method or statistical procedure.

This primer is designed to help students and others in the helping professions who will be practicing in the field, doing research and writing about their work.

But more specifically, I wrote this book for students taking their first course in research for helping professionals because the majority of bachelor, master, and doctoral education programs that train helping professionals require experiential learning activities in their research courses. Many students actually conduct or participate in a research study. However, this type of class assignment creates a problem for both students and teachers because the students are doing two things at once: trying to learn research methods and statistical procedures while trying to do a research study.

You will find this research book to be different from other researcher books.

Most research textbooks for the helping professional are written for the traditional didactic model of teaching. They are **not** written as a source of quick information on research procedures, nor are they written to show one how to do a research study. *Most research texts are written so teachers can teach you about the research process.* This puts the student in the awkward position of having to design a research project before he or she has any idea what it should look like. This book will help alleviate that problem.

This book should be the first one you turn to when you have a research or statistics question. When you need to understand or find information on a research or statistical question, it will get you started. It will help you determine what a journal article is reporting as research methods and statistics. It will be a good reference and companion text to other research methods and statistical texts purchased in the future. This primer can be your starting point when you want to do a research project. The methods and techniques can help you learn more about human behaviors, human processes, human services, and human problems. You will be better able to determine the impact of a new social service, or to measure change using behavioral interventions.

What Is Different about This Research Primer

Fields of practice in the helping professions have expanded and become more specialized since the 1970s. Likewise, research conducted in the human services has become more sophisticated with each passing year. The statistical procedures we use today, thanks to computer technology, are far more sophisticated than those available only a few years ago. Even so, we must still learn the fundamentals; luckily, these fundamentals have not changed much.

To help you with these often intimidating though fundamental subjects, there are sundry books on research methods and statistics. Unfortunately, rather than clarifying the concepts, these texts—with their in-depth treatment of each subject—often leave the reader in a state of shock, frustration and confusion. Such texts often meet one need but create additional problems. **This primer meets the need for a basic social science research text for the helping professional. It is easy to use, has a clear summary overview, and briefly introduces basic research methods and statistical procedures.** This book is designed as a single source for a clear, understandable explanation of research procedures that helping professionals use.

What You Can Expect from This Primer

The two bywords for this primer are *clarity* and *parsimony.*

In this research primer, **only the essential information on each subject is presented.** The extent of the information presented on each subject is limited to what is needed to provide a clear basic understanding. For more in-depth explanation and for reading on related topics, references are provided at the end of each chapter.

Plan and Organization of Primer

This research primer for the helping professional is designed to be a learning tool, as well as a reference book. As a learning tool, the material is presented so that you can walk through each phase of a research project from beginning to end. As a reference book, it gives you easy access to *understandable* explanations of the research methods, statistical terms, and research procedures used by those in the helping professions.

The first chapter is an overview of the scientific method, the standard on which social science research is based. The second chapter reviews the ethical issues related to social research in the helping professions. Chapters in Part II take you through each phase of a qualitative and quantitative research project. You start with problem formation (identifying a problem that can be and needs to be studied) and move through each research phase, ending with data analysis.

Closely examining each phase of a research project has a number of advantages. An overview of the research process will facilitate planning a research study. It will help you identify different research designs, choose an appropriate design for your own research, and help you avoid a number of simple and common mistakes.

After guiding you through a sample qualitative and quantitative research project, the book provides chapters (Part III) on the basic quantitative research methods, including chapters on the most common methods used to conduct human service research. Part IV provides content on major research statistical topics. The final chapter presents an accepted format for writing about the results of a research study for a class paper, dissertation, or professional journal article.

This text is designed to help you navigate through the social science research process.

Each chapter is organized in a similar way. On the first page of each chapter is a brief table of contents for that chapter. The titles of the subtopics vary slightly from chapter to chapter to better fit the material, but in each chapter, the following questions and issues will be presented:

Example of Chapter Table of Contents
- What is Sampling? [or the topic of the chapter]
- How you can use Sampling [or the topic of the chapter]
- Background
- Fundamentals
- Analysis (if appropriate)
- Postscript
- Advanced level materials
- References

Additionally, if the topic is complex, the material is presented at two levels: basic and advanced. The majority of this book is written at the basic level.

The advanced level material uses the typical jargon and vernacular found in most research texts to round out the explanation of complicated material. Advanced level material will be indicated in the text but placed at the end of each chapter.

You do *not* need to read the more advanced level to understand the content in the basic level. I do recommend, however, that you read basic explanations before going to the advanced level material.

You will also find bywords throughout the book that are similar to sound bites. These bywords appear in the margins to help you identify and remember important ideas and issues. Boxes are included in most chapters to present research examples and material to help explain what is being presented.

How to Use This Research Primer for Helping Professionals

After you have read Chapters 1 and 2, you will be introduced to the basic designs for conducting research in the helping professions. Once you have reviewed the research designs available, you will be ready to experience the research process. Chapter 4 will take you through the *five phases* of a qualitative (naturalistic)[1] study, and Chapter 5 will take you through the *nine phases* of a quantitative (statistical) research study. You will approach each *phase* in this experience just as if

---

[1] To help you remember the difference; *Qualitative* is followed by (naturalistic) to indicate this methods reliance on heuristic, phenomenological, ethnographic and field methodologies to describe reality. *Quantitative* is followed by (statistical) to indicate this method's reliance on statistical procedures to describe reality. I hope that this approach will make it easier for you remember the difference.

you were making decisions for doing a research project. Each chapter will contribute to your understanding of empirical research for the helping professions.

The decisions you need to make during each *phase* of research are explained in detail in Chapter 4 and 5. If you choose to conduct a qualitative (naturalistic) study, Chapter 4 provides you with a good model to conduct such a study. Chapter 4 also has information on where to find other models and texts. The rest of this primer will benefit you as a qualitative (naturalistic) researcher because of the comprehendible explanations about quantitative research.

If you choose to conduct a quantitative (statistical) study, the methods and statistics you will need are presented in the remaining chapters in Part III, "Research Methods For Helping Professionals," and in Part IV, "Statistics For Helping Professionals." Parts III and IV cover the vast majority of quantitative (statistical) methods and statistical procedures. The chapters include discussions of statistical procedures and tests that are as simple as frequency distribution and as complicated as discriminate and cluster analysis.

Part V, Chapter 28, contains an outline to help you write a research paper, along with a presentation of the *nine parts* that make up a class research paper, a professional journal article, or a dissertation. Each of the *nine parts* is explained, and you are referred to pertinent chapters in Part III and Part IV that will help you write about your research findings.

Besides being helpful for your research courses, this text will also be useful in your professional practice. The research skills you acquire and the information in this text will help you in your counseling, supervisory, and administrative roles in the helping professions.

INTRODUCTION TO RESEARCH IN THE HELPING PROFESSIONS

Chapter 1

THE NATURE OF SOCIAL RESEARCH IN THE HELPING PROFESSIONS

WHAT IS DIFFERENT ABOUT SOCIAL SCIENCE RESEARCH IN THE HELPING PROFESSIONS?

Considering yourself weak in math or disliking math will NOT prevent you from being a great researcher. Researchers use knowledge, organization, conceptualization, and intuition much more than they use math skills.

Funny you should ask! I have been trying to figure that out for years, and I think I have come up with a fairly understandable answer. Research in the helping professions is social science research that focuses on areas of interest to helping professionals. Social science research involves the application of the scientific approach for analyzing, explaining, and predicting individual and group behavior. It is the approach that helping professionals use to gather reliable knowledge about the human experience. Reliable knowledge is acquired in an objective, logical, and systematic way.

For the student and helping professional, social science research is a source of new information that promotes knowledge development and helps build professional skills. If you are in an education program or if you are already a helping professional, social research has affected and will continue to affect your life as a professional.

SOCIAL SCIENCE RESEARCH SKILLS: A PROFESSIONAL TOOL

As a student and a member of the helping professions, it is important that you understand, evaluate, and develop new knowledge about the services you provide your clients. Research skills will help you in your effort to become a human service professional. Once you begin your career, research skills will help you maintain a high level of professional expertise. These skills are especially important in times when the knowledge base is expanding at a rapid pace.

Basic research skills are viewed as being so important that *almost every national association in the helping professions that accredits educational programs at the bachelor and master education level requires that research education be included in the curriculum.* Accordingly, many of these associations have committees that accredit college curricula, or have educational standards that must be met for a person to be a member of the association. Following are a few of the associations that helping professionals belong to:

- American Association for Counseling and Development
- American Association for Marriage and Family Therapy
- American Counseling Association
- American Mental Health Counseling Association
- American Psychological Association
- American Society of Criminology
- Council on Social Work Education
- National Association of Cognitive-Behavioral Therapists
- National Association of Social Work
- National Association of Black Social Workers
- National Association of Alcoholism & Drug Abuse Counselors

3

1.1   *Fields of Practice*

Although members of several different professional organizations are considered helping professionals, we tend to work with similar client populations. For example, as a helping professional you could work with those in need of the following:

- Addiction treatment and services
- Case management services
- Child development services
- Juvenile services
- Immigrant services
- Individual and family services
- Medical hospital services
- Mental health treatment and services
- School based services
- General human services

Leaders and members of these professional organizations assume that with the knowledge they gain in research courses, helping professionals will be better equipped to provide the best care and services to their clients (see Box 1.1).

USING RESEARCH SKILLS IN YOUR PROFESSIONAL PRACTICE

When you are working as a practitioner in the helping professions, you will be able to use your research skills:

1. To study your caseload using grounded theory
2. To describe your caseload using frequencies and crossbreak tables
3. To improve your grant writing by including tables, graphs and statistics as evidence of need (In grant proposals, statistics are invaluable when showing need, cost versus benefits, the utilization of services, and outcomes.)
4. To enhance quarterly and year-end reports to funders by adding tables, graphs, and statistics about the clients you serve and the outcomes from the services clients receive.

As helping professionals, we can better serve our clients when we have basic research knowledge and skills that help us document and analyze the services we are providing.

Your clients might need your research skills. Your research skills could be important for maintaining and/or enhancing client services.

Your job might depend on your research skills. Staff members might lose their jobs if you are unable to show that clients need your services and that the services are beneficial and cost effective. If you lose your job because you cannot show a need or positive outcomes, future services to your clients could be lost.

Hypothesis: A statement declaring a new relationship between two or more variables or conditions. What we expect to occur if specific concepts and relationships are true and accurate.

Reliability: That quality of a measurement method suggesting that the same data would be collected each time in repeated observations of the same phenomenon. In other words, the reliability of a measure or a scale depends on its ability to produce consistent results each time it is used.

Validity: Term describing a measure that accurately reflects the concept it is intended to measure. For example, your IQ would seem a more valid measure or your intelligence than would the number of hours you spend in the library.

Your agency might depend on your research skills. Your agency might need your research skills to fulfill a service grant. Such grants are often lost because of poor reporting of services and a failure to keep appropriate client statistics. The loss of a grant could result in the agency's having fewer financial resources to provide a needed service.

BACKGROUND—THE SCIENTIFIC METHOD AND SOCIAL SERVICE RESEARCH

To best help our clients, we must possess a practice knowledge that is grounded in reality (ontology). The question is, how do we recognize knowledge that is grounded in reality (epistemology) (Kuhn, 1970)?

The foundation of knowledge and skills in the helping professions has, for the most part, been developed using the five general strategies listed here, which assist in confirming or disproving our perceptions of reality. With the exception of the scientific method, you have already used these strategies to test what you think is *real* and what you think is *not real.*

1. Intuition/Common Sense— "It just seems right." "It seems to make sense."
2. Tradition—Culturally accepted knowledge about the workings of the world.
3. Authority—Accepting information as knowledge because of the status of the discoverer.
4. Logic—The use of philosophical reasoning to determine reality—inductive and deductive reasoning.
5. The Scientific Method—This is the core of the scientific approach. The scientific method is concerned with the cause of specific problems, the data related to problems, and the inferences from the data. *Social science research is based on the scientific method.*

The *scientific method* is a way to do scientific research that helps you avoid the mistakes that cause erroneous research findings. It is an accepted approach by the scientific community for doing social and human research (see Advanced Level 1.1 p. 17).

⇨ **Advanced Level**
see page 17

A Brief History of Social Research

The history of social research can be broken into three broad historical periods. The beginning phase of social research (around the beginning of the twentieth century) was characterized by the development and attention to mass social reform. In the second phase (starting in the 1930s), social research of all kinds lost its effectiveness and credibility. The present phase (starting in the 1970s) is characterized by looking for new models of social research that can accommodate our professional commitment to the development of knowledge and social justice.

The Beginning Phase   The tradition of social research in the United States began with the large-scale social reform movements that took place in this country during the first 30 years of the twentieth century. Sociologists and social workers conducted research intended to help bring about social change, and in many cases it did.

These social researchers were inspired by the success and social reform resulting from social surveys conducted in London, England, by Charles Booth (1840–1916) and later in the United States by Paul U. Kellogg (1879–1958). Kellogg replicated Booth's London survey in Pittsburgh (1906 to 1914). The statistics they collected and disseminated on income, crime, disease, and other social maladies were powerful and brought about numerous social reforms. The success of the community social survey stimulated the "survey movement" and early social research (Polansky, 1975).

The settlement house surveys, which were far less encompassing than the larger community surveys, were motivated by direct contact and a one-to-one familiarity with the people who lived in the communities around the settlement houses. The settlement house surveys like the larger community surveys were helpful (if not instrumental) in promoting social reforms in such areas as child welfare, labor, and sanitation (Tyson, 1995).

The Middle Phase   By the 1930s, however, the survey movement had lost its impact and credibility. It was easy to demonstrate for the umpteenth time that all sorts of social problems tended to be concentrated in the same "part of town" (Polansky, 1975; p. 11). Even more problematic was the attitude, "Let's get the facts and do something about them" (Polansky, 1975; p. 10).

During this period, social service research was stagnant, and it lost much, if not all, of its previous status. Researchers in other fields, such as psychology and the behavioral sciences, were using the "scientific method" and were beginning to produce knowledge and theory grounded in the logical consistency of the new science (Polansky, 1975). By the late 1940s, Alfred Kahn and others, in what became known as the Social Work Research Group, were calling for a model of social research that would embrace social science theory. They proposed the use of the scientific method (an empirical model) in the development and validation of knowledge (Maas, 1966).

This model did not exclude case studies, a major source of knowledge in the helping professions. Nonetheless, it obliged social researchers to conduct their inquiry in a scientific way, which meant a value-free or neutral way. One of the primary tasks of the social researcher under this rubric is to observe facts without letting one's bias influence the findings.

The Current Phase   Since the 1970s, there have been three major influences on research in the human services: (1) managed care, (2) program evaluation, and (3) the postpositivism movement.

1. *Managed care organizations,* such as Health Maintenance Organizations (HMOs), demand accountability. They pay only for psychosocial or behavioral interventions that can show effectiveness. For human service workers, this means being able to show that the intervention used with an individual has had a positive effect on his or her problem. One approach acceptable to

---

1.2   *Documenting Treatment Effectiveness per HMO*

Counselors treating clients for depression and/or anxiety can use reliable and valid psychometric scales to measure the degree of severity of these disorders. By measuring depression and/or anxiety before, during, and after treatment, the clinician can show HMO representatives whether or not the counseling they paid for is helping or was beneficial to the client, family, or group.

---

managed care organizations is the "single subject design." As presented in Chapter 6, the single subject design can monitor the impact of a planned intervention on one individual, one family, one group, or even one organization. (See Box 1.2.)

2. *Evaluating social programs* has also had a major impact on human service research. The demand by funders that human service programs be evaluated has influenced the way human services are provided. Even so, as a workable component of human service programs, program evaluation is still in the developmental stage. Although most human services funders require an evaluation of the programs they fund, typically the approach to evaluating the program either is not specified or is so vague that it is of little use in determining effectiveness. This situation will not be true in the future. Funders and human service providers are learning better approaches and are refining evaluation procedures.

Evaluation designs are typically a combination of compatible research methods. The methods often used in evaluation research are addressed in Parts III and IV of this primer. (See Box 1.3.)

Two primary types of program evaluations are typically used to evaluate social programs: the *process evaluation* and the *outcome evaluation* (see Box 1.4).

- *Process Evaluation.* The process evaluation is a description of the intervention, target population, and staff of a social service project from the inception of the program. Such an evaluation will answer the question, *"What services are actually delivered?"* The process evaluation will clearly and comprehensively document the relationship of the resources and program activities to the project objectives to permit any adjustments needed to optimize project implementation and ultimate replication.

- *Outcome Evaluation.* The outcome evaluation plan should have sufficient rigor to permit drawing valid conclusions concerning the effectiveness of the various intervention strategies. The purpose of the outcome evaluation is to demonstrate the extent to which the intervention(s) affected those involved in the social service project. Outcome indices should be

---

1.3   *A Program Evaluation Using Compatible Research Methods*

The following is an example of combining compatible research methods in a program evaluation. A fairly standard and effective program evaluation design was used in 1994 to evaluate the effectiveness of a family builders program. The program provided case management services to prevent, if possible children's removal from their homes by the state child-protection agency. Evaluating and determining the effectiveness of the program would involve using an evaluation design that employed several different research methodologies.

In this type of program evaluation, you would gather data from clients, the clients' worker(s), supervisors, administrators, records, and databases. You would use insights from the interviews, results of psychosocial scales, and information from a measure of client satisfaction as your data. You would be looking for information to describe how services were delivered and how they were accepted. You would also be looking for information on outcomes and the effectiveness of the services provided.

---

selected to match the measurable objectives of the project. This part of the evaluation answers the questions: *Do the interventions make a difference?* and *What interventions work best?*

3. *The postpositive movement* is affecting research in the helping professions. Its focus on the advantages of qualitative (naturalistic) research has helped clarify some of the limitations of quantitative (statistical) research.

   The postpositive movement grew rapidly throughout the 1990s (see Chapters 3 and 4 for more detail about postpositive perceptions and qualitative methodology). Members of the postpositive movement maintained that there has been an over-reliance on statistical studies. They argue that statistical studies have limited use in the analysis of human processes. They point out that statistical methods are poorly suited for studying some aspects of human processes, like family life. See Box 1.5.

   Their dissatisfaction with the findings from statistical investigations will no doubt continue to influence scientific research in the helping professions. Using both statistical data and observational data collected by trained investigators can only improve our research efforts. The postpositivists also have a point about what is considered "scientific." This issue is part of a larger modern critique of scientific "truth," the influence of the scientific method, and its European traditions and history.

1.4   *Two Evaluation Studies*

An Evaluation of the Effectiveness of Head Start: There are several well-known evaluation studies that have helped shape current program evaluations. The expensive Westinghouse study of Head Start used a large nationwide sample to evaluate the effect of Head Start on the low-income children it served as compared with middle-class children who did not attend Head Start. This study found that the children attending Head Start did do better in the first grade than children not attending Head Start, but the study showed little impact on their learning in the second grade. Because of this finding, other studies of Head Start were conducted with the finding that gains made by the Head Start children lasted over several grades. These replicated findings proved useful when social programs were challenged during the Reagan administration. Although a large number of social programs were cut or discontinued, Head Start because—of the evaluation evidence showing its effectiveness—was left intact (Gustavsson & Segal, 1994; Chambers, Wedel & Rodwell, 1992, pp. 4–7).

An Evaluation of a Guaranteed Annual Income Program: Another major study devised to test economic theory in a social setting was the evaluation of the "guaranteed annual income" programs. The economic theory tested suggested that people would work less if they were given a guaranteed income. This experiment, which ran for ten years during the 1960s and 1970s, was carried out in several cities around the United States (e.g., Denver, New Jersey, Seattle) (Skidmore, 1975).

There were seven experimental groups and one control group. Each group's level of guaran-teed income was varied in relationship to the level of poverty, with several groups guaranteed income equal to the poverty level. One group received 125% of the poverty level, while two groups received less than the poverty level. Their guaranteed income levels were 75% and 50% of the poverty level.

The belief to be tested was that the amounts of benefits were an important determinant in the "labor-leisure choice." "When faced with a choice of spending time earning money or being at leisure, what determines the choice?" (Chambers, 1995, p. 829).

Although the findings must be interpreted with caution (Aaron, 1975), they suggest that the guaranteed annual income had little effect on the productivity of the primary wage earners. Overall, the primary wage earner reduced the weekly hours worked by 6% to 7%. Single mothers, the primary wage earners, reduced their hours worked by only 2%. Interestingly, secondary wage earners (female spouses with children, for the most part) reduced the hours they worked by 17%. It was speculated that mothers with young children chose to stay home when the family income was ensured.

What this experiment suggested is that welfare benefits themselves do not destroy work incentives. Consequently, in the 1970s the Nixon Administration supported a "negative income tax" proposal. The negative income tax was viewed as a way to fold all social welfare benefits into one easy-to-manage benefit. This proposal failed to become law by a single vote (Chambers, 1995, pp. 829–831; Chambers, Wedel & Rodwell, 1992, p. 13).

1.5 *Needs of Caregiver of AIDS Patients*

Using analyst-constructed categories with case study observations, Matocha (1992) identified five categories of need that caregivers of people with AIDS have in common. The five categories of "observed recurring events" are as follows:

1. Physical effects: During the period when the person with AIDS was newly diagnosed, caregivers tended to experience a deterioration of physical health.
2. Psychological effects: The psychological well being of the caregivers deteriorated. They experienced increased stress from attempting to cope with the diagnosis. They felt alone. They thought about the future demands of providing care. They thought about the person's death and about life without the person.
3. Social effects: Caregivers often experienced social isolation.
4. Economic effects: The economic effects on the caregivers were minimal.
5. Spiritual effects: Spiritual strength was defined as hope and emotional strength. The spiritual strength of the caregiver increased as the health of the person with AIDS improved. Spiritual strength decreased when the health of the AIDS patient deteriorated.

FUNDAMENTALS OF THE SCIENTIFIC METHOD

The qualitative (naturalistic) approaches come from the phenomenological perspective and research traditions, while the quantitative (statistical) methodologies come from the traditions of the scientific method. Although the two traditions have different orientations, proponents of both approaches support assumptions that promote rigor and accuracy. Both groups agree that if the research is not conducted in a rigorous way, the findings could be flawed and inaccurate. Flawed research findings are of no use to helping professionals.

The scientific method can be described as "an objective, systematic method of analysis of phenomena devised to permit the accumulation of reliable knowledge" (Sedlack & Stanley, 1992). Generally, it involves the formulation of a hypothesis concerning a phenomenon, the observation of the phenomenon, tests to demonstrate the truth or falseness of the hypothesis, and a conclusion that validates or modifies the hypotheses.

The definition above sets up a strict standard for calling a research study "scientific." When a quantitative (statistical) research study meets these standards, the findings might explain and predict social and human events. The quantitative (statistical) approaches presented in this primer meet these standards.

ASSUMPTIONS OF THE SCIENTIFIC METHOD

A number of assumptions are necessary to meet the demands for scientific rigor required by the scientific method. The ten important assumptions that follow will help illustrate the rigor of the scientific method as it applies to research in the helping professions.

1. Principle of Objectivity: Social science professionals develop the ability to examine facts impartially. They also delay judgement about their activities, observations, and conclusions.
2. Principle of Consistency: Social science professionals believe that the functioning of the universe is not erratic, but that it is understandable in terms of consistent laws. For example, when two sets of conditions are the same, the same consequences may be expected to occur.
3. Principle of Tentativeness: Social science professionals do not consider generalizations as conclusive, and they are willing to modify them if the generalizations are contradicted by new facts.
4. Principle of Causality: Social science professionals believe that every phenomenon results from a discoverable cause.
5. Principle of Parsimony: Social science professionals select simple and widely applicable explanations of phenomena. They attempt to reduce their picture of the world to simple and clear terms. The simplest answer that accounts for the most known facts is the best answer.
6. Principle of Practicality: Social science professionals expect that in any situation involving competition among elements that vary in effectiveness, for example, behaviors, those that work best under the existing conditions (whether considered to be good or bad behaviors) will tend to survive and perpetuate themselves.
7. Principle of Dynamism: Social science professionals expect nature to be dynamic rather than static and to show variation and change.
8. Principle of Relativeness: Social science professionals think of their universe as sets of relative relationships rather than as absolutes.
9. Principle of Continuous Discovery: Social science professionals believe that it will be possible to go on learning more and more about the material universe of which they study.
10. Principle of Social Limitation: Social science professionals realize that their social framework might impact and limit the kinds of problems on which data are collected. They also recognize that bias and social influences might be reflected in their findings.

THREE LEVELS OF RESEARCH IN THE HELPING PROFESSIONS

Research most often cited in the helping professions is conducted on one of three levels. The three levels can be thought of as hierarchical. The *exploratory* level is the ground level that produces a broad picture. Exploratory procedures can also

1.6   *The Homeless Studies in the Early 1990s*

A good example of how different levels of research can provide a clearer picture of a social phenomenon is found in studies conducted to understand homelessness in the late 1980s and early 1990s. Exploratory, descriptive and explanatory research approaches were used to increase our knowledge and understanding of homeless people in general. Moreover, without basic information about the numbers of needy homeless people and about the services needed, it was difficult for government and traditional social service agencies to respond to the needs of the homeless.

By the late 1980s, the homeless phenomenon was obvious to more than just human service workers. The number of homeless people had grown alarmingly in the cities, where the homeless tended to concentrate by downtown businesses and around public buildings. This made it difficult for the local governments to ignore the homeless.

In 1987 in Miami/Dade County, Florida, a tax evasion trail ended in the conviction of a prominent businessman. As part of his sentence, he was to perform several hundred hours of public service. To fulfill his duty, he learned about the homeless. He also had to pay to have a wide ranging study conducted to learn as much as possible about the homeless in South Florida.

The study was broken down into six independent sub-studies. Study 1, a field study using qualitative (naturalistic) research methods, examined several individual homeless people living in street. Study 2 collected data from open-ended interviews with providers of homeless services. Study 3 collected data from open-ended interviews with political and community leaders. Study 4 was an epidemiological study that counted and provided descriptive data about the homeless. Study 5 documented the incident rate of mental illness among the homeless. Finally, study 6 measured the harm done to the children of the homeless.

give a detailed part of the larger picture. The *descriptive* level is the middle level; it produces a clearer picture of a group as a whole or a composite picture. The *explanatory* level is the upper level; it explains cause and effect.

We decide on which level to conduct our research based on what is already known about a topic. For example, how much do we know about processes that affect the lives of our clients? If we know very little about our clients, we will use an exploratory approach. If we already know a good bit about our clients, however, we might attempt to explain some part of the processes by using an explanatory research approach. See Box 1.6 for an example of a research study.

Exploratory Research

The exploratory approach is very useful when we know little about a new phenomenon or a group of people that begin to emerge with similar human service needs. Exploratory research gives us a broad picture of what is going on. In the case of the homeless studies mentioned in Box 1.6, the exploratory research helped put faces on the homeless people living on the streets of Miami, Florida. It brought to life their struggle, and it helped explain the circumstances that resulted in their living on the streets. Most often, this approach is qualitative (naturalistic) [see Chapter 3 for an overview of the qualitative (naturalistic) methodologies and Chapter 4 for more detail]. The exploratory level is not used to collect data for sophisticated statistics analysis.

Descriptive Research

The next level is descriptive research. The descriptive approach produces a clearer picture of a group as a whole or produces a composite picture. In the homeless studies, we selected several descriptive methods to ensure collecting objective information on the demographic and descriptive variables found among the homeless. Descriptive research often takes the form of a survey. It is useful for describing the characteristics of a group or the extent of general or specific conditions. Surveys can be used to gather large amounts of data from individuals, records, etc.

The descriptive information collected on the homeless in South Florida consisted of a fairly accurate count of the homeless in the community and a picture of the population based on data from closed-ended questions.

Information gained from descriptive research is like your impressions of a picture where you can make out the individuals but the details are still not very clear. You try to look closer at a certain area of the photograph (explanatory research). Yet, the closer you look at one area, the more the rest of the picture blurs.

Explanatory Research

Explanatory research answers questions about cause and effect. This type of information allows us some ability to predict events. Quantitative (statistical) research approaches are used to predict events (see Chapter 3 for a brief overview of the quantitative approaches and Chapter 5 for more detail). Quantitative approaches use statistical procedures that have been adopted to help determine causation or the effect of events. The quantitative approach adheres to the principles of the scientific method. Explanatory research begins with a hypothesis, followed by the gathering of data, which are then used to test the hypothesis statistically.

In the homeless studies, the effect of homelessness on child development was studied. Homeless children were compared to children of similar gender, race, economic background, and other pertinent characteristics of children who had not experienced homelessness. The study attempted to determine if any child developmental problems were caused by the child's being homeless.

CULTURAL, ETHNIC, AND GENDER SENSITIVE RESEARCH

One of the primary purposes for doing research in the helping professions is to give practitioners another view of reality. An accurate picture of reality can assist you in providing better services to your clients (individuals, groups and organizations). The important term here is "reality." It is impossible to conduct a research study in the helping professions that truly reflects "reality" (the characteristics of a population, the events, the process, etc.) if we are not *sensitive to racial and ethnic, cultural and gender differences.* Ignoring these differences and the oppression experienced by members of some groups has produced biased research that has harmed and continues to harm members of *racial, ethnic and minority groups, and women in general.*

Being sensitive to differences in the people you serve and wish to describe objectively is also a requirement of scientific research. According to accepted scientific research standards, if you use a sample—for example, to describe your agencies' client population—the people you describe are expected to be representative of the people served by the agency. The degree of representativeness tells us to what degree your sample is like the population as a whole.

THE INFLUENCE OF RACE, ETHNICITY, CULTURE, AND GENDER ON PERCEPTION

The literature and research on the differences in *cultural perspective* and its impact on attitudes and behavior has been growing over the last 30 years. These studies have clearly pointed out that there is a strong relationship between behavior and culture, values, beliefs, and traditions. Furthermore, we find that a group's cultural beliefs affect the group's behavior and the behavior of each individual in the group.

Attention to cultural factors can change perceptions, research questions, and evaluations. These factors can elucidate the multi-dimensionality of individual and group behavior.

Culture acts as a filtering system that shapes one's perception of experiences and environments. Because cultures influence our perceptions of the world, our perceptions vary according to our cultural group.

To recognize how cultural and ethnic differences alter individual behavior, we must avoid global assessments and measures of behavior. Different sociocultural and gender worldviews among the people we work with can affect the way they understand, use, and evaluate the services and information we as helping professionals provide. Whether or not a client uses your services as a helping professional depends to a great extent on how well you understand the worldview of your client.

Examples of How Race, Ethnicity, and Culture Impact the Helping Professions

A great deal of research has been conducted to aid understanding of the different perceptions among racial and ethnic groups. How people view human services and social research plays a major role in how the services are received and used. The perceptions of human services and the negative impact of poorly conceived human service programs on the lives of the people being served are ongoing concerns among helping professionals. The findings from these types of studies are not

---

1.7   *Disturbing Differences*

In 1991, the percentage of addiction and dependency among adult Americans who were white, African American, and Latino was the same (Anthony & Helzer, 1991).

In 1993, African Americans were found to be twice as likely as whites to have high blood pressure. Even more disturbing, African Americans were seven times more likely than whites to experience severe hypertension (Leary, 1993).

In 1995, the risk of AIDS among Latino men was more than twice that among non-Latino white men (Popple & Leighninger, 1996).

In 1995, the risk of AIDS among African American men was four times higher than that among white men (Popple & Leighninger, 1996).

---

attempts to stereotype ethnic and racial groups but are intended to identify their unique differences.

When people seek out services from helping professionals, they expect the helpers to be aware that some of their strengths and tensions are related to the racial, ethnic, and cultural aspect of their lives (Devore & Schlesinger, 1991). As responsible professionals, we are obligated to be sensitive to these governing factors and the effect they may have on the services we provide. (See Box 1.7.)

Unlike common stereotypes used to denigrate a group (which are often made up of untested "truths" and often involve an underlying political agenda), the descriptions below have increased our understanding and appreciation of human differences and diversity.

- *Ethnicity:* Definitions of ethnic groups tend to include the elements of history, culture, and other shared experiences or some combination of these characteristics (Alba, 1985).
- *Ethnicity and Culture:* As members of racial, ethnic and cultural groups, people experience an essential bond to others that have a common history. Ethnicity and culture are two of the components that shape an individual's perception of an experience. Other components are race, social class, minority status, education, etc. (Brookins, 1993).
- *Biculturalism:* People in minority groups generally function in two different cultures, a minority and a majority culture. The different cultures might require different behaviors to cope and survive (Ho, 1987).
- *Social Class and Ethnicity:* Devore and Schlesinger (1991) suggest that the intersection of social class and ethnic identity is for that person or group "ethnic reality."

1.8   *Gender Issues*

Gender issues bring together situations that structure the relationship between women and men. Hooyman (1994) describes three frameworks often used to examine women's affairs:

1. *Women's Issues:* Using this framework, independent attention is devoted to comprehending the distinct issues that pertain to women.

2. *Nonsexist Perspectives:* Based on this perspective, many of the "problems experienced by women are rooted in and influenced by societal expectations of women . . ." (p. 321).

3. *The Feminist Perspective:* This perspective proposes that social reality is formed by the male viewpoint, a perspective recognized as androcentricity (man as norm).

GENDER DIFFERENCES

Add to the *cultural perspective* the differences in gender and we are closing in on the "person-in-environment" (Karis & Wandrei, 1995). Although the reasons for differences between males and females have been debated down through the centuries, there is little dispute that observable and measurable differences exist. Men and women differ in the way they communicate and behave.

Biological theories view the differences as innate. Psychological theories propose that the differences result from cognitive stages of development and reinforcement procedures. Sociologists view the differences as being similar to cross-cultural differences related to sociolinguistic sub-cultures' having learned different rules for engaging in and interpreting conversations. Highly formalized female and male sub-cultures are especially apparent in places like the Middle East where men and women are more segregated than in the West.

A few of the differences noted in North American culture is that men use less eye contact. Women ask more questions and tend to maintain the conversation. Women tend to initiate topics of conversations, while men tend to control the topic. Men tend to talk more than women do and tend to interrupt more. Women tend to engage in more self-disclosure (Buechier, 1990; Goldberg & Kremen, 1990; Hooyman, 1994).

See Box 1.8 for three frameworks for studying the relationship between men and women.

HOMOSEXUALITY

The oppression of racial, ethnic and cultural groups, and females is closely linked to the oppression of gays and lesbians. Sexual orientation is a critical issue that influences the life experiences of all individuals (Newman, 1994). How an individual deals with the treatment of the dominant society at various phases of life becomes an important issue in counseling and in providing human services (Ashford, Lecroy, & Lortie, 1997).

Language shapes thought.

POSTSCRIPT

Research in the helping professions can provide information and knowledge that has made and continues to make a difference in the lives of the people we serve. Both benefits and limitations are inherent in social science research. One of the primary restraints and controls on research with human subjects is the professional code of ethics of the researchers. Ethics, the subject of Chapter 2, needs to be taken into consideration before any research project with human subjects is started.

ADVANCED LEVEL MATERIAL

Advanced Level 1.1

The *scientific method,* as it is known, is a rigorous, reliable and valid approach for testing hypotheses. It requires that you clearly state what you think to be *real.* Then it requires you to test your assumptions (hypotheses) about reality. At the same time it requires that you control biases (conscious or unconscious) so that biases do not change the outcome of the test of your assumptions (hypotheses) (see the section "Fundamentals of the Scientific Method," presented in this chapter.

REFERENCES

Aaron, H. J. (1975). Cautionary notes on the experiment. In J. A. Pechman & P. M. Timpane (Eds.), *Work incentives and income guarantees* (pp. 168–189). Washington, D.C.: Brookings.

Alba, R. D. (1985). *Italian-Americans: Into the twilight of ethnicity.* Englewood Cliffs, NJ: Prentice Hall.

Anthony, J. C., & Helzer, J. E. (1991). Syndromes of drug abuse and dependence. In L. N. Robin & D. A. Regier (Eds.), *Psychiatric disorders in America: The epidemiologic catchment area study* (pp. 116–154). New York: Free Press.

Ashford, J. B., Lecroy, C. W., & Lortie, K. L. (1997). *Human behavior in the social environment: A multidimensional perspective.* Pacific Grove, CA: Brooks/Cole.

Brookins, G. K. (1993). Culture, ethnicity and bicultural competence: Implications for children with chronic illness and disability. *Pediatrics, 91,* 1056–1062.

Buechier, S. (1990). *Women's movement in the United States.* New Brunswick, NJ: Rutgers University.

Chambers, D. E. (1995). Economic Analysis. In L. R. Edwards (Ed.), *Encyclopedia of social work* (pp. 829–831). Washington, D.C.: NASW.

Chambers, D. E., Wedel, K. R., & Rodwell, M. K. (1992). *Evaluating Social Programs.* Boston: Allyn & Bacon.

Devore, W., & Schlesinger, E. G. (1991). *Ethnic-sensitive social work practice* (3rd ed.). New York: Macmillan.

Goldberg, G. S., & Kremen, E. (1990). *The feminization of poverty: Only in America?* New York: Praeger.

Gustavsson, N. S., & Segal, E. A. (1994). *Critical issues in child welfare.* Thousand Oaks, CA: Sage.

Ho, M. K. (1987). *Family therapy with ethnic minorities.* Newbury Park, CA: Sage.

Hooyman, N. R. (1994). Diversity and population at risk: Women. In F. Reamer (Ed.), *The foundations of social work knowledge.* New York: Columbia University Press.

Karis, J. M., & Wandrei, K. E. (1995). Person-in-environment. In L. R. Edwards (Ed.), *Encyclopedia of social work* (19th ed. pp. 1818–1827). Washington, D.C.: NASW.

Kuhn, T. S. (1970). The structure of scientific revolutions (2nd ed.). Chicago: University of Chicago Press.

Leary, W. E. (1993, October 22). Black hypertension may reflect other ills. *New York Times,* p. B6.

Maas, H. S. (1966). *Five fields of social service: Review of research.* New York: National Association of Social Work.

Matocha, L. (1992). Case study interviews: Care for persons with AIDS. In J. Gilgun, K. Daily, & G. Handel (Eds.), *Qualitative methods in family research* (pp. 66–84). Newbury Park, CA: Sage.

Newman, B. S. (1994). Diversity and populations at risk: gays and lesbians. In F. Reamer (Ed.), *The foundations of social work knowledge.* New York: Columbia University Press.

Polansky, N. A. (1975). *Social work research* (2nd ed.). Chicago: University of Chicago Press.

Popple, P. R., & Leighninger, L. (1996). *Social work, social welfare, and American society.* Boston: Allyn & Bacon.

Sedlack, R. G., & Stanley, J., (1992). *Social research: theory and method.* Boston: Allyn & Bacon.

Skidmore, F. (1975). Operational design of the experiment. In J. A. Pechman & P. M. Timpane (Eds.), *Work incentives and income guarantees* (pp. 168–189). Washington, D.C.: Brookings.

Tyson, K. (1995). *New foundations for scientific social and behavioral research.* Boston: Allyn & Bacon.

SOCIAL SCIENCE RESEARCH ETHICS AND THE HELPING PROFESSIONAL

WHAT ARE SOCIAL SCIENCE RESEARCH ETHICS AND HOW DO THEY APPLY TO HELPING PROFESSIONALS?

As helping professionals, we might be from different fields of the social sciences, receive radically different training, belong to different professional associations, or work with different groups of people. Nonetheless, our various professional *codes of ethics* inform us that if we wish to be called professionals, we are ethically obligated to protect the rights and well-being of those we serve.

To some extent, we are able to protect our clients by observing the ethical standards of the professional associations to which we belong. The same is true when you are working as a researcher in the helping professions. If you are trained as a social worker and if you conduct research as a member of the National Association of Social Workers (NASW), you are required to follow the Social Work Code of Ethics. If doing research as a member of the American Counseling Association (ACA), you are required to follow the ACA code of ethics while conducting your research. The same is true for psychologists and sociologists.

Fortunately, the ethical codes of all of the helping professional associations are similar. They are based on the results of ethical dilemmas that have been debated over the years, and resulting legal decisions.

> Ethics emerge from value conflicts among those in a profession. These conflicts are expressed in discussions and decisions that relate to individual rights. For example, when conducting a research study the researcher tries to minimize the risk to individual rights. However, there is a conflict between a person's right to privacy versus the researchers need to know. Researchers must try to minimize risks to participants, colleagues, and society while attempting to maximize a quality of information they produce. (Gillespie, 1995, p. 884)

In addition to learning about social research, another way to prepare yourself for a career in the helping professions is to learn about the application of professional ethics in your chosen profession. Dealing with ethical dilemmas is exponentially more complex than one thinks when beginning a career in the helping professions.

Among helping professional associations, ethical standards have been adopted that cover the professions' particular fields of study and practice. Even so, these codes of ethics are similar for each professional organization. When we conduct research the **code of ethics supported by our professional association is our guide in the effort to develop accurate, verifiable knowledge without violating the rights and well-being of those who participate in our research.**

BACKGROUND ON THE DEVELOPMENT OF ETHICS IN THE HELPING PROFESSIONS

Moral principles and values are the foundation of a complex society. One must deal with not just one value system, but with numerous ones that sometimes overlap and compete, using slightly different principals and ethical standards. Both the reform efforts and criticism described in Box 2.1 were guided by accepted (although competing) ethics and values.

> ### 2.1   *An Example of Competing Ethical Values*

The Personal Responsibility and Work Opportunity Act of 1996 was much different in focus and intent from the 1964 Economic Opportunity Act passed during President Lyndon Johnson's Administration. The Economic Opportunity Act was the centerpiece in President Johnson's War on Poverty. Many social conservatives regarded Lyndon Johnson's Personal Responsibility and Work Opportunity Act, designed to abolish poverty in the United States, as naive in its conception (many do not believe that poverty can be abolished) and unhelpful for the people it was intended to serve.

With similar resolution, many in the helping professions view the Personal Responsibility and Work Opportunity Act of 1996 as mean spirited and harmful to the people whose lives the Act would change. For instance, based on the Personal Responsibility and Work Opportunity Act of 1996, a 1998 provision of the Temporary Assistance to Needy Families Federal Block Grant seemed especially harsh. One of the more severe provisions of that Block Grant stipulated that single parents (typically women) who were on public assistance would either be employed

or in a "Welfare-to-work" program within two years. If not, in most cases they would lose their cash assistance (Ewalt & Mulroy, 1997).

Social libertarians were opposed to the Personal Responsibility and Work Opportunity Act. For this group, the Act did not address issues like the number of entry-level jobs needed by the single parents losing their welfare or the need for affordable and adequate housing of these working poor.

An entry-level job is defined by the Federal Government as a job that pays minimum wage. The Federal Government considers housing affordable if it costs no more than 30% of the household income.

Based on the above standards and on the fact that many of the single parents going off welfare would earn minimum wage, DeParle (1996) calculated the funds a single-parent family would have for housing. He made the point that a single parent working full-time at minimum wage would have approximately $250 a month for rent and utilities. At that time (in 1996) 5 million families were paying more than 30% of the family income for rent and utilities.

A BRIEF ACCOUNT OF ETHICS IN THE HELPING PROFESSIONS

The concept of professional ethics has a long history. Some forms of professional standards existed verbally even before the Hippocratic Oath. Different codes of honor—like those in government, the military, and religious orders—were imposed on members of those organizations down through the centuries. Nonetheless, not until the Nuremberg trials in 1946 revealed the outrageous, depraved, and inhuman Nazi medical research did *written* ethical standards become the norm for professional associations. The requiring of ethical standards by the Nuremberg Code (which were based on the prosecution and the defense of

2.2   A Personal Experience

The effect on the lives of the African American men in the Tuskegee syphilis study was devastating. In the late 1970s at a mental hospital where I worked, I cared for a man in his mid-50s who had been a "subject" in the Tuskegee syphilis study. As a result of Public Health researchers' withholding treatment for syphilis, he suffered severe brain damage from the infection and had to be hospitalized. He was so brain damaged that he was unable to communicate and to care for himself. He would follow simple instructions, but he never responded in any other way to those around him. His family visited him often, but he was unable to respond to their attention and affection. He never improved and died in the late 1970s.

Nazis on trial) was an effort to prevent the recurrence of the pain, injury, disability, and death caused by the Nazi medical experiments during the Holocaust (Chambers, Wedel & Rodwell, 1992; Faden & Beauchamp, 1986).

Although the Nuremberg Code was written to guide medical and human research in the civilized world, it did not stop unethical medical research in the United States and other countries. For instance, the ethical standards that grew out of the Nuremberg Code did not prevent the United States Military from conducting unethical research using LSD on unsuspecting soldiers in the 1950s (Brecher, 1972).

Nor did the Nuremberg Code stop the U.S. Public Health Service from continuing to fund the Tuskegee Syphilis Study for approximately 50 years. The study, begun in 1932, ended because of U.S. Senate hearings in the mid-1970s.

In this study, researchers working for the Federal Public Health Service promised treatment for syphilis to hundreds of African American men in Tuskegee, Alabama. In reality, the researchers were studying the effects of syphilis when it is left untreated, and they never intended to treat the men. They continued this experiment even after penicillin was found to cure syphilis (Jones, 1981). (See Box 2.2.)

UNETHICAL SCIENTIFIC RESEARCH

Numerous unethical scientific research projects have been undertaken since the writing of the Nuremberg Code. In the United States for example, "the Office of Scientific Integrity Review of the National Institutes of Health had investigated 174 allegations of scientific misconduct" by 1991 (Baker, 1994, p. 77). What's more, we must expect that unethical research will continue to be proposed and conducted.

2.3   *Is Participation Truly Voluntary?*

A major tenet of social science research is that participation in a research study must be voluntary—that is, no one should be forced to participate in a research study. How often is participation truly voluntary? Take, for instance, an instructor of a class on social policy asking students to fill out a questionnaire that he or she hopes to analyze and publish. Students should always be told and assured that their participation in such a survey is completely voluntary. Even so, some students may fear that nonparticipation will somehow influence their class grade.

Consequently, there will always be a need for helping professionals committed to upholding professional ethics. Such professionals serve on human subjects research review committees, often referred to as Institutional Review Boards. This type of committee is formed at the institutional level to review research proposals. Its purpose is to ensure that proposed research meets ethical and legal standards, especially when humans are involved as participants. For more information on the Institutional Review Board, see the section under this heading later in this chapter.

SEVEN ETHICAL ISSUES

Significant changes have occurred in the helping professions over the last 100 years, with the organization of many new associations. Each of the helping professions has parts of its code of ethics that are specific to its professional field of interest. Nevertheless, there is a set of values and ethics central to all helping professional associations; thus, all codes of ethics in the helping professions address the following legal and ethical issues related to research.

1. Voluntary Participation

No matter how careful we are, if our research involves humans, we are intruding into their lives. Human service research often asks people to reveal personal information about themselves, even information that they might have kept from their friends and associates. (See Box 2.3.)

2. No Harm to the Participants

A research study should never cause injury to the people being studied, even if they volunteered to participate in the study. Revealing personal information collected on a survey is a clear example of how a participant could be harmed. Revealing

2.4   *Technology and Confidentiality*

Today and in the near future, *technology* will be a source of many ethical dilemmas in providing human services. Given the current problems in protecting individual privacy, we only expect that maintaining individual privacy will become more difficult and complicated. Manning (1997) suggests that transformations in health care and social welfare institutions are occurring rapidly. "Technology can offer opportunities for treat- ment, choice, and the potential for longer life, but also can bring profound ethical dilemmas about access to and refusal of services and informed consent" (p. 223). Access to technol- ogy and control of the results of technology can create ethical dilemmas. For example, when one counsels people who are HIV positive, is it pos- sible to control access to their personal informa- tion when it is entered into an agency database?

information that participants might have kept confidential and that would embar- rass or endanger a participant is clearly a violation of ethical standards.

3. Protection of Participants

One of the primary concerns in social research is the protection of the participant's interests and well being. This is typically thought of as protecting the participant's identity, especially in survey research. This protection is usually provided in one of two ways: anonymity or confidentiality. Although very different, they are often confused.

4. Anonymity

If a researcher cannot identify participants in the research effort, then the partici- pant is considered anonymous. An example is a mail survey where there is no way to connect any of the participants with the questionnaire they filled out. In this sit- uation, the participants are anonymous.

5. Confidentiality

A research study where the primary researcher is able to identify a given partic- ipant's responses but promises not to do so is an example of confidentiality. In a face-to-face interview survey, for instance, the interviewer could make public a respondent's self-diagnosis even if the respondent was assured that this would not be done. Personal information revealed under the promise of confidentiality to a principal researcher or the assistant(s) should be protected by that promise. (See Box 2.4.)

6. Deceiving Subjects

Deceiving participants is unethical, but in some social research studies, deception is involved. For example, some researchers admit that they are doing research but fudge about why they are doing it or for whom. Any deception, no matter how insignificant it may seem, needs to be justified by compelling scientific or administrative concerns. Even so, the approach should be questioned and the justification argued.

7. Right to Receive Services versus Responsibility to Evaluate Service Effectiveness

By and large, the codes of ethics of most professional associations do *not* suggest that clients have a right to receive safe and effective—empirically validated—treatment. Even if the ethical codes did require safe and effective interventions, however, would it be possible to evaluate the effectiveness of interventions both *ethically* and *empirically?*

There are many ethical questions to tackle when you set out to evaluate the effectiveness of an intervention used by helping professionals. For example, if the researcher chooses a methodology that tests the experimental services by withholding services from people placed in a control group, you face an ethical dilemma, *the right of clients in need of services to receive services.*

This dilemma addresses the question about the long-term benefits. Do the long-term benefits outweigh the costs to people in the experiment (benefits vs. cost)? Even if the research helps verify the value of the intervention, is it ever justified to withhold (or delay) educational, medical, or social services from clients placed in a control group? (See Box 2.5.)

Two Values in Conflict: The Experimental Design

Of all the approaches that have been used to treat specific phobia, empirical evidence suggests that Systematic Desensitization is the most effective (Myers & Thyer, 1997; Wolpe, 1990). This is not to say that there might not be good untested treatments, but Systematic Desensitization was tested and was found effective.

On the one hand, let us say that in your practice you choose to use Insight Therapy to treat a person distressed by social phobia. You decide to use Insight Therapy because you are not trained in Systematic Desensitization. If you are aware that little empirical data (qualitative and quantitative) supports the effectiveness of Insight Therapy in the treatment of specific phobia, your decision is unethical (Myers & Thyer, 1997).

It is an unethical decision because there is a question as to whether or not you are meeting your professional obligation to provide the best treatment to your client. It would be ethical to refer the person to a therapist who is trained in Systematic Desensitization and who could treat social phobia.

On the other hand, if you wish to test the effectiveness of Insight Therapy versus Systematic Desensitization with people who are distressed by social phobia,

2.5   *Ethics of Withholding Services*

In 1982 a large-scale study, the Physician's Health Study, was begun. Its purpose was to evaluate the role of aspirin in preventing death from cardiovascular disease. Some 22,000 doctors in the United States took part in the study. It was a double-blind study, where the participants were assigned to the aspirin group or assigned to a placebo group. Each person in the aspirin group took 325 milligrams of aspirin every other day. A 325 milligram aspirin is like the regular strength aspirin you buy over the counter at any store.

Although the study had been planned to continue to 1990, it was discontinued in 1988 because of the "extreme beneficial effects." The data revealed that physicians who were taking an aspirin every other day had 47% fewer heat attacks than physicians taking a placebo (Hennekens et al., 1988).

THE ETHICAL DILEMMAS

What are the ethics involved in stopping a research study? It did solve one dilemma, the problem of withholding beneficial services from the placebo group, but it did not help the physicians who had been taking a placebo and who

suffered a heart attack during the study. Nor did it help the physicians who suffered strokes because of taking an aspirin every other day. The physicians had a 15% increase in the risk of stroke when taking aspirin.

Of course, when the study began, there was the chance that taking an aspirin every other day could increase the number of heart attacks but it did not. It did, however, slightly increase the risk of stroke.

What are the ethics of stopping the study before the researchers had the information necessary to make the best decision about who should use aspirin and who should not use aspirin? A lot of doctors were put at risk and some died, thinking the intent of the research was to determine the role aspirin played as a prevention for heart attacks. It met its goal in some ways but the study was stopped before it was clear, for example, who should take aspirin and who is put at greater risk of having a stroke when taking aspirin. This creates another ethical dilemma. By stopping the study early and not meeting their goals, did the researchers fulfill their implied promise to the 22,000 physicians who participated in this study?

An ethical dilemma is a problem because there is no clear or easy way to determine the correct course of action. If we knew the ethical answer, it would not be an ethical dilemma.

you have to ask the same question. If you place people distressed by social phobia in the experimental group, are they receiving the best treatment?

The impact on your clients as a practitioner will be the same as the impact on the people in your research experimental group. Why would you as a practitioner be considered unethical, while as a researcher you could be considered ethical? The difference hinges on the fact that the public and the professional organizations demand that clinicians use effective interventions when treating clients.

2.6   *Legal Decisions on Valid Consent*

Early legal decisions regarding disclosure of information to patients maintained that valid consent was based on the "reasonable physician"(*Salgo v. Stanford University Board of Trustees,* 1957)— that is, information that the average, reasonable physician felt was adequate and appropriate for a patient to make a decision about whether to consent to any given treatment. In the United States and Canada, this standard was later replaced by the "reasonable patient" standard (*Canterbury v. Spence,* 1972; *Hopp v. Lepp,* 1980). Disclosure now must include all information that an objective, reasonable person in a patient's situation would consider important in reaching a decision to accept or refuse the proposed treatment, including all material risks of that treatment, and the risks of available options (Regehr & Antle, 1997, p. 302).

Confidentiality: You cannot promise anonymity if you know who the person is. In such cases, you can promise confidentiality.

Anonymity: If you and others cannot identify the person participating in the research study under any circumstance, you can promise anonymity.

Confidentiality versus Anonymity

It is incumbent upon the researcher to maintain the participant's confidentiality and to safeguard the information collected on each person. In the Statement of Informed Consent, a clear promise should be made to the participants stating that their identity will remain confidential.

THE ISSUE OF INFORMED CONSENT

Requiring researchers in the helping professions to obtain Informed Consent from people participating in their research studies is not a straightforward solution for ensuring that the ethical conditions delineated above will be followed. Tyson (1995) and many other authors have pointed out that the "power differential between professionals (practitioners or researchers) and clients" (p. 227) can compromise the client's freedom to evaluate and to reject a request to participate in a research study. The client's motive for requesting help and the mental distress of the problems they face may reduce their ability to make informed decisions (Heatherington, Friedlander, & Johnson, 1989). The question of informed consent is especially problematic when the participants in the research study are young children or people requiring medical or psychological treatment and having no alternative treatment resources (Munir & Earls, 1992). (See Box 2.6.)

OBTAINING INFORMED CONSENT

Information collected from individuals who agree to participate in your research study can be highly sensitive. As a result, you have an ethical and legal obligation to fully inform the person about how you intend to use the information they are divulging to you.

If you plan to interview people for your study, I suggest that you ask the participants to sign a "statement of informed consent." Furthermore, if you tape record the interviews, the explanation of "informed consent" by the research interviewer and the participant's agreeing to participate in the "research interview" should be a part of the total recorded interview.

If your data gathering approach calls for collecting field observations, it might not be practical or advisable in some cases to ask for signed consents—for instance, in observing the behavior between drug addicts and criminals. Obtaining consent in such instances could put the researcher in danger. At minimum, the validity of the observations would be threatened because of the likelihood that "giving consent" would influence the behavior of those being observed.

GUIDELINES FOR DEFINING INFORMED CONSENT

To obtain "informed consent" the participant must be given, at least, the following information:

1. A description of the study
2. What the participant will be asked to do
3. How long it will take
4. The risks involved in participating in the study
5. That participants can withdraw at anytime without penalty
6. The consent form signed by each participant should contain the name and telephone number of a person to contact if the participant has any questions about his or her participation in the study
7. Each participant should be given a copy of the consent he or she signed.

The following is an example of a consent form that was used in a research project. This consent form was approved by an Institutional Review Board. The following is an "Informed Consent Statement" that describes the relationship between the participant and the researcher.

EXAMPLES OF AN INFORMED CONSENT DOCUMENT

The informed consent statement should be in a language that the participants can understand. The wording needs to be clear and understandable. It is a contract that you make with the person who agrees to participate in the study. Figures 2.1

FIGURE **2.1**

STATEMENT OF INFORMED CONSENT FOR PARENT/GUARDIAN OF PARTICIPANT

Dear Parent/Guardian:

My name is Name of Researcher; as a graduate student at Barry University School of Social Work, I am requesting permission for your child to participate in a research study. I am conducting a study on cognitive development and sexual activity between two groups of Black adolescent females. The specific aim of the study is to identify social psychological variables that influence sexual behaviors among Black adolescent females. The information obtained from the study will be useful to the field of social work.

If you should decide to allow your child to participate in this study, please be advised of the following:

- Your child will be considered a participant in the research study and asked to complete the survey.
- It will take approximately one hour and thirty minutes for your child to complete the survey.
- Participation in the research study is voluntary. Your child may decline or discontinue participation at any time during the study without any negative consequences.
- Your child will not be asked to give her name or any information that could identify who she is.
- Any published results of the research study will refer to group averages only. Your child's name will not be included in the study.
- The survey completed by your child will be kept in a locked file cabinet.
- Participation in the research study may stimulate your child to examine her thoughts and feelings. A video that will provide positive encouragement and reinforcement of the belief in her capacity for positive change and successful life outcomes will be shown to her immediately after completion of survey by research staff.
- Upon completion of the research study, the results will be provided to you if you request them.

I am available to answer any questions you may have regarding the research study. My telephone number and that of my supervisor are provided below.

If you are satisfied with the information provided and are willing to have your child participate in this research study, please sign the enclosed Parent/Guardian Consent Form. Please have your child return the Participant's Assent Form, along with the Parent/Guardian Consent Form, to her primary care counselor in the enclosed envelope. Thank you.

Sincerely,

Name of Researcher

Researcher

Telephone: (000) 000–0000

Andrew L. Cherry, DSW, ACSW
Professor
Barry University
Telephone: (305) 899–3902

Parent/Guardian Consent Form

I acknowledge that I have been informed of the nature and purpose of this research by Name of Researcher, that I have read and understood the information presented and that I have received a copy of the Parent/Guardian Consent letter and the Participant's Assent letter for my records. I give consent for my child to participate in this study.

_____   _____

Parent/Guardian Consent   Date

FIGURE **2.2**

STATEMENT OF INFORMED CONSENT FOR TEEN PARTICIPANT

Dear Prospective Participant:

My name is <u>Name of Researcher</u>; as a graduate student at Barry University School of Social Work, I am requesting that you participate in a research study. I am conducting a study on cognitive development and sexual activity between two groups of Black adolescent females. The specific aim of the study is to identify social psychological variables that influence sexual behaviors among Black adolescent females. The information obtained from the study will be useful to the field of social work.

If you should decide to participate in this study, please be advised of the following:
- You will be considered a participant in the research study and asked to complete the survey.
- It will take approximately one hour and thirty minutes for you to complete the survey.
- Participation in the research study is voluntary. You may decline or discontinue participation at any time during the study without any negative consequences.
- You will not be asked to give your name or any information that could identify who you are.
- Any published results of the research study will refer to group averages only. Your name will not be included in the study.
- The survey you complete will be kept in a locked file cabinet.
- Participation in the research study may stimulate you to examine your thoughts and feelings. A video that will provide positive encouragement and reinforcement of the belief in your capacity for positive change and successful life outcomes will be shown to you immediately after completion of survey by research staff.
- Upon completion of the research study, the results will be provided to you if you request them.

I am available to answer any questions that you may have regarding the research study. My telephone number and that of my supervisor are provided below.

If you are satisfied with the information provided and are willing to participate in this research study, please sign the enclosed Participant's Assent Form. Please return the Participant's Assent Form, along with the Parent/Guardian Consent Form, to your primary care counselor in the enclosed envelope. Thank you.

Sincerely,

Name of Researcher

Researcher

Telephone: (000) 000–0000

Andrew L. Cherry, DSW, ACSW
Professor
Barry University
Telephone: (305) 899–3902

Participant's Assent Form

I acknowledge that I have been informed of the nature and purpose of this research by <u>Name of Researcher,</u> that I have read and understood the information presented and that I have received a copy of the Child's Assent letter for my records. I give assent to participate in this study.

_____   _____
Participant   Date

and 2.2 are examples of informed consents used in a study of pregnant and never-pregnant teens (Croskey, 1999).

Two consent forms were used. One consent form was signed by the parents of the teen participants. The other was signed by the teenager who participated in the study. The forms are similar to each other.

THE INSTITUTIONAL REVIEW BOARD

Before you start a research project, check to see if your school or institution has an Institutional Review Board that serves to protect human subjects. You might be required to submit a proposal of your research project to the committee for ethical review.

Most educational and medical facilities, especially research facilities have developed what is often called an Institutional Review Board. These oversight committees were originally called Human Subject Committees. These boards or committees are typically made up of a group of professionals from different fields within and without the institution. The members review potential research projects with the purpose and duty of protecting the people participating. A committee similar to an Institutional Review Board is required for federal research and research for many states and foundations.

POSTSCRIPT

As researchers in the helping professions, we must follow the code of ethics of the professional associations to which we belong. These ethical codes are similar to one another in terms of protecting the rights and well-being of the people who participate in our research.

Even with the principals and ethics as guides, dilemmas continue to arise in both practice and research. On the one hand, we are expected to provide the best services available. On the other hand, we are expected to evaluate the services by withholding from a control group an experimental intervention that might help the very people to whom we pledged to do no harm.

One of the ways in which we as helping professionals can meet our ethical obligations to provide safe and effective—empirically validated treatment—is to develop our research skills. In Chapters 4 and 5, you will find an *overview* of the steps involved in doing a research study in the helping professions. These *phases* are presented as a guide for planning and conducting a research study. Once you have an idea of what you will be doing on a research project, you can use the following chapters to design your research study and to choose the statistical procedures to analyze the data you collect.

REFERENCES

Baker, T. L. (1994). *Doing social research* (2nd ed.). New York: McGraw-Hill.
Brecher, E. M. (1972). *Licit & illicit drugs*. Boston: Little, Brown.

Canterbury v. Spence, 464 F. 2d 772 (D.C. Cir. 1972).

Chambers, D. E., Wedel, K. R., & Rodwell, M. K. (1992). *Evaluating social programs.* Boston: Allyn & Bacon.

Croskey, L. (Spring 1999). *An analysis of personal psychological and cognitive factors between pregnant and/or parenting and never pregnant black adolescent females.* Barry University School of Social Work, Miami Shores, FL. Available from University Microfilm International, Mich.

DeParle, J. (1996, October 20). Slamming the door: The low-wage jobs of the new economy cannot pay the rent. *New York Times.* [Sunday Edition], p. 6–52.

Ewalt, P. L., & Mulroy, E. A. (1997). Locked out: Welfare reform, housing reform, and the fate of affordable housing. (Editorial) *Social Work, 42*(1), 5–6.

Faden, R. R., & Beauchamp, T. L. (1986). *A history and theory of informed consent.* New York: Oxford University Press.

Gillespie, D. (1995). Ethical issues in research. In L. R. Edwards (Ed.), *Encyclopedia of social work* (19th ed., p. 884). Washington, D.C.: NASW.

Heatherington, L., Friedlander, M. L., & Johnson, W. F. (1989). Informed consent in family therapy research: Ethical dilemmas and practical problems. *Journal of Family Psychology, 2,* 373, 385.

Hennenkens, C. H., and members of the Steering Committee of Physicians' Health Study Research Group. (1989). Final report on the aspirin component of the ongoing physicians' health study. *New England Journal of Medicine, 321*(3), 129–135.

Hopp v. Lepp, 112 D. L. R. 3d 67 (1980).

Jones, J. (1981). *Bad blood: The Tuskegee syphilis experiment.* New York: Free Press.

Manning, S. S. (1997). The social worker as a moral citizen. *Social Work, 42*(3), 223–230.

Munir, K., & Earls, F. (1992). Ethical principals governing research in child and adolescent psychiatry. *Journal of the American Academy of Child and Adolescent Psychiatry, 31*(3), 408–414.

Myers, L. L., & Thyer, B. A. (1997). Should social work clients have the right to effective treatment? *Social Work, 42*(3), 288–298.

Regehr, C., & Antle, B. (1997). Coercive influences: Informed consent in court-mandated social work practice. *Social Work, 42*(3), 300–306.

Salgo v. Stanford University Board of Trustees, 317 P. 2d 170 (1957).

Tyson, K. (1995). *New foundations for scientific social and behavioral research: The heuristic paradigm.* Boston: Allyn & Bacon.

Wolpe, J. (1990). *Practice of behavior therapy* (4th ed.). New York: Pergamon.

PART two

CONDUCTING A RESEARCH STUDY IN THE HELPING PROFESSIONS

Chapter 3

DESIGNING A RESEARCH STUDY IN THE HELPING PROFESSIONS

DOING RESEARCH IN THE HELPING PROFESSIONS

In the helping professions, research is most often guided by questions about phenomena or events occurring among the people we service. Because scientists or practitioners from different helping professions sometimes work in the same field of human study, their research efforts overlap. (See Box 3.1.)

Unlike psychologists and sociologists, however, most people in the helping professions do not do a lot of *pure scientific research.* Pure scientific research often deals with phenomena that has little application to our day-to-day world. Although the findings from pure science might be very beneficial in the future as a building block of knowledge, they might have little use in the present. An example might be the sighting of a new meteorite. It is interesting, but in and of itself, it does not help me understand the makeup of the universe.

In the helping professions, we are more likely to wonder about how people are affected by the services we provide or about the living conditions of a specific group of people. In the case of human behavior, we are always trying to understand why one person behaves one way in a situation while another person behaves differently in the same situation. (See Box 3.2.)

RESEARCH AS AN ORDERLY PROCESS

Conducting research in the helping professions is an orderly process. The research procedures most often used by today's helping professional have five generally accepted components:

1. Identifying a phenomenon you need to learn more about. Deciding on whether you will use a qualitative (naturalistic) approach, or a quantitative (statistical) approach
2. Selecting the parameters of the study—a part of a qualitative (naturalistic) approach; or formulating a hypothesis—a part of a quantitative (statistical) approach
3. Collecting data
4. Analyzing the data
5. Generating a theory about recurrent themes and patterns in qualitative (naturalistic) data—a part of a qualitative (naturalistic) research outcome; or confirming/disconfirming a hypothesis—a quantitative (statistical) research outcome.

RECOGNIZING AND DEFINING CLINICAL ISSUES OR AREAS OF INQUIRY REQUIRE CRITICAL THINKING SKILLS

There is a broad need for continuous research in the helping professions concerning the effectiveness of interventions and the needs of those we service. This type of research is often conducted by the scientific practitioner—a clinical person who

---

3.1   *Many Different Professionals Might Work with One Client*

Research efforts among the helping professionals overlap because although we have a general professional focus, we also have a field of interest and study.

For instance, you might be a crisis counselor interested in the addictions field. When you work as a counselor at a comprehensive addiction treatment center, you find that you work with social workers, mental health and family counselors, psychologists, and medical and psychiatric staff. You also find out very

quickly that as professionals they or their colleagues are engaged in addiction research.

It is common to find a social worker conducting biofeedback experiments with addicts (in the past this was generally considered the domain of the psychologist). Or a mental health counselor might be studying the characteristics of single mother households of addicted women without family support that were serviced by her agency (in the past this was generally considered the domain of the sociologist).

---

is also trained in basic scientific thinking and the application of social science research methodologies to their research questions.

Critical or scientific thinking is a skill that all counselors must develop to maximize their effectiveness. Critical thinking skills are essential for processing information you gather about your clients and for determining the effectiveness of your interventions (Heppner, Kivlighan, & Wampold, 1992). The cognitive process used by the effective counselor is not selective or biased in the information collected about clients because one does not gather information to confirm beliefs or to discount information contrary to one's beliefs. Scientific thinking will help us in our clinical efforts to evaluate the effectiveness of human service interventions "more objectively and with less personal or subjective bias" (Heppner, Kivlighan, & Wampold, 1992, p. 20).

Identifying, refining, and stating the hypothesis takes skill but these skills are transferable. Thus, it does not matter in what context you learn them; the important thing is that you learn them, whether in a research class or in a practice class. These skills will be essential to you as a clinician and a researcher in the helping professions. In Chapter 5, in the section called "Phase 1: Selecting a Manageable Research Project," there are some helpful tips on developing a research topic.

The Role of the Literature Review

Once you have identified a possible research question, it is important to become knowledgeable about any previous research done on the topic. This is where the literature review is important. The social science literature review has three primary roles: (1) to educate you about previous research on the topic, (2) to lay out

| 3.2 | *Asking a Research Question* |

Research in the helping professions typically starts with a question. In 1988, few services were provided to the homeless, although the numbers of homeless seemed to be growing. Local governments did not want to get involved providing money or services to the homeless because they disputed the number of homeless people in their communities. The homeless providers in South Florida were claiming that 20,000 to 30,000 homeless people were living in the streets of South Florida. The local governments claimed that fewer than 5,000 people were homeless in South Florida and that the majority of those were "snowbirds." ("Snowbirds" are tourists and homeless people from the north who live in Florida only during the winter.) Without accurate numbers, the local government leaders argued that they had no idea what services to provide the homeless. They maintained that the variation in the estimate of the number of homeless, from 5,000 to 30,000, made it impossible for them to plan and provide effective services.

One way to move the debate from arguing about how many homeless were in South Florida was to go out into the community and count them. Hence, my research question became, "Who are the homeless, and how many are living in South Florida streets?" Although it is a good sounding research question, how do you count people who have no home? This was a major research design problem that had to be overcome. Once fairly accurate numbers were provided to both sides, however, the debate moved from questions about how many homeless there were to how best to provide services to the 10,000 homeless living in South Florida in 1989. Almost 85% were from South Florida, so very few could be considered "snowbirds."

the rationale for the research study, and (3) to help formulate and refine the research questions and hypotheses. References should be included only if they add to the research question or the method being considered. "The framework for the rationale [of a research study] is built through the logical interconnectedness of empirical results and theory that leads to a critical unanswered question" (Heppner, Kivlighan, & Wampold, 1992, p. 378).

Using a Computer to Search the Literature

Today few people conduct a literature review without using computer databases. On-line databases are available from many libraries and from commercial sources on the World Wide Web. These central databases provide many thousands of references and abstracts of journal articles, books, dissertations, government records, newspapers and other materials. A number are available for research in the helping professions. Some of the important databases are *The Psychological Abstracts, Sociological Abstracts, Social Work Abstracts, Educational Resources Information Center, Medline,* and *The Dissertation Abstract International.* These databases (and others) can be found online in all university libraries and in most public libraries. Computer-generated searches can be done in minutes. The output of references and abstracts can be printed out on paper or downloaded to a disk.

In Chapter 5, in the section called "Phase 2: Conducting the Literature Review," there are some helpful tips on doing a literature review.

FORMULATING A HYPOTHESIS

Although not as commonly used in qualitative (naturalistic) research as in quantitative (statistical) research, research hypotheses are declarative statements that tentatively answer questions about the empirical relationships between the independent and dependent variables or that predict outcomes. They are considered tentative answers because hypotheses can be tested empirically to verify or disprove the stated relationships.

Common Characteristics of Good Hypotheses

Nachmias & Nachmias (1987) suggest that all good hypotheses have four common characteristics: they are "clear, value-free, specific and can be empirically tested using available methods" (p. 65).

Hypotheses Must Be Clear   It is important that the hypotheses define the expected relationships among the variables as well as the circumstances under which the relations are expected to be evident. Precision in defining the relationships identified in the hypothesis is required so that reliable and valid observations can be made and the hypothesis test can be replicated.

Hypotheses Must Be Value Free   Although this is more difficult than once believed, a researcher's biases, and subjective preference should not influence the formulation of the hypothesis. The hypothesis should be based on objective observations, data, previous research, and practice experiences.

Hypotheses Must Be Specific   The hypothesis must be specific; it must propose that an association, relationship, or difference exists among variables, or that change in one variable predicts change in a different variable. The strength of the association/relationship between two quantitative variables can be determined using statistical tests (chi-square, correlations, t-tests, and so on) that are discussed in Part IV of this primer.

The direction of the relationship among the variables is also important. The direction of the relationship among sets of variables can be positive or inverse (negative). An example of a positive relationship between four variables would be, "As poverty increases, suicide, addiction, and crime increase." An example of an inverse (negative) relationship would be, "The more education a person has, the less likely he or she is to participate in crime, to become addicted, or to commit suicide."

Variable: The logical grouping of characteristics such as gender. For example, gender is made up of the attributes of female and male.

Independent Variables: These are thought to cause or to determine change in the characteristics of a *dependent variable*. For example, when you pay your bills (an independent variable), the money you have in the bank (the dependent variable) goes down.

Dependent Variables: The dependent variable is the variable that is affected or changed by the *independent variable*. For example, if the average student's level of education is dependent in part on family income, then family income is an independent variable, and of course, the average student's level of education is the dependent variable.

Intervening Variables: An intervening variable (B) is a variable that exists between an independent variable (A) and a dependent variable (C). Consequently, the independent variable (A) affects the dependent variable (C) only by affecting the intervening variable (B) and the intervening variable (B) affects the dependent variable (C).

Hypothesis: A statement about the nature of things typically based on theory. It is a testable statement about the relationship between two or more variables.

Research Question: A question about a problem or condition that is NOT based on any theoretical framework, such as asking young women without college plans and who score in the upper quartile on the SAT why they do not plan to attend college.

A research question or hypothesis does NOT have to be complicated to be a good research question or hypothesis.

Hypotheses Must Be Testable Using Available Methods   Although a hypothesis might have merit in the helping professions, if no method is available to test it, the hypothesis has little utility. It cannot be used to explain relationships among variables nor as a means of predicting events.

You Can Use a Hypothesis or a Research Question

Though you can use either a hypothesis or a research question to guide your research efforts, there is more than a semantic difference in these two terms. ***Hypotheses*** are statements based on theoretical assumptions about the impact of specific conditions. In the helping professions, we often think of the conditions in terms of individual or social problems. Hypotheses are logical deductions consistent with theoretical assumptions.

The section in Chapter 4, "Formulating the hypothesis or a testable research question," has some helpful tips on how to develop and state research questions and hypotheses.

CHOOSING A QUALITATIVE (NATURALISTIC) OR A QUANTITATIVE (STATISTICAL) METHOD

Once you have formulated a testable hypothesis, or have selected an area for comprehensive investigation, you must select the design of the research project. The selection of the research design depends on whether you are going to study a phenomenon (qualitative) or test a hypothesis (quantitative).

In the helping professions, we use qualitative (naturalistic) methods to study social processes and complicated human systems such as families, organizations and communities (Reid, 1987). The qualitative method is also used to describe and understand the ways that people give meaning to their own and others' behavior (Heppner, Kivlighan, & Wampold, 1992).

We use quantitative (statistical) methods to test hypotheses and answer research questions. These studies use statistical methods to test relationships between the independent variables and dependent variables stated in the hypotheses.

The design you will use depends on the choice of method. The choice of method depends on whether you are testing a hypothesis (deductive) or generating theory (inductive). Ordinarily, inductive, qualitative methods are best for generating a theory and deductive, quantitative methods are best for testing hypotheses and answering research questions.

WHAT ARE RESEARCH METHODS AND DESIGNS?

The terms *research design* and *research method* are often used interchangeably to describe the same process. The difference, which is not really that important, could be described as the difference between the "plan" and "carrying out the plan." A

Research Design: The research design is a detailed plan outlining how the research hypothesis will be tested or the *method* that will be used to test the hypothesis. It is composed of the concepts and techniques employed in the research study.

research design is the "plan." A research method is the procedure for "carrying out the plan." In other words, the differences are more semantic than real.

The research design you choose is important. The research design is the plan you intend to use to test your hypothesis. For instance, if you touch my forehead and hypothesize that I have a temperature, you might want to check your assumption more accurately. One way to test your hypothesis accurately is to design a plan for using a thermometer made to measure the human temperature. The method would be to use the thermometer to check my temperature once an hour for four hours. The data from this design using these methods will help either confirm or disconfirm your hypothesis about my temperature.

CHOOSING YOUR RESEARCH METHOD

After you have selected a *working hypothesis* or *research question,* you are ready to design a plan to test your hypothesis. You need to make at least two decisions when you choose the method for your research study.

1. Will the study be a qualitative or a quantitative study?
2. What design will you use?

Each method has different philosophies and characteristics. The differences are important because a number of research designs based on each approach have been developed. These designs lend themselves to answering specific types of research questions.

If you decide to do a qualitative or quantitative research study, you will need to make further decisions when selecting your research design. Answering the questions below will save you a lot of time and effort:

Questions to Ask When Choosing a Research Method

1. What types of research designs were used in previous studies to examine research questions similar to yours?
2. Will your design allow you to collect the type of data you need to identify patterns and recurrent events, or to test your hypotheses?
3. Do you have the resources to carry out the research design?
4. Is the design too ambitious or too complicated to be doable given the circumstances under which the study will be conducted?

CHOOSING A QUALITATIVE (NATURALISTIC) RESEARCH DESIGN

The qualitative (naturalistic) designs that helping professionals use are variations of the phenomenological approach to research. One of the most popular variations of this method is what Glaser and Stauss (1967) call "grounded theory." The purpose of grounded theory is to systematically observe a phenomenon to identify trends and patterns that suggest a tentative theory about the patterns. It is a "process of constant comparisons." Each new case is compared to past cases and studied until it yields no new insights. Then a new case is selected and submitted to the process of constant comparison.

This and other qualitative research approaches are grounded in the German term *verstehen* as used by Max Weber (Bhaskar, 1989). *Verstehen* means "empathetic insight," an important concept in qualitative (naturalistic) research. The postpositivists (qualitative researchers) maintain that empathy is a reliable tool in the study of human behavior. Qualitative researchers argue that one cannot understand some human experiences in any other way. Positivists (quantitative researchers) argue that empathy is not a reliable research tool because it cannot be standardized, as it varies from research to researcher.

If you select a qualitative research method, you will use observation or unstructured interviews to collect your data. Typically, your sample will be small, but the data collected on each participant will be voluminous.

Many researchers conducting qualitative research studies collect volumes of "field" notes based on observations of natural interactions, processes, and events. Although these approaches may not use numbers like quantitative research methods, the qualitative observations must be made with a great deal of accuracy. Then the collected observations are analyzed to identify common patterns across cases and recurring events.

The basic qualitative approaches used by helping professionals are grounded theory, naturalistic, ethnography, and heuristic.

The designs, procedures and methods for analyzing data used in qualitative research are presented in detail in Chapter 4.

CHOOSING A QUANTITATIVE (STATISTICAL) RESEARCH METHOD

The quantitative (statistical) designs used by helping professionals are variations of three basic research designs:

1. The experimental design
2. The cross sectional/survey design
3. The time-series design

Almost all quantitative research in the helping professions uses some form of these three basic designs (see Chapter 5 for more information).

THE EXPERIMENTAL DESIGN

The most sophisticated research approach used in the helping professions is the experimental design, which can be used to study cause-and-effect. Most of us know it as the before-and-after comparison, pretest and posttest, or group

TABLE 3.1   THE QUALITATIVE VERSUS QUANTITATIVE METHODS CHART

Qualitative	Quantitative
Data: Subjective, verbal, from observations and unstructured interviews, and so on.	**Data:** Objective, numbers, from structured interviews, . questionnaires, case records, and so on
Samples: Single subject or small group (5 to 25 people)	**Samples:** A population or large samples (100 to 150+ people)
Types of Studies: Descriptive, survey, single case, historical, and so on.	**Types of Studies:** Experimental, quasi-experimental, statistical survey, and so on.

Experiment: A research technique or method that attempts to isolate the impact of an independent variable on a dependent variable under fixed and controlled conditions.

Quasi-Experimental Design: An experimental design in which some condition required to be a true experiment is not met. Most often, this condition is the inability to randomize group assignments.

comparison. Using this approach, the researcher can isolate and systematically manipulate specific characteristics (independent variables) and then verify whether systematic changes have occurred in the dependent variable. The classical social science experimental study typically uses a group comparison design. It may also be called a *pretest-posttest control group design.* In this experimental design, participants are randomly assigned either to the experimental group or to a control group. The experimental group members are given a service, treatment, or intervention, while it is withheld from the control group members. After a specific period of time, the groups are posttested and the scores on the pretest and posttest are compared to determine the effect of the service, treatment, or intervention.

Researchers use control groups to reduce outside influences from affecting the dependent variable (in the example above, the posttest). In research, control is the process by which a researcher eliminates unwanted influences on the dependent variable. For example, the researcher might remove gender from being an influence on income because males have consistently been shown to earn more money than females for the same work.

There are variations on the experimental design, such as the *quasi-experimental* design. This research effort is designed and conducted as an experiment, but it does not meet the standards of an experimental research study. Quasi-experimental studies typically do not meet all the variable controls that are required in the experimental standard.

Examples of Experimental Research

Experiment in Physics   The true experiment comes from the field of physics. In an experiment the researcher controls all conditions in the environment, sometimes changing one condition or characteristic to see what systematic changes occur in the dependent variable.

Medical Experiment   To test the effects of a new drug, the medical researcher often uses two groups of genetically identical white mice. While living in identical environments, one group of mice receives a new drug (the experimental group); the other group (the control group) does *not* receive the drug. Any changes that occur in the experimental group are attributed to the drug.

Psychotherapeutic Experiment   To test the effectiveness of two different psychotherapeutic approaches (psychoanalysis versus cognitive therapy) in the treatment of severe depression, a mental health center researcher randomly assigns clients to one of two groups. Then the clients are observed, using measures from a depression scale, over the next three months to see which group shows the most improvement.

Educational Quasi-Experiment   To test the effectiveness of two different ways of teaching research (didactic versus hands on), a professor decides to use two classes of students taking a foundation course in research. Although other experimental standards are met, the professor cannot control how the students are assigned to each class.

Much like the group example described above (the "Psychotherapeutic Experiment") this kind of study seeks information on effectiveness, in this case the effectiveness of various teaching approaches. A pretest and a posttest design could be used to test knowledge and skills of the students in each research class. To test the hypothesis, the difference in scores between the pretest and posttest of each class would be compared. If mathematically large enough, the difference would indicate that the students in the experimental class learned more than the students in the control class.

THE CROSS SECTIONAL OR SURVEY DESIGN

This is the oldest type of social research, dating back at least to the ancient Egyptian censuses. It continues to be the most widely used type of social research design. Often taking the form of survey research, it is typically used to study the demographics and/or characteristics of large groups of people.

The *survey research design* is very flexible. It can be modified to find new relationships between variables (*exploratory research*), to describe a population (*descriptive research*), or to explain a population's behavior or attitude (*explanatory research*). Researchers administer questionnaires or interview a **representative sample** of a larger population of people (for example, 1,000 people out of 1,000,000).

A *representative sample* is much the same as or has the distribution of characteristics found in the larger population from which the sample was selected. Because of this relationship between the sample and the larger population, descriptions and explanations obtained from an analysis of the sample may be assumed to adequately describe or explain the population from which the sample was selected. The likelihood of representativeness is enhanced using probability sampling techniques. An extremely important point: a probability sample meets one of the assumptions necessary to use inferential statistics to analyze the data collected from the sample. These procedures allow the findings to be generalized to the larger population.

A *cross sectional study* is based on observations representing a single point in time. Thus, the study gathers the data for the analysis at one point in time. This differs from a longitudinal study, which gathers data over a long period of time.

A *survey* is a data-collecting technique used to gather information from individuals who respond to specific questions related to the focus of the study.

Examples of Survey Research

An Exploratory Survey   An example of how survey research can do different research jobs is the way it has been used in AIDS research. Here surveys have been used in exploring medical and psychosocial patterns that affect the symptoms and the quality of life of people with AIDS.

A Descriptive Survey   In 1980 when little was known about people with AIDS, survey research methods were used to identify individual characteristics of people with AIDS.

Explanatory Survey   Later information and knowledge gained from survey research helped explain the health issues related to AIDS. Survey data also helped explain the relationship between some human behaviors and AIDS. For example, it was found that a loving and caring support system would enhance the health and extend the life of a person with AIDS.

THE TIME-SERIES DESIGN

Single-Subject Design:
A quasi-experimental design featuring continuous or near continuous measurement of the dependent variable on a single research subject over a time interval that is divided into a baseline phase and one or more phases during which the independent variable is manipulated. The experimental effects are inferred by comparisons of the subject's responses between the baseline and intervention phases.

The *time-series design* is an extended case of the pretest and posttest design (the experimental design). The strength of this design is the multiple measurements. Instead of taking two measurements, the researcher takes three or more measurements at similar intervals over time. This design can help measure the short-range, medium-range, and long-range effects of an intervention.

One of the most popular time-series designs in human service research is the *single-subject design,* which is typically used to monitor changes in one subject. "One subject" may also refer to one group, one agency, one class, or one product.

Examples of Time-Series Research

Single-Subject Design   In the field of social work, the single-subject design has become an important tool for practitioners who want to improve their clinical skills. Jayaratne, in a paper called *Single-Subject and Group Designs in Treatment*

Evaluation (1977), demonstrated how the practitioner could both carry out individualized treatment plans with individuals and groups and at the same time conduct a research study on the effectiveness of the intervention (see Chapter 6, Box 6.2 for this example).

Longitudinal Study: This type of study continues over time. One study to help develop and evaluate a strengths-based substance abuse prevention program lasted over six years (Cherry, Cherry, & Sainz, 1998). This study was an examination of a community-based prevention approach utilizing small-group interactive workshops for parents, children, and service providers. The workshops focused on normative educating, resistance training, and increasing the participants' understanding of basic cognitive approaches.

In years one and two of the study, the empirical data guided refinement of the instruments and the workshop presentation. As feedback, the findings guided improvement of the content and delivery of workshop material. In year three, the empirical data on satisfaction with the workshops, learning, and integration of material was significantly increased. Based on the analysis of data collected during the third year, final adjustments were made in the workshops' content and delivery. In years four, five, and six the analyses showed increasing levels of satisfaction, along with high levels of learning and an integration of workshop materials that was consistent over time and across workshops with different workshop leaders.

TRIANGULATION

Triangulation is especially useful for dealing with problems related to systematic error. The reliability of a study is improved if several different research methods are used to collect data on the same phenomena. We tend to have more confidence when data are collected from several sources and when they all point to similar descriptions or explanations of the phenomena.

One form of triangulation for doing qualitative research is the use of observation data and interview data. Another approach might be using records, observations, and interviews. One of the most ambitious approaches to triangulation is to use qualitative *and* quantitative methodologies to study a phenomenon. Typically, it is more expensive and time consuming (basically, you are doing two different studies). Applied research studies and program evaluation studies have often employed triangulation approaches.

APPLIED RESEARCH

Human service research tends to be applied research (as opposed to pure research). It is the study of a problem or situation that will hopefully result in a benefit for individuals or groups. It is often used to assist in developing new interventions, programs, and approaches to solving problems. It also can be used to evaluate and validate the degree of success of a new program or intervention.

Intervention research as conceptualized by Thomas and Rothman (1994) has six stages:

1. Use existing research to learn about target populations and services being provided.
2. Conduct preliminary trials of a new or modified social service intervention.
3. Collect data on the process and apparent outcomes.
4. Use data to improve the intervention.
5. Test the intervention using more rigorous research approaches.
6. Disseminate and adopt the research findings (see Chapter 5 for another brief description).

EVALUATION RESEARCH

Evaluation research is an example of applied research. One of the most notable characteristics of evaluation research in terms of design is that a program evaluation plan can include the use of several research methodologies. The plan might call for conducting individual interviews with staff to identify broad issues and to be able to better describe the context in which the program is operating.

Additionally, the plan might call for using self-administered questionnaires to determine client satisfaction and client perception of the program being evaluated.

The plan also could call for an examination of the program case records so as to obtain a description of the clients. This could suggest what types of clients return for services and what types of clients tend to complete the program.

The evaluation plan might also include an experimental design. The experimental design could be employed to identify changes in clients receiving services from the program as opposed to clients on a waiting list.

In other words, evaluation research is not a method but rather an approach for combining research methods to evaluate a program. Typically, a combination of research designs is needed because most programs are made up of several components, each component needing to be evaluated.

POSTSCRIPT

Now that you have some idea of the different research methods available, you need more information about the two major approaches: the qualitative (naturalistic) and the quantitative (statistical) approach. The qualitative approach is presented in Chapter 4 and the quantitative approach is presented in Chapter 5. These two chapters will give you a brief overview of the two methods and will take you through the phases involved in doing research in the helping professions.

REFERENCES

Bhaskar, R. (1989). *Reclaiming reality: A critical introduction to contemporary philosophy.* London: Verso.

Cherry, A., Cherry, M. E., & Sainz, A. (Jan. 1998). *A six-year longitudinal study of a substance abuse prevention program: Instrument construction and measuring effectiveness.* A conference presentation at the Research for Social Work Practice International Conference, Miami, FL.

Glaser, B., & Strauss, A. (1967). *The discovery of grounded theory.* Chicago: Aldine.

Heppner, P. P., Kivlighan, D. M., & Wampold, B. E. (1992). *Research design in counseling.* Pacific Grove, CA: Brooks/Cole.

Jayaratne, S. (1977). Single-subject and group designs in treatment evaluation. *Social Work Research and Abstracts, 13*(3), 35-44.

Nachmias, D., & Nachmias, C. (1987). *Research methods in the social sciences.* New York: St. Martin's.

Reid, W. (1987). Research in social work. In A. Minahan (Ed.), *Encyclopedia of social work* (18th ed., Vol. 2, pp. 474–487). Silver Spring, MD: National Association of Social Work.

Thomas, E. J., & Rothman, J. (1994). An integrative perspective on intervention research. In J. Rothman & E. J. Thomas (Eds.), *Intervention research* (pp. 1–15). New York: Haworth.

A MODEL FOR CONDUCTING QUALITATIVE (NATURALISTIC) RESEARCH IN THE HELPING PROFESSIONS

Five Phases of a Qualitative Study

WHAT IS QUALITATIVE RESEARCH?

Two types of research methods are used in the helping professions: *qualitative (naturalistic)* and *quantitative (statistical)*. They are used to collect and analyze data either in the form of words (that is, descriptions of recurrent events) or numbers (that is, the times an event is repeated).

You would use a qualitative (naturalistic) approach if you wanted a deeper and fuller understanding of a social process or human interaction, or if you were seeking to identify patterns, identify recurrent themes, or describe events over time.

If you are interested in knowing whether two or more variables correlate (repeatedly occur together), or if you want to know whether one variable could predict the other variable, you would use a quantitative (statistical) research design.

Your choice of design is determined by your decision either to **generate new theory** (qualitative/naturalistic) or to **test hypotheses** (quantitative/statistical). If you choose to study a complicated human system or process, such as family life, and you are hoping to generate new tentative theory, you would select a qualitative methodology. In this chapter on qualitative research, you will be introduced to qualitative methods, data collection procedures and approaches for analyzing qualitative data. Here we will present an example of a qualitative study using grounded theory.

Qualitative (naturalistic) methodology is based on the direct observation of behavior as it occurs. Its roots are in *field research*. Today it is most often referred to as *naturalistic* research. Qualitative (naturalistic) research is based on phenomenological research traditions. "Phenomenological researchers attempt to understand how participants make meaning of and through their interaction" (Heppner, Kivlighan, & Wampold, 1992). In the helping professions qualitative research is characterized by an emphasis on inductive observation and description (Hoshmand, 1989). Qualitative research is a process where systematic observation of human behaviors is used to identify underlying meaning and patterns of relationships (see Chapter 5 for a definition of quantitative [statistical] research).

> Do not be fooled into thinking that *qualitative* research is easier because qualitative methodologies use little or no math. Qualitative research is difficult and labor intensive.

FOUR QUALITATIVE METHODS

The following are four of the main qualitative approaches used by helping professionals:

1. The **Grounded theory** approach compares each new case to the previous case(s) until no new information can be obtained from new cases. New cases are chosen for their degree of similarity to or difference from previous cases. Likewise, the participants are chosen either because they are similar to each other or because they are different from those used in other cases.
2. **Naturalistic** approaches are used if the study's emphasis is to record the development of everyday events. This approach is useful for recording events in real time. Studies of family-life have used this approach and other qualitative approaches with good success (McRoy, 1995).
3. **Ethnography** is used to study a culture from the perspective of the people who belong to that particular culture. Studies of cultures existing within

---

4.1   *A Qualitative Study of a Preschool*

Preschool has been popular in the United States since the 1960s. In many preschool programs for low-income families, parents are required to participate. Longitudinal studies have reported that children who are in these programs benefit substantially. Few studies, however, have examined the impact of these programs on the parents. In a qualitative exploratory investigation, 24 parents and caregivers were interviewed to see if empowerment was an outcome of participation in a cooperative preschool. Empowerment was defined as adults becoming self-sufficient and developing mastery over personal affairs. The study found that such programs helped parents attain and maintain self-sufficiency. The study also identified what program components promoted empowerment (Dunlap, 1996).

---

groups have demonstrated a different but undeniable reality. Cultures also exist around behaviors. For example, family violence has been studied as a culture. McGee (1997) focused on the value system that defines family violence. Using a cross-cultural perspective, McGee examined the impact of cultural beliefs and social rules on family violence.

4. **Heuristic** approaches might have a grounded theory, a naturalistic, and/or an ethnographic focus, but they also encompass the philosophy that researchers are not detached observers; rather, they experience the phenomena they are studying as a first-hand witness. To increase the accuracy of their observations, they examine their own thoughts and feelings about the phenomena as they are experiencing it. Lindsey (1997) attempted to incorporate feminist principals into her qualitative study of "the process of successful restabilization among formerly homeless mother-headed families."

The qualitative approaches highlight internal mental events of people as the foundation of reality. For the qualitative researcher, knowledge is actively constructed from people's internal perceptions; thus, researchers try to retain the perspective of the people being studied. See Box 4.1 for an example of a qualitative study.

FIELD RESEARCH

Field Study: The process of collecting and analyzing detailed and descriptive observations of individuals and groups in a given setting.

"Field Study" has been a more common name for qualitative research. Even today, field research connotes research conducted in the natural environment—the field. In the helping professions, it also denotes that the researcher

4.2   *Classical Field Studies*

Some of the classic field studies are still interesting and relevant to our work today. Two of these are Margaret Mead's *Coming of Age in Samoa* (1933) and Elliot Liebow's *Tally's Corner* (1967).

ANTHROPOLOGY

Mead's often criticized study, *Coming of Age in Samoa* (1933), as mentioned above is a good example of a field study. In this case, Mead lived with a tribe of Samoans for a short period of time and recorded what to her was an idyllic life style. In later research using records and interviews, Derek Freeman found that Samoan life had *not* been as angelic as Margaret Mead

had thought she observed (Cote, 1992; Theodoratus, 1997).

SOCIOLOGY

In the exemplary field study, *Tally's Corner* (1967), Liebow explored a culture we thought we knew something about. The researcher did his study in a "blighted section of Washington's inner-city during the early 1960's." "The Carry-out shop on Tally's Corner was a fixed spot around which their complex but limited lives ebbed and flowed" (Liebow, 1967, p. vii). At the time, this study was heralded as the best available information on African-American life in the inner cities.

is observing people as they go about their everyday affairs. Field researchers immerse themselves in a naturally occurring situation to gain firsthand information and often to understand the world as their subjects see it. The trained observer identifies underlying meanings and patterns of relationships. Box 4.2 describes some classical field studies.

BEST USES FOR QUALITATIVE METHODS

Qualitative research is especially useful for the study of social processes, particularly processes that occur over time. Lofland and Lofland (1995) list several practical units of study for qualitative studies. These "units" also known as "units of analysis" are also relevant to quantitative research.

1. Practices: Various kinds of common behavior
2. Episodes: Common events, such as, divorce, crime, and illness
3. Encounters: Two or more people interacting, such as, mothers and their children in grocery stores
4. Roles: Position in society, such as, occupation, family, or groups
5. Relationships: Behavior in relationships, for example, mother/daughter, mother/son, friendships, or sibling relationships

6. Groups and Organizations: Ranging from small groups to large formal organizations, such as, cliques, athletic teams, hospitals, or universities
7. Societies: Villages, neighborhoods, ghettos

GROUNDED THEORY

One of the most popular variations of the qualitative method is grounded theory (Glaser & Strauss, 1967). The purpose of grounded theory is to systematically observe a behavior or social process (phenomenon) and to identify trends and patterns that suggest a tentative theory about the patterns. Because the tentative theory is derived from the data, the theory is said to be grounded in the data. It is a "process of constant comparisons." Case one is compared to case two; then each new case is compared to past cases. The comparison continues until new cases yield no new insights (Heppner, Kivlighan & Wampold, 1992).

FUNDAMENTALS OF THE GROUNDED THEORY APPROACH

Rennie, Phillips, and Quartaro, (1988) list five steps for doing grounded theory research:

1. Data collection
2. Categorization
3. Memoing (recording the ideas that occur to the researcher during the categorization process)
4. Movement toward parsimony
5. Writing the theory

Adding more detail to the procedures involved in doing grounded theory research, Gilgun (1990) listed 12 steps for conducting a grounded theory study:

1. Identification of area under investigation
2. Literature review
3. Selection of parameters of study
4. Collection of data
5. Comparison of patterns of the first case with those of the second case
6. Development of working hypothesis as common patterns emerge across interviews
7. Formulation of additional questions and modification of questions, based on analysis
8. Continuation of theoretical sampling
9. Review of relevant literature when patterns appear to stabilize
10. Linking of relevant literature to the *empirically* grounded hypotheses
11. Testing of theoretical formulations derived from preceding steps
12. Revision of theoretical formulations as needed to fit empirical patterns in each subsequent step (p. 11)

4.3   *Empirical/Empiricism*

The clear difference between scientific inquiry and theological and philosophical inquiry is that scientific inquiry is based on empiricism. Empiricism is a way of knowing and understanding the world around us. Empiricism relies directly or indirectly on what we experience through our senses (hearing, sight, smell, taste, and touch). In science, acceptable data must be gathered under specific conditions by people possessing normal sensory apparatus, intelligence, and skills (Singleton, Straits, & Straits, 1993).

Selltiz, Wrightsman, and Cook (1976) use an example that makes the difference between scientific (empirical) and nonscientific (nonempirical) easy to understand.

Empiricism: On the one hand, you see a baseball, so you can employ all of your senses to test the existence of a baseball empirically.

Additionally, even if you cannot see a neutron directly, you can observe the photographic representations of the paths the neutrons leave.

Nonempiricism: On the other hand, ghosts are not observed under normal conditions. Nor do they leave any other observable or tangible evidence of their existence. Consequently, there can be scientific theory about baseballs and neutrons, but there can be *no* scientific theory about ghosts.

In other words, empiricism does not accept as scientific evidence data supported by appeals to authority, tradition, revelation, intuition, and other nonempirical ways of knowing (for example, theology and philosophy). According to this viewpoint, the best way to obtain knowledge about the world is "by carefully looking at the world, not by looking at someone's idea of the world" (Katzer, Cook, & Crouch, 1991).

When using grounded theory, a researcher stops the process when new cases do not yield new information or insights. The previous two lists of steps for doing grounded theory research help us form a clear picture of how the grounded theory approach is used in scientific inquiry.

FIVE PHASES OF A QUALITATIVE RESEARCH PROJECT

If you plan to do a qualitative study, it would increase your understanding of the process to read about similar phases in quantitative research (Chapter 5, Phases 1 to 9).

Phase 1: Identifying Your Area of Investigation

Qualitative research can be useful in answering *exploratory* and *descriptive* research questions and in developing viable tentative hypotheses. Although the descriptions are very different, both qualitative (naturalistic) and quantitative (statistical) approaches can yield excellent descriptive data. Qualitative descriptions tend to provide context, for example, and then to depict the circumstances and the meaning of the participant's interactions. Quantitative (statistical) descriptions tend to be demographic and to use statistical values—such as percentages, averages, distributions, correlations, and psychosocial measures—to describe the participants (Tyson, 1995). In qualitative studies that use more than five participants, however, there is typically a descriptive section to describe the participants statistically. Demographic characteristics are reported using frequency statistics, tables, charts and graphs.

Phase 2: Selecting a Qualitative Sample

When choosing a sample for a qualitative study, you must first decide what group of people you are going to study. Will you study *resiliency* in children or the role of peer relationships among resilient children? Will you study the interactions between the homeless and the police or a homeless community under a bridge? Are you interested in drug use ritual or the dynamics involved in a family where one of the members is addicted to amphetamines?

The general purpose of choosing a sample for a qualitative (naturalistic) study is the same as the purpose of choosing a sample for a quantitative (statistical) study. The task is to select people (participants) who are representative of a group of people that interest you. One qualitative research approach is to select new cases that resemble previous cases so that the participants are similar to each other.

There are at least two schools of thought on qualitative sampling: (1) the traditional social science approach, and (2) the phenomenological approach. The *traditional social science approach* is to select a representative sample of the population you are studying. Then you attempt to gather data from all persons identified as members of your sample.

If you use a *phenomenological approach* like grounded theory, you employ a sampling technique called "theory based data selection." With this approach only part of the sample is determined before the study is started. In addition, the selection of new cases is determined partly by the outcomes of the analysis of previous cases (Heppner, Kivlighan & Wampold, 1992). Using *theory based data selection,* the researcher selects new cases that resemble previous cases so that the sample of participants are similar to each other. In this way, participants are likely to represent "ideas" of the phenomenon being studied (Rennie, Phillips, & Quartaro, 1988).

Sample Size   A major difference between the qualitative sample and the quantitative sample is the number of people in the sample. Qualitative approaches typically use small numbers of people in their studies. This is, in part, because so much in-depth data are collected in qualitative studies; only data from small samples are manageable. Larger sample sizes are typically found in quantitative (statistical) research studies.

A sample of under 100 participants would be small for a quantitative (statistical) study. Such a study might be criticized as not being representative of the population under study because the sample is too small. Generalizations about a large population from a small sample are problematic. A sample of 25 participants in a qualitative (naturalistic) study, however, is considered a good size sample. The sample size must be restricted to a smaller number of people, agencies, or social groups because of the sheer volume of data collected.

In some qualitative studies, you may not need to select a sample. The population you want to study may already be few in number. In the study (presented later in this chapter), *Moving from welfare to work: Six years later in two housing projects,* the 14 mothers who were involved in the intervention program were known to the researchers by name. The problem the researchers faced was finding the mothers six years after the two-year intervention program ended. The sampling plan in this study focused on a design to secure interviews from as many of the 32 mothers who participated in the intervention program as possible. To accomplish this task, we used snowball sampling. We located several of the mothers (the first group of participants) from contacts with key informants. While interviewing the first group of mothers, researchers obtained addresses of other mothers who had been involved in the intervention program. Then they obtained addresses for additional mothers who had been involved in the intervention program from this second group of mothers. In this way, researchers located a cohort of mothers and key informants who were able to describe and validate the impact of the intervention program on the lives of the mothers who participated in it.

Phase 3: Collecting Qualitative Data

Qualitative data are typically: (1) descriptions of observations made by researchers or (2) the open-ended answers of participants to questions about their experiences.

Qualitative data are typically observations or narration of those who have ownership or experience with the phenomenon. It is collected by observing the phenomena taking place or interviewing those who have experienced the phenomenon.

Unobtrusive Observation: A situation in which the observer's discretion prevents those being observed from knowing it. An example is gathering data about the educational level of health center clients from their case records.

Two Approaches for Collecting Qualitative Data
Qualitative data are collected as *field observations* of participants, and from *interviews* with participants, or from both. Qualitative methodology is designed to distinguish the patterns, recurrent themes, and typologies that exist in observations. Other sources of unobtrusive qualitative data, such as case records, documents, and photographs are all good sources of qualitative data.

The typical data gathering approaches in qualitative research are: (1) field observations and (2) interviews. There are a number of more exotic approaches, but these two will help the new qualitative researcher get started.

The Field Observation Approach
Because field studies require that researchers use themselves as the data-collecting instrument, you need to make a decision as to how much you will be involved in the social process you are observing. Will you be a non-participant observer? Will you be a participant observer? Alternatively, will you use an approach that is somewhere between the non-participant and participant approach?

NONPARTICIPANT OBSERVATION   Using this method, the researcher observes the process without becoming a part of the process in any way. If possible, the subjects of the study should be unaware of the researcher's presence.

In the effort to be a nonparticipant observer, the researcher may run into an ethical problem. If the people being observed want to know what the researcher is doing, the ethical question is, "Is it all right to lie to maintain your anonymity as a researcher?" There is no clear-cut answer here; the researcher should decide situation by situation. Although honesty is always the first choice, there could be exceptions—for instance, when observing a corner where drug dealers do business. In this case, the researcher risks jeopardizing the quality of the study by revealing his or her purpose because people tend to change their responses if they know they are being observed.

PARTICIPANT OBSERVATION   Using this methodological approach for gathering your data, you would participate in the activities of the process under study, and the people you are observing would be aware of your identity as a researcher.

Problems faced by the participant/observer: It is difficult at times to separate biased feelings and perceptions from observations. This problem can be offset because of the ownership one feels as a participant. Additionally, once those being observed realize they are a part of a research project, they may change their behavior to try to help the researcher.

A MIXED APPROACH   The approach used most often is a mixture of these two approaches. In this situation, some of the people being observed for the research study realize that you are a researcher and that you are there to make observations and collect information. This is similar to the role a newspaper reporter takes when gathering information to do a newspaper story.

The Qualitative Interview Approach: Three Designs   For a novice, one of the best approaches for collecting qualitative data is to do interviews. It is a fairly simple process. You select key informants and interview them with a set of predeveloped interview questions that might help to answer your research questions.

The three most common approaches for organizing a qualitative interview are the following: unstructured, structured, or a mix of the unstructured and structured interviews.

UNSTRUCTURED INTERVIEW   Unstructured interviews are based on questions that are broad in scope and non-specific. They include open-ended questions that cannot be answered with a "yes" or "no." An example of this type of question would be "How would you describe your early childhood?"

After asking this wide-ranging question, the interviewer would use probing questions to get clarifications on statements made by the participant about his or her early childhood. The interviewer would follow the lead of the participant and ask probing questions until a fairly clear descriptive picture of the subject's early childhood was completed.

STRUCTURED INTERVIEW   Structured interviews are most often based on questions that are fairly specific and focused on collecting specific information. In qualitative research studies that use structured interviews, the questions are usually open-ended questions as opposed to closed-ended questions (that is, questions with fixed response categories). A qualitative researcher may, however, use both open-ended and closed-ended questions during an interview.

The open-ended questions, although difficult to analyze, are easier to analyze than the broad, wide-ranging questions typically used in the unstructured interview. For instance, an open-ended question might read, "Describe your typical morning on a day you go to work" as opposed to a broader, wide-ranging question that might read, "Tell me about yourself."

Data collected using structured interviews can be analyzed more easily because the major categories are already defined by the questions. In this case, the analysis focuses on finding the underlying patterns that exist in the collection of comments made in response to each open-ended question asked during the interview.

MIXED UNSTRUCTURED AND STRUCTURED INTERVIEW   With this approach, we typically think of the "area of inquiry" and "how to get the clearest picture" of what we are studying. Mixing both structured and unstructured interview techniques—using both observations and a structured interview—to gather data can result in a more in-depth picture of the people you are studying.

For instance, in one study where we wanted background information on the participants, we used a life history type of interview: "Tell me about yourself." In addition, the questionnaire was broken down into life stages, and each stage was accompanied with a variety of questions to be covered such as participant's family, education, and social background.

Typology: A typology is a systematic classification of characteristics and traits that the participants or groups of participants have in common.

Using this approach, the questions are open-ended and are written so that they can be asked in a way that produces similar information from all participants in the study. If we were doing a quantitative (statistical) study, this would be demographic data and we would report frequency information. In a qualitative study, we describe a typology or several typologies of those who participated in the interviews.

UNSTRUCTURED VERSUS STRUCTURED INTERVIEWS   In the continuum from unstructured to structured interviews, you need to keep several points in mind:

1. The more structured the interview, the more up-front work you have to put into the interviewing instrument or questions.
2. All three approaches require that the interviewer be trained to use the questionnaire; however, the more unstructured the questionnaire, the more training is needed by the interviewer. In the case of *Tally's Corner* (Liebow, 1967), a field study described in Box 4.2, all data, observations, and descriptions were written by one person. Fortunately, Elliot Liebow was a well-trained sociologist.

Procedural Considerations   You need to know about several elements in a qualitative research project before you venture forth on this often rocky road of qualitative exploration. It is extremely important that the interviewer/researcher be able to develop a relationship with the person to be interviewed and be able to effect a positive termination of the interview, all within a given time period.

INTERVIEWER TASKS   When a qualitative study uses open-ended questionnaires to gather data during one or several interviews, the research interviewer must achieve at least four tasks in a short time:

1. Establish rapport with the participant.
2. Ask the questions on the interview questionnaire.
3. Take notes on the responses and the participant being interviewed.
4. Complete a positive termination process at the end of the interview.

CONFOUNDING EFFECTS OF BEING OBSERVED   Sometimes participants react to being observed, thus confounding the researcher's efforts. This circumstance is sometimes called the reactive effect (often referred to as the Hawthorne effect). The participants might also react to the questions being asked, or to the person doing the interview, or both. Although there are techniques to bolster reliability (improve the chances that the findings can be reproduced across studies and researchers), this unwanted *reactive effect* cannot be totally controlled or eliminated. We can reduce the impact of some of these confounding effects, however, by considering the gender, race, ethnic group, and language of the people that will be interviewed, and then selecting research interviewers that are acceptable (similar, if possible) to the people we expect to interview.

In addition, training interviewers can help control the potential impact of confounding characteristics like gender, race, ethnic group, language, etc. The longer the professional interviewer can spend with the participant, the more likely the interviewer will be able to overcome the *reactive effect* to develop an open and honest relationship.

THE TIME FACTOR   If you use a structured interview, the interview should usually last no longer than one hour. This is about all a participant can handle at one sitting.

Plan on spending roughly eight hours organizing and analyzing each hour of taped interview material.

The less structured and organized the data collection effort, the less time needed to begin the qualitative study. You may need more time after the data are collected, however, for organizing and analyzing your less structured and organized data.

Phase 4: Analyzing Qualitative Data

The major task of analyzing qualitative interviews or observations is *data reduction*. Because the amount of qualitative data tends to be voluminous, the data might seem unmanageable in the early stages of organization. Several approaches, including computer programs, have been developed for analyzing qualitative data. These computer programs help transform data from interview and observational transcripts into sets of organized "sum and substance" that reveal common patterns and recurrent events.

The following is a process for organizing and analyzing qualitative data collected by questionnaire or interview. With slight variation this process can also be used for organizing observational field notes. This systematic procedure will help you better understand how to organize and analyze qualitative data. First, take the time to review the abbreviated example of the qualitative study in Box 4.4 (on page 60).

Organizing Interview Data   For the study outlined in Box 4.4, a questionnaire was used to conduct the interviews. If you use a questionnaire to conduct interviews or collect observations, the best way to begin your data reduction procedure is to organize the content from the interviews under the questions on the *questionnaire* you used in your study. If you have 32 questions on the interview questionnaire, start with 32 basic categories by making each major question into one of the 32 categories. Then, organize the interview material into *descriptive categories*.

Next, based on the themes found in the descriptive categories, organize the descriptive categories into *construct categories.* Often, analyst-constructed categories explain the groupings of descriptive categories.

Finally, using the descriptive and construct categories, the researcher identifies *central categories,* which explain the phenomenon being studied.

- **Descriptive Categories**—Categories made up of sets of participant remarks that are similar and that come directly from the language used by the participants. These are also referred to as "indigenous typologies" (Marshall & Rossman, 1989; Patton, 1990).
- **Construct Categories**—A cluster of items organized together to characterize and/or measure aspects of a broader concept. These categories are made up of "analyst-constructed typologies." Construct categories are formed out of the *descriptive categories;* construct categories "should explain the descriptive categorizing and their interrelations" (Heppner, Kivlighan, & Wampold, 1992).
- **Central Categories**—The final categories to be constructed. "The ultimate goal of this process is the identification of core categories that explain the phenomenon" (Heppner, Kivlighan, & Wampold, 1992).
- **Constant Comparison**—A method of qualitative data analysis consisting of a systematic method for deductive data analysis (Glaser & Strauss, 1967). Using this approach, the researcher begins to develop concepts and working hypotheses based on patterns emerging from inductive observations. Next the researcher conducts more interviews or collects more observations. These new data are compared to the concepts and tentative hypotheses developed from earlier interviews and observations. This approach continues until the researcher reaches "theoretical saturation" (Glaser & Strauss, 1967; Rubin & Babbie, 1997).
- **Inductive Reasoning**—A reasoning process where one uses specific observations to propose generalizations that apply to the whole. Qualitative researchers often use inductive reasoning. Based on the information gathered from a few mothers with children who were living in a housing project one might suggest that a lack of education and of marketable job skills was the reason these families were living in poverty.
- **Deductive Reasoning**—A reasoning process where one moves from the general to the specific. Quantitative researchers use deductive reasoning when they combine several independent variables to predict change in a dependent variable. For example, we know that in the general population there is a strong correlation between level of education and life satisfaction. Accordingly, one might deduct and hypothesize that helping mothers with children living in housing projects obtain a basic education and marketable job skills would result in the mothers and their children moving out of poverty. Testing this hypothesis would require a large quantitative study of an intervention to provide education and marketable job skills to a large, stratified random sample of mothers with children living in public housing.

Box 4.5 describes how to tape record qualitative interviews.

4.4   *An Example of a Qualitative Study*

MOVING FROM WELFARE TO WORK: SIX YEARS LATER IN TWO HOUSING PROJECTS

What happens to families when the programs designed to move them from welfare to work end? What services help and what services hinder them from becoming independent and self-sufficient? This qualitative study was conducted six years after the close of a two-year coordinated social service program designed to move families from welfare to work. The paper describes the experiences of 14 females and their children, who lived in two housing projects where the intervention was carried out.

The in-depth interviews were guided by 32 open-ended questions covering the life of the participant. A second questionnaire with 17 open-ended questions about the intervention program was used to guide interviews with nine key informants. The key informants were helping professionals, community leaders, and a local police department member who had been involved in carrying out the original intervention program. To gather the data, a social work professor and a doctoral student were trained and conducted the interviews. The addresses and/or telephone numbers of five mothers who participated in the intervention came from the key informants. The addresses and/or telephone numbers of the remaining nine mothers came from the first five mothers interviewed. This was a simple form of snowball sampling.

With the use of grounded theory (Glaser & Strauss, 1967), patterns and themes emerged about the lives of the 14 women who participated in this study. Each mother-headed family interview was typically two hours long. The interview questionnaire was designed after McCracken's (1988) "life interview" format.

Short descriptive paragraphs (indigenous quotes, statements, and/or descriptive material) were created directly from the content of the interviews. Based on these and self-memos, the short descriptive paragraphs were organized into *descriptive categories* (Tyson, 1995).

The descriptive categories used in this study were typical: age, education, number of children in the family, experience with the intervention program, life since the intervention, and how they are doing today?

Analysis-construct categories and themes explained the experience of this small group of mother-headed families (Lofland & Lofland, 1995). The construct categories were individual capacity, family function, community involvement, education, employment, and quality of life over eight years.

The family of origin category provided a history of sorts that contributed to our core themes. For instance, the women tended to come from large families with six to eleven siblings. Although more than half of the women grew up in an intact family, *their family of origin was impoverished.*

Eleven of these women showed potential for educational achievement when they were in junior high or high school. However, only one finished high school and went to college. She dropped out in her first year.

The concrete services that helped these mothers were educational opportunities, childcare, transportation, and entry-level jobs.

Important patterns and themes were observed in the six areas of inquiry.

1. *Individual capacity:* All of these women made some changes during the intervention. Eight women changed dramatically in terms of self-perception and in their view of the possibilities for their future. The intervention had some minor long lasting effect on all of the women.
2. *Level of family function:* The level of dysfunction went down in six of the families. Four of the mothers could still explain how to use the cognitive approach they were taught during the intervention years earlier.
3. *Community involvement:* The women advocated for change at their housing project. They organized cookouts and block party activities on a regular basis. They became less tolerant of criminal activities in the projects.
4. *Education:* All of the women became involved in some type of education and/or job training.
5. *Employment:* Five of the women were hired to work as outreach workers by social service agencies that participated in the intervention programs. None of the women moved into the private business sector.
6. *Quality of life:* The quality of life improved for six of the women. The intervention program was a positive experience for all of the women.

These data are clearly drawn from a small and biased sample (14 women with children living in a housing project). It is by no means representative of all women on welfare. Moreover, these findings cannot be generalized to any other group. Based on the responses from these participants, however, it is possible to say that all of the women and their children who were interviewed benefited in some way from the intervention program. It is also clear that these women were not middle class mothers who fell on "hard times" and ended up in a public housing project. One of the concluding central themes suggests that the life experiences of these mothers were not the product of intergenerational welfare but the results of intergenerational poverty (Kamerman, 1995). This study suggests that for many single mothers with children living in a housing project, the goal should be NOT to get them off welfare but to move them out of poverty.

REFERENCES FOR THE STUDY

Glaser, B. & Strauss, A. (1967). *The discovery of grounded theory.* Chicago: Aldine.

Kamerman, S. B. (1995). Gender role and family structure changes in the advanced industrialized west: Implications for social policy. In K. McFate, R. Laeson, & W. J. Wilson (Eds.) *Poverty Inequality and the future of social policy: Western states in the New World order* (pp. 231–256). New York: Russell Sage Foundation.

Lofland, J., & Lofland, L. H. (1995). *Analyzing social settings* (3rd ed.) Belmont, CA: Wadsworth.

McCracken, G. (1988). The long interview. *Qualitative research methods series No. 13.* Newbury Park, CA: Sage.

Tyson, K. (1995). *New foundations for scientific social and behavioral research: The heuristic paradigm.* Needham Heights, MA: Allyn & Bacon.

4.5	*Tape Recording Qualitative Interviews*

If you are going to do a qualitative study using the interview for gathering data, consider tape recording the interviews. Although it is more expensive and not quite as convenient, I would suggest you videotape the interviews. If you have the ability to videotape and if it is practical, videotape both the participant and the research interviewer during the interview. With videotape you can both collect your data and make observations of both interviewer and subject.

Do not be surprised, however, if you meet resistance to a research proposal to videotape participants. All potential research projects should go before some type of Institutional Review Board process to protect human subjects. Some members of your Institutional Review Board might be opposed to videotaping participants. In some situations, particularly with a vulnerable population, there may be good reason not to use these technologies (see Chapter 2 for information on the Institutional Review Board).

Qualitative researchers select their sample in one of two general ways.
1. A sample to reflect the real world. In this type of sample, the choice of participants is based on difference.
2. A sample to study some aspect of a phenomenon. In this type of sample, the choice of participant is based on similarities (Bromley, 1986).

STEP 1: ANALYZING QUALITATIVE DATA   After you have completed two to five taped interviews, type transcripts of the taped interview material. Once the tapes are transcribed, the interview material can be organized and analyzed. The knowledge gained from these first few interviews will also be used to identify new persons to add to your sample. This process will also help you identify people to sample who have a different view or different opinion about the phenomenon under study. As a qualitative researcher, you must always be alert to differences or similarities in your sample.

This preliminary analysis might also yield information on the best and most descriptive information of, let us say, the participants' experiences. It will also be used to develop constructs and tentative hypotheses to be tested with data from additional interviews.

As you would expect, transcribing tape-recorded interviews is extremely time consuming and expensive, especially if you hire someone to transcribe the tapes for you. Limited financial resources and questions regarding the use of verbatim transcripts have resulted in variations in this step of the analytical procedure. (See Box 4.6.)

STEP 2: ANALYZING QUALITATIVE DATA   For this step it does not really matter how you created the short descriptive paragraphs, whether from a verbatim transcript or from listening to the taped interviews and typing short descriptive paragraphs about the responses. What matters most is that you have the descriptive paragraphs in a raw database that you can organize under descriptive categories.

After you have the interview material organized in a raw data file, you can use the *process of constant comparisons* to better organize the raw data into meaningful sets of events and recurrent themes. *Constant comparisons* are used to

4.6   *A Sensible Approach for Analyzing Qualitative Data When Transcribing Interviews Verbatim Is Not Practical*

After an interview is recorded on tape, the preferred analytical approach is to transcribe each interview verbatim. The cost of transcribing 50 hours of taped interviews is staggering. A less expensive approach is to listen to the taped interviews and develop short descriptive paragraphs (indigenous quotes, statements, and/or descriptive material) directly from the content on the tapes. Each of the short descriptive paragraphs should be assigned an identification number. This number should identify the interview and the question under which each short paragraph is located in your raw database.

Using this technique, the research analyst listens to the tape of the first person interviewed and organizes the responses to Question 1 into short descriptive paragraphs (indigenous quotes, statements, and/or descriptive material) under Question 1. These short descriptions are taken directly from the taped interview, and they reflect the responses to the interview questions. Often, they are direct quotes.

Additionally, as you listen to the taped interviews you makes notes on any observations or thoughts that occur to you while listening to the interviews (memoing yourself) (Rennie, Phillips, & Quartaro, 1988).

Repeat this process with Question 2 from the first person interviewed. Continue this process with each question answered by the first person interviewed.

When the responses to all of the questions from the first interview are organized into short descriptive statements for each question, go to the tape of the second person interviewed and repeat the process described above. The short descriptive responses of the second person interviewed under each question become your raw data file. This process is repeated with each taped interview.

After you have a raw database, the next step is to develop *descriptive categories* (see definition on p. 159) to organize your short descriptive paragraphs. The descriptive categories explain the relationships between the short paragraphs you have developed of the phenomenon being studied. (See "Step 2: Analyzing Qualitative Data") for suggestions on how to develop descriptive categories.)

help identify the underlying themes and patterns in the data collected using qualitative methods.

Constant comparison is the process of starting with the first interview and developing descriptive categories. Then you analyze the second interview in the same way. Instead of developing additional descriptive categories, however, you try to place the descriptive categories created for the second person interviewed into the categories created for the first person. If not all of the descriptive categories from the second interview fit, add new descriptive categories. While organizing the data you collected from each respondent, you increase the number of categories and subcategories under each question as needed.

You repeat this process with the third interview and continue until all the interviews have been analyzed and their descriptive paragraphs organized under descriptive categories and subcategories. In the example above, you will have descriptive categories from all of the interviews organized under the 32 basic questions on the interview questionnaire.

For instance, in the study presented in Box 4.4, *Moving from Welfare to Work,* the first question on the interview form was, "Tell me about yourself." Among the descriptive responses related to their family and the part of the United States where they came from, one descriptive category became "Family of Origin."

At this point, you are looking for patterns that all participants in the situation share. Do all of the participants lack job skills? Do the children share common strengths and problems? Do all of the mother-headed households receive (or have received) welfare assistance, and so forth?

> Organization and analysis are interlaced processes in qualitative research. As you organize the responses or field observations, the organization gives you clues for better organizing the data.

STEP 3: ANALYZING QUALITATIVE DATA   Even after using the constant comparison technique, you will still have a large number of descriptive categories and subcategories under each of the questions used to conduct the interviews. This is typical in the qualitative data reduction procedure.

The next step is to study the descriptive categories and subcategories and see if they can be collapsed or reorganized to be categories that are more descriptive.

Once you have the best set of descriptive categories, you can devise, you will be ready to develop *construct categories* (see the earlier definition). Construct categories are brief explanations for the different sets of descriptive topics under each question of the questionnaire.

One approach for developing construct categories is to identify sets of descriptive categories and memos that exist under each question. Then, move descriptive statements and memos into their respective construct categories based on characteristics, patterns, and/or themes found in the descriptive categories.

STEP 4: ANALYZING QUALITATIVE DATA   Next you refine the construct categories by expanding and collapsing categories until you cannot learn anything new from more cases or from adding and collapsing descriptive and construct categories. At this point, you have reached *data saturation.* No new information or better descriptive or construct categories add to the analysis. The work toward an optimum number of descriptive and construct categories meets one of the requirements of the scientific method, *parsimony.*

STEP 5: ANALYZING QUALITATIVE DATA   The last step is to develop several *central categories.* These are "core categories" that help explain the phenomenon you are studying.

One of the core categories in the study *Moving from Welfare to Work* was related to welfare and work. It declared, "For these women, their story is NOT one of intergenerational welfare but one of intergenerational poverty."

> Remember, nothing can take the place of reading and rereading the descriptive paragraphs that make up the descriptive and construct categories.

This completes a brief overview of the process used to organize and analyze the study *Moving from Welfare to Work* (Cherry & Dillon, unpublished manuscript, 1999). Following are more tools that make data collection, organization, and analysis more efficient.

Qualitative Reliability and Validity: When qualitative research procedures are used, steps are taken to ensure reliability and validity. You might use triangulation, compare and contrast patterns of observations among groups, check extreme cases, or determine if the findings are repeated.

Reliability and Validity Issues   The reliability and validity of qualitative research has always been considered a problem by its detractors. Can another qualitative researcher replicate the observations (reliability), and to what extent did the research situation influence the participants or subjects being studied (ecological validity)?

Qualitative researchers deal with the *reliability* issue by using purposive sampling based on knowledge of those being studied, review of the literature related to the participants, and using teams of observers. They have dealt with the *validity* issues by using a "member validation" technique in which participants are asked to read and comment on the observations. They also use *triangulation* to address both reliability and validity. Using this technique, several different qualitative research methods are used to collect data on the same phenomena (see "Triangulation" in Chapter 3).

Tools of the Trade   Although personal computers have come a long way since the 1970's, before computers a number of other approaches were around to collect and organize qualitative data. These approaches are still useful and important today. Computers might replace a lot of the manual work, but the reason for organizing the data on note cards has not changed: to help organize the data so you could find themes and patterns in it.

USING COMPUTER WORD PROCESSORS IN QUALITATIVE RESEARCH   First, you process the tape-recorded interviews into descriptive paragraphs. Make sure to use identification numbers to identify the participant and the paragraph number of the interview. This is important when you are shuffling the paragraphs in and out of categories. Moving descriptive paragraphs in and out of categories is easily done using a computer word processing package. I make two working computer files and at least two backup files. One raw data file and a companion backup file are created for the original observations, with the descriptive paragraphs in the order they occurred during the interview. Once completed, this file never changes.

The second computer file, a working file, and a second backup file are made of the categories developed for reorganizing the descriptive paragraphs. The descriptive paragraphs are copied into the categories of the working file from the raw data file.

If a descriptive paragraph seems like it should go into two categories, go ahead and put it into two categories. As you refine the categories, your goal is to have only one paragraph in each category, but this may not be possible in some cases.

During the analysis, when you are looking for underlying patterns, try to develop categories with subcategories. In this way, you could talk about three or four overarching categories and the particular details of the subcategories. For example, we might have a category called "neighborhood environment" and under that category, we might list several subcategories, such as concerns for "safety" and "cleanliness."

COMPUTERS AND QUALITATIVE ANALYSIS   Two of the earliest computer programs designed to help organize and analyze qualitative data were Ethnograph and Nudist. TextSmart, a newer program, was developed by SPSS, Inc., to analyze opened-ended survey responses. This program is good at filtering words of apparently little semantic value from the text and creating a list of key terms that capture the meaning of the data. It is able to organize important terms and group responses into meaningful categories that can be converted into tables, charts, and graphs. These computer programs are noteworthy because the resulting analysis is consistent and bias free. Thus, they are able to deal with two of the major problems that plague qualitative studies.

Although computer programs designed to assist with qualitative studies are more efficient than they used to be, they do not substitute for careful planning; nor do they correct poorly thought-out research methodologies. If the data collected are flawed, the analysis will also be flawed and will lack validity.

Programs for analyzing qualitative data are improving and changing all the time. To find the latest information on computer programs for qualitative research, use any search engine on the Internet and type in "qualitative research." This search will give you a listing of software, user groups, chat groups, and organizations that promote and develop computer programs for qualitative research.

In addition, a number of resources, both in print and on the computer, will be helpful in developing skills to do qualitative research. Check your university Web sites for library and other qualitative resources.

> Remember to back up your computer files. We have all lost computer files to what could be called a "cyber swamp." The objective is to lose as few files as possible.

USING INDEX CARDS   Although not as convenient, you can also organize your data using index cards. To use index cards, type out your descriptive paragraphs on paper, and tape each paragraph on an index card. As you develop descriptive categories, simply place the index cards into the appropriate category.

USING FIELD NOTES   When you are using a tape recorder, the recorded field notes are considered the same as recorded interviews. These field notes or recorded interviews are then processed into raw data (descriptive paragraphs) that are organized, categorized, and used to describe the different themes that emerge during the periods of observation.

USING A RESEARCHER'S LOG   As mentioned earlier you will also want to keep a log or a diary in which you record the steps and procedures you used to gather the data. These notes reflect the experiences that might give the reader a picture of what was going on when you were gathering your data. This information will be invaluable to you when you are writing up the methodology and findings section of your report.

RESEARCHER'S INTERVIEW OBSERVATIONS   The research interviewer should also keep a field log. The field notes of the interviewer should be taken during the interview itself and additional notes made immediately after the interview. These notes would at least include the following:

1. A description of the surroundings in which the interview was conducted
2. Observations about the participant
3. Observations of nonverbal responses
4. Observations of any reaction to the questions
5. Observations of any reaction to the research interviewer
6. Observations of any reaction to the interview as a whole

4.7   *Protecting the Confidentiality of Those Who Refuse to Be in a Study*

To protect the confidentiality of Persons With AIDS (PWA), Matocha (1992) used a third party to recruit family members who cared for persons with AIDS. The third party was a person who had direct contact with the PWA or family member. The third parties approached the PWA or family member about being in the study. If the individuals did not want to be involved in the study, the confidentiality of that person with AIDS was protected.

Ethical Considerations   The information collected from the individuals who agree to participate in your research study can be highly sensitive. Therefore, you have an ethical and legal obligation to fully inform the people about how you intend to use the information they divulge.

If you promise confidentiality, you have the ethical and legal duty to protect their confidentiality. You are also legally required to protect the confidentiality of persons who decline to be involved in your study. (See Box 4.7.)

STATEMENT OF INFORMED CONSENT   If you plan to interview people for your study, I suggest that you ask the participants to sign a "statement of informed consent" (see Chapter 2 for an example). Furthermore, if you are tape recording the interviews, the explanation of informed consent by the research interviewer and the participant's agreeing to participate in the research interview should be a part of the total recorded interview.

If your data gathering approach calls for collecting field observations, it may not be practical or advisable in some cases to ask for signed consents—for instance, if you are observing the behavior between drug addicts and criminals. Obtaining consent in such instances could put the researcher in danger. At minimum, the validity of the observations would be threatened because of the likelihood that giving consent would influence the behavior of those being observed.

RESEARCHER BIAS   One of the best ways to avoid researcher bias from slipping into your field notes is to describe what you see or what the participants say rather than your rationalization for what you think is going on (see Box 4.8). You need to give up all interest in outcome and concentrate on collecting accurate data.

Make separate notes and records for

1. What you saw
2. What you heard
3. What you felt

In the descriptive paragraphs that I develop from observations or interviews, I try to use verbatim statements to maintain the integrity of the description of the

4.8   *Being Open about Research Bias*

In the journal article, *Case study interviews: Caring for persons with AIDS*, Matocha (1992) is clear about emotions and experiences that could bias the findings of her study. In the section, "Becoming an Active Participant," Matocha states, "I experienced strong emotions while conducting this research. I cried, laughed, and exhibited anger and confusion along with each participant. I did not remain untouched or removed from the participants. The sessions were full of sharing. I felt accepted by families. For short periods of time, the family system seemed to open to include me." p. 73

topic of the conversation. Later, in the findings section of my report or paper, I report some of the statements that reflect the experiences and perceptions of the people who were studied.

It is more difficult to avoid research bias with qualitative data than it is with quantitative data. I say this because quantitative data are typically straightforward. It is not as easy to inadvertently give a matrix of numbers in a data file a particular twist or slant. It can be done, but it is not easy.

CULTURAL SENSITIVITY   As stated in Chapter 1, there is no way to conduct a social research study that truly reflects the characteristics of a population if we are not sensitive to cultural, ethnic, and gender differences. This is true for both qualitative and quantitative research. In qualitative studies, the data gathered by a researcher from an individual of a different cultural, ethnic, and gender group can be seriously flawed. Without knowing it, one's bias can filter data to present a negative view of the individual's cultural, ethnic, or gender group. Training and a willingness to challenge our biases can help us as individuals check our work for discriminatory slants. Self-regulation is not enough in the academic and professional world. The institution that attempts to control bias in the professional press and thus somewhat control it in the professional communities is the peer review process used by most legitimate publishers.

A culturally sensitive qualitative methodology might suggest matching interviewers of the same racial, ethnic and/or gender group as those being interviewed. It might also suggest a bilingual interviewer; and it might even suggest a dress code for the interviewers. The purpose of these suggestions, however, is to enhance the data gathering process so that the findings come as close as possible to matching reality.

Phase 5: Writing about Theory That Emerges from the Data

A qualitative paper published in a journal is in many ways similar to any other professional paper published in a professional journal. It is written in a scholarly way and is rigorous and empirical.

A Model for Writing a Qualitative Research Paper   A qualitative paper for a research class or a paper for a professional journal can be written using a model similar to that presented in Chapter 27. The introduction and literature review could easily follow the format described in Chapter 27, however, there are several differences that you will want to keep in mind when you are writing your qualitative paper.

STATEMENT OF THE HYPOTHESIS OR RESEARCH QUESTION   Rather than a hypothesis, qualitative papers usually have a research question that guides the study. Typically, there is a general (broad) research question and specific research questions to answer the broader research question. For example in the study, *Moving from Welfare to Work,* there were two general research questions: "What happens to families when the programs designed to move them from welfare to work end?" "What services help and what services hinder them from becoming independent and self-sufficient?" To answer these questions, we explored the characteristics of the mothers who were head of their household. We examined their involvement in the training programs, as well as the effects of the training on their lives and on their families' lives. We also documented the events in their lives and the lives of their families for six years after the interventions were discontinued.

THE METHODOLOGY SECTION   Here you describe the process that you used to carry out the study. The procedures involved should be described in enough detail that another researcher could follow your research design and replicate your study.

The details are also important so that your colleagues can evaluate both your research design procedures, and findings. You will find the following in most qualitative studies in the methods section.

1. *Section on Sampling.* The section on how you selected your sample should clearly state your reasons for choosing the participants for your study. Did you want your sample to reflect the "real world" or were you studying some aspect of a phenomenon. Your approach and sample must be able to answer the research questions.
2. *The Protocol.* Under the generic heading "Protocol" in a qualitative paper, you explain how you collected the data and under what circumstances the data were gathered. "Why were some participants interviewed earlier than others?" "How did the analysis of those earlier interviews impact the selection of additional participants, if at all?"

   If you used a questionnaire, you discuss any changes made in the questionnaire during data collection. In qualitative research, it is acceptable to adjust a data-gathering instrument between participant interviews. The objective of qualitative methods is to reflect reality. Reality is viewed as being more important than consistency.

3. *Field Procedures.* Field procedures in a qualitative study are typically explained in greater detail than in quantitative studies. You might need to address questions on procedure in some detail. "What data were collected in what time period?" "Under what conditions were the persons interviewed and taped?" "Were they interviewed by phone or in person?"

4. *Role of the Researchers.* What role did you play in the system that you studied? How did your being a part of the environment affect those you were observing or interviewing? We know that a field researcher is an outsider who is attempting to violate a system that is typically closed to researchers. "How much did we as researchers impact the people who we were observing?" "How much of the observation was because they knew you were watching?"

THE FINDINGS SECTION   In a qualitative study, this section is very different from that found in a quantitative paper. Rather than reporting the statistical results of the data analysis as you would in a quantitative study, in a qualitative study the actual descriptions of the categories of the data collected are presented. The findings section of the qualitative research paper is where the categories are presented and described.

1. *Characteristics of the Participants.* In this section, you describe the participants of your study. How similar or how different were the participants? What were their ages, gender, and education? In general, you try to describe the people who participated in the study. You can also use frequency data and graphs to describe your population (see Chapter 15 on frequency distributions).

2. *Defining the Broad Categories Identified.* These categories are presented with the supporting data. These broad categories are the "Analyst Constructed" categories supported by the subcategories and the descriptive statements from the participants.

THE CONCLUSION AND DISCUSSION SECTION   This part, similar in both qualitative and quantitative research papers, is for interpreting and discussing your findings. In a qualitative research paper, you also interpret the meaning of the categories of observations collected during the study.

In qualitative research, it can be difficult to tell if the descriptions of the observations were impartial. Because of the nature of qualitative research, you could be unaware of the bias. Make every effort to describe your observations in an unbiased way. Following this rule, other researchers can read your observations and draw their own conclusions, just as researchers do when they read the statistical findings in a quantitative research paper.

1. *Distinguish Between the Findings Section of the Research Paper and the Discussion Section.* Qualitative reports and papers clearly have a *findings section* and a *discussion section.* The finding section should contain an unadulterated description of what the data analysis produced rather than an interpretation of what you observed.

2. *The Discussion Section of the Research Paper.* In the discussion section of the qualitative research study, you assess if the methodology worked as well as expected. How flexible was the design?
3. *The Limitation Section.* In the limitation section, you want the reader to know what problems you encountered and in what way you deviated from the design. Will replication be a problem? What are your recommendations for future researchers?

Could Your Findings and Conclusions Be Replicated?

In all social science research, you need to give up all interest in what emerges out of the data. You must try to find patterns and meaning that would be clear to any trained observer with the same data that you collected. Your insights and conclusions should be so logical that other researchers would come to the same conclusions. Although an unpleasant thought, you must remember that if your interpretation is biased the finding will not likely be replicated. Others will dispute and perhaps even attack your findings. You should feel comfortable enough with your conclusions that you would be willing to allow your data to be analyzed by any of your colleagues.

Alternative Methods

Two other qualitative approaches are historical research and the use of focus groups. Historical research has a long tradition, but the use of focus groups to gather qualitative data is fairly new.

Historical Research: A technique that uses previous observations and records (archival data) to address questions about events and the meaning of events in the past.

HISTORICAL RESEARCH   In this chapter, the focus thus far has been on field research. *Historical research* is another widely used qualitative research approach. Historical research, which depends upon records kept by others, is rigorous, systematic, and exhaustive. Two questions must be addressed by the researcher: (1) Are the records or data *authentic?* and (2) Are they *accurate and relevant?* The purpose is to establish facts and reach defensible conclusions. Historical researchers might begin their research by stating a hypothesis.

The book *Regulating the Poor: The Function of Public Welfare* (1971), by Frances F. Piven and Richard A. Cloward is an excellent example of historical research. Piven and Cloward hypothesized that a social institution allegedly developed to help the poor in this country, was also instrumental in oppressing the poor.

A more recent historical paper using the qualitative approach is Carlton-Laney's (1997) thesis on the contributions of Elizabeth Ross Haynes, an African-American reformer in the early 1900's. This is a history of a reformer interested in women's labor issues and in social services provided to women. Her work and advocacy were based on her "womanist" consciousness.

FOCUS GROUPS   The *focus group* is another useful qualitative approach for gathering data. The focus group approach involves a group of people selected by the researcher for their knowledge about a specific issue or problem. The *key to success* is that the researcher promotes group dynamics. For example, less structured groups tend to pursue those issues that are important, relevant, and of interest to the group members.

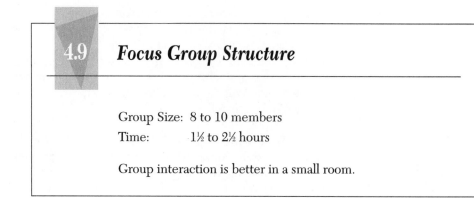

4.9   *Focus Group Structure*

Group Size: 8 to 10 members
Time: 1½ to 2½ hours

Group interaction is better in a small room.

The term *focus* implies that the process is limited to a small number of issues. The term *group* implies that the moderator/researcher uses the group process as a device for eliciting pertinent information from the participants.

Given the loose nature of the group process, it is imperative to have a good tape recorder with microphones and plenty of recording tape. Remember, when the focus group discussion heats up, without a tape recorder, you will miss some important information.

The focus group process usually begins with a series of general questions; the moderator/researcher gradually directs the discussion to more specific issues as the group solidifies into a functional unit. The only rule is that members do not criticize the ideas generated by other group members. (See Box 4.9.)

Focus groups have been used for many years to determine the best approach for marketing products. It was probably developed or at least refined by Robert Merton in the early 1950's. The focus group became famous as a powerful research tool when it was used by Vice President George Bush's political consultants in his presidential race against Massachusetts Governor Michael Dukakis in 1988. It is alleged that at a Republican focus group meeting in Dukakis's home state of Massachusetts, a group member made the statement that he was not going to vote for Dukakis because he let Willey Horton out of prison on a weekend furlough and Willey Horton raped and killed a woman. The focus group member blamed Dukakis for the prison furlough program in Massachusetts, although the furlough program had been implemented before Dukakis was elected governor of Massachusetts. The Willy Horton incident so infuriated other members of the focus group that Republicans began a campaign at the national level to link Dukakis with the Willey Horton murder. The now famous Willey Horton campaign is credited with virtually destroying Dukakis's chances of becoming president (Miller, 1992).

See Boxes 4.10 and 4.11 for examples of focus groups.

4.10   *A Focus Group Example*

Although a focus group might be considered similar to *brainstorming*, it is a more structured approach than brainstorming to get the group to focus on problems, needs, and gaps in services. This approach often uses a task to solicit new ideas. In the early 1990s, I used focus groups to explore and suggest better approaches to AIDS prevention education in South Florida. The Ford foundation was willing to provide funds to two South Florida Community Foundations; however, they first wanted to know where the money would be spent to meet unmet needs. The focus group approach was selected because of the need to develop a broad picture of community needs and gaps in AIDS prevention education.

The focus groups began with the following observation of the community efforts to that point. *The current AIDS prevention efforts are not effective with the most at-risk population in our community. What needs to change?* The following is the outline used to conduct the focus groups.

OUTLINE FOR AIDS PREVENTION EDUCATION FOCUS GROUPS

Use four focus groups made up of providers and consumers from different segments of the community. The members should be selected for their knowledge about and representativeness of the relevant segments of the community.

I. Deferment: In the beginning of the session, look for viewpoints or perspectives, rather than solutions.

A. General problems and general needs
   1. What AIDS prevention education is being provided in your community?
      a. What materials are available?
      b. What populations are being serviced?
      c. What types of media are being used?
   2. AIDS prevention education gaps in your community and area of interest.
      a. What materials are not available?
      b. What populations are not being served?
      c. What types of media are not being used?

Let the discussion take on a life of its own.

B. Tasks to generate a list of priorities.
   1. What would be the ideal set of AIDS prevention education materials? Prioritize.
   2. How would the material best be delivered? Prioritize.
   3. What groups would be served? Prioritize?

C. Tasks to generate new ideas.
   Put yourself in the place of the people you serve.
   1. What types of AIDS prevention education would you find acceptable and useable?
   2. What types of AIDS prevention education would you find unacceptable?

II. Go over the prioritized list developed by the focus group to obtain group consensus.

4.11   *Focus Groups to Identify HIV Risk Reduction Behavior*

Carey, Gordon, Morrison-Beedy, and McLean (1997) used focus groups to learn more about low-income women and HIV risk reduction. Qualitative analysis identified six themes related to HIV risk reduction that emerged across focus groups with 45 young, single, low-income women. They found: (1) misinformation, (2) risk perception, (3) uncertainty regarding risk reduction, (4) fatalism, (5) recognition of the importance of discussing HIV related topics with children, and (6) inconsistent communication regarding HIV transmission and prevention with partners. These factors are important when developing an HIV risk reduction program for low-income, at-risk women.

POSTSCRIPT

The qualitative research method can contribute a great deal to the knowledge base of the helping professions. It is the best approach if you need or want a deeper and fuller understanding of social processes and human interactions. Qualitative research puts a face on a few members of the population as they go about their daily lives. The drawback is generalizability.

If you need more precise information to be able to predict events, the best approach would involve quantitative (statistical) research methods (using probability theory and statistical procedures to identify relationships between variables). Chapter 5 will briefly sketch out quantitative (statistical) methods. The subsequent chapters will be related primarily to understanding and applying the quantitative methods in the helping professions.

REFERENCES

Bromley, D. B. (1986). *The case-study method in psychology and related disciplines.* New York: John Wiley.

Carey, M. P., Gordon, C. M., Morrison-Beedy, D., & McLean, D. A. (1997). Low-income women and HIV risk reduction: Elaborations from qualitative research. *AIDS and Behavior, 1*(3): 163–168.

Carlton-Laney, I. (1997). Elizabeth Ross Haynes: An African American reformer of womanist consciousness. *Social Work, 42*(6): 573–583.

Cherry, A. L., & Dillon, M. E. (unpublished manuscript, 1999). *Moving from welfare to work: Six years later in two housing projects.*

Cote, J. E. (1992). Was Mead wrong about coming of age in Samoa? An analysis of the Mead/Freeman controversy for scholars of adolescence and human development. *Journal of Youth and Adolescence, 21*(5): 499–528.

Dunlap, K. (1996). Supporting and empowering families through cooperative preschool education. *Social Work in Education, 18*(4): 210–221.

Gilgun, J. F. (1990). Steps in the development of theory using a grounded theory approach. *Qualitative Family Research Newsletter, 42*(2): 11–12.

Glaser, B., & Strauss, A. (1967). *The discovery of grounded theory.* Chicago: Aldine.

Heppner, P. P., Kivlighan, D. M., & Wampold, B. E. (1992). *Research design in counseling.* Pacific Grove, CA: Brooks/Cole.

Hoshmand, L. L. (1989). Alternative research paradigms: A review and teaching proposal. *Counseling Psychologist, 17*: 3–79.

Katzer, J., Cook, K. H., & Crouch, W. W. (1991). *Evaluation information: A guide for users of social science research* (3rd ed.). New York: McGraw-Hill.

Liebow, E. (1967). *Tally's corner.* Boston: Little, Brown.

Lindsey, E. (1997). Feminist issues in qualitative research with formerly homeless mothers. *AFFILIA Journal of Women & Social Work, 12*(1): 57–75.

Lofland, J., & Lofland, L. H. (1995). *Analyzing social settings* (3rd ed.). Belmont, CA: Wadsworth.

Marshall, C., & Rossman, G., (1989). *Designing qualitative research.* Newbury Park, CA: Sage.

Matocha, L. K. (1992). Case study interviews: Caring for persons with AIDS. In J. F. Gilgun, K. Daly, & G. Handel (Eds.), *Qualitative methods in family research* (pp. 66–84). Newbury Park, CA: Sage.

McCracken, G. (1988). The long interview. *Qualitative Research Methods Series No. 13.* Newbury Park, CA: Sage.

McGee, C. (1997). Children's experiences of domestic violence. *Child and Family Social Work, 2*(1): 13–23.

McRoy, R. (1995). Qualitative research. In L. R. Edwards (Ed.), *Encyclopedia of social work* (pp. 2009–2015). Washington, D.C.: NASW.

Mead, M. (1933). *Coming of age in Samoa.* New York: Morrow.

Miller, M. C. (1992). Political ads: Decoding hidden messages. *Columbia Journalism Review, 30*(5): 36–39

Patton, M. (1990). *Qualitative evaluation methods.* Newbury Park, CA: Sage.

Piven, F. F., & Cloward, R. A. (1971). *Regulating the poor: The function of public welfare.* New York: Vintage.

Rennie, D. L., Phillips, J. R., & Quartaro, G. K. (1988). Grounded theory: A promising approach into conceptualization in psychology? *Canadian Psychology/Psychologie Canadienne, 29*: 139–150.

Rubin, A, and Babbie, E, (1997). *Research methods for social work.* Belmont, CA: Wadsworth.

Selltiz, C., Wrightsman, L. S., & Cook, S. W. (1976). *Research methods in social relationships* (3rd ed.). New York: Holt, Rinehart, and Winston.

Singleton, R. A., Straits, B. C., & Straits, M. M. (1993). *Approaches to social research* (2nd ed.). New York: Oxford Univ.

Theodoratus, R. J. (1997). Not even wrong: Margaret Mead, Derek Freeman, and the Samoans. *Social Science Journal, 34*(1): 344–443.

Tyson, K. (1995). *New foundations for scientific social and behavioral research: The heuristic paradigm.* Boston: Allyn &Bacon.

A MODEL FOR CONDUCTING QUANTITATIVE (STATISTICAL) RESEARCH IN THE HELPING PROFESSIONS

Nine Phases of a Quantitative Study

WHAT IS QUANTITATIVE RESEARCH?

It is difficult to conduct human service research in the laboratory (experimental research). Most human service problems and processes do not lend themselves to experimental design (Gyarfas, 1983; Rubin & Babbie, 1997). However, quantitative research statistical techniques have been developed so that quantitative methods can be applied using *experimental* approaches, *cross sectional/survey* designs, and *time-series* designs (see Chapter 3).

WHERE DO QUANTITATIVE METHODS EXCEL?

Quantitative (statistical) research is best at testing hypotheses that require measurement of content. It is best at measuring amount, percentages, or quantity and at determining the degree of statistical significance in the relationship between characteristics or behaviors.

The findings derived from quantitative research techniques are based on *representativeness of the sample, reliability and validity of the measures* being used and *statistical analysis*.

Representativeness: The degree of representativeness tells us to what degree the sample is like the population as a whole. If a psychotherapeutic group to increase family bonds was effective with a *representative,* experimental group, it probably will work with many similar families.

RELIABILITY, AND INTERNAL AND EXTERNAL VALIDITY

In quantitative research, three questions should be asked about the *reliability and validity* of a measure (e.g., psychosocial and behavioral scales).

Question 1. *Reliability* Is the data collected by the scale you wish to use, the same data that would have been collected each time the questions were asked of the same type of participants?

Question 2. *Internal Validity* Does the scale measure what it is alleged to measure with the given population?

Question 3. *External Validity* Can the findings from the scale be generalized to people beyond those in the study?

Reliable and Valid Measures: These measures tend to be psychosocial scales that measure such things as *self-image, locus of control, depression,* and *motivation to study.* These scales show the level of intensity and direction: The depression and motivation scales show a level of intensity of feelings. The self-image and locus of control scales show the direction to which the participants lean. These measures give the researcher some assurance that what the scales reveal is a reliable indicator for the feeling of those who answered the questions on the scales.

THE RESEARCH PROCESS BROKEN DOWN INTO NINE PHASES

This chapter presents a brief *overview* of the steps involved in a quantitative (statistical) research study that could be conducted by a helping professional. These steps are presented to help readers organize the research process in their own minds. These *phases* are a guide for planning and conducting a research study, though they might change slightly from one study to another. Even so, this overview will show you how the majority of the quantitative (statistical) studies are organized. In this case, *social science research is more of a case of form following function.*

| 5.1 | *Small Quasi-Experimental Research Design in Family Counseling* |

In your work at Family Counseling Center, you believe that an intervention to improve family bonds would affect school grades and behavior. To test your idea, you design an intervention to increase family bonds. You then select 40 families whose children receive poor grades and have numerous behavioral problems in school.

Then you randomly select 20 of these 40 families to participate in a family group intervention to build family bonds and 20 families to be in a control group. The control group receives the regular counseling sessions.

Both groups would be pretested and posttested. In this case, you might use a family bond scale. To pretest and posttest the children you might use the Wide Range Achievement Test (WRAT) along with verbal reports from teachers, parents, and children about problem behavior at school. What you are trying to find out is the degree of the relationship between the variables you have decided are important to study.

For example, let us say you find there is a relationship between an increase in family bond and an increase in WRAT scores, accompanied by a reduction in reported behavioral problems at school. Given this finding there is good reason to believe that the same intervention might work with other similar families at your agency.

A clock that reads 1:00 P.M. when it is actually 1:10 P.M. is reliable if it continues to be 10 minutes fast, but the clock is not a *valid* measure of time because it is incorrect.

Once you have an understanding of where you are going or what you will be doing when you begin a research project, you can make informed decisions about the tools that you will need to do research. Like a map, this overview will not take you where you are going, but it will give you a lot of information about how to get there as well as great assistance in planning a research project.

By familiarizing yourself with the phases involved in a quantitative study in the helping professions, you will be better able to see how the pieces fit together. You will be able to see what skills, tools, and resources you will need to complete a similar research project on your own or with a group.

The chapters dealing with topics related to designing your quantitative research study and the statistical procedures you can use to analyze collected data are found in Parts III and IV of this text.

The last stage of the research process is presented in Chapter 27, "A Model for Writing a Research Paper for a Class, a Dissertation, or an Article for a Professional Journal or Research Class." This chapter will guide you in disseminating the findings from your research study. It presents a format for writing a paper for a research class or for submitting a paper to a professional journal.

NINE PHASES OF A QUANTITATIVE RESEARCH PROJECT

Keep a log or diary of your work on your research study. All scientists conducting research with rigor and veracity keep a record of their experiences and efforts.

The phases of a quantitative research project are selecting a manageable research project, reviewing literature, formulating the hypothesis or research question, selecting a research design, choosing the population or the sample, choosing scales and measures to test the hypothesis, gathering data, analyzing the data, and drawing conclusions from the analysis.

Phase 1: Selecting a Manageable Research Project

Begin with a Question   Start your project by selecting a tentative research question. It is important that your question be considered a general starting place until you have completed your literature review. **As you conduct the literature review, you will refine the tentative question into a *testable research question or hypothesis.***

Be good to yourself. In your first research effort or two, pick a people-type question that you are somewhat familiar with and interested in learning more about. If you are interested in the helping professions, research is much more interesting and fun if you hope to get an answer to a question you have pondered in the past.

LOOKING FOR ANSWERS   Most research questions come from personal work experiences or the reported work related experiences of others. We may look at the process or development of a human situation or the causes for problems related to individuals, groups, families, and communities. Social, economic and political changes and their accompanying unanticipated consequences produce a never-ending flow of social conditions and problems for study and for understanding.

Ordinarily, we try to find answers to the perplexing questions in our respective fields of study and work. In the first place, we know a good bit about our field. In the second place, there are thousands of unanswered questions in human services and related disciplines. The answers to these questions can help solve human problems and improve their condition.

Nonetheless, do not be over ambitious. If this is your first research effort, you might think your research project is too simple. If that is what you think, you (like most of us when we started doing research) probably have picked a project that is too complicated rather than too simple.

Moreover, remember that in the helping professions, some questions cannot be answered. Our current research tools are inadequate and our knowledge base too limited. Even so, if we use the tools we have, we can learn a great deal more about our community and ourselves.

SOCIAL RESEARCH PROBLEMS AND QUESTIONS   You can also start your research study with a field-of-practice question, a good foundation for developing your research question and hypothesis. Hold off on refining your research question and hypothesis, however, until after you have completed your literature review. Let it evolve out of support in the literature.

Plan your research project so that it adds *a brick* to the house of knowledge. Do NOT try to build the house—at least not on your first attempt.

Research Problem:	Hyperactivity and juvenile delinquency.
Research Question:	Does hyperactivity in a pre-teen predict delinquency as a teenager?
Research Problem:	High rates of Teenage Pregnancy.
Research Question:	What role do social bonds play in teens experiencing an unwanted pregnancy?
Research Problem:	Supports that are needed to live with AIDS.
Research Question:	What social supports do people living with AIDS find the most beneficial?
Research Problem:	School failure in junior high school students.
Research Question:	Is an external locus of control significantly related to success in school?
Research Problem:	Child and spouse abuse.
Research Question:	Is there less child and spouse abuse among families that are members of a larger family network who live in the same community?

WHO SAYS IT IS A GOOD QUESTION?   Here, a solid literature review is essential. You will find out what others have published in the professional literature. You will find out what others think about the question you plan to study and what they have done to answer the same question or a similar question. Additionally, you will be able to see the kinds of research done to date to test the concepts. Someone might have already done the kind of study you wish to do, but you will never know it without doing a thorough literature review.

Following are two general types of questions that lend themselves to research in the helping professions:

1. Questions that emerge from one's natural curiosity to know and understand
2. Questions that the researcher hopes will provide information to increase our understanding of a situation

SOME BASIC CRITERIA FOR SELECTING A RESEARCH QUESTION   A question suitable for social science research needs to meet several basic criteria:

1. It should be important.
2. It should be relevant.
3. It should be ethical.
4. It should be measurable.
5. Prudent research methods should be available to carry out the study of the research problem.
6. You should have adequate financial resources and time to do the study.
7. An adequate number of participants should be available to test the hypothesis.

Some Procedural Problems to Keep in Mind

As you go through the process of refining your tentative research question, you will need to make at least four basic decisions related to your research question:

1. Does your research question (hopefully in an area you have an interest) support the need for a research study?
2. Do you have the means and resources to conduct the research study? Research in the helping professions is a time consuming task. You need support on many levels: identifying and accessing a sample, consultation on methodology and the statistical analysis. Even if you do all of the work yourself, it can still cost a good bit of money—for example, to pay for making copies of a questionnaire, computer facilities, travel, postage, and other unforeseen expenses.
3. Should you describe the characteristics of a group of people with the problem to add new information? If so, your first level of research might be a descriptive study. If little is known about the numbers and characteristics of a population or problem, this is a first approach. This is also the simplest research study to conduct. These studies tend to be manageable for researchers with few or limited experience and resources.
4. Do you want to try to show a relationship between two variables or show that an independent variable causes changes in a dependent variable? This is a sophisticated research project that calls for a correlational study (see Chapter 3 for a definition and an explanation for the term, *variable*). This type of research examines the effect that an independent variable has on a dependent variable. This can be a bivariate or multivariate research study.

Feasibility Checklist   Once you have selected a tentative research question or social problem to study, use the following feasibility checklist before you commit to the research project.

	Is there literature on the topic?
_____	Is there previous research on the topic?
_____	Can you better define the area you wish to study?
_____	Are there scales or measures to help answer the question?
_____	Is there a population available for you to study?

If you answer "no" to any of the above questions, you might want to select another tentative research question before you do a thorough literature review. See Box 5.2 for a list of common mistakes researchers make in developing a research project.

Phase 2: Conducting the Literature Review

For most of you, conducting a literature review of a specific topic and then writing about your findings in a formal paper will be familiar. It is *similar to writing a college term paper*. Writing a term paper, as I am sure you remember, is broken down into a two-part task. First, you identify a topic you are somewhat interested in, and then you go to the library and find as many books and articles as you can on the topic. In research in the helping professions, this is called *conducting a literature review*. Secondly, you write a paper on what you found in the literature on the topic from your library search. In this guide, it is called, *writing-up the literature*

Become best friends with a librarian in the reference department. He/she wants to help you.

5.2   *Common Mistakes in Developing a Tentative Research Project*

1. Putting off selection of a tentative research question until after the literature review is a mistake because a good tentative research question helps to focus the literature review.
2. Beginning to work on the first research idea that comes to mind without assessing its feasibility.

3. Picking a topic not really of interest to you.
4. Choosing a topic that is too ambitious, too general, too broad in scope, or too complicated.
5. Failing to thoroughly review the existing literature related to the tentative research question.

As you do the literature review, carefully record the citations of the books, articles and references related to your study. If you do not, you will regret it when you write your research paper or report.

review, a step that has its own section in the chapter on writing a research report (Chapter 27).

When doing a literature review for a research study in the helping professions, we typically confine ourselves to scientific books and articles on our topic.

Why Do a Literature Search?   There are at least 10 reasons to do a good literature review before you begin your study.

1. To find any studies that address a similar research question
2. To find the most central and important studies related to your general research question
3. To find any rival explanations to your research question
4. To familiarize yourself with the theoretical frameworks that have been used to study similar research questions
5. To identify the methodological approaches used to answer similar research questions
6. To assess design issues
7. To assess the populations and sample sizes used in previous studies
8. To assess the measures used
9. To survey the statistical analyses used
10. To see what research direction or research questions others suggest.

Locating an Exemplar Study   One approach that can be useful to a new researcher is to find a previous study that addresses the same or a similar research question and use it as a model.

For the student or for the new or occasional researcher, finding one or several exemplars (a research study something like the one you want to do) is a big help. It can be used as a kind of rough road map for your research project. Why reinvent the wheel? If a study has been done with a similar population, has used similar measures, and has employed a method that worked well in the study, why not use similar tools?

Replicating A Previous Study: Trying to reproduce a study in every way to see if you get the same results.

Replicating a Previous Study

Using a study for an *exemplar* and *replicating* a previous study are very different. When you replicate a study, you try to do the same study to see if the results are the same. Replicating a study is theoretically important in terms of validating findings and of knowledge building (although such studies are difficult to get published). Most good studies are, in part, a replication of previous works and studies. These approaches use the best variables from the previous studies and test additional new variables that might contribute to the overall explanation. This approach also fits the scientific method's approach to knowledge building.

Covering the Areas Important to Your Study

In most cases, a plethora of literature exists on the topic or problem you wish to study. Therefore, you need to keep several criteria in mind when selecting material to include in your literature review.

1. Articles, books and research studies that cover the general and specific *background* of the area that you wish to research. Find the most recent studies, especially by leaders in the field.
2. Articles, books and research studies that support the *importance* of your proposed study.
3. Related articles, books and research studies that explicate *theoretical* considerations you may employ in your study.
4. *Hypotheses* that have been tested in previous research studies.
5. Articles, books and research studies that examine or use *measures* to test hypotheses in similar research studies.
6. Articles, books and research studies that use different *methodological approaches* to study similar problems.

Put to good use the computerized reference databases in your library.

Common Mistakes in the Literature Review

1. **Becoming overwhelmed by the swamp of literature.** Most of us have had the experience of being lost in the literature swamp. We collect so many studies, articles, and books that we lose focus of the problem. If this happens to you, pick out a few articles that are exemplars and refocus.
2. **Trying to base your study on a mass media article.** You might find interesting statistical material or ideas in newspapers or popular magazines; however, you do not want to base your study on the writings of journalists. They do not follow procedures of the scientific method. They have a different approach to collecting data and presenting material.
3. **Using loosely related literature.** Although there is typically a great deal of literature on most topics, some students will pick a topic that might be a bit obscure—for instance, "Using biofeedback to teach a dually diagnosed substance abuser how to meditate." It will be difficult to find many studies on this specific intervention. You might have to go to several library databases. The psychology

literature will have numerous studies on biofeedback, perhaps not on biofeed-back to teach the dually diagnosed substance abuser how to meditate, but many articles that could support using biofeedback in an effort to teach the dually diag-nosed to meditate. The substance abuse literature would be more related to occurrence and treatment interventions with dually diagnosed substance abusers. You might even find one that is an example of using biofeedback.

Phase 3: Formulating the Hypothesis or a Testable Research Question

Now that you have completed a thorough literature review, you are ready to define a testable research question or hypothesis.

One of the primary characteristics of a good researcher in the helping profes-sions is a natural inquisitiveness, combined with the discipline to follow the steps of the scientific method. After the researcher has reviewed the literature related to the question, he or she moves to the next step in the scientific method: Stating a testable research question or hypothesis. The scientific method calls for the researcher to state the research question or hypothesis before collecting data. *Stating the research question or hypothesis before collecting our data helps us avoid finding what we are looking for in our data—when there is nothing there.* All too often, when we find a relationship in data that we were not looking for, the relationship is an artifact of the situation. It was a fluke, a quirk, or an accident.

We test our hypothesis by going out and gathering data that will either sup-port our hypothesis or disprove our hypothesis. The hypothesis is one of the basic tools of the helping professional researcher. It provides the vehicle that allows us to test our ideas about causes or contributors to social phenomena or social prob-lems. Box 5.3 gives some examples of research hypotheses and questions.

Four Criteria for Hypothesis Development

1. Is the hypothesis stated accurately, clearly, and without ambiguity?
2. Does the hypothesis describe a single relationship? Compound, complex and multiple type relationships used as a hypothesis can be almost impossible to test.
3. Are the hypotheses stated so that they are testable? That is, are they stated in terms of values on scales and measures (see later for examples of hypothesis statements).
4. Will the appropriate scores or values be available to quantitatively test the hypothesis?

Box 5.4 gives some examples of hypothesis statements.

Common Mistakes in Formulating a Research Hypothesis or Question

1. Choosing a hypothesis that is fuzzy or untestable.
2. Failing to review the existing literature related to the hypothesis or research question.

Alternate hypothesis: A substitute explanation for a phenomenon if the origi-nally stated hypothesis is not supported by the data when the hypothesis is tested.

Null hypothesis: A pro-posal based on theory, stating that there will be NO relationship between characteristics. The *null hypothesis* is the reverse of the hypothesis. For example, if we hypothe-size that there is a relation-ship between poor family/social bonds and whether a child partici-pates in delinquent behav-ior, the null hypothesis is that there is **no** relation-ship between poor family/social bonds and a child participating in juve-nile behavior.

Hypothesis Testing: The effort to determine if the expected relationships as described in the hypothe-sis are found to exist in the real world.

5.3   *Examples of Research Hypotheses and Questions*

In explanatory research, a research question can often be the basis for stating several hypotheses. Each hypothesis states one possible answer to the research question (Baker, 1994).

Studying at-risk children, several of my master's students broke down the larger question and decided to examine one aspect of the relationship between children in juvenile detention and their mothers.

> *Research Question:* How many adolescents in juvenile detention were born to teenage mothers?

Or, phrased as a hypothesis,

> *Hypothesis:* More adolescents in juvenile detention will have been born to teenage mothers (mothers who gave birth to a child while a teenager) than to older mothers.

This hypothesis is based on the knowledge that most teenage mothers have fewer emotional and physical resources to share with their children than most older mothers have. The children of teenage mothers who are deprived of adequate emotional and physical support often participate in delinquent behavior that results in detention.

One of my doctoral students did a follow-up study of the effect and outcome of *real burden and perceived burden* of "family caretakers" of the frail elderly.

> *Research Question:* Do caregivers who report they feel overburdened by the necessity of caring for their frail elderly relative express an interest in institutionalizing their relative?

Or, phrased as a hypothesis,

> *Hypothesis:* Caregivers who score significantly higher on the Subjective Burden Inventory will indicate higher levels of interest in the institutionalization of their frail elderly relative.

This is a true hypothesis because it is based on *Caregiver Burden,* which has its foundation in Stress Theory. In this case, Subjective Burden is operationalized for this hypothesis test using the Subjected Burden Inventory developed by Montgomery, Gonyea, and Hooyman (1985).

---

3. Failing to develop a theoretical framework.
4. Collecting data without stating a research hypothesis or question or beginning to collect data without a clear plan for doing the study.
5. Not recognizing the limitation of approaches that could be used to answer the research question.
6. Failing to consider rival answers that could explain the research question.
7. Not making sure suitable statistical procedures are available to analyze the data collected.

Now you are ready to decide how to test your hypothesis.

5.4 *Examples of Hypothesis Statements*

1. *Hypothesis:*   High school graduates will have a statistically significant higher score on the Buss and Perry's (1992) Aggression Questionnaire (AQ) than college graduates will.
2. *Hypothesis:* Women who participant in a child education class will have statistically significant lower scores on Thyer's, (1992) Clinical Anxiety Scale (CAS) than will males who participant in the class.
3. *Hypothesis:* Among eighth graders, those from families with higher levels of family income will obtain statistically significant lower scores on Plake and Parker's, (1982) Mathematics Anxiety Rating Scale-Revised than children from families with lower incomes.

4. *Hypothesis:* There will be a positive statistically significant correlation between life satisfaction and scores on Cherry's Individual Bond Scale (1987), Cherry's Family Bond Scale (1987), and Cherry's Community Bond Scale (1987).
5. *Hypothesis:* African-American and Hispanic female victims of sexual assault will have statistically significant lower scores on measures of depression (Hakstian & McLean, 1989) and will have statistically significant higher scores on intimacy (Miller & Lefcourt, 1982) than will white females who were victims of a sexual assault.

Phase 4: Selecting a Research Method

Chapters 7 and 8 will give you additional help in selecting a research method.

Selecting a *research method* to test your hypothesis, is a bit like selecting a restaurant for dinner. When you select a French Bistro, you still have many decisions you need to make before eating dinner. Choosing the research method helps narrow down your choices, but there are a number of additional decisions to make. If you choose an *experimental* or a *survey* research method, two of many you can choose from, your choice of samples would be different. Your hypothesis would be different. You would use a different approach to gather your data and the instrumentation would be different.

Design or Method, Which Is It?   As already stated, the terms *research design* and *research method* are often used interchangeably to describe the same process. The difference, which is not very important, could be described as follows: A *design* is the plan, whereas the *method* is the procedure for carrying out the plan. In other words, the differences are more semantic than real.

Ten Common Research Methods   Before making a final selection of one of the research methods presented below, you might want to review Chapters 1, 3, and 4 to determine if the method should be qualitative or quantitative. The following are brief descriptions of the most commonly used qualitative and quantitative methods.

1. **The Historical Study**—A method used to reconstruct the past objectively and accurately. This is a qualitative method discussed in more depth in Chapter 4.

2. **The Field Study**—A method used to gather and analyze descriptive observations of individuals and groups in a given natural setting. This qualitative method was discussed in more depth in Chapter 4.

3. **The Descriptive Study**—A method of systematically describing a problem, population, or characteristics of interest, most often based on actual counts of characteristics and events. This method can be used in both a qualitative and a quantitative study. It is briefly discussed in Chapters 3 and 15 (Frequency Distribution).

4. **The Correlation Study**—A method that allows the researcher to mathematically determine the extent to which one or more variables correspond with variations in another variable.

5. **The Causal Study**—A method to mathematically test for *cause-and-effect* relationships between independent and dependent variables.

6. **The Experimental Study**—A method in which two or more groups of subjects that are identical on all variables, but the experimental group is exposed to a treatment intervention, while the control group is not exposed. After the experiment, the groups are compared to determine the effect of the treatment intervention.

7. **The Quasi-Experimental Study**—An experimental method that does not meet all the criteria to be called a true experimental design. A quasi-experimental study might not control for all of the important independent variables.

8. **The Time-Series Study**—A method to investigate patterns and sequences of growth or change as it occurs over time. Currently, the most popular approach in the helping professions is the *single-subject-design* (see Chapter 6).

9. **The Applied Research Study**—A method utilized to assist in the development of new interventions, programs, and knowledge that will help alleviate some type of human problem. It can be used to validate the degree of success or failure of a new program or intervention. This research approach may use several of the methods previously mentioned. This approach is incorporated into the design of a new program or intervention to test its effectiveness.

10. **The Evaluation Research Study**—This approach is used to determine the effectiveness of a model program, an existing program, or an agency. Typically the program to be evaluated has been in operation for a period of time, and the researcher develops an approach for evaluating the program. This approach does not involve a fixed set of steps. It typically incorporates a combination of these methods to evaluate a program.

Phase 5: Choosing the Population or a Sample

In Chapter 13, you will find a more in-depth treatment of sampling issues. The chapter on sampling is in the statistical section of this text because it is a statistical procedure.

In this *phase* of planning a research project, you need to make major decisions about your target population and sample.

1. What population will you study?
2. Will you study the entire the population or a sample of the population?
3. If you choose to use a sample, how large does it need to be?
4. What sampling technique will you use?

In almost all cases, a large carefully selected sample is better than a small carefully selected sample.

Choosing the Population or Sample You Will Study   Following is a checklist of five questions you need to answer before selecting a population and sample. Your answer to four of the questions should be "yes," before you make any additional decisions about your research effort.

1. The people you select to participate in your study need to have ownership of the problem and a first-hand knowledge of the problem. They should be directly linked to the cause or effect of the problem. Alternatively, they need to possess the characteristics of interest you are studying. If we are trying to learn how sexual assault affects women, we study women who were sexually assaulted; we might compare them to women who have *not* been sexually assaulted, but we do not study women who have not been sexually assaulted.

   Do the participants have ownership of the problem or situation you are going to study?
   Yes _____ No _____

2. You need to determine if the people you wish to learn about are accessible and if they will cooperate in your research effort. It is very difficult to gain access to some groups of people—for instance, college seniors who use illegal drugs, or politicians who have taken a bribe and have not been apprehended. These are examples of groups that are almost impossible to access and even harder to get to cooperate in a research study.

   Are the people you wish to study accessible, and will they cooperate?
   Yes _____ No _____

3. You need to decide if you are going to try to use the entire population or a sample of the population. If you plan to study a group of 100 to 200 or more people, depending on your financial backing, you might be wise to select all of the people in the group. If you are planning to study a group of say, 2,000 people, however, unless you are well financed, you will probably need to use a sample of the 2,000 individuals. You should be able to answer "yes" to one of the following questions:

If you are planning to use the entire population, have you reviewed the sections in Chapter 13 on "generalizability" and "nonprobability sampling"?
Yes _____ No _____ Not App _____

If you are going to use a sample of a population have you reviewed Chapter 13, "Probability and Sampling" and sampling issues?
Yes _____ No _____ Not App _____

4. If you plan to conduct research with human subjects, most academic and government related institutions require the research plan to be approved by a committee, often called an Institutional Review Board or Human Subjects Committee. This committee is to protect the rights and safety of the participants. This is typically a formal procedure.

Have you checked to see if your research study would fall under the auspices of a Institutional Review Board or Human Subjects Committee?
Yes _____ No _____ Not App _____

Parameter: A specific value of a population that is used as a reference to determine the value of other population variables.

Parametric Test: Hypotheses tests (in the form of tests of significance) based on assumptions about the parameter values of the population. These tests of statistical significance require that at least one variable is an interval or ratio level of measure. The sample distribution of the interval or ratio variable(s) must be normally distributed. If you are comparing different groups, the members should be randomly assigned to each group. This will help meet the assumption that group members are independent of one another. The t-test, the analysis of variance, and the Pearson product-moment correlation are examples of parametric tests.

Deciding on the Size of Your Sample
If you plan to use the entire population to test your hypothesis, you do not need to be overly concerned with issues related to sample size. If you plan to use a sample of a larger population, however, you will need to know:

1. How large a sample you will need to be able to generalize to the larger population you are trying to study
2. How large a sample you will need for an adequate sample for the statistical analysis

The size of your sample is a very important component of your research plan. If you have an inadequate sample, the entire research project can be questioned as to representativeness and adequacy in terms of the statistical analysis.

The section in Chapter 13, "Selecting a Good Sample Size" will provide you with a mathematical formula to help you determine the sample size you will need.

The sample size needed for a parametric test is another issue.

Sample Size Based on the Number of Groups in the Study

1. If you plan to use a *one-group sample,* for instance in a survey research study, the minimum size of the sample must be large enough to meet the requirements of the statistical procedures used to analyze the data. This requirement is in addition to the assumptions about the data that must be met to use parametric testing to analyze your data (for example, the sample must also be representative of the population under study). A sample of between 100 and 150 randomly selected individuals who are representative of the larger population is an adequate sample size for most studies where parametric statistical procedures are used. For this reason, your chances of locating a professional journal to publish a paper based on a sample of *less than* 100 cases is not very good.

2. If you plan to *compare two or more groups,* it is best to use 25 to 50 participants in each group because that number will meet the requirements of statistical procedures that can be used to analyze data in a group comparison study.

3. When deciding on sample size, be sure to take into consideration those in your sample who might refuse to participate in the research study or who will not complete the study or questionnaire. The attrition rate (see the following description) of your sample is very important. If a substantial number of people selected for your study do not answer the survey questions (that is, do not participate in your study), this sampling problem will threaten the generalizability of your findings because there will be no way to know if the sample is representative of the population. Thus, the findings will *not* be generalizable to the population under study.

Choosing Your Sampling Technique   After you have decided on the population or the size of your sample, you need to determine what sampling technique you will use to select the participants in your study. You must decide if you will use a *probability* or *nonprobability sample.*

There are several common-sampling approaches based on probability sampling that you could use: (1) simple random sampling, (2) systematic sampling, and (3) proportional stratified sampling.

The most common nonprobability sampling approaches are (1) quota sampling, (2) snowball sampling, and (3) available/judgmental sampling. These approaches are discussed in detail in Chapter 13, "Probability and Sampling."

SIX CONSIDERATIONS FOR CHOOSING YOUR SAMPLE

1. **Generalization:** To what population do you want to generalize the findings from your study? For example, if you want to generalize your findings to inner city adjudicated adolescent females, your sampling approach needs to be very precise. If you only want to describe a single group of inner city adjudicated girls in Miami, Florida, the sampling approach need not be so rigorous.

2. **Cost of Precision:** The more precisely you design your sampling techniques, the more it will cost. Precision is related to sample size.

3. **Availability:** Are the possible participants accessible? Is a list of the population available? What is the estimated dropout rate of the people you want to participate in the study?

4. **Attrition Rate:** This is the number of people randomly selected for inclusion in a study but who did not (for one reason or another) participate in the study. This is a serious threat to the generalizability of the findings to the population under study.

5. **Geographic Location:** Be careful of selecting participants that cover a large geographic area. A sample spread over a large area is difficult to manage in terms of administration and follow-up. The population in a large geographic area is probably made up of different subgroups. Sampling people over a large geographic area is best handled using a more complex stratified or cluster sampling approach; however, this typically increases cost.

6. **Knowledge of the Population:** It is important to know the subjects you wish to study. Demographic information on the population is a real

advantage. For example, if you want to study the opinions of social work students on the privatization of human services, you need to know the demographics of students majoring in social work. At the individual university level, demographics are available on those students as well as on the entire student body. This information will allow you to compare those majoring in social work to the entire student body. Additionally, if you look hard enough, you will find demographics on students majoring in social work throughout the United States. Lists of members of a population that you wish to study and demographic information on them gives you a real advantage when selecting a sample.

Phase 6: Choosing Scales or Measures to Test Your Hypothesis

Never construct a scale before doing an exhaustive search of the literature to see if someone else developed a similar scale and has already tested or used it.

In Chapter 8, you will find a more in-depth treatment of issues related to choosing appropriate measures and scales.

You must make several decisions about the measurement of characteristics or variables related to your hypotheses.

1. What demographic data will you need to be able to clearly describe the participants in your study?
2. What demographic data will you need to help test your hypothesis (that is, control variables)?
3. Which measures/scales are the best measures to test your hypotheses for your quantitative study?
4. What is the best layout and wording for your questionnaire?
5. Which data-gathering method is the best approach for testing the hypothesis and for meeting the needs of the participants?

Particularly for new researchers, it is important to find models or studies that have used a method, sample, and measures or scales that you would like to use in your research. This approach will save you a great deal of time and confusion. I spent several months developing and testing a scale on "loneliness" only to later stumble on the Loneliness Rating Scale (Scalise, Ginter, & Gerstein, 1984).

Before you begin the process of choosing the scales or measures that you will use to test your hypotheses, you will want to review Chapter 8.

Phase 7: Data Gathering

Chapter 9 will describe data-gathering approaches in much more detail.

The Five Approaches to Collecting Data
1. Personal interviews
2. Group administration (giving the questionnaire to a group of participants at the same time, such as students in your human service research class)
3. Mailing questionnaires to participants
4. Telephone interviews
5. Case record "interviews" (using archival data)

The data collecting approach you select, can make or break you. Consider a researcher's decision to do personal interviews with several hundred people. Without considerable time and money, this type of study would be very difficult, if not impossible.

Consider this example of a practical approach: A student who needs to do a small research project for a mental health research class asks members of the research class to participate in the study as a sample. The students are asked to answer a survey questionnaire with 25 close-ended items, and the questionnaires are collected as students leave the classroom.

This is a very practical approach to doing a small study. There are no data gathering problems because the participants return the questionnaires as they leave the classroom.

To make the best choice of a data collecting method for your project, you will need to know how the different data collecting methods affect accuracy, cost, generalizability of findings, and time spent gathering the data.

Statement of Informed Consent   When I was doing my dissertation at Columbia University, signed consents were required unless the signed consent would jeopardize the anonymity or confidentiality of the participant. Please review the section "The Issue of Consent in Social Research," in Chapter 2.

Phase 8: Analyzing the Data

After taking a course on statistics, if you do NOT feel comfortable doing the statistical analysis of your data, GET HELP! If you do get help, be sure to have your *analyst* teach you what he or she did as he or she does it. You get double your money's worth.

The material in this chapter is not meant to explain the statistical procedures. Part IV has specific chapters on the most often used statistical procedures. (Actual statistical tests are presented in these chapters.) This presentation is intended to help you *plan and carry out your statistical analyses.*

Preparing the Data for Analysis   Setting up the data file is the first thing you do. It is not complicated, but certain procedures can save you a great deal of time. (See Chapter 9.)

Hopefully, you will use a computer program to help you do the statistical analysis. You should follow the format that the computer program requires for inputting your data into a suitable computer file. Most computer statistical programs, such as SPSS and SAS, are written for Windows. If you use Windows, you can use these programs to input your data. They have fairly easy ways of setting up a data file.

Steps for Analyzing Your Data   The question of how to analyze data has perplexed many a new researcher. Generally, five steps can be followed when analyzing data to help you identify the statistical procedures you will need.

STEP 1.   Use a questionnaire to organize the statistical analysis. Set up a notebook and assign one page to each item and scale on the questionnaire. This procedure will help throughout the analysis.

STEP 2.   Begin the statistical analysis by finding the frequency distribution of each item and scale on your questionnaire.

A frequency table and bar graph should be constructed for each question on which you gathered data. If you are using a computer statistical program, request output that gives you both a frequency table and a bar graph or a histogram for the responses to each question and scale in the analysis. Bar graphs are used to display nominal data and histograms are used to display rank, interval, and ratio data. A frequency analysis is called a univariate analysis.

When you have the frequency output, make notes describing your sample in terms of the information collected on the demographic questions on the questionnaire. To express the statistical findings use the actual numbers produced for each question, frequency of each response to each question, averages, the median, and standard deviation to describe your sample.

STEP 3.   Conduct a bivariate analysis. Examine the relationship between pairs of questions. To find the relationship between two variables (or items on your questionnaire) use crosstabs (also called crosstabulation or crossbreak) and statistical tests such as chi square, *t*-test, or correlations and their levels of significance (see Chapters 17, 18, and 19). Record any statistically significant relationships between any two variables/questions and scales that may be related.

Findings from these tests describe your sample in terms of relationships between questions and responses to questions. List the bivariate coefficients between the items, and between items and scales that have statistically significant values of between $p \leq .050$ and $p < .000$.

STEP 4.   Check the reliability of each scale you used in your study. List the reliability coefficients of your measures/scales. The better the reliability, the more likely the scales are reflecting the perspective of your participants (see Chapter 19, the section on reliability).

STEP 5.   Test your hypothesis about variables found in one group using multiple regression analysis. Record any statistically significant coefficients (β coefficients) between the hypothesized variables—items and scale scores on the questionnaire (see Chapter 20). If you hypothesize a relationship between three or more variables, you might use the F values, and their levels of significance from a MANOVA (multiple analysis of variance) (see Chapter 21). The above are both multivariate analyses.

Before you decide on your plan for analysis, review the statistical procedures you will use. The procedures are explained in the chapters in Part IV.

Once you have completed the data analysis, you are ready to begin to interpret your findings.

Phase 9: Drawing Conclusions from the Analysis

In the conclusion section you combine your informed opinions and the statistical findings from your data to produce a better understanding of the hypothesis or research question. Remember that all results are findings even if they disprove your hypothesis. All findings—those that support the hypotheses or disprove them—are judged on the methods and procedures used to produce those findings.

Your major task in Phase 9 (the last phase of a research project) is to draw conclusions from your *data analysis*. The question for most new researchers, however, is *How do I figure out what I found from the data analysis?* Do not feel too bad; for most of us, doing this task is difficult. Even so, there are ways to organize the process that will help.

(Chapter 27 presents a model for writing up the results of your conclusions.)

The following approach will help get you started. It will not tell you what you have found, but it will tell you what to look for and how to organize the results of the data analysis in a logical way.

Until this point in the research process, we could say that you have turned the people in your sample into numbers. You have taken individual characteristics and individual opinions and given them number values. When making decisions about what the data analysis indicates, you need to turn the numbers back into "composite" people. This is a mathematical picture of the typical individual or individuals in your sample. When drawing conclusions, you will need to tell the people's story revealed in your data.

Step 1. Before you draw conclusions about your findings, you should review the procedures you used to do the research. Compared to the ideal, what limitations did your research method have? How does your sample stack up against what you believe would be the ideal sample? What are the limitations of the measures/scales used in the study? Compare your level of research with what you would have liked to do. Make notes on these limitations under a heading you will use later in your report: *Limitations of the study*.

Step 2. Use the *frequency data* on demographic items to sketch a mathematical, demographic picture of the participants in your study. This will be useful later. Compare your sample with the population you were trying to study. Is your sample similar enough to the total population to be able to generalize findings from your research to that population? Notes on these issues will help you and others decide if the findings can be generalized to the population you are trying to study.

Step 3. Next, examine the outcome of the statistical tests of the hypotheses. Make notes on the coefficients between the hypothesized *independent* and the *dependent* variables. During this process, you ask questions of the findings of the data analysis. Some questions about your study you would try to answer are the following:

- How do the relationships between the hypothesized variables compare to what you expected to find?
- How do the items and scales (variables) relate to each other? Make notes of the actual statistical coefficients and their levels of significance for each relationship between the variables (that is, Education and Income: $r = .48$, $p \leq .008$).
- What do your findings tell about the population you were studying? The above ($r = .48$, $p \leq .008$) would tell us that a moderate correlation existed between education and income, and that there are only 8 chances in a 1000 that the relationship exists because of an accident or chance (see Chapter 12).

Step 4. Make notes on any other relationships identified in your bivariate analysis that are of interest, even if you did not include them in a hypothesis.

Step 5. Make notes on how your statistical findings are supported by similar or previous research you found in the literature. This is another place where the literature review is very important. If your findings are very different from those found in the literature, check your findings at least three times very carefully.

Step 6. Quantitative reports and papers clearly distinguish between the *findings section* and the *discussion section* of the report or paper. In quantitative (statistical) research papers, the findings section is the report of the statistical analysis and tests. The discussion section is the conclusions drawn from the statistical findings.

In the finding section, it is easy to be caught up in interpreting what you observed rather than writing an unadulterated description of what the data analysis produced. This mistake becomes obvious when you find yourself repeating in the discussion section what you said in the findings section.

POSTSCRIPT

In this chapter, in addition to reviewing the nine phases of a quantitative research project, you have also reviewed how the scientific method is used in the helping professions. Briefly, we first hypothesize that a relationship exists between two or more variables. Next, the hypothesis is tested to see if the relationship exists. Finally, the statistical results of the hypothesis tests are compared to the hypotheses with which we began the study.

In Chapter 6, you will find the steps involved in conducting and analyzing a study of a single-subject (one individual, group, agency, or program). This is considered a weak quantitative study because of the sample size (N = 1). However, it is a very useful approach in the early stages of developing an intervention and in determining the effectiveness of your intervention with a single client. The remaining chapters will cover the methods and statistical analysis used in quantitative research.

Good luck with your research project!

REFERENCES

Baker, T. L. (1994). *Doing social research* (2nd ed.). New York: McGraw-Hill.

Buss, A. H., & Perry, M. (1992). The aggression questionnaire. *Journal of Personality and Social Psychology, 63,* 452–459.

Cherry, A. L. (1987). Social bond theory and alcohol use among college students. *Journal of College Student Personnel, 28*(2), 128–135.

Gyarfas, M. (1983). The scientific imperative again. *Social Service Review, 57,* 149–150.

Hakstian, A. R., & McLean, P. D. (1989). Brief screen for depression. *Psychological Assessment, 1,* 139–141.

Miller, R. S., & Lefcourt, H. M. (1982). The assessment of social intimacy. *Journal of Personality Assessment, 46,* 514–518.

Montgomery, R. V., Gonyea, J. G., & Hooyman, N. R. (1985). Caregiving and the experience of subjective and objective burden. *Family Relations, 34*(1), 19–26.

Plake, B. S., & Parker, C. S. (1982). Mathematics anxiety rating scale-revised (MARS-R). *Education and Psychological Measurement, 42,* 551–557.

Rubin, A. & Babbie, E. (1997). *Research methods for social work* (3rd ed.). Pacific Grove, CA: Brooks/Cole.

Scalise, J. J., Ginter E. J., & Gerstein, L. H. (1984). A multidimensional loneliness measure: The loneliness rating scale (LSR). *Journal of Personality Assessment, 48,* 525–530.

Thyer, B. (1992). Clinical Anxiety Scale (CAS). In Hudson, W. W. (Ed.). *The WALMYR assessment scales scoring manual.* Tempe, AZ: WALMYR.

RESEARCH METHODS FOR HELPING PROFESSIONALS

Chapter 6

SINGLE-SUBJECT RESEARCH DESIGNS

WHAT IS A SINGLE-SUBJECT RESEARCH DESIGN?

The single-subject design is as easy to understand as it is to use. The key to understanding it is to remember that the researcher takes *repeated measures* over time on the same target behavior or characteristic on the same person or on one unit of analysis. The targeted behavior must be a characteristic that can be counted or that can be given a mathematical value, like the scores on a psychometric scale. The data must have mathematical value so that it can be presented in a time flow chart, like a line graph or bar chart for visual examination, and so that it can be used in a statistical analysis.

To evaluate the effectiveness of a treatment intervention using the simple A-B single-subject design, you first collect data on the behavior prior to beginning your intervention/treatment. This is called the "A" phase or the *baseline phase*. The baseline is evidence for how frequently the behavior or problem occurred before the intervention is implemented.

The next step is phase B or the *intervention phase*. While continuing to collect data on the same variables at the same intervals, you start the *intervention*.

After the intervention phase, the data collected during that phase is compared with the data collected during the baseline phase. The analysis consists of plotting a graph. The scores obtained during the baseline and intervention phase are used to determine if a statistically significant change occurred in the targeted behavior after the introduction of the intervention.

In this way, the single-subject design can help verify that a planned change did or did not occur. If the expected change took place during the intervention phase, the single-subject design provides objective support that the behavioral change was related to the treatment intervention. In a clinical setting, it allows us to better understand the events and circumstances that might aggravate or reduce the targeted behavior(s).

> The single-subject design was devised to measure change in one person or one unit of analysis over time using *repeated measures* of the same target behavior or characteristic.

USING THE SINGLE-SUBJECT RESEARCH DESIGN

The *single-subject research design* can help you study changes in one person, or one family, or one group. It is an easy way to tell if changes a person makes over time are a part of an ongoing pattern or if they are a real change in behavior. That is, it can be difficult to tell if a person or group changes because of an intervention you are using or because they change every so often on their own. The single subject research design can help you determine if the change is so great that it could not have been an accidental change. It will help support your assertion that the change was brought about because of an effective intervention intended to change the behavior (Barlow & Hersen, 1984).

See Advanced Level 6.1 on page 112.

➡ **Advanced Level**
see page 112

99

BACKGROUND ON THE SINGLE-SUBJECT RESEARCH DESIGN

The use of the single-subject design began during the early 1970s when behavior modification techniques were adopted by psychologists and social workers in the field of mental health. Using behavior modification techniques requires the practitioner to employ repeated measures of the behavior to be extinguished or reduced. In the 1980's, this approach became extremely popular in the field of mental retardation and in group homes where household tasks and concrete behavior needed to be monitored.

The single-subject design was adopted by human service professionals in the 1980's because it strengthened their role as clinician-researchers. Prior to the elaboration of the single-subject design, the primary source of clinical knowledge came from "practice wisdom" based on clinical experience and from group experiments. Practice wisdom varies with the personality of the clinician, however, and group experiments were not practical for therapeutic interventions with individuals. Moreover, group experiments tend to obscure individual changes because group experiments produce averages of change for the entire population of the group (Levy & Olson, 1979).

By the mid 1980s, the single-subject design became the centerpiece of what was called the *clinical-research model.* This model proposed that it was the responsibility of the human service professional to hypothesize and test the interventions used in practice. The single-subject design is viewed as an essential tool in this process (Bloom, Fischer, & Orme, 1995).

FUNDAMENTALS OF THE SINGLE-SUBJECT DESIGN

The single-subject design is an experimental research design and is often called an *interrupted time-series design.* Single-subject studies are typically carried out in three phases called an A-B-A design. The first letter "A' stands for a period where *no* treatment is given; typically, it stands for the baseline phase. The letter "B" stands for the period when the person is receiving the treatment. The second letter "A" stands for the period after the treatment is stopped. Other common designs are the A-B, the A-B-A-B, and some variation of the A-B-C-A design. In the A-B-C-A design, the letter "C" stands for a second treatment phase that is different from the "B" treatment phase. Box 6.1 gives an example of an intervention.

▷ **Advanced Level**
see page 112

See Advanced Level 6.2 on page 112.

VALIDITY ISSUES RELATED TO THE SINGLE-SUBJECT DESIGN

When specific interventions are used to change behavior and the behavior actually changes, it is important to rule out other causes for the changes. Conditions other than the intervention may have caused the change in behavior. These causes are considered threats to the internal and external validity of the intervention.

6.1   *An Intervention for Excessive Water Consumption*

In one case, when working at a mental hospital, I collected baseline data for two days on a patient's water drinking behavior. Excessive water intake is dangerous. If this behavior is not controlled, it will cause the death of the patient. The data consisted of observations of the person drinking water or other liquids. We estimated the amount of intake of water for each incident.

Data were collected for 6 staggered 30-minute intervals over a 24-hour period. This gave us a baseline of how often and approximately how much water the person was drinking a day. With this data as an objective estimate of liquid intake, we initiated an intervention to reduce water intake by educating the person on the problems of drinking too little or too much water and requesting that the person drink only 10 cups of water a day. The person also was asked to record on a flowchart each cup of water he drank. His recording of his own behavior alerted him to the need to control his water intake, and he did so with the support of the staff.

There are at least four types of threats to the *internal validity* of the single-subject design: *maturation, reactivity, regression toward the mean,* and *history.* You can control for these threats by using a baseline as a comparison.

When an intervention works, the graph using single-subject design often looks like the Figure 6.1. The behavior is stable during the baseline phase. Then the target behavior is reduced over several days once the intervention is introduced.

Maturation would appear as a continual change occurring in both the baseline phase and intervention phase. As you can see in Figure 6.2, the behavior was declining in the baseline phase and continued to decline during the treatment phase. This change is probably caused by *maturation* rather than by the influence of the intervention.

Reactivity appears as an initial change in behavior when the intervention is first introduced. The behavior will revert back to baseline levels, however, when the novelty of the intervention wears off and before the end of the intervention phase. In Figure 6.3, the behavior drops for the first three days of the intervention and then slowly returns to the baseline level. Changes like these are best explained as *reactivity* rather than as the effect of the intervention.

Regression toward the mean is seen as an extreme score followed by a score closer to the mean score. Figure 6.4 shows a cycle of behavior that increased and decreased through the baseline and intervention phase but was not interrupted by the intervention. The behavior is observed as many as five times a day and as few as one time per day. Even so, the behavior tends to occur two to three times a day on average. These changes in behavior are best explained as *regression to the mean* rather than as the impact of the intervention.

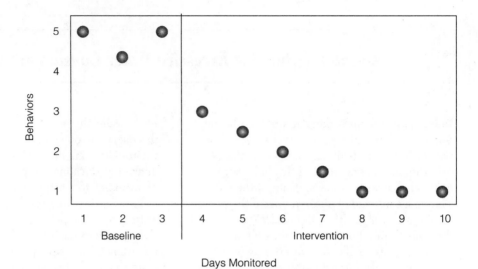

FIGURE **6.1**

CHANGE EXPECTED AS A RESULT OF AN EFFECTIVE INTERVENTION

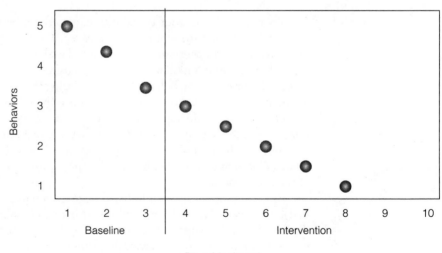

FIGURE **6.2**

CHANGE CAUSED BY MATURATION

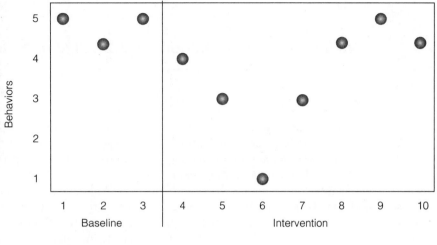

FIGURE **6.3**

CHANGE CAUSED BY REACTIVITY

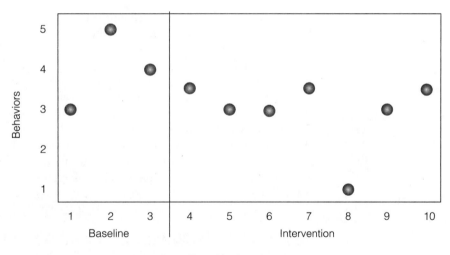

FIGURE **6.4**

CHANGE CAUSED BY REGRESSION TOWARD THE MEAN

6.2   *History as an Explanation for a Change in Behavior*

A mother of a five-year-old boy went to a child psychotherapist requesting help to curb the child's threatening and aggressive behavior toward his younger sister, a fairly common problem among siblings. The boy had recently become more aggressive and had begun hitting his three-year-old sister. After a medical examination that found no biological problems related to the behavior, baseline data on the number of occurrences of aggressive behavior per day were collected over a two-week period. Then the intervention began. The intervention had two components, the first consisting of a set of activities intended to help develop a relationship between the two children. The second component was a system of rewards and time-outs developed to help extinguish the boy's aggression toward his sister.

Within two weeks after the intervention was begun, the aggressive behavior virtually stopped; however, the effectiveness of the intervention had to be questioned. At the same time the aggressive behavior was reduced, the boy began preschool, so he was out of the home and separated from his sister most of day.

> If you use the single-subject design, multiple baseline measures increase your ability to pinpoint unlikely coincidences, and they give more support for suggesting the cause for any change in the behavior.

The single-subject design cannot rule out all threats to validity. Even with a baseline measure, one cannot altogether rule out the internal threat to validity known as *history*. A historical event might have occurred exactly when the intervention began. If this happens, the target behavior might change because of the historical event rather than because of the intervention. (See Box 6.2.)

To counter these types of historical threats, we can monitor several related behaviors that will give us several baselines to be used for comparison. In the case outlined in Box 6.2, the psychotherapist could have also monitored the amount of time per day that the two children were together. If she had monitored the time variable, she would have seen that when the amount of time the two children spent together was reduced, the number of aggressive acts committed by the boy was also reduced.

REPLICATION INCREASES EXTERNAL VALIDITY

Using the single-subject design with a single case to evaluate the effectiveness of an intervention lacks external validity. Replication of the intervention can support a finding that the intervention works or does not work. That the intervention worked with one client does not mean it will work with other clients. If the intervention and outcomes are similar in other cases, however, we would have some justification for believing the intervention had some external validity.

HOW LONG IS A GOOD BASELINE?

A good baseline has enough repeated measures to allow you to rule out extraneous factors that could explain changes in behavior caused by factors other than the intervention. The baseline should be as long as is practical and ethically possible. For example, it would not be ethical to withhold treatment in the case of a person who is a suicide risk to acquire a good baseline.

When monitoring behaviors that seldom occur, you will need a longer baseline phase to show up cycles and variations in the frequency of that behavior. You will need a shorter baseline when monitoring behaviors that occur very frequently. At any rate, the baseline data should be gathered until a stable baseline appears.

VARIATIONS OF THE SINGLE-SUBJECT DESIGN

Remember, although the single-subject design is a variation on the experimental design, it has many of the weaknesses inherent in both the qualitative and quantitative study. A single-subject study cannot be generalized because one person under study does not make the whole. This is a quantitative weakness. The single-subject design is a univariate analysis, and that does not provide context or conditions. This is a qualitative weakness.

The basic single-subject design is the A-B design. Although this is a weak design, it still provides an objective method of observing changes or a lack of change in behavior. The classic single-subject design is the A-B-A-B design, and the weakest single-subject design is the B design. In this design, no baseline data are collected.

The A-B-A-B design (often called the *withdrawal/reversal design*) helps us rule out extraneous causes for the change in behavior. With the A-B-A-B design, after the first baseline and intervention phase, the intervention is stopped. Theoretically, if the intervention was the only reason for the change in behavior then the behavior would revert back to baseline levels in the second A phase, the "withdrawal phase." Then after the behavior is again stable, the intervention is introduced a second time to see if the behavior changes in the same way. If it does, the researcher can assume that the intervention caused the change.

In most cases when we are dealing with human behavior, however, a complete reversal of behavior does not always occur when the intervention is withdrawn. In many cases, once the behavior changes, it stays changed or it continues to improve. Sadly, this lack of reversal of behavior when the intervention is withdrawn suggests that the intervention may *not* have caused the change. Something other than the intervention could have caused the change, and it is maintaining the change. For example, in the case presented in Box 6.2, although it was a good intervention and though it might help the mother develop other child management skills, separation of the siblings is the more likely cause for the reduction in the five-year-old boy's aggressive behavior toward his younger sister.

An Example of the Single-Subject Design

An actual example of how a single-subject design was used in a treatment situation can provide another way for you to remember and understand how this approach works. This case was published as a paper in the journal *Case Analysis: In Social*

Science and Social Therapy titled, "Separation Anxiety and School Phobia: An Intervention to Revive the School Bond" (Cherry, 1992).

In this case, it came to the attention of the school social worker that one of the third-grade students was showing the signs of a child who was school phobic. The eight-year-old boy had been progressively missing more and more school because of transitory illnesses, such as stomach problems and headaches.

Early in October, the parents asked for a conference with the school social worker. They stated they were "at their wits' end" trying to deal with their son's problem. They said that their son, Mark* seemed to be obsessed with a fear that they would be killed, or that he would come home from school and something terrible would have happened to members of the family.

When he did attend school, he typically became physically ill during the school day and had to be sent to the school nurse. Too often, he would become so ill that his mother or father would have to leave work and pick him up before the end of the school day.

The only thing that calmed him down for even short periods of time when he attended school was the school nurse's allowing him to call his mother at work. These calls became a problem for the child's mother, who indicated that they were interfering with her job. The father, torn between disciplining his son with a "heavy hand" or treating him with "kid gloves," stated, "I don't know how much pressure to put on him!"

After meeting with the parents and Mark, it became evident that for at least six months Mark had increasingly shown signs of an attachment disorder. As the school year passed, the symptoms became worse. Both Mark and his parents asked the school social worker for help.

The intervention that was developed in conjunction with the parents, Mark, and the school personnel consisted of the following components:

1. For two weeks, Mark was to report to the school social worker's office every morning upon arriving at school and at lunchtime. During these periods, which lasted from five to ten minutes, Mark and the school social worker would talk about what Mark was feeling at the time, and they would discuss the forthcoming day's activities.
2. If Mark was not feeling well, he could report to the nurse's office. His time there was limited to 10 minutes for each visit, however, and then (unless in the nurse's judgment he was severely sick) he would be sent back to the classroom.
3. Three-minute telephone calls to his mother were allowed during the first week, but only at noon. In the case of extreme anxiety, after consultation with the school nurse and school social worker, additional telephone calls would be permitted. All telephone calls would be made from the social worker's office.
4. During the second week, the three-minute telephone calls would be limited to every other day during the lunch hour.

---

*Not his real name.

5. In addition to the intervention with the school social worker, as described above, Mark's self-esteem and attachment to the school were bolstered by arrangements for him to become involved in a "public service project." Each day upon his arrival at school, Mark was one of several students who were assigned to help children in a Head Start class go from their bus to their classroom. Mark looked forward to this responsibility. It also helped him get his mind off himself and his anxieties.

This multilevel intervention had two specific strengths: It set limits on the problematic behaviors, but also provided support for the anxious child. While time in the nurse's office and telephone calls were being restricted, counseling sessions and day-to-day contact with the school social worker offered Mark a more appropriate form of support and reassurance. The intervention also provided for emergencies; if Mark's anxiety was truly unmanageable, exceptions could be made without scrapping the intervention.

To determine the effect of the intervention, the school social worker monitored any changes in behavior by using a single-subject design. The intervention was to last eight weeks. Data would be collected on three target behaviors.

The first step was to gather *baseline* data. Single-subject methodology would usually require that the three behaviors be monitored for several weeks to gather the baseline data before starting the intervention phase. Because of the nature and seriousness of the problem, however, it was deemed unethical to withhold treatment to collect baseline data. Instead, it was decided to develop a baseline on data that already existed. In this case, there were excellent school records of the number of *days that Mark had missed school,* the number of *times he visited the school nurse,* and a good estimate of the number of *times he had called his mother* over the previous four weeks.

As stated earlier, the best approach to verify change when using a single-subject design is to use several related measures. In this case, three behavioral measures were used.

The second step was to collect data on the targeted behaviors for eight more school weeks while the intervention was being used. Three line charts were developed.

Figure 6.5 is a record of the number of school days Mark missed. Figure 6.6 is a record of the actual amount of time he spent in the nurse's office each day. Figure 6.7 is a record of the number of telephone calls he made to his mother each day.

Based on a visual examination, the results were rather dramatic. Although things got off to a slow start, after the third week there was a drastic reduction in the time Mark spent in the nurse's office. By the fourth week, the first without mandated sessions with the school social worker, Mark reported being much happier upon his arrival at school, and his attitude was much more positive and relaxed.

After the fifth week of the intervention, the school social worker talked openly with Mark about the changes that were observed in his behavior and attitude. Mark told the school social worker that he had no idea why he had been so anxious, nor did he know why he no longer felt that way. When he finally got his

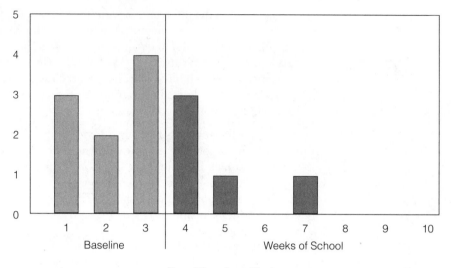

FIGURE **6.5**

DAYS MISSED PER WEEK

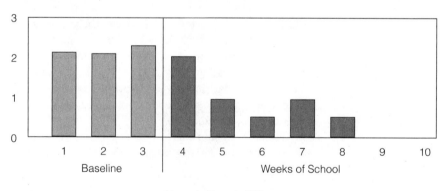

FIGURE **6.6**

HOURS MARK SPENT IN THE NURSE'S OFFICE

anxiety under control, Mark was as happy about it as were his parents and school officials. Even without the flow charts or the objective findings of the single-subject methodology, it was obvious from talking with Mark that a change had taken place. Nevertheless, the data collected using the single-subject design is another view of events, and it can be used to suggest that a statistically significant change did or did not occur.

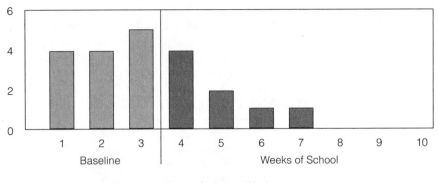

FIGURE **6.7**

NUMBER OF PHONE CALLS MARK MADE PER WEEK

ANALYZING SINGLE-SUBJECT DATA

Four basic questions can be asked of the data to determine if a single-subject experiment was successful.

1. Is there an observable pattern of behavior that suggests a change in behavior after the intervention began?
2. What are the possibilities that the observed change was merely a part of an ongoing fluctuation in the behavior?
3. If the change is related to the intervention, is the change statistically significant?
4. Did the change make a practical difference? Although statistically significant, the intervention would not be considered a success if it only increased Mark's school attendance from two to three days a week.

➪ **Advanced Level**
see page 113

WEAKNESSES OF THE SINGLE-SUBJECT DESIGN

1. The findings from a single-subject study are somewhere between qualitative and quantitative. The findings are not derived from a method that meets the statistical assumptions of quantitative research, nor do they have the depth of a qualitative study although it is a study of one person or one group.
2. Another problem is the placebo effect. A placebo effect will cause some change. The question that must be answered is, Does the intervention have more of an effect on the experimental group than the placebo has on the control group?

3. There can be significant change without its making a real difference in the problem being treated. In the earlier case, the intervention would not be considered a success if it increased Mark's school attendance only from two to three days a week. (See the Glossary for an in-depth explanation of **placebo**.)

Postscript

The single-subject design is an excellent method for testing the effectiveness of an intervention on one person. It is useful when you are working with individual clients to help develop your skills as a practitioner. It is useful for demonstrating the effectiveness of the intervention you choose to use with your client. It is also a good way to show a managed care organization that might be paying for the treatment that the treatment is working.

In Chapters 7 and 8 you will learn more about actually gathering your data and the scales and measures that are useful in this task. These chapters will be followed by further discussion to help you understand how to analyze your data once you have collected it.

Advanced Level Material

Advanced Level 6.1   With the single-subject research design, you can take the analysis of what would otherwise be a qualitative study of one person, or one family or one group and collect data so that you can also do a quantitative analysis of your one-person study. In other words, the single-subject design is an objective approach for monitoring specific behaviors of any single entity. The sample size is one (N = 1). Time-series data are collected over several weeks or months, before, during, and after an intervention to change a behavior.

Presently, it is the best approach available for measuring change over time in one person or one system. Consequently, since the early 1980s, single-subject methodology has gained popularity among clinicians. In part, its popularity stems from the need to demonstrate the effectiveness of a clinical treatment for one person. It is not enough to know that a new treatment for depression is effective on the majority of people treated. In a managed care environment, clinicians need an objective way to show how the treatment works in each individual case. The single-subject design helps meet that need.

Advanced Level 6.2   The single-subject design relies on *repeated measures of a targeted behavior.* When the repeated measures taken during the baseline phase are compared to the measures taken during the intervention phase, the differences in the measures reveal variations in behavior occurring before and after the intervention. When baseline measures are used in this way, they act similar to a control group. They control for some threats to internal validity.

Data for a single-subject study can be gathered by self-report, by unobtrusive observations or case records, or by a trained observer. The data are collected at equal intervals, perhaps each day or each week or during specific parts of a day, say when a child is at play with other children.

Advanced Level 6.3   ## *Simple Mathematical Tests for Analysis of Single-Subject Data*

There are a number of statistical approaches for testing the level of significance of "change over time" using data from a single-subject design study. The two tests presented here should meet most of your needs: The Bartlett's Coefficient is used to rule out autocorrelation among the variables (Matyas & Greenwood, 1991) and the Two Standard Deviation Test (Boom, Fischer & Orme, 1995) is used to determine statistical significance.

In the following two examples, data found in Figure 6.5, "Days Missed Per Week," is used for the example.

Bartlett's Coefficient (Testing for Autocorrelation)

The Bartlett's Coefficient (r_k) is used when you are concerned that the data you collected is autocorrelated. It is dependent on the value of the variable that was measured previously. Autocorrelation is similar to the concept of correlation. A correlation is a situation in which changes in one variable can be predicted by changes in another variable to the extent of their correlation. An autocorrelation is a situation where later change in a variable is dependent on earlier change in the variable.

For example, a researcher has been testing the hypothesis that exercise and fresh air will increase a child's height. For data, using a single-subject design, the researcher collects on a weekly basis over the school year the height of 15 children in a Therapeutic After School Program.

The hypothesis is that the longer a child is in the Therapeutic After School Program, the greater will be the child's increased height because of the regular exercise and fresh air that the children get when in the Program.

The flaw in this hypothesis is obvious. The data is autocorrelated. The researcher can *predict* the future height of a child by knowing the child's current height. Time, rather than the Therapeutic After School Program, causes the change in height. Although the Program might contribute, using the single-subject design makes it appear that the Therapeutic After School Program caused the change.

If you analyzed the data using statistical tests to detect significant change in single-subject data, the autocorrelation would not be identified as a problem. That is because statistical tests to detect significant change in a single-subject data assume that the observations are independent of one another. In fact, if your baseline is flat, you can assume there is no autocorrelation in the observations and skip using the Bartlett's Coefficient to determine if the data you collected is independent or dependent.

To determine if your data is autocorrelated you would use the Bartlett's Coefficient. This test can detect whether or not the early scores in a time-series analysis tend to predict the scores that follow.

This approach is not perfect. The smaller the number of observations, the less accurate the Bartlett's Coefficient is in detecting autocorrelation. The autocorrelation has to be very large for Bartlett's Coefficient to detect it if you have less than 7 observations. Bartlett's Coefficient can be used with either baseline or intervention phase data if you want to determine if your data from either the baseline or intervention phase data may be autocorrelated.

The following example is another situation where the data could be autocorrelated. The longer a child is in the After School Program, the fewer days the child will miss attending regular school. The Intervention phase (B) of Figure 6.5 will be calculated to find the Bartlett's Coefficient.

We are looking to see if the Bartlett's Coefficient (r_k) is *significant*. If the coefficient is significant, this will indicate that there is a serious autocorrelation problem with the data. If the child's school attendance has radically improved, however, it does not matter whether there is autocorrelation or not. The objective was to improve the child's attendance at school.

Step 1:   Calculate the Bartlett's Coefficient (A Lag 1 Autocorrelation Coefficient) for the data from the intervention phase in Figure 6.5.

Step 2:   Now find the Bartlett's Coefficient

Equation 6.1. The formula for the Bartlett's Coefficient:

$$\frac{d^2}{X \times X} =$$

$$\frac{.37575}{5.3125}$$

The Bartlett's Coefficient = .07061

Step 3:   Now find the Bartlett's Value.

Equation 6.2. The formula for obtaining the Bartlett's Value:

$$\frac{2}{\sqrt{8}} =$$

$$\frac{2}{2.83}$$

The Bartlett's Value = .70671

Step 4:   Now compare the Bartlett's Coefficient to the Bartlett's Value. If the variable is *not* autocorrelated the Bartlett's Coefficient will be smaller than the Bartlett's Value.

In this example, the Bartlett's Coefficient (.07061) is much smaller than the Bartlett's Value (.70671). This is what we were hoping to find. This indicates that

| TABLE 6.1 | **CALCULATION OF BARTLETT'S COEFFICIENT** | | | | |

Weeks	Days Missed	Subtract Mean	Remainder/ Difference Values (*d*)	X • X*	d2**
5	3	−.75	2.25		5.0625
6	1	−.75	.25	.5625	.0625
7	.5	−.75	−.25	−.06245	.0625
8	1	−.75	.25	−.06245	.0625
9	.5	−.75	−.25	−.06245	.0625
10	0	−.75	0	0	0
11	0	−.75	0	0	0
12	0	−.75	0	0	0
Total of 8 Weeks	Mean = 6 / 8 = .75	Do Not Total	Do Not Total	Total = .37515	Total for Bartlett's Coeff. = 5.3125

* To find the value for "X • X," multiply the remainder from day 5 by the remainder from day 6, which equals .5625. Then multiply the remainder from day 6 by the remainder from day 7, which equals .06245. Then multiply the remainder from day 7 by the remainder from day 8, which equals .06245. Then multiply the remainder from day 8 by the remainder from day 9, which equals .06245. Continue this process until you have the values for each pair (in this case all the remaining values are zero).

** You find the "d^2" values by multiplying the remainder (*d*) times itself. The remainder (*d*) from day 5 is 2.25. To find the d^2 value for day 5, multiply 2.25 x 2.25 which equals 5.0625.

there is *no* autocorrelation and that you can now use the Two Standard Deviation Test to determine if a statistically significant change took place after the intervention phase was started.

The Two Standard Deviation Test

You can use this approach when you have data that can be used as a stable baseline phase (A) and reliable data from an intervention phase (B). Using this analysis, you compare the *mean of the baseline* to the *mean of the intervention.* If the difference in the mean of the intervention is two standard deviations from the mean of the baseline, the difference is considered to be statistically significant at the .05 level of probability. This statistical finding suggests that a change took place after the intervention phase was started.

This approach uses familiar mathematical concepts. The first of four steps is to find the *mean* and *standard deviation* of the baseline phase and the intervention phase. These statistics will be used in the formula.

Step 1:   Calculate Means and the Standard Deviations (SD).

Baseline (A)	**Intervention (B)**
Mean = 3.00	Mean = .38
SD = .82	SD = .44

Step 2:   Next, find the value of two *standard deviations* from the mean of the baseline phase.

2 *standard deviations* from the mean of the baseline (in this case) = .82 x 2 = 1.64

Step 3:   Subtract two standard deviations from the mean of the baseline.

Baseline mean = 3.00 (-) 2 SD or 1.64 = 1.36

Step 4:   Compare the values. When the value of two standard deviations is subtracted from the mean of a normal population curve 2.28% of the population is left at each end of the normal curve. This tells us that only 4.56% people out of 100 are not included in two standard deviations on either side of the normal curve.

If the mean of the intervention falls outside of two standard deviations from the mean of the baseline (in this example it does), such a finding suggests that there is a 95.44% chance out of 100 that a real behavior change did take place during the intervention phase of the study. Thus, the findings suggest that a statistically significant behavior change occurred at the p < .05 level.

In this example, the mean for phases "A" and "B" are quite different. Moreover, the mean of the intervention phase (M = .38) is more than two standard deviations (2 SD = 1.69) from the mean of the baseline. In fact, it is more than three standard deviations from the mean of the baseline. This indicates that the chance that a real behavior change took place is very good. Now all you have to do is to determine if, in fact, it was the intervention that caused the change. The validity issues discussed earlier in this chapter still apply.

REFERENCES

Barlow, D. H., & Hersen, M. (1984). *Single case experimental design: Strategies for studying behavioral change.* New York: Pergamon.

Bloom, M., Fischer, J., & Orme, J. (1995). *Evaluating Practice: Guidelines for the accountable professional* (2nd ed.). Boston: Allyn & Bacon.

Cherry, A. L. (1992). Separation anxiety and school phobia: An intervention to revive the school bond. *Case Analysis: In Social Science and Social Therapy, 3,* 3–10.

Levy, R. L., & Olson, D. G. (1979). The single-subject methodology in clinical practice: An overview. *Journal of Social Service Research, 3,* 25–49.

Matyas, T. A., & Greenwood, K. M. (1991). Problems in the estimation of autocorrelation in brief time series and some implications for behavioral data. *Behavioral Assessment, 13,* 137–157.

TECHNIQUES FOR COLLECTING YOUR QUANTITATIVE (STATISTICAL) DATA

QUANTITATIVE DATA COLLECTION TECHNIQUES

Data gathering techniques are methods used to gather data from individuals or other sources. The techniques presented in this chapter are the most commonly used and best tested approaches in the literature, and there is a great deal of literature on each technique presented. These techniques have been developed to a high level of sophistication over the years through trial and error.

The data collecting method you choose will, in part, be based on the population (see Chapter 13) and the type of questionnaire or data gathering instrument (see Chapter 8) you plan to use in your study.

To make the best choice of a data collecting method, you will need to know how the different data collecting methods affect precision, cost, and the time involved in gathering the data.

HOW CAN YOU USE DATA COLLECTION TECHNIQUES?

Five commonly used data gathering techniques will be discussed in this chapter. There might be other approaches, but these are good examples of the most practical techniques available. The five approaches are

1. Personal interviews
2. Group administered (giving the questionnaire to a group of participants at the same time, such as a psychology class)
3. Mailing questionnaires to participants
4. Telephone interviews
5. Case record "interviews" (archival data)

Personal Interviews

In this process you or an associate gathers the data by personally interviewing each person who participates in the study. You typically ask the participants questions and record their answers. This approach is often used in qualitative studies with small samples of 20 or so.

One of the difficult tasks using this data gathering approach is developing the questions. A good approach is to ask the questions sequentially. What happened first? What happened next? McCracken (1988) calls it the "long interview."

The most difficult task (a real killer) is organizing the findings so that similar stories and responses from the participants will lead you to or help you reach some defensible conclusions.

7.1   *Example of Gathering Data from the Homeless*

The following is an example of how a survey of homeless people in South Florida was conducted. After identifying the areas where groups and individual homeless people were located, trained interviewers went to the homeless areas and, using a combination of closed-ended and open-ended questions, interviewed and made observational notes on 350 homeless men and women. The interviews lasted about 10 minutes. This type of on-the-street interview questionnaire was constructed like a telephone interview questionnaire. Because closed-ended questions were used, a part of the data could be easily coded and analyzed by computer.

Positives *(personal interviews):*

- The completion rate is typically higher when trained research assistants conduct individual interviews.
- Your interviewers also have the opportunity to gather observational data. For example, they would record "race" and "gender" and if trained, they could make observations about possible mental illness, retardation, level of interest in answering the questions, the environment where the interview was conducted, and so on.
- As a supplemental data gathering approach, personal interviews of 10 to 20 typical people who participated in the larger, survey-type study can add a great deal of information to the percentages and other statistical findings from the study.
- The personal interview is the best approach to use if you have long, complicated, open-ended questions.

Negatives *(personal interviews):*

- The interviewers must be trained so they read the questions in the same way to all participants to insure reliability.
- This approach is time consuming and expensive.
- It is not a good method to use with large samples. The exception is a short-type questionnaire, such as those used in shopping centers and in the telephone interview.
- It is not a good method to use if the participants are spread over a large geographic area.

Group Administered

This is a data gathering approach where you ask a group or gathering of people to fill out a *self-administered questionnaire.* This approach almost limits one to a

7.2 *Administering a Questionnaire to a Large Group*

The following is an example of a study of the elderly and disabled living in public housing in Northeastern Pennsylvania. With this population, a team of master-level social workers went to group meetings of residents and asked them to participate in a study of their needs. This was a good approach because the master students were able to assist residents who had difficulty filling out the survey questionnaire. Some were sight-impaired, others were physically unable to deal with the tasks involved in answering the questions and filling out the questionnaire. Elderly residents who could not complete the questionnaire were asked to answer the questions in an interview where the closed-end questions and responses were read to them. It would have been difficult for a large number of the elderly to participate without help.

survey type questionnaire that can be completed by the participants with little or no assistance. The type of group you might collect data from could be a psychology class, a service club, or a church group. The best method is to ask the members of the group to fill out the questionnaire while you have them together as a group. If you send the questionnaire home with them, you will get a low return rate, 40% if you are lucky. If they fill it out while you wait, and it only takes 10 to 15 minutes to complete, your return rate could be 90% or more.

Positives (group administered):
- The group administered approach to collecting data is fast and relatively accurate.
- Survey type questions are typically used so the answers can be coded for statistical analysis.
- It is low in cost and cost effective.
- Traditionally, the group administered approach is accepted, particularly in educational research in the classroom.
- The procedures used to collect data from a group (explanations to the participants, the setting, and the physical task of the participants filling out the questionnaire) can be easily controlled, and little reliance on others is necessary.

Negatives (group administered):
- The group administered approach tends to be limited to gathering specific types of data.
- It tends to be restricted to using self-administered questionnaires to collect data.
- The group members must be able to follow directions, to understand the questions, and to complete the tasks. Many people in the world do not meet this requirement.
- If the participant gives a unique, interesting, or confusing answer on the questionnaire, there is no way to follow up on the question or probe for more

information. Both the questionnaire used in this approach and the type of questionnaire used in a mail survey have the same limitation.

- Using the group administered approach, it is difficult to make a case that the members of the group in the study are typical of a larger population and that the findings can be generalized to a larger population (that is, it is a convenient sample).

Mailing Questionnaires

As is obvious from the name for this approach, you *mail* a questionnaire to people selected as the sample of the population you wish to study. They fill out the questionnaire and return it to you, typically by return mail.

This approach involves meticulous planning, and it can take several months to collect the data. Of course, all approaches to data gathering need to be done meticulously. With approaches where you meet the respondent in person, however, you have the opportunity to clear up a question about what is being asked or how the participant is to indicate an answer. When you mail the questionnaire to the participant, any chance of clearing up a misunderstood question is lost.

You should also remember to plan for plenty of time for data collection. Your returns will come in for about three weeks after the questionnaires reach the participants. After three weeks, you need to begin follow-up activities to encourage people who did not return the questionnaire to do so. This may take another month or so depending on the number of follow-up contacts. One follow-up contact is typical; however, I have been known to make several follow-up contacts when desperate to get a decent return rate.

The number of questionnaires completed and returned can be very low. This is called a *low response rate*. A low response rate is a threat to the representativeness of those who filled out the questionnaire. If you picked a random sample of 100 students to be representative of all 400 people in a master's program for family therapy, and if only 50 return the questionnaire, you will not be able to tell if the 50 people who responded are still representative of the 400 you wanted to study. As a group, the 50 who returned questionnaires were different on one level: They were more motivated to return the questionnaire or possibly more compliant.

To successfully collect the data you need using a questionnaire that you mail to those you want to participate in your study, you must—with painstaking care—attend to the following tasks:

1. The directions or instructions used in the questionnaire need to be absolutely clear; leave no room for questions about what you want the person to do.
2. Each individual question or item needs to be clear and unambiguous.
3. Choose the types of scales and measures that are familiar in appearance and form, and are easy for the person to understand and respond to.
4. Plan the layout of the questionnaire (eye appeal) so that the form that it takes will make it easy for a person to complete.
5. Plan an intensive follow-up effort to maximize the rate of questionnaires returned to you.

7.3 *Example of a Mailed Survey*

The following was used to study alcohol and other drug use among college seniors. To gather the data, an official college list of all seniors (640) in the fall term was selected as the population pool. Each senior was sent a package containing a letter of explanation, a questionnaire with instructions, and a self-addressed, stamped envelope. The letter explained the research project, how participants' confidentiality would be maintained, and how the data would be used in a dissertation study.

At the same time, an article was printed in the school paper about the project. Additionally, posters were put up around campus notifying seniors that they would be receiving the questionnaire package. Professors who would possibly teach classes with seniors were asked to announce the beginning of the study.

Two weeks after the questionnaire was mailed, a follow-up post card was sent to each senior asking him or her to fill out the questionnaire if he or she had not already done so. A week later, students who were helping on the project called every senior for which there was a telephone number listed. In this way, we reminded them to return the questionnaire and we found out who had already sent it in. When a senior was contacted by telephone and said he or she had already returned the questionnaire, the person was thanked and the name added to the list of returns. Those who had not completed and returned the questionnaire were asked if they would complete it and return it, and if they needed us to send them another questionnaire. Returns came in over a three-month period. The rate of return was approximately 80%. At 1985 postage rates the cost of sending the questionnaire through the mail was almost $2.50 per package. Almost 800 packets were sent out to 640 seniors (Cherry, 1987).

Positives (mailing the questionnaire):

- Mailing questionnaires allows the respondent the privacy and convenience to complete the questionnaire at leisure.
- Mailing questionnaires costs less than training and paying interviewers by the hour.
- It is the most effective way to reach some populations.
- In most cases the questionnaire you mail can be longer than a telephone interview—although one must be careful about the length and take into account the population's motivation, interest, and ability to follow the instructions.

Negatives (mailing the questionnaire):

- Mailing lists used for identifying a sample might be biased, depending upon the source of a list.
- Only interested persons will return the survey form, and this may seriously bias the sample.
- Follow-up is necessary to encourage returns of the surveys. This process can be very time-consuming and expensive.
- Even with follow-up, mail surveys have had notoriously low response rates.

7.4   *Example of Gathering Data by Telephone*

The following is an example of gathering data by telephone interview. In 1987, a telephone survey was used to identify the attitudes and knowledge of the Death Penalty among Catholics living in Pennsylvania. A short interview questionnaire was used to gather the data. The participants were selected from five representative parishes. A proportional, random sample was selected from the parish lists. Interviewers were trained to conduct the interview that was made up of 30 closed-ended questions. The interview lasted approximately 15 minutes.

Telephone Interviews

Using the telephone survey approach to collect data typically takes less time, can cover a large geographical area, and can deal with a diverse population with varying skills for responding to self-administered questionnaires (Sedlack & Stanley, 1992). It can be more expensive, however, because you need to hire and train interviewers.

The cost of long-distance telephone calls also can be very expensive. It is the most popular data collection method among political and marketing researchers.

To maximize the effectiveness of the telephone interview, start with well-trained interviewers. A short questionnaire is critically important because the telephone interview should last no more than 15 minutes. Learning how to engage a participant quickly, asking the same question in the same way to every participant, and ending the interview, all within 15 minutes takes training.

When planning to use this method, allow extra data collection time for re-contacting unavailable respondents. You also might want to contact a sub-sample of respondents to check reliability of the data being gathered by the interviewers.

Positives (telephone interview):
- Using a telephone administered questionnaire to collect data has the advantage of speed.
- The sample of participants can be spread out over a large geographic area.
- Questions or comments can be handled by trained interviewers, which adds to the quality of the data collected.

Negatives (telephone interviews):
- There could be a problem with biasing the sample because it is a list of telephone numbers. Some people who should be in the sample might not have a telephone or might have an unlisted telephone number. Using random digit dialing techniques, if possible, eliminates the problem of unlisted numbers.
- People sometimes screen their telephone calls with answering machines or caller I.D. equipment.

7.5 *Example of Gathering Data from Case Records*

The following is an example of gathering data from case records of juveniles. All of the teens to be studied had been in one community detention facility. Their case records were the source of data for a study of "teen parenting." Among other findings, those juveniles in detention tended to be from families where the mother had been in her teens when she had her first child. Even this simple information was difficult to obtain. To find the age of the mother at the birth of her first child, we had to find the birth date of the mother and a list of siblings with birth dates. Even well-kept records can be weak in collecting that kind of information from clients. Furthermore, there are all kinds of reasons for a person to give a wrong birth date. Even so, a lot of good descriptive data were collected and analyzed.

- Even with training, one cannot rule out interviewer bias.
- The cost can be fairly high if long-distance calls are required.

Case Record "Interviews"

This is the least intrusive method for gathering data on individuals. The source of data is case records, face sheets, school records, employee files, etc. Using this approach, one would not have to contact the participant unless one has to obtain consent to collect data from a person's case record. Typically, permission is obtained from the agency that has possession of the case records. As well, the clients' names and other data that could identify them would not be used or collected for the study.

Data gathering, using this approach, can work just like a survey. Instead of asking individuals about themselves, you find the answers to your survey questions in their case files.

The most reliable approach is to develop a questionnaire that can be used to gather the data from the case records. The questionnaire would look like any survey questionnaire. Of course, the answers to the items on the questionnaire must be found in the case records. A given item you might choose—for example diagnosis—might not be listed in all records or there might be several diagnoses listed in the records.

Additionally, to read case transcripts and answer questions about the meaning of the text can be very difficult. Carelessness at this stage could reduce reliability. The case record narratives also vary greatly by worker. Some workers will be very thorough, but other workers will be brief and might leave out information that would suggest a different answer.

This approach lends itself to pilot testing the questionnaire. A pilot test will help determine the feasibility of finding answers to the research questions and will give you an idea of how much missing data you can expect.

Positives (case record "interviews"):
- Using case records as a source of data has a lot of potential. In terms of convenience, the records are not going anywhere.
- As long as answers to your questions are easy to find on the face sheet, it can be a reliable source of data.
- It can provide quantitative information and the findings can be based on the number of occurrences of an answer. With a sample of 50 or more, frequencies and percentages are necessary to describe the sample. At times, this type of quantitative data can also support conclusions based on qualitative impressions.
- Program databases kept on computer are becoming more available.

Negatives (case record "interviews"):
- Limits you to the information in the case records.
- Trying to glean the same information from several hundred case records can be difficult, even if the records are well-kept.
- No matter how well the case records are kept, missing data can be a problem unless you limit the investigation to information that is always recorded and present in the case records. The more you limit the types of data you collect, however, the fewer hypotheses you can test.
- At times, getting permission from an agency to collect data from their case records can be tricky and difficult. This, of course, depends on your position at the agency. Whatever the circumstance, make sure you have permission and make sure it is in writing.
- An agency might feel threatened by your request to have access to their records. They might be concerned that you will find something that will embarrass the agency.
- If you use assistants to collect the data, they must be trained in going through the records and collecting the data.

POSTSCRIPT

Gathering your data is often time consuming and costly. Moreover, the accuracy of the data will be a major determinant in the accuracy of your findings. Choosing the right instrument and measures to gather your data are extremely important. Chapter 8 will help you decide what scales and measures are available and how to select them.

REFERENCES

Cherry, A. L. (1987). Social bond theory and alcohol use among college students. *Journal of College Student Personnel, 28*(2): 128–135.

McCracken, G. (1988). The long interview. *Qualitative Research Methods Series No. 13.* Newbury Park, CA: Sage.

Sedlack, R. G., & Stanley, J. (1992). *Social research: theory and method.* Boston: Allyn & Bacon.

THE QUESTIONNAIRE

Scales and Measures

WHAT ARE SCALES AND MEASURES?

In research in the helping professions, psychological scales, sociological scales, and psychosocial scales are used to measure human behavior and characteristics.

Many of the concepts and variables we rely on as indicators or evidence of human characteristics, attitudes, and psychosocial perspectives have been converted into *standardized measures*. These scales or measures work on the same principal as any yardstick, bathroom scale, or thermometer. The words "scale" and "measure" are used interchangeably. For example, Beck's depression scale is used to measure a person's "level of depression." Though not as accurate, this scale is similar to the thermometer we use to measure the level of a person's body temperature.

HOW CAN YOU USE SCALES AND MEASURES?

Using measures and scales is one way to operationalize abstract concepts used in your hypothesis.

One of the difficulties researchers in the helping professions have faced is the task of finding accurate ways of measuring human characteristics, behaviors, and problems. The best method to measure human characteristics and the best scales to use have been debated for almost a hundred years—that is, in the modern sense of the term "measure." Fortunately, today there are some widely accepted measures/scales that you can use to research most topics related to human nature. The *good news* is that if you know a little about research and measurement, you, too, can pick out good scales. The *bad news* is that you have to choose from a field of scales ranging in quality from the ridiculously bad to the very good.

See Advanced Level 8.1 on page 131.

➡ **Advanced Level**
see page 131

BACKGROUND ON SCALING

When reviewing issues that can get as convoluted as issues related to measurement can, REMEMBER that your objective is to select measures or scales that will best test your hypothesis.

The measures and scales we use today are the result of a merger (during the last half of the twentieth century) between techniques developed by sociology and those developed by psychology. Sociologists refined the techniques used in survey research; psychologists refined experimental research techniques applicable to humans. Therefore, standards for scales have been developed. *Currently, social science standards require that measures and scales used in human research be both reliable and valid.* To review the mathematical issues related to *reliability,* see the section in Chapter 19, on "Testing the Reliability of Measurements and Scales."

THE QUESTIONNAIRE OR YOUR DATA GATHERING INSTRUMENT

Measures and scales are one part of a typical research questionnaire. In addition to the items in the psychosocial scales, research questionnaires are constructed using selected *demographic questions*.

Demographic questions solicit objective information from the participants. They are common questions, seen on virtually every questionnaire and relating to general characteristics such as age, gender, education, work, income, family, and health. These concrete questions help to describe individual and group similarities and differences. These are not abstract measures such as a scale to measure I.Q. or a scale to measure an individual's level of depression. "Female" and "29 years old" are not abstract concepts, but being "mildly depressed" is an abstract concept.

FUNDAMENTALS OF QUESTIONNAIRE CONSTRUCTION

Before you develop a questionnaire on your own, find several questionnaires (that have been used by other researchers) and use them as examples. Most well constructed surveys, those that at least look professional, are good models of how to ask demographic questions. The questions in these surveys are typically items that have been used in the same way in many different questionnaires over a number of years. They might add a few demographic questions of their own; but most researchers do not "reinvent the wheel." See Chapter 9 for an example of how demographic questions on a questionnaire might look.

In a quantitative study, demographic variables that characterize the participants can take on two important roles:

1. They can be used to describe the population or sample
2. They can be used as control variables.

Tailor your questionnaire to meet the needs of the research effort.

CONTROL VARIABLES

You might also want to review the sections on control variables found in Chapters 16, 21, and 26.

In addition to using demographic characteristics (variables) to describe the population or sample, the values of these variables can be controlled for with specific statistical procedures. When you mathematically control for variation in a variable, it is much like selecting people who have the same values on the variables. It is similar to selecting participants of the same age (for example, people who are all 29 years old). If all the participants are the same "age" (all 29 years old), then age cannot be a factor nor can it have impact on their "level of depression." This characteristic (age) can be eliminated as a possible explanation for the difference in depression among this group of 29-year-olds.

At times, it is not possible to select a homogeneous sample. Yet, our sample meets the assumptions necessary to perform bivariate statistical analysis. In these cases, we can use statistical techniques to mathematically control for the variation in variables, such as age of the population or education, with much the same results as physically controlling the variation by choosing people of the same age

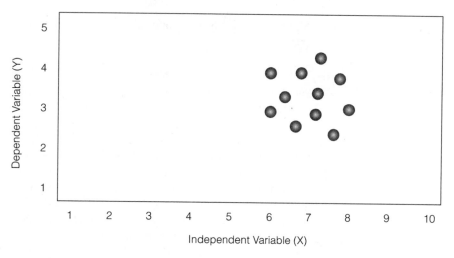

FIGURE **8.1**

HOMOGENEOUS GROUP

Homogeneous: Of the same or similar nature or kind.

Heterogeneous: Consisting of dissimilar elements or parts; not homogeneous.

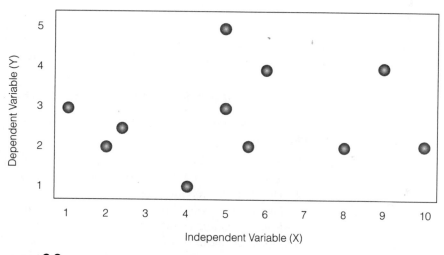

FIGURE **8.2**

HETEROGENEOUS GROUP

and education. Using a statistical procedure such as regression or MANOVA to control for differences, for example, in the pay of teachers would be like selecting a sample of teachers who all made the same amount of money.

Figure 8.1 shows the people are similar on two variables age (X) and depression (Y); whereas Figure 8.2 shows the people are NOT similar on the two variables of age (X) and depression (Y).

SELECTING PSYCHOSOCIAL MEASURES AND SCALES TO TEST YOUR HYPOTHESES

See the list of books of scales and measures at the end of this chapter.

Locating good scales in today's helping professional research environment is a fairly easy proposition, as long as your research is in well-defined areas. The best time to find measures or scales is during the literature review on your research topic. Similar studies will have gone through the same process. Keep a list of the scales the researchers in the journal article used to study the problem.

If you want to measure a characteristic that is not widely studied, finding a good scale can often be a hit and miss proposition. On the one hand, a good scale may exist, but it is buried in the literature. On the other hand, how long do you look before spending both the time and money to develop your own scale? Considering the cost to develop a scale, you will be wise to exhaust every avenue looking for a good scale. Developing reliable and valid scales is a science unto itself.

Scale development is a long and slow process. Developing a set of questions (measure/scale) that are theoretically based and congruent, with a high level of reported reliability and validity, could take years. Before you start, ask yourself if you want to go to the trouble of developing a measure/scale when someone else has already done so. Developing a scale while knowing that similar scales exist is one thing; developing a scale because you have not put forth the effort to find one already in existence is another (Robinson, Shaver, & Wrightsman, 1991).

Five Criteria for Selecting Published Measures and Scales

If you do decide to use a published scale, the following are good criteria for judging it.

1. Have the scales been used in similar studies in the past to measure similar topics of interest, characteristics, or perspectives?
2. Do the scales you are considering have reported reliability and validity in journal articles and books? This information will be included in your research paper, dissertation, or journal article.
3. Do the scales/measures you wish to use have a reliability coefficient equal to .70 or above? The closer to .90 the better. Typically, reliability coefficients are expressed in a range from .01 to .99.
4. Is the scale reasonably short: 20 to 30 items? Look for the shortest version of the scale. Very often researchers will develop shorter versions of a measure with many items. Shorter scales (10 to 20 items) that have similar reliability and validity and that measure the same thing are better. People tend to finish them more often.
5. Are the scales/measures available for anyone to use (public domain), or do you need to get permission to use them? Some scales must be purchased from publishers or the researcher that developed them. Most of the time, the publisher makes it clear if you must pay to use a scale. If you hope to use a

8.1 *Example of Questionnaire Development*

Let us assume that you wish to identify the strength of the relationship between level of "self concept" and "expectation of academic achievement" among high school sophomore males. If such a study has never been done before, your best approach will be to look in the counseling literature for "self concept" scales that have high levels of reliability and reported validity, and that have been successfully used with a similar population. Next, you go to the education literature to find scales related to expectation of academic achievement among high school students.

To develop the questionnaire, use these two psychosocial measures/scales together. Add demographic questions to the questionnaire that both describe the boys and control for possible differences—for example, age, family income, members in household, grade point average, and membership in school related clubs and/or sports teams. Note: you do not need to ask the boys for their gender or grade level in school.

THE FINDINGS

The demographic data combined with the two scale scores from the two psychosocial measures can tell a very interesting story. Using a simple statistical analysis, such as the Pearson's Correlation procedure or partial correlation procedure, it is easy to see if grade point average (GPA) changes the correlation coefficient. Does it make the correlation either stronger or weaker between level of self-concept and expectation of academic achievement among high school sophomore males? This statistical analysis will answer the question, does GPA alter the relationship between level of self concept and expectation of academic achievement among high school sophomore males?

In this case, if it strengthens or weakens the statistical correlation, this indicates that level of self concept and expectation of academic achievement are affected by GPA.

If Controlling GPA Weakens the Correlation = GPA is suppressing contributing to the level of "self concept," resulting in specific levels of "expectation of academic achievement."

If GPA Strengthens the Correlations = Concerns about GPA is suppressing the level of "self concept" as it relates to "expectation of academic achievement."

If Controlling GPA does NOT Change the Correlation = GPA is NOT important to the relationship between the level of "self concept" and "expectation of academic achievement."

scale in a dissertation, book, or journal article, you will want to get permission to use the scale from the author, even if you do not pay for it. If the scale has been published in the past, someone probably has a copyright on it. See the section in this chapter on "Copyright Laws and Psychosocial Scales."

Common Mistakes Choosing Scales

1. Picking scales that are difficult to score.
2. Picking too many scales, making the questionnaire too long.

3. Picking scales that have too many items.
4. Picking scales that have NO reported reliability and validity.
5. Picking scales that are wrong for the population.
6. Picking scales that are too personal.

WHAT IS THE BEST LAYOUT FOR THE QUESTIONNAIRE?

Questionnaires must be simple to understand and easy to complete. For an example of how intimidating and bad a questionnaire can look, think of trying to understand the 1040 tax form. Another way to critically evaluate your questionnaire is to try to recall other questionnaires that you have filled out. What did you find difficult and problematic in filling them out? One good approach is to find a questionnaire that works well for you, and if it fits the research effort, use it as a model to develop your questionnaire.

Although it may be tempting, never crowd the pages of your questionnaire. Crowded pages interfere with the ability of the participants to complete the questionnaire accurately and they cause fatigue. Crowded pages are the reason a number of people do not even attempt to answer the questions. Poorly constructed questionnaires reduce the reliability and validity of your questionnaire.

The last step is a pilot-test of your questionnaire. Ask a few friends or people who will not be in your study to complete your questionnaire. After they have finished, do a debriefing. Ask them to tell you what problems they had answering the questions or filling out the questionnaire. You can catch many silly errors using this pilot-test approach before finalizing your questionnaire.

COPYRIGHT LAWS AND PSYCHOSOCIAL SCALES

When you are selecting scales or measures, check to see if the scale is copyrighted. The copyright laws became a great deal more restrictive in the early 1990s. Before *reproducing* a scale, you may need to request permission from the holder of the copyright. Typically, this means writing a letter to the author. If it is a commercial scale like the *Interpersonal Behavior Survey (IBS)*, the *Children's Depression Inventory,* or the *Minnesota Multiphasic Personality Inventory (MMPI)*, it is distributed by companies who make a profit on the sale of the scale.

If in doubt about whether or not you need permission, write the author and ask permission to use the scale. It is also a way of extending to the author the courtesy of letting him or her know you will be using one of his or her scales. To use the vast number of scales and measures in your research you need only cite the original source. You cite the source or author of a scale just as you would a quotation from a book.

If you have questions about copyright law, a good person to ask is your librarian.

POSTSCRIPT

Now that you have determined the best approach to gathering your quantitative (statistical) data and the types of scales and measures you can use in this process, you are ready to learn about data analysis. Data analysis begins with an understanding that we most often are attempting to measure human characteristics. These characteristics are known as variables. Part IV of this text is written to help you understand the data analysis.

ADVANCED LEVEL MATERIAL

Advanced Level 8.1

For today's human service professional, modern scales and measures are an attempt to narrow the gap between guessing and the reality of a given situation (Blythe & Tripodi, 1989). Scales and measures are tools used by the helping professional practitioner and researcher to measure social phenomena. It is no longer good enough to know in your heart that you helped a needy family. Today, in addition you must be able to show it in an unbiased, scientific way.

For example, it is logical to speculate that minority people will experience increased levels of anxiety when viewing the videotape of the March 3, 1991, Rodney King beating by the Los Angeles Police. This speculation is an educated guess, a hypothesis, based on *conflict theory*. The researcher's task, however, is to move beyond mere speculation. The goal is to find out if anxiety levels increase and by how much. To do this, you must devise a means to test the hypothesis. First, you must operationalize "anxiety." In this case, let us say, you select the *Clinical Anxiety Scale* (Fischer & Corcoran, 1994) to measure the level of anxiety. This approach is an objective standardized measure of "anxiety." Next, you ask a group of carefully selected individuals to complete the *Clinical Anxiety Scale.* This is a pretest. Then you ask your sample of individuals to view the videotape of the beating. After the subjects see the video tape, you ask them to complete the scale a second time as a posttest. Now, by comparing the levels of anxiety in the pretest and posttest, you have far more convincing evidence than speculation about the reactions of minority individuals to this example of police brutality.

These scales are created as objective standardized measures; yet, as times change, the vocabulary used in the scales can become outdated. This occurs because the definitions of everyday words change from generation to generation and from group to group. The difference in what words mean to one generation and what they mean to another, for example, can clearly be seen in popular music over the last 100 years.

BOOKS OF SCALES AND MEASURES

Conoley, J. C., & Kramer, J. J. (1987). *The tenth mental measurements yearbook.* Lincoln, NE: Buros Institute of Mental Measurement.

Fischer J., & Corcoran, K. J. (1994). *Measures for clinical practice: A sourcebook* (2nd ed. Volume 1: Couples, families and children). New York: Free Press.

Fischer J., & Corcoran, K. J. (1994). *Measures for clinical practice: A sourcebook* (2nd ed. Volume 2: Adults). New York: Free Press.

Fredman, N., & Sherman, R. (1987). *Handbook of measurement for marriage and family therapy.* New York: Brunner/Mazel.

Holdman, A. D. (1982). *Family assessment: Tools for understanding and intervention.* Newbury Park, CA: Sage.

Hudson, W. W. (1982). *The clinical measurement package: A field manual.* Homewood, IL: Dorsey.

Magura, S., & Moses, B. S. (1986). *Outcome measures for child welfare services: Theory and applications.* Washington, D.C.: Child Welfare League of America.

Miller, D. (1991). *Handbook of research and social measurement* (5th ed.). Newbury Park, CA: Sage.

Sweetland, R. C., & Kendis, D. J. (1991). *Test: A comprehensive reference* (3rd ed.). Austin, TX: Pro-Ed.

REFERENCES

Blythe, B. J., & Tripodi, T. (1989). *Measurement in direct practice.* Newbury Park, CA: Sage.

Fischer J., & Corcoran, K. J. (1994). *Measures for clinical practice: A sourcebook* (2nd ed. Volume 2: Adults). New York: Free Press.

Robinson, J. P., Shaver, P. R., & Wrightsman, L. S. (1991). *Measure of personality and social psychological attitudes.* New York: Academic.

part four

STATISTICS FOR THE
HELPING PROFESSIONAL

VARIABLES, DATA, AND DATA ORGANIZATION

What Are Data?

The word "data" is a plural noun—thus, "Once the data *are* collected . . . " The singular noun is "datum."

Data are the count of characteristics, occurrences, facts, or measurements of events that take place and that can be counted. For example, the information collected using the survey questionnaire for the study *Child rearing practices among Haitian and Jamaican immigrants* (McPherson-Blake, 1991) is the data collected for the study—information equals data.

The collection of data is based on one of the guiding principles of the scientific method: The scientist must clearly specify and define what he or she is observing. We call what is being observed the *variable of interest*.

Measurement used in this way is one of the fundamental elements of all sciences. In research in the helping professions, we use the scientific method to learn about ourselves. In this pursuit of knowledge, we measure and collect data on variables of interest such as the behaviors of individuals, families, groups and organizations.

We call this collection of data, a *data set*. A data set is at least two or more recorded observations on a variable of interest. A data set could be made up of thousands of observations (Burning & Kintz, 1987).

What Is a Variable?

A *variable* is a characteristic that can be counted by some form of observation. The count or value is the *datum* that makes up our data and data set/data file.

In quantitative research, the *variable* has two or more values. Each value is called a *datum*. For example, Gender is a variable with the *values* being Female and Male. Another example: Age in Years of participants in a study is a variable. The values are the age of each participant.

See Chapter 3 for a more detailed explanation of variables (dependent and independent variables) and how they fit into the overall research effort.

How Can You Measure Human Characteristics?

The scientific method requires that scientists state precisely how they measured the variable of interest. In research in the helping professions, typically the variable of interest is a count of human behaviors or activities, or the results of a psychosocial scale used to measure human likes and dislikes, perceptions, or attitudes.

Fundamentals for Organizing Your Data

Once the data are collected, it must be organized in some usable way. The questionnaires (*n* = 356) returned in the study *Child rearing practices among Haitian and Jamaican immigrants,* are of little use unless the information from the questionnaire is organized in a summarized form.

Not by chance but by design, the questionnaire was constructed so that the individual items (variables) could be coded into uniform numbers (values). The

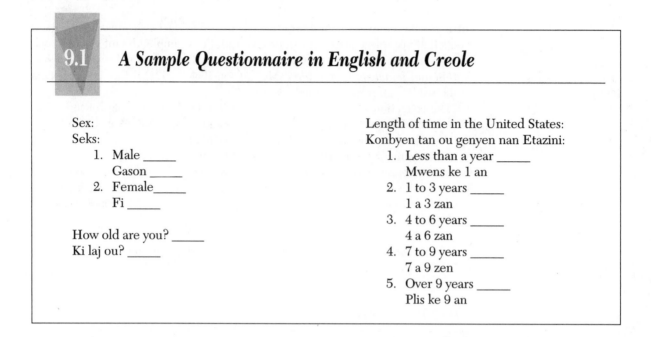

9.1   A Sample Questionnaire in English and Creole

Sex:
Seks:
   1. Male _____
      Gason _____
   2. Female_____
      Fi _____

How old are you? _____
Ki laj ou? _____

Length of time in the United States:
Konbyen tan ou genyen nan Etazini:
   1. Less than a year _____
      Mwens ke 1 an
   2. 1 to 3 years _____
      1 a 3 zan
   3. 4 to 6 years _____
      4 a 6 zan
   4. 7 to 9 years _____
      7 a 9 zen
   5. Over 9 years _____
      Plis ke 9 an

resulting data could then be organized into a data set that could be used as a data file so that the data could be analyzed by a computer-based statistics program.

Sample Questions and Items

A sample of *questions* on a survey-type instrument that are specifically designed to be used to construct a data set is presented (see Box 9.1). Notice how easily the answers are turned into numbers that can be entered into a data file.

The questions and items in the box are samples of questions from which the data were collected and organized into the data file for the study *Child rearing practices among Haitian and Jamaican immigrants*. The questions on the questionnaire were in English for the Jamaican participants and in English and Creole for the Haitian participants.

COMPUTERS AND YOUR DATABASE

Almost all of the commercial statistical packages used by helping professionals have a computer program for setting up a data file. SPSS (Statistical Package for the Social Sciences) and SAS are the two best and most popular statistical packages for designing, collecting, and inputting your data for analysis (Gravetter & Wallnau, 1985).

Computer programs devoted to simplifying data entry, such as DBase, MS Access, Quattro Pro, and MS Excel, use a data base concept. The better statistical programs will also allow you to use databases and spreadsheet programs to enter your data. Then you download the data to the statistical program for transformation into the preferred data file form.

There are also computer programs to help you develop and set up your questionnaire. These programs, which help the researcher design questions for data analysis, typically use the "drag and drop" form development approach found in Windows. To develop the form, you select from a variety of response options and customize the questionnaire layout to fit your study. One caveat: if you are doing a survey and do not plan to do other studies in the near future, using these programs can be less than efficient. It can take you longer to learn these programs than to construct a quality questionnaire and enter the data in a standard database.

An Example of a Data File

A data file is a set of numbers organized in blocks of rows and columns, a matrix of numbers, so that the same type of data or the data from the same question is always found in the same column for each individual. The data are organized so that each individual case occupies a ROW and data on each variable are placed in the COLUMN (Craft, 1992).

In this example, the variables (questions) are listed across the top. The identification number for each individual who answered the questions (variables) is listed in the first column. The numbers in the squares are the answers given by each person to the questions (values).

DATA ORGANIZATION MATRIX

ID of Indiv	Sex	Age	Place of Birth	Time in U.S.	Marital Status	No. of Children	INC
01	2	24	1	3	2	4	2
02	1	35	1	2	1	2	3
03	2	37	2	4	1	6	5
04	2	29	2	2	1	2	3

Values representing "Length of time in the United States" are found under the column variable "Time in U.S." for each person who answered the question. For instance, the person with the "ID of Indiv" number 01, indicated on the questionnaire that she (Sex: Female = 2) had been in the U.S. between 4 and 6 years. Person number 02 indicated he (Sex: Male = 1) had been in the U.S. between 1 and 3 years.

Setting up a data file is simple, but it must be done with care, because the reliability of data analysis depends on the accuracy of the data file. The data analysis is based on the accuracy of the data file.

POSTSCRIPT

The data file is a set of numbers representing variables and human characteristics. Constructing the data file is the first step in analysis, but before beginning the analysis, it is important to have a basic understanding of the rudimentary concepts involved in the data analysis. The normal curve is an important concept, both to data analysis and to understanding the underlying concepts involved in selecting a representative sample from a larger population. In Chapter 10, the principals that allow the use of the normal curve in statistical analyses are explained. In Chapter 13 (the chapter on sampling is in the statistical section of this book because it is a statistical procedure), the application of the normal curve in the selection of a representative sample is explained.

REFERENCES

Burning, J., & Kintz, B. (1987). *Computation handbook of statistics* (3rd ed.). Glenview, IL: Harper Collins.

Craft, J. (1992). *Statistics and data analysis for social work.* Itasca, IL: F.E. Peacock.

Gravetter, F. J., & Wallnau, L. B. (1985). *Statistics for the behavioral sciences.* St. Paul, MN: West.

McPherson-Blake, P. (1991). *Psychosocial factors associated with the immigration of Haitians and Jamaicans to South Florida and changes in their parental role.* Barry University School of Social Work, Miami Shores, Florida. Available from *Dissertation Abstracts International, 52-11A,* page 4092, 00229 pages.

THE NORMAL CURVE AND LEVELS OF MEASUREMENT

A *normal curve* is often referred to in layman's terms as a "bell curve" because of its bell-like appearance.

Advanced Level
see page 146

Advanced Level
see page 146

Descriptive statistics:
Statistical computations describing either the characteristics of a sample or the relationship among variables in a sample. Descriptive statistics merely summarize a set of sample observations.

Inferential statistics:
Inferential statistics move beyond the description of specific observations (descriptive statistics) to make inferences about a larger population based on a representative sample drawn from that population. Inferential statistics use an assortment of statistical computations for making inferences regarding the larger population from findings based on the sample data.

WHAT IS THE NORMAL CURVE?

The *normal curve* is the "bell shaped"' curve that our teachers used to "curve" our poor test scores (if we were lucky). In this graph the average person shows up the most and in the middle of the curve (see a graph of a normal population curve later in this chapter).

See Advanced Level 10.1, page 146.

HOW IS THE NORMAL CURVE USED IN RESEARCH?

The normal curve is the basis for sampling and most inferential statistical tests we use in research in the helping professions. The normal curve and its mathematical equation allows us to describe what we find in terms of ***descriptive statistics*** or ***inferential statistics*** (Gay, 1987).

See Advanced Level 10.2, page 146.

BACKGROUND ON USING THE NORMAL CURVE TO PREDICT HUMAN BEHAVIOR

The effort to devise a way of beating the odds in gambling gave rise to the development and study of statistical methods. Linking statistical methods to the study of humans occurred accidentally in the 1800's. While pouring over various *state records* on the physical measurements of army recruits (*state*-istics or statistics), the Belgian scientist Adolphe Quetelet (1796–1874) saw that the soldiers' measurements fell into a specific pattern. When he plotted the frequency distribution of the chest expansion size of Scottish soldiers, taking note of the number of cases that fell into various intervals, two new phenomena concerning human beings became apparent:

1. The measurements tended to cluster around a central value (the mean, median or mode).
2. The clustering tendency was by no means perfect; there was variability around the average. This variability formed a bell-shaped curved on his scattergram.

Quetelet's symmetrical shaped distributions of chest expansion sizes of Scottish soldiers is the basis for what we call a normal curve (Cherry, 1994).

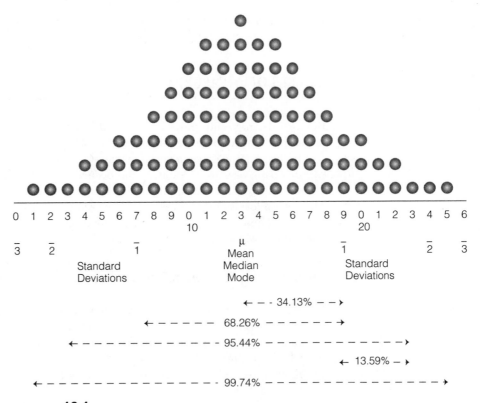

FIGURE **10.1**

A NORMAL POPULATION CURVE

In this scattergram you can see approximately what Quetelet saw when he plotted the chest sizes he had collected.

A GRAPH OF THE NORMAL CURVE

The normal curve can be represented graphically as a scattergram (Brase & Brase, 1991). This simulation of Quetelet's graph (Figure 10.1) shows that the *range* of chest expansion is from zero (0) to 26 inches. It also shows the mean, median, and mode, which all represent the average size. It also shows the three standard deviations that lie on either side of the mean.

This graph shows the average expansion size to be 13 inches. Approximately 68% of individuals had chest expansion sizes of between 7 and 19 inches. This 68% represents the number of individuals who had scores between one standard deviation below the mean (arithmetic average) and one standard deviation above the mean (Craft, 1992).

This is a fairly perfect normal curve. In almost perfect symmetrically shaped normal curves, you will find that the mean, median, and mode all have the same value. The mathematical properties of the normal curve, *central tendency,* and *variability,* are presented in Chapter 11.

LEVELS OF MEASUREMENT

Before we can go into more detail about how the normal curve is used in social research, we need to be clear about the *levels of measurement.*

In the social sciences, a *variable* is an observable event that has more than one *characteristic* or value. Counting the occurrences of a characteristic or value is called measurement. The type of value it is determines the level of measurement. There are 4 levels of measurement: (1) *nominal,* (2) *rank/ordinal,* (3) *interval,* and (4) *ratio.* These levels of measure are important when you choose the statistical method you will use to analyze your data (Rubin & Babbie, 1997).

An Easy Way to Remember the Levels of Measurement

The *level of measure* is important and useful because it determines the statistical analysis you use to analyze your data.

- *Ratio*—A continuous measure where the value of that measure can be divided and multiplied. Ratio is the highest level of measurement.
- *Interval*—A ratio variable that has been divided into equal intervals. We know where each interval begins and ends.
- *Rank/Ordinal* —Has intervals but we do not know exactly where the intervals begin and end.
- *Nominal*—Has no mathematical value, but is simply a number that represents a name. Any number could be used to represent "Single" as a value of marital status.

Example of Ratio Scale Variable

1. What is your age in years? _____
2. How many children live in your household? _____
3. How many months has it been since you visited Jamaica? _____

Example of Interval Scale Variable

1. Length of time in the United States:
   (1) Less than a year _____   (2) 1 to 3 years _____
   (3) 4 to 6 years _____   (4) 7 to 9 years _____
   (5) Over 9 years _____

2. Total annual family income:
   (1) under $5,000 _____
   (2) $5,001 to $10,000 _____

TABLE 10.1	BRIEF EXPLANATIONS FOR LEVELS OF MEASUREMENT
Nominal Level:	A name—for example, race, marital status, (yes or no)
Ordinal/Rank Level:	An order of unequal intervals—for example, questions with answers (none, sometimes, often), military rank*
Interval Level:	A measure with equal intervals—a collapsed ratio measure—for example, questions with answers (1–5 yrs, 6–10 yrs, 11 or more years)*
Ratio Level:	A continual unit of measure with a zero point—for example, a dollar, a pound, an inch*

* These levels of measure allow for arithmetic operations on the data

(3) $10,001 to $15,000 _____

(4) $15,001 to $20,000 _____

(5) $20,001 to $25,000 _____

(6) $25,001 to $30,000 _____

(7) $30,001 to $35,000 _____

(8) $35,001 or more _____

Example of Ordinal/Rank Scale Variable

1. Since you have migrated to the U.S., has there been a change in the type of food you eat?
   (1) None of the time _____
   (2) Sometimes _____
   (3) Often _____

2. If you were in Jamaica, would you encourage your child to be independent?
   (1) Strongly Agree _____
   (2) Agree _____
   (3) Disagree _____
   (4) Strongly Disagree _____

Example of Nominal Variable

1. Gender:
   (1) Male _____
   (2) Female _____

2. Marital Status:
   (1) Married _____   (2) Single _____
   (3) Separated _____   (4) Divorced _____
   (5) Common Law _____   (6) Widowed _____
   (7) Other _____

POSTSCRIPT

Now that you are more familiar with the role of the normal curve in inferential statistics and the levels of measures used in quantitative research, you are ready to examine central tendency and the statistical variability among characteristics. The mean/arithmetic average, medium, and mode are easy to understand and are very useful descriptors in both qualitative (naturalistic) and quantitative (statistical) research.

ADVANCED LEVEL MATERIAL

Advanced Level 10.1   The normal curve is a symmetrical curve in which the greatest frequency of scores or events occur in the middle. Fewer and fewer scores or events occur as you move to either extreme from the middle of the curve. In a normal curve, the left and right side of the curve are mirror images of each other. Because the normal curve can be expressed in a mathematical equation, it is the basis for inferential statistics.

Advanced Level 10.2   The phenomena of variation in nature result in a distribution. Mathematically, because of this "distribution phenomena" which has identifiable "distribution properties," a sample can be employed to predict the distribution of the whole population (Gravetter & Wallnau, 1985).

The equation for a normal curve is presented here just to show you that such an equation exists.

$$Y = \frac{1}{\sigma \sqrt{2\pi}} e^{-(X - \mu)^2 / 2\alpha^2}$$

REFERENCES

Brase, H. B., & Brase, C. O. (1991). *Understandable statistics: Concepts and methods.* Lexington, MA: D. C. Health.

Cherry, A. L. (1994). *The socializing instincts: Individual, family, and social bonds.* Westport, CT: Praeger.

Craft, J. (1992). *Statistics and data analysis for social work.* Itasca, IL: F.E. Peacock.

Gay, L. R. (1987). *Educational research* (3rd ed.). Columbus, OH: Merrill. (Chapter 12 has a very good discussion of the importance of the normal curve.)

Gravetter, F. J., & Wallnau, L. B. (1985). *Statistics for the behavioral sciences.* New York: West.

Rubin, A., & Babbie, E. (1997). *Research methods for social work* (3rd ed.). Pacific Grove, CA: Brooks/Cole. (Pages 156–161 deal with levels of measurement.)

CENTRAL TENDENCY AND VARIABILITY

WHAT IS CENTRAL TENDENCY?

The most common statistical term used in research in the helping professions is *mean*. The mean, however, is the same as an ***average*** or *arithmetic average*. Using the mean, we can find the average score, the average person, the average perception, the average attitude and so on. We can do this because in almost all groups of scores, people, or things, there is an average, which in statistics and research is called the mean. The three different types of central tendency are mean, median, and mode (Wilkinson & McNeil, 1996).

⇨ **Advanced Level**
see page 151

See Advanced Level 11.1, page 151.

EXAMPLES OF THE MEAN/AVERAGE, MEDIAN, AND MODE

When the participants in the study *Child rearing practices among Haitian and Jamaican immigrants* (McPherson-Blake, 1991) were asked their age, it was possible from their responses to determine the mean age of those who participated: Haitian Mean Age = 39 and Jamaican Mean Age = 38.

The mean/average age of 38 years and 39 years tells us that the respondents were middle-aged, mature adults. Both groups were approximately the same age. Although some were younger and some were older, their average age was almost the same. As adults, they had plenty of time to appraise their parenting skills both in their country of origin and in the United States.

Mean

The **mean** is the arithmetic average. If your data are fairly *normal,* the mean is the best statistic for the average or typical score. Even the simplest computer program will give you a mean.

If you need to compute a *mean for a population* (μ) by hand, it is very easy to do (μ is pronounced "mu"). If you wanted to compute a *mean for a sample* ($\bar{X}$)(pronounced X-bar) by hand, it is also very easy to do.

Let us say you had to find the average age for Haitians. The mathematical procedure (see the following formula) is to *sum* (Σ) or add together all of the ages for all Haitians *(X)* and divide that sum by the total number *(N)* of Haitians who revealed their age.

$$\bar{X} = \frac{\Sigma X}{N}$$

This equation for finding a mean or average calls for us to sum the ages of each person in the study and divide that sum by the total number in the study (Craft, 1992). Thus, in this case,

$$\bar{X} = \frac{7995}{205} = 39 \text{ years}$$

| 11.1 | *A Study of Rich Cocaine Addicts* |

Consider a dissertation about a study of cocaine addicts with an average income of over $100,000 a year. If you work in a public drug rehabilitation facility, you might read the article to see if rich cocaine addicts have any similarities to the people with which you work. You might even read the article out of morbid curiosity, but, you would not read the article because you believe that the findings from the study of cocaine addicts with an average income of over $100,000 a year would have a lot of relevance to your clients, especially if the majority of your clients are poor and homeless.

You would consider the findings irrelevant to your clients because the people in the study have a *mean* income of approximately $100,000 a year more than your clients. This difference in mean income tends to make a person's life experience different. The statistic of average yearly income tells us immediately that we should not generalize the findings to poor and homeless drug addicts.

The mean, median, and mode are different ways to talk about the average person in these populations.

Median

If scores are organized from high to low, the **median score** is the point where 50% of scores are below it and 50% are above it. For example, the median age for people in the previous study is 35 years. This suggests that the number of Jamaicans younger than 35 is equal to the number of Jamaicans older than 35.

Mode

The **mode** is the easiest to remember. It is the score or number most often occurring; in this case it is the age that occurred most often among the Haitians or among the Jamaicans. If the age of 28 occurred more often among Jamaicans than any other age, 28 would be the *modal* age.

Facts about Mean, Medium, and Mode

1. In many texts, the authors refer to central tendency as the description of the average score (Burning & Kintz, 1987; Gravetter & Wallnau, 1985). In these statements, the authors are using the word "average" to indicate a typical score. When it is used as a way of indicating a mean, however, the writers intend it to be understood as the arithmetic average.

2. If the distribution of scores in a normal curve form a perfect bell shape on a scattergram, the mean, median, and mode will all be the same score. In the case of the age of Jamaicans, if age was perfectly distributed among this group of Jamaicans, the mean, median, and mode would all be the same, 38 years of age (mean = 38, median = 38, mode = 38). In this case, the fact that the mean age was 39, the median age was 35, and the mode was 28 indicates that age is not normally distributed. A scattergram of age will not form a perfect bell shape.

The mean, median, and mode all have the same value on a normal curve or in a normally distributed population.

Variability/Dispersion/Spread: Range and Standard Deviation

Whereas central tendency gives us an idea of the average or typical response, *range* and *standard deviation* tell us to what extent individual scores depart from or are spread out above and below the mean.

Range

The simplest measure of dispersion is **range**. Range encompasses the highest and lowest values of a variable in a data set. Among the Jamaican participants, the range was 20 years of age to 61 years of age. In other words, the youngest person(s) who participated in the study was 20 years old. The oldest person(s) in the study was 61 years old. It would appear in text as: (Range "age of Jamaicans" = 20 to 61).

Standard Deviation

Standard deviation is the most important and commonly used measure of variability in research in the helping professions. Based on the mean as a point of reference, standard deviation is computed by determining the average distance of each score from the mean. Using standard deviation, we can determine if the scores cluster around the mean or are scattered widely above and below the mean.

An easy way to visualize standard deviation is to remember that a small standard deviation would indicate that the scores of the people in a study were very similar because they all had close to the same score. By the same token, a large standard deviation would indicate that the scores of the people in a study were very different because the people had scores that were very different from the average score. See Advanced Level 11.2, page 151.

▷ **Advanced Level**
see page 151

POSTSCRIPT

Now that you are more familiar with central tendency—mean/arithmetic average, median, and mode—the way they are used in hypothesis testing and sampling will be easier to understand. Chapter 12 will familiarize you with hypothesis testing, and Chapter 13 will show you how the normal curve and central tendency and variability apply to selecting a representative sample from a larger population.

ADVANCED LEVEL MATERIAL

Advanced Level 11.1

The three most commonly used measures of *central tendency,* the *mean/arithmetic average, median,* and *mode,* tell us the average response to a specific question. These measures work best with *ratio* levels of measure (Singleton, Straits, & Straits, 1993).

The mean, median, and mode can also be used to describe the people who participated in the study. In this way, we can determine if people we might want to generalize the findings to are similar to people who participated in the study.

Advanced Level 11.2

A small standard deviation would indicate a *homogeneous* population; similarly, a large standard deviation would indicate that the population is *heterogeneous.*

The equation to find the standard deviation depends on first finding the mean:

$$\sigma = \sqrt{\frac{\Sigma(X-\mu)^2}{N}}$$

Skewed Distribution and Kurtosis

If the distribution of data points on a scattergram do not form a normal curve, but fall to the left or right of the mean score, the distribution of scores is said to be *skewed* (see Figure 11.1).

A *positive kurtosis* value indicates that the population curve has a peak higher than a normal curve.

A *negative kurtosis* value indicates that the population curve is flatter than a normal curve.

The skewed distribution in Figure 11.1 is said to be *negatively skewed* because the mean is smaller than the median. If it were skewed in the opposite direction, it would be positively skewed because the mean would be larger than the median (Craft, 1992). This is opposite of what most of us would guess.

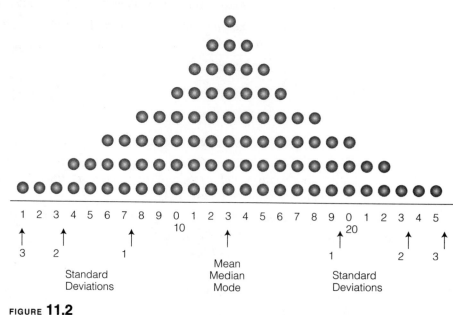

FIGURE **11.1**

GRAPH OF THE MEAN, MEDIAN, MODE IN A SKEWED DISTRIBUTION

You can compare the above graph of a skewed population distribution (Figure 11.1) to a graph of a normal population distribution (Figure 11.2). As you can see on the graph of the skewed distribution, the mean, the median, and mode have different values. On the normal curve the mean, the median, and mode all have the same value.

FIGURE **11.2**

A NORMAL POPULATION CURVE

REFERENCES

Burning, J., & Kintz, B. (1987). *Computation handbook of statistics* (3rd ed.). Glenview, IL: Harper Collins.

Craft, J. (1992). *Statistics and data analysis for social work.* Itasca, IL: F.E. Peacock.

Gravetter, F. J., & Wallnau, L. B. (1985). *Statistics for the behavioral sciences.* New York: West.

McPherson-Blake, P. (1991). *Psychosocial factors associated with the immigration of Haitians and Jamaicans to South Florida and changes in their parental role.* Barry University School of Social Work, Miami Shores, Florida. *Dissertation Abstracts International, 52-11A,* page 4092, 00229 pages.

Singleton, R. A., Straits, B. C., & Straits, M. M. (1993). *Approaches to social research* (2nd ed.). New York: Oxford University Press.

Wilkinson, W. K., & McNeil, K. (1996). *Research for the helping professions.* Pacific Grove, CA: Brooks/Cole.

PROBABILITY AND TESTING YOUR HYPOTHESIS

WHAT IS PROBABILITY?

The most common way of thinking about *probability* is to think of it as taking a *chance* that something will happen, such as the type of chances you take when you are gambling. In my case, what is the chance/probability that I will hit the lotto? I almost never buy a lotto ticket, and when I do I either forget to check it or I lose it, so the likelihood of me "hitting the lotto" is very small. If my chances/odds of winning the lotto are 7,000,000 to 1, however, and I buy 7,000,000 lotto tickets with 7,000,000 different numbers, I would win the lotto.

Probability can also be thought of as the knowledge on which to predict events that will occur. For instance, if you flipped a U.S. quarter 5 times, how much would you be willing to bet that it would come up heads 5 times out of 5 flips? My guess is that you would not bet your first born that heads will come up 5 times out of 5. It might, but the *odds are only about 3 out of 100* that 5 flips of a fair coin will result in 5 heads (Twaite & Monroe, 1979).

The probabilities on flipping a coin are the following:

0 heads in 5 flips	3.125%
1 head in 5 flips	15.625%
2 heads in 5 flips	31.250%
3 heads in 5 flips	31.250%
4 heads in 5 flips	15.625%
5 heads in 5 flips	3.125%

See Advanced Level 12.1, page 160.

⇨ **Advanced Level**
see page 160

HOW CAN YOU USE PROBABILITY?

⇨ **Advanced Level**
see page 160

Probability is the basis of the statistical procedures we use to test our hypotheses. You can also use it as it was first used by humans—to improve your chances if you gamble. See Advanced Level 12.2, page 160.

FUNDAMENTALS FOR TESTING YOUR HYPOTHESIS

Hypothesis: A statement about the nature of things based on a theory. It is a testable statement about the relationship between two or more variables or "constructs."

Hypothesis testing: The procedure of determining whether the stated relationship between two or more variables is indeed found to exist in the real world.

Testing your hypothesis is the practice of making a prediction and testing it mathematically to see if your prediction is right or wrong.

For a discussion of how a hypothesis is used in research in the helping professions, see Chapter 5, "Phase 3: Formulating the Hypothesis or a Research Question."

One of the hypotheses for the study *Child rearing among Haitian and Jamaican immigrants* is an example of a clearly stated hypothesis.

> Representative groups of Haitians and Jamaicans living in the U.S. will be influenced in their children rearing practices by U.S. culture (operationalized as living in the U.S.) at a statistically significant level as determined by the scale, *Children Rearing Report,* a 25 item scale developed by Block, Block, and Roberts (1984), revised by McPherson-Blake and Cherry (McPherson-Blake, 1991).

153

To test a hypothesis, first we state the hypothesis that we wish to test. Then we test it. In the helping professions, testing a hypothesis typically means doing a statistical test.

When you state this hypothesis, you are stating that you believe it is possible that cultural influence is an important factor in children rearing. In addition, you are saying that this influence can be measured by the scale *Children Rearing Report.*

Accepting the Hypothesis

For you to accept this hypothesis, we offer some proof. We have a scale that can compare child-rearing practices of participants in the U.S. as opposed to their child-rearing practices in Haiti and Jamaica. Using this scale and a sample of Haitians and Jamaicans living in the U.S., we found that the chances of these participants *not* being influenced in their child-rearing practices by residence in the U.S. are only 5 out of a 100. In other words, if you picked a hundred random samples of Haitians and Jamaicans living in the United States, at least 95% of those samples would have scores on the scale *Children Rearing Report* that are statistically significant at the probability level of .05 (p = .05).

The Null Hypothesis

Although it can be confusing, all research texts and all statistical tests refer to the *null hypothesis.* We talk about the null hypothesis because all of the statistical tests we use to determine level of significance are based on the beginning assumption that there is *no difference* (Twaite & Monroe, 1979).

What do we mean when we reject the null hypothesis? It means that we accept the hypothesis as being true. In short, our prediction (the hypothesis) is correct. We are right in suggesting there is a relationship between the two variables being studied.

Level of significance:
When referring to tests of statistical significance, the level of significance is the proportion of chance that an observed, empirical relationship can be attributed to sampling error. If a relationship is significant at the .05 level (p = .05), there are only 5 chances in a 100 that the relationship is occurring by accident or because of sampling error.

  Advanced Level
see page 160

LEVEL OF SIGNIFICANCE

Although simple in concept when explained, **level of significance** can be one of the most confusing issues to understand for people who are new to the use of mathematical expression in the helping professions and what it means. This type of expression, which may seem to be double talk, gives statistics a bad name. Nevertheless, there is an easy way to think of it.

A research finding that culture and child-rearing practices are highly related, and that the relation has a level of significance at the $p \leq .05$, tells us that we should accept the finding that the two are related. The two occurred together in the study because they are related. There are only 5 chances in a 100 that the relationship between culture and child-rearing practices will not be found in other populations. See Advanced Level 12.3, page 160.

Acceptable Levels of Significance

Any probability statistic that is between 5% and .000001% of an event occurring is considered to be statistically significant [e.g., (p ≤ .05), (p ≤ 049), (p ≤ .048) . . . (p ≤ .4) . . . (p ≤ .35), (p ≤ .34) . . . (p ≤ .2) . . . (p ≤ .1) . . . (p ≤ .001) . . . (p ≤ .0001)].

These significant probabilities are read this way:

(p = .05)	True 5 out of a 100 times.
(p < .05)	True less than 5 times out of a 100 times ("<" is the symbol for "less than").
(p ≤ .05)	True 5 times or less out of a 100 times ("≤" is the symbol for "less than or equal to").
(p ≤ .04)	True 4 times or less out of a 100 times.
(p ≤ .03)	True 3 times or less out of a 100 times.
(p ≤ .01)	True 1 time or less out of a 100 times.
(p ≤ .001)	True 1 time or less out of a 1000 times.

Accepted social science convention has set p = .05 as the minimum level of statistical significance. Anything greater than 5 chances in a 100 of it NOT occurring (i.e., 6 in 100) is NOT statistically significant. If we find anything more than 5 chances in a 100, it is NOT significant and it is reported as a non-significant finding.

Unacceptable Levels of Significance

(p ≥ .06)	Not acceptable as a statistically significant finding. There is too great a chance that it was an accidental finding.
(p ≥ .07)	Not acceptable as a statistically significant finding. There is too great a chance that it was an accidental finding.
(p ≥.051)	Although it is very close to .05, it is still over the cut off of .05. Where .05 equals 50 out of 1000, .051 equals 51 out of a 1000. It may be close in horseshoes but it is *not* significant in social science research.
(p ≥ .10)	Not significant. Not true more than 10 times or more out of a 100 times.

In the helping professions, for a relationship to be significant it must have a level of significance at the p ≤ .05 or greater. In some cases, such as in international economic research, a researcher might report a p ≤ .10 as "worthy of note." This means that there is a possibility that with a larger sample this may have been a significant relationship. There is not a large population of nations from which to select a larger sample.

Type I error: A Type I error (level of significance), is based on the statistical probability of the relationship occurring by chance. The Greek letter alpha (α) symbolizes Type I error.

Type II error: A Type II error is called *power.* This suggests there is power in the ability to reject the null hypothesis when it should be rejected. In statistical jargon we say, *a Type II error is taking the risk of rejecting a null hypothesis.* The Greek letter beta (β) symbolizes Type II error.

TYPE I AND TYPE II ERRORS

This is another way of talking about whether the relationship that was found in the study happened by accident or because the two are really related to one another.

If you make a Type I error, you believe it is a true relationship but, in fact, it really happened by accident.

If you make a Type II error, you do NOT believe there is a real relationship but the two really are related. See Advanced Level 12.4, page 161.

 Advanced Level
see page 161

Type I and Type II errors can be compared to the "legal dilemma"of trying to convict the guilty and not convict the innocent. A Type I error would be a legal system such as is used in the United States where some guilty persons go free to avoid convicting an innocent person. A Type II error would be employing a legal system that would convict as many of the guilty as possible even if it means convicting some people who are innocent.

Type I errors can be thought of as a fine screen that rejects untrue events, but because it is so fine it may reject some true events.

Type II errors, thought of in the same way, are like a coarse screen that lets some untrue events slip through because it is so coarse, but only a few true events will be rejected.

A Type I error is taking the risk of accepting a null hypothesis. In our example, there are 5 chances out of a 100 (p = .05) of accepting the null hypothesis when it should be rejected. In this example, the null hypothesis is, "Culture does NOT influence child rearing practices."

We run the risk of picking a loser 5 out of a 100 times with a Type I error. We run the risk of missing a winner 5 out of a 100 times with a Type II error.

There is an inverse relationship between the Type I error and the Type II error. As can be seen from the definitions, a large Type I error (β = .06) would be bad, while a large Type II error would be good (β = .95).

To increase power and maintain an acceptable level of significance we can increase the sample size.

THE ONE-TAIL AND TWO-TAIL TEST OF THE HYPOTHESIS

The decision to use a *one-tail* or *two-tail test* depends on whether your hypothesis is a test of a correlational relationship. A correlational relationship is a relationship between two variables. In the two-tail test, the critical regions of the correlation hypothesis are located at both the right and left tails of the population distribution (see Figure 12.1).

You would use a two-tail test if you were unable to specify the direction of the correlation. For example, we hypothesize that a relationship (correlation) exists between family bond and school grades, but we do not know if the variables will be positively or inversely related.

If it is a positive relationship, high levels of family bond will be correlated with *good* school grades. On the other hand, if it is an inverse relationship, high levels of family bond will be correlated with *poor* school grades. If the correlation that exists between the two variables could be either positive or inverse, you would use a (nondirectional) two-tail test.

If you use a two-tail test, you will accept the hypothesis that a statistically significant correlation exists between the two variables if the relationship occurs at *either end* of the distribution graph. Using a two-tail test, the alpha (α) is .025 at either end of the sample population distribution (see Figure 12.1).

If you use a one-tail test, you will accept the hypothesis that a statistically significant correlation exists between the two variables if the relationship occurs at *one end* of the distribution graph. Using a one-tail test, the alpha (α) is .050 at one end of the sample population distribution. Figure 12.2 is a one-tailed test that reflects a positive relationship between the two variables. It can be referred to as a *right-tailed test.*(Nachmias & Nachmias, 1987).

For example, in the case of a child's age and its influence over height, we would use a one-tail test of the effects of age because as children grow older they grow taller, not stick out. In a one-tail test the critical region is .05 twice that of a two-tail test. If the change occurs at the left end of the tail, however, you will not have tested for that event.

Testing your hypotheses (a tentative answer) is important for determining whether the relationships you propose are true or false. It is a mathematical way of describing reality.

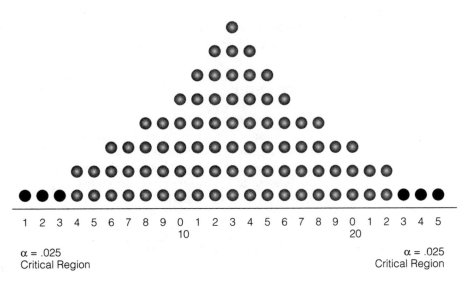

1 2 3 4 5 6 7 8 9 0 1 2 3 4 5 6 7 8 9 0 1 2 3 4 5
                    10   20

α = .025
Critical Region

α = .025
Critical Region

FIGURE **12.1**

A TWO-TAIL TEST

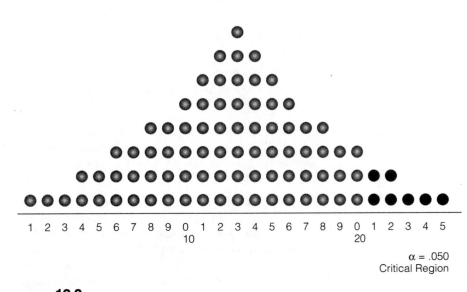

1 2 3 4 5 6 7 8 9 0 1 2 3 4 5 6 7 8 9 0 1 2 3 4 5
                    10   20

α = .050
Critical Region

FIGURE **12.2**

A RIGHT-TAILED TEST

If we were testing the relationship between elderly adults' (over 60 years of age) age and its influence over height, we would use a one-tail test (a left-tailed test) of the effects of age because as the elderly grow older they lose height. In this situation, Figure 12.2 would be a left-tailed test. The dark region would be on the left side of the population distribution graph. In most research studies, we use a two-tail test of significance (Craft, 1992).

POSTSCRIPT

The relevance of probability theory to hypotheses testing is an important concept to understand when conducting quantitative research or when selecting a representative sample. This will become clear to you in Chapter 13. Probability theory can be used to tell us how close our sample is to being representative to a larger population we want to study.

ADVANCED LEVEL MATERIAL

Advanced Level 12.1   Probability can be defined as the ratio of successes to total number of events. Probability can be written as the equation

$$0 \leq P(A) \leq 1$$

Using this equation, the probability that event (A) will occur is more than zero (0) % of the time and less than 100% of the time.

Probability theory is the underlying mathematical structure of the statistical tests we use in research in the helping professions to test research hypotheses.

Advanced Level 12.2   In research in the helping professions, probability allows us to determine the risk we take when predicting events from a sample of observations. We could not observe every possible 5 flips of a quarter, but we can predict the chances mathematically.

When we predict that child-rearing practices are in part influenced by culture, the risk of being wrong in our prediction is the obstacle we must overcome. How do we convince you that there is a very good possibility that culture affects child rearing? In this case, we are predicting that culture has a social influence on child rearing practices. We offer as proof a study that shows the influence of U.S. culture on Haitian and Jamaican parents in terms of the way they raise their children. We offer as proof a measure of the impact of U.S. culture on child rearing practice among a sample of Haitians and Jamaicans. In this study, we found that on all measures the chances were less than 5 in 100 that culture was *not* affecting child-rearing practice in these two groups of people. In the text of a research paper it is written (p = .05).

Advanced Level 12.3   In this case, there are only 5 chances in 100 that the finding occurred by accident. What we mean when we say that the probability is greater than .05 (p ≤ .05) is that the chances are greater than 95 out of 100 it will occur again. It may occur 96, 97, 98, 99, or even 100 times out of 100 times.

The level of significance is the proportion of chance that an observed, empirical relationship should be attributed to sampling error.

In the example used here, the level of significance ($p \leq .05$) tells us that the chances of finding that U.S. culture influences the child-rearing practices of a sample of Haitians and Jamaicans living in the U. S. are 95 out of 100. As a rule, given this finding, out of 100 samples of Haitians and Jamaicans, 95 will be influenced by U.S. culture and 5 samples will *not* be influenced in their child-rearing practices by U.S. culture.

Advanced Level 12.4   Type I error (level of significance) (called the *alpha level*) is determined by the mathematical chances that the relationship you found in your study was an accident (Burning & Kintz, 1987). The sample size influences the statistical significance. The larger the sample, the smaller the difference that will be needed to have a statistically significant difference.

Type II error (power) (called the *beta level*) is influenced by the size of your sample. It determines if an error occurred in the findings because your sample was mathematically too small to statistically represent the population from which you picked your sample.

As researchers, we can set the alpha level at any level we judge to be appropriate. There is a problem, however, with setting the alpha level too high. A high alpha level ($p = .05$, $p = .04$, $p = .03$, . . . $p = .01$) may reduce a Type I error, but it will increase the likelihood of making a Type II error.

A Type II or beta error (also called power) comes into play when we fail to reject the null hypothesis when it is actually false. If we reduce the likelihood of making a Type II error, however, we will increase the chances of making a Type I error.

The way to reduce the chances of making either a Type I error or a Type II error is by increasing the sample size. When you increase the sample size appropriately you can increase the alpha level without increasing the likelihood of making a Type II error. Cohen (1969) has developed tables to help us decide what sample size we need to maintain high alpha levels while at the same time reducing the chances of making a Type II error. There are computer programs as well that help you with decisions you need to make related to power.

REFERENCES

Block, J. H., Block, J., & Roberts, G. (1984). Continuity and change in parents' child rearing practices. (Rev., McPherson and Cherry, 1991). *Child Development*, 55 (2), 586–597.

Burning, J., & Kintz, B. (1987). *Computation handbook of statistics* (3rd ed.). Glenview, IL: HarperCollins.

Cohen, J. (1969). *Statistical power analysis for the behavioral sciences.* NY: Academic.

Craft, J. (1992). *Statistics and data analysis for social work.* Itasca, IL: F.E. Peacock.

McPherson-Blake, P. (1991). *Psychosocial factors associated with the immigration of Haitians and Jamaicans to South Florida and changes in their parental role.* Barry University School of Social Work, Miami Shores, Florida. *Dissertation Abstracts International, 52-11A,* page 4092, 00229 pages.

Nachmias, D., & Nachmias, C. (1987). *Research methods in the social sciences.* New York: St. Martin's.

Twaite, J. A., & Monroe, J. A. (1979). *Introductory statistics.* Glenville, IL: Scott, Foresman.

PROBABILITY AND SAMPLING

PROBABILITY THEORY AND SAMPLING

We can use probability theory to make sure that the sample of people we select are representative of the population we wish to study. It helps prevent us from selecting a biased sample.

For an illustration, suppose I want to know how undergraduates feel about social research statistics. Should I ask students who are majoring in math? Why not? Could it be that the opinion of math majors would not reflect the general opinion of undergraduates? If this is what you think, you are right. Asking only math majors would bias the findings because most math majors probably think statistics are "neat!"

WHAT IS SCIENTIFIC SAMPLING?

If you do not know the people you wish to study, get to know them firsthand before you make decisions about sampling. The more you know about the characteristics (variables) within the population you wish to study, the more sophisticated your sampling design can be.

Most of us use some form of sampling theory on a daily basis. For instance, if you took a sip from a container of sour milk, you would not need to drink the entire container of milk to determine that the milk was sour. Sampling in research in the helping professions works in much the same way. We use samples to tell us about the whole.

When probability theory is applied to the sampling process, it is called *scientific sampling*. This careful and systematic approach to sampling allows us to gain information about a large population by studying a small select group of the population. This type of sample is typically called a *representative sample* (Burning & Kintz, 1987); see Chapter 3, page 43, for a definition and description.

USING PROBABILITY TO IMPROVE YOUR SAMPLE

 Advanced Level
see page 169

 Advanced Level
see page 170

Sampling allows you to study a small number of people (often called *sampling units*) from a large population and to imply that the findings from the sample are true for the larger population. See Advanced Level 13.1, page 169.

Sampling allows you to concentrate your efforts on the members of your sample. Studying a small, well-selected (representative) sample is better than studying a large sample that is not representative. See Advanced Level 13.2, page 170. Box 13.1 describes an argument for samples.

A SIMPLE MATHEMATICAL FORMULA FOR SAMPLING ERROR

$$s = \sqrt{\frac{P \times Q}{n}}$$

<table>
<tr><td>13.1</td><td>An Argument in Favor of Sampling</td></tr>
</table>

It is much easier to obtain completed questionnaires from 30% of your sample of students (n = 300) who did not return the questionnaire during the first wave, than it is to obtain completed questionnaires from 30% of the entire student body (N = 6,000). Contacting 90 students for a second or even a third time would be possible, although a lot of work, but contacting 1,800 students two or three times would take a tremendous amount of time and resources.

P & Q	=	The population responses on a dichotomus variable (for example, a "yes" or "no") question:
P	=	Percent of "yes" answers
Q	=	Percent of "no" answers
n	=	The number of units (that is, people) in each sample. The small n stands for "sample population." The large N stands for the "total population" from which the "n" sample was selected.
s	=	The standard error.

⇨ **Advanced Level**
see page 170

See Advanced Level 13.3, page 170.

SELECTING A GOOD SAMPLE SIZE

A good sample size is one large enough to be similar to the total population you wish to study. In Chapter 3, I suggested that if you are doing a one-group study, you should try to select a sample of 100 to 150. If it is a group comparison of two or more groups, I suggested between 25 and 50 per group with all group members adding up to at least 100.

The life experience of one person might be important for some forms of therapy, but the problems that a Haitian parent is having adapting to U.S. culture give us no sense that she or he is representative of all Haitian parents. We may want to believe so, but there is no offer of proof that the life experience of one Haitian parent is similar to that of all Haitian parents living in the United States.

A sample larger than one person is surely needed. Although it is possible that a one-person sample could be representative of the opinion of his or her group, this would be difficult to prove. Another reason to go to the trouble to select an acceptable size sample is that a bad sample may cause the findings to be erroneous. See Advanced Level 13.4, page 171.

⇨ **Advanced Level**
see page 171

Probability and Nonprobability Sampling Designs

If you use probability sampling, you have to follow established social research procedures. If you do, your study will have met one of the criteria for empirical research. Furthermore, this will meet the expectations of professionals in your field who might want to read about your study.

Using a nonprobability sample, on the other hand, can be as simple as standing on the street corner, stopping people who pass by, and asking them to be in your study. This is a sample, but a sample of what population? Unless you have some compelling reason for randomly interviewing people on the street, it would be a sample that most researchers would think is worthless. See Advanced Level 13.5, page 172.

⇨ **Advanced Level**
see page 172

Probability and Simple Random Sampling

Sampling frame: A list of known units comprised of a population from which the sample is selected. If the sample is to be representative of the population from which it is selected, all units of the population must be included in the sampling frame.

One of the easiest ways to understand sampling theory is to remember that all samples are compared to a perfect **simple random sample.** The question is: How close does the sample come to being as good as a perfect simple random sample? A good way to think of a simple random sample is to think of the familiar procedure where you pick names out of a hat for your sample. Using this simple random sampling approach, you put each person's name in a hat and draw out the names randomly until you select the total number of units (that is, people) you want in your sample.

Simple random sample: The simplest probability sampling approach. It is a sample where each unit (for example, people) found in a population of interest has an equal chance of being selected to be members of the sample for the study.

Three Probability Sampling Designs

Three basic probability sampling designs are presented here. The one thing that all probability sampling designs have in common is that all of them incorporate randomization in the plan as much as possible. Furthermore, it is not unusual for these approaches to be mixed together in one way or the other.

A Simple Random Sample

The simple random sample is the easiest way to select a probability sample. It is also the basic sampling process that probability theory and its related statistics depend on. All other sampling designs are compared to the perfect simple random sample—that is, it is the standard by which to judge the other sampling designs.

In addition to picking names from a hat, you can use several approaches that are more conventional. Assign different numbers to all the members of the total population you wish to study and have a computer generate a list of random numbers that can be used to identify the matching numbers of people in the population and select them for your sample.

Systematic sample: A type of probability sample where after a random starting number is selected, every "*k*th" unit on a list is selected for inclusion in the sample. "*k*th" in research jargon stands for an equal interval used to select the sample. For example, if we choose every 100th person on a list of students, "*k*th" = 100. If we choose every 25th person on a list of students, "*k*th" = 25.

⇨ **Advanced Level**
   see page 172

⇨ **Advanced Level**
   see page 172

Sampling interval: The equal distance between units from a population for a sample, selecting every *k*th person.

Proportionate stratified sampling: A sample in which the units (for example, people) from a larger known population are separated into homogeneous groups (or strata) before a proportionate sample is drawn from each group. This procedure is most often used in conjunction with a simple random sample or systematic sampling approach. Combining these approaches can improve the representativeness of a sample.

Another approach is to use a *random numbers table*. You randomly pick a number to start with and then go down the column of numbers on the table using them to select your sample. A random numbers table is not as convenient as a computer list of random numbers, but if you need to use a table of random numbers, such a table can be found in virtually all of the traditional texts on research methods.

Systematic Sampling

The easiest way to remember how systematic sampling works is to think of choosing every other name from a list of 300 people in your graduating class. You would have a sample list of 150 people. A **systematic sample** is a type of probability sample with a random starting number. See Advanced Level 13.6, on page 172.

Proportionate Stratified Sampling

This approach can be broken down into two different approaches—a *proportionate* and a *stratified* approach—and then used individually, but it makes little sense to do so. Most of the time we use them together. See Advanced Level 13.7, page 172.

THREE NONPROBABILITY SAMPLING DESIGNS

In certain situations a nonprobability sample is acceptable, and it might be the only way to learn about some groups of people. If we wanted to obtain a representative sample of people who drink over the legal limit and drive how would we go about it? We could send out self-administered questionnaires to a randomly selected group from the telephone book. How do we know that everyone who drinks and drives will answer the questions honestly or even tell us that they do drink and drive?

This kind of sample might be impossible to obtain. We could easily get a sample of people who were caught driving and drinking but they might be very different from people who are not caught. It is logical to assume, however, that we could learn a lot from people who were caught even if we do not know if they are representative of all people who drink and drive.

Snowball Sampling

Consider trying to find the homeless in your community. One way to find where homeless people stay is to ask homeless people you find on the street where other homeless people might be found. They will know better than most.

As another example, we wanted to gather information on long-term gay relationships. After trying a number of approaches like advertising, we used the *snowball* approach successfully. We started with the few gay couples who responded to our ads and asked them to help us identify other gay couples who would participate in our research.

Quota Sampling

A *quota sample* is based on a number of characteristics common to the population of interest, such as gender, race, and education. Once we have identified these characteristics, the sample is selected by choosing people from each subgroup:

> Group 1 = Female, African-American, college educated
> Group 2 = Female, African-American, non-college educated
> Group 3 = Male, African-American, college educated
> Group 4 = Male, African-American, non-college educated
> Group 5 = Female, Hispanic, college educated
> Group 6 = Female, Hispanic, non-college educated
> . . . and so on until all groups are represented

Then you select people from each subgroup to make up your sample. Although this approach is similar to the stratified approach, it does not meet the provision of randomness.

Convenient/Available/Judgmental Sampling

The name of this approach, the one most often used by students in my research classes, tells the story. It is a sample that is *available* and that, in the *judgment* of the researcher, is representative.

Suppose we wanted to known how social work students in the United States feel about social work licensure. We could get together a list of every social work student in the United States and select a random sample, or we could use a sample of social work students at a local university and ask them what they feel about professional licensure. The social work students at the local university are available. They may not be representative of the social work students in the rest of the United States, but in my judgment they have more of a chance of reflecting the opinion of all U.S. social work students on social work licensure than, say, students in accounting or history at the same university.

Returning to the illustration of the sample of "sour milk," it would be more scientific for me to taste the milk in a randomly selected sample of glasses of milk from that container before drawing any conclusion. The sample I had available to me (in my judgment) is probably like all other glasses of milk from that container. The one taste would be enough to convince me not to drink the rest of the milk in the container.

This type of sample may also be called a *convenient* or *accidental sample*.

Generalizability: The degree to which a research finding can be assumed to exist in a broader population than the sample from which the finding was obtained. As an example would you generalize the findings about college students in a southern university to all the college students in the U.S.?

GENERALIZABILITY

Representativeness, mentioned earlier is very much like *generalizability*. Whereas representativeness speaks to how similar the sample is to the whole population under study, *generalizability* speaks to whether the findings from your sample can be used to draw an inference concerning the total population. In other words, are

---

13.2 *Generalizing Your Findings*

The sample of Haitians and Jamaicans for the study *Child Rearing and Culture* were selected so that they would be representative of a larger population of Haitian and Jamaicans who were raising or had recently raised children. Of course, you need to make up your own mind about the sample. Looking at the demographic information on the participants in the study will help you to get a picture of the people in the sample.

If you think the sample is fairly representative, then you can determine how many (if any) of the findings you would attribute to all Haitians and Jamaicans raising children.

---

the findings from the sample relevant to a larger population? Box 13.2 describes generalizing findings.

POSTSCRIPT

It is obvious that selecting a sample representative of the population you wish to study is important. The problem occurs when one tries to select the sample. As you realize from this chapter, there is more to selecting a sample than merely picking a few people from the population.

Furthermore, the degree of normalcy of the population distribution as seen in this chapter and Chapter 12 is important when using inferential statistical tests (Chapters 14 through 26) to analyze the data collected from the people in your sample.

In Part IV, Chapter 14 inferential statistics is introduced. It is not as difficult as you have been led to believe. Remember you do not need to be good at math to learn to use statistical tests to analyze your data.

ADVANCED LEVEL MATERIAL

Advanced Level 13.1   The term *unit* or *element* is used to represent people, groups, organizations, interventions, and so on. The individuals in the study or the individual units in your sample are called the *units of analysis.* It is easier to gain information on a lengthy questionnaire from a small sample of college students than from the entire student body.

Advanced Level 13.2 ## Fundamental Sampling Issues

The most important issue associated with sampling can be stated in the nagging question: Can what we learn from the observations of a few units be translated into knowledge about a larger population of units?

Without comparing the information gained from the sample to the larger population from which the sample was selected, there might be no exact way of knowing the answer to the above question. If we apply probability techniques to the problem of selecting a representative sample, however, we can at least get some idea of how close our sample is to reflecting reality, in other words, how close our sample is to reflecting the same characteristics as the population from which the sample was selected. One way to check the sample is to use an estimate called, *sampling error* (also called *standard error*) (Singleton, Straits, & Straits, 1993).

Sampling Error

Probability theory makes two major contributions to scientific sampling:

Contribution 1: The larger the number of randomly selected individuals chosen from a known group, the greater the chances that the majority of individuals and their characteristics will be distributed around the same mean as that of the population from which the sample was selected.

This phenomenon is also known as the *Law of Large Numbers* and is derived from the normal curve phenomena. This phenomenon is what causes the characteristics of a majority of a known population (for example, Haitians or Jamaicans) to cluster around the mean of that population. When a truly random sample is selected from that population, the attributes of the sample will cluster around the same mean/arithmetic average as those found in the population.

In our example study of the U.S. population of Haitians and Jamaicans, the chances of randomly selecting Jamaican parents who were 38 years old were greater. Why? Because many more people between the ages of 30 years and 50 years are parents currently rearing families than are people below 30 or above 50 years of age.

Contribution 2: Statistical techniques based on probability theory provide a mathematical formula for telling us how close our sample mean is to being the same as the mean of the population from which the sample was selected. The *standard error formula* gives an estimate of how closely our sample mean is clustered around the mean of the population from which the sample was selected.

Advanced Level 13.3 In the study, *Child rearing practices among Haitian and Jamaican immigrants* (McPherson-Blake, 1991), if we wished to know if the percentage of U.S. citizens in our sample was similar to the percentage of U.S. citizens in the total population of Haitians, we could use the formula for standard error to find out (Rubin & Babbie, 1997). In our sample, about 35% were citizens and approximately 65% were non-citizens of the United States. To find out how close the sample is to the total population, we can use the following procedure:

$$s = \sqrt{\frac{35 \times 65}{205}} = \sqrt{\frac{2275}{205}} = \sqrt{11.10} = s = 3.33$$

Based on the findings of a standard error of 3.33%, we can say that for the Haitian population from which this sample of Haitians was selected, the percentage of those who are citizens of the U.S. will be between 32% and 38%. This means that the 35% found in the sample is fairly close to what we could expect if we were to ask all Haitians in the population to answer the question about their citizenship. If we want our confidence interval of "3" to be even better, for instance "2," we can simply increase the number in the sample.

Advanced Level 13.4 Instead of picking the number of people you want in your sample out of thin air, you can use a mathematical formula to determine the sample size you need for your study. The formula allows you to determine how large your sample needs to be, depending on how accurate you want your sample to be. The formula helps you answer the question, "What are the chances of my sample being representative of the total population?"

Although the mathematical techniques can be very complicated, the concept is simple. You want a sample that is large enough to be representative of the larger population.

To determine the sample size we want or will need, we could use a variation of the standard error formula presented above. Suppose we have census data suggesting that an estimated 35% of Haitians living in the U.S. are U.S. citizens. Say we wanted a sample of Haitians in which the number of U.S. citizens in the sample was within 2 percentage points of 35%. The formula will tell how many Haitians we need to randomly select from the total population.

A Simple Mathematical Formula for Selecting an Appropriate Sample Size

If we increase our sample size, the chance of making a Type II error will be decreased (see Chapter 12 for more information on Type I and Type II errors). A larger sample size would increase the closeness of our sample's mean to the true population mean. Using a variation on the formula for standard error presented above, we would calculate the following:

$$n = (P \times Q) / s^2$$
$$n = 2275 / 2^2 = 568.75$$

Although the increase in sample size will decrease the standard error from 3.33% to 2%, I do not know if the increase in confidence that we are now within 2 percentage points of the true population arithmetic mean is worth the effort. Even though we are now able to say that the true population arithmetic mean of the sample will be between 33% and 37% of Haitians who are U.S. citizens, we have had to increase the sample size from 205 to 568 randomly selected Haitians to be able to say so. It might be worth it under some circumstances, but it would greatly increase the expense and time to do the same study. It might also be more difficult to collect data from a high number of people from this population. This is a decision the researcher must make.

Advanced Level 13.5   Two general categories of sampling design are important. The *probability* and *nonprobability* sample. Identifying a sample as a probability sample tells us that the sample meets the assumption of randomness and thus tends to be representative of the population from which it was selected.

Choosing a nonprobability sample indicates that we do not know how close the sample is to being representative of the population we wish to study. Even so, nonprobability sampling can be useful.

Advanced Level 13.6   There are *specific criteria for using a systematic sampling approach* that you must include in the design. You must use equal interval. To determine the interval for your systematic sample, you divide the size of the population by the number you want to use as a sample. For instance, if you have a list of 3,000 names and you want to draw a sample of 300 names, you pick every 10th name on your list.

You also need to have a randomly selected starting number. To be as random as possible, using a systematic sampling approach you need to randomly pick the number you will use to start the selection process. In the example we are using here, you would pick a number between 1 and 10 as your starting place. If you randomly picked 4 as a starting place, you would then pick the 4th name from the list and every 10th name after that. In this example, you would pick the 4th name, and the 14th, 24th, 34th, 44th, 54th, 64th name and so on until you picked the 300 names out of 3000 for your sample.

Advanced Level 13.7   The easiest way to remember how the *proportionate stratified sampling* approach works is to think of separating people into homogeneous groups such as seniors, juniors, and sophomores. Then you use the previously discussed systematic sampling approach to draw 50% of your sample ($n = 100$ sophomores) from the sophomore group because sophomores make up 50% of the total population of the three groups ($N = 1000$). You draw 30% of your sample ($n = 60$ juniors) from the junior group because juniors make up 30% of the total population of the three groups. You draw 20% of your sample ($n = 40$ seniors) from the senior group because seniors make up 20% of the total population of the three groups.

REFERENCES

Burning, J., & Kintz, B. (1987). *Computation handbook of statistics* (3rd ed.). Glenview, IL: HarperCollins.

McPherson-Blake, P. (Spring, 1991). *Psychosocial factors associated with the immigration of Haitians and Jamaicans to South Florida and changes in their parental role.* Barry University School of Social Work, Miami Shores, Florida. *Dissertation Abstracts International, 52-11A,* page 4092, 00229 pages.

Rubin, A., & Babbie, E. (1997). *Research methods for social work* (3rd ed.). Pacific Grove, CA: Brooks/Cole. Chapter 8 is a good overview of sample procedures.

Singleton, R. A., Straits, B. C., & Straits, M. M. (1993). *Approaches to social research.* New York: Oxford University Press.

UNIVARIATE, BIVARIATE, AND MULTIVARIATE ANALYSIS

What Are Univariate, Bivariate, and Multivariate Analysis?

Social research is more conceptual than mathematical. In fact, most concepts in social research are intuitive and are used by all thoughtful people.

You use these levels of analysis in your everyday life to understand and predict events. You might not have a crystal ball, but you use univariate, bivariate, and multivariate analysis when making predictions. Even more bewildering, we use these levels of analysis every day of our lives without knowing it.

Box 14.1 shows an example of how you might use univariate, bivariate, and multivariate analyses in your everyday life.

Univariate Analysis

Univariate analysis: The analysis of one variable at a time. It describes one characteristic of a population or sample at a time.

The **univariate analysis** uses *frequencies* to analyze data. You most often see the frequencies expressed in *percentages* or *marginals* (for example, upper 25%, lower 25%) and *ratio* comparisons [for example, a ratio of (1 : 3) or read, 1 in every 3 tries].

A univariate analysis can give us some useful information, alhtough it is limited information:

- 179 people in a study had been living in the United States for more than 9 years.
- 5 people in the study were in the United States for less that 1 year.
- 37% of the Haitian participants and 67% of the Jamaican participants had lived in the U.S. for more than 9 years.

This is excellent information, but we can learn a great deal more from a bivariate analysis.

Bivariate Analysis

Bivariate analysis: The analysis of two variables at the same time to determine the empirical relationship between the two variables. Statistical procedures such as *Crosstabs table, t-test,* and the *Pearson's product moment correlation* (r^2) are typically used for bivariate analyses.

Multivariate analysis: The analysis of three or more variables at the same time so as to determine the empirical relationship between the three or more variables. Statistical procedures such as multiple regression and multiple analysis of variance are typically used for multivariate analyses.

More sophisticated statistical procedures are used if you want to do a **bivariate analysis.** Statistical tests such as chi-square (χ^2), *t*-test, and a Pearson's correlation (r^2) are examples of statistical procedures used to do bivariate analyses (Twaite & Monroe, 1979).

In a national sample of people in auto accidents, it was found that more men than women get into auto accidents. This finding is interesting. It is also interesting to find out that people who drive more than 100 miles per week get into more auto accidents than do people who drive less than 100 miles per week. Finally, finding out that more men than women drive more than 100 miles per week puts a different twist on the original bivariate finding that, "More men than women get into auto accidents."

Although these relationships are based on three different bivariate analyses, they do help us form some ideas about those who are involved in auto accidents. This information helps focus our thinking and probably will change our earlier explanations for the possible causes for auto accidents.

14.1   *The Office Meeting: An Example of Univariate, Bivariate, and Multivariate Analysis*

We might attend an office meeting and, upon entering the room and making an initial observation, remark to ourselves, "Most of the people at this meeting are from out of town. Hmm, I wonder what this means."

Our univariate analysis alerts us that something is different, but, it does not give us many answers.

UNIVARIATE DATA:

1. People are from out of town.

When we are told that they are accountants and computer people, we now have two bits of information.

BIVARIATE DATA:

1. People are from out of town.
2. They are accounting and computer people.

When we put the two pieces together, we are doing a bivariate analysis. Given this bivariate data, we can reanalyze the situation and propose several possible reasons why the out-of-town people are at the meeting.

PRELIMINARY ANALYSIS:

1. The bookkeeping system is down and these people had to be called in to fix it.
2. It could be an audit of the accounts.
3. Alternative explanations could also be possible—they are here to "praise me, not to fire me."

Next, when we sit down our supervisor tells us that the out-of-town people are from a private company that sells computer software for bookkeeping. We now have three pieces of data that we can put together to allow us to do a multivariate analysis.

MULTIVARIATE DATA:

1. People are from out of town.
2. They are accounting and computer people.
3. They are from a private company that sells computer software.

We now put all three pieces of data together. This is a multivariate analysis and it suggests an even more plausible explanation for the presence of the out-of-town people at the meeting.

PRELIMINARY ANALYSIS:

1. They are here to try to sell us some new software.
2. They are here to install and train us on new computer software.

There could be competing explanations, but as the bits of data increase and we put them together, the analysis becomes stronger and more convincing. Additionally, we feel more confident in our predictions as to why the people are at the meeting. The same logic of putting together the facts we know in a multivariate way also works in research in the helping professions. Furthermore, by employing statistics we can estimate the chances that our predictions are going to come true. See Advanced Level 14.1, page 175.

▷ **Advanced Level**
see page 175

Multivariate Relationships and Analysis

The most sophisticated statistical procedures available are needed to do a **multivariate analysis.** The statistical procedures typically used to simultaneously analyze three or more variables at a time are the *multiple regression,* and *multiple analysis of variance* procedures (Singleton, Straits, & Straits, 1993) (see Table 14.1).

FOUR TYPES OF DATA TO ANALYZE

Selecting the best statistical procedure to analyze data often seems mysterious to the new researcher. If you organize your decisions around the type of sample or participants, however, it is a little easier. Do the participants represent 1 group, 2 groups, or 3 or more groups?

To keep it simple, there are basically four types of data that you will probably collect in your research effort.

1. Data from *one group*
2. Data from *two groups* on the same measures (for example, items on a questionnaire)
3. Data from *three groups or more* on the same measures (for example, items on a questionnaire)
4. *Time-series data* on the same measure (for example, data from a pre- and posttest).

Although selecting the best statistical procedure to analyze your data may seem complicated, it is not. "What kind of statistics are used with what kind of data?" is often easier to determine than you would think. Keep in mind, there are only four major types of statistical approaches that you will probably use. These are the most often used statistical procedures in the helping professions. If you are just starting out, you would be wise to design your study so you are using one of the four approaches presented in Table 14.2.

TIME SERIES ANALYSIS

The best way to remember what a time-series analysis can do is to think of an example like the FBI yearly report on crime in the United States. In each issue, the current year's crime rates are reported, and these rates are compared to years in the past. Using this approach, crime rates over the last 10 years, 20 years, or more can be compared year by year.

⇨ **Advanced Level**
see page 177

The statistical procedures you will use are for analyzing data from three or more groups. In this analysis each year is considered a "group." See Advanced Level 14.2, on page 176.

TABLE 14.1	DETERMINING STATISTICAL PROCEDURES BASED ON THE NUMBER OF VARIABLES IN THE ANALYSIS	
Number of Variables	**Statistical Procedure to Use for Analysis**
Univariate	Frequencies
Bivariate	Crosstabs, *t*-test, Correlations, and Analysis of Variance (ANOVA)
Multivariate	Multiple Regression and Multiple Analysis of Variance (MANOVA)

TABLE 14.2	DETERMINING STATISTICAL PROCEDURES BASED ON GROUPS BEING STUDIED		
Number of Variables	**(1) Group Analysis**	**(2) Groups Analysis**	**(3) Groups or More & Time-Series**
Univariate	Frequencies	Frequencies	Frequencies
Bivariate	Crosstabs, Correlations	Crosstabs, *t*-test Correlations, and ANOVA	Crosstabs, Correlations, and ANOVA
Multivariate	Multiple Regression	Multiple Analysis of Variance (MANOVA)	MANOVA

POSTSCRIPT

In this chapter, you were introduced to the three types of analysis: univariate, bivariate, and multivariate analysis. You were also presented with examples of how the four types of data can be analyzed: data from one group, data from two groups, data from three or more groups, and time-series (pretest-posttest) data.

Chapter 15 ("Frequency Distributions") will show you how to do a univariate analysis. Although frequency distributions can be used in both qualitative (naturalistic) and quantitative (statistical) research, they are most often seen in quantitative research.

ADVANCED LEVEL MATERIAL

Advanced Level 14.1   If I employ multivariate statistics and find that three bits of data (independent variables) explained 80% of the reason why out-of-town people (dependent variable) are attending the office meeting, I might be wrong, but I would be willing to bet that they are there to either sell or install computer software. Explaining 80% of the variance of the reason why is quite good in the human sciences—but not perfect.

Advanced Level 14.2   For a study like this if you treat the data from each year as a group, you could use the various forms of Multiple Analysis of Variance (MANOVA) or Regression Analysis (in regression analysis, time is the independent variable). If the crime rates were stable over the past 10 years, the MANOVA would find no significant differences between the years. If crime rates declined, the MANOVA would show that a statistically significant difference existed between the years. If you examine the crime rates for each year, you should see a decline over the last 10 years.

If you use Regression Analysis, this procedure would tell you how much of the variance the independent variable "time" would explain in the changes over time. With regression analysis, you can also obtain curvilinear estimates.

Although the time-series analysis requires that we collect data in a different way—the data are collected on the same variable over time—it gives us a different view of a relationship. It may reveal that the relationship fluctuates over time (Stark & Roberts, 1996).

An example of a more informative study, would be to test the hypothesis that crime rates and unemployment are related. What would your hypothesis say about the relationship between crime and unemployment?

REFERENCES

Singleton, R. A., Straits, B. C., & Straits, M. M. (1993). *Approaches to social research* (2nd ed.). New York: Oxford University Press.

Stark, R., & Roberts, L. (1996). *Contemporary social research methods.* Bellevue, WA: MicroCase Corporation.

Twaite, J. A., & Monroe, J. A. (1979). *Introductory statistics.* Glenville, IL: Scott, Foresman.

FREQUENCY DISTRIBUTIONS

WHAT IS A FREQUENCY DISTRIBUTION?

Frequency relates to such questions as How many? How many times did people answer the question? How many were female? How old were they? *Your first statistical analysis should be a frequency analysis of your data.*

A *frequency distribution* will tell you how often an event occurred in the data that were collected. For example what was the number of Haitians and Jamaicans in the study *Child rearing practices among Haitian and Jamaican immigrants* (McPherson-Blake, 1991).

A frequency distribution is typically constructed for each quantitative variable or question used in a study. Quantitative variables are questions that have a number for an answer (a count or value). These questions often tell us how many times something occurred.

SELECTING GOOD ITEMS AND QUESTIONS

The items used in frequency distributions are questions set up so they are easy to count. We typically use questions that relate to numbers of events, levels of agreement, etc. A few typical questions should make the point.

- **Age.** The answer can be the exact age of the participant. This is a ratio level variable.
- **Gender.** A closed-ended question in which the options are provided to the participant. This is a nominal level variable.
  - (1) Female
  - (2) Male
- **Level of Income.** This question could be either a ratio level or interval level variable. In this case, it is also a closed-ended question and the options are provided to the participant. Though interval data are vague about a specific amount of income within each interval, there are clear lines separating each level. The options should also be exhaustive. Option #1 takes in everyone below $25,000 and #5 takes in everyone above $100,000. Everyone will be able to find one and only one interval that describes him or her (an interval level variable).
  - (1) Less than $25,000
  - (2) Between $25,001 and $50,000
  - (3) Between $50,001 and $75,000
  - (4) Between $75,001 and $100,000, and
  - (5) Above $100,000
- **Level of Interest in Research in the Helping Professionals.** Another closed-ended question where the options are provided. This is a rank/ordinal level variable. These variables are not only vague within the ranks but also the line between the ranks is a bit vague. It might be difficult for people to find a rank that they believe describes their level of interest.

(1) Low
(2) Medium
(3) High

BACKGROUND ON FREQUENCY DISTRIBUTIONS

The frequency distribution is the oldest and most popular approach for summarizing data. The extensive use of frequency distributions has occurred because they are easy to understand and to explain. Another reason frequency distribution continues to be used is that it tells us how many times something has occured better than a raw count or raw numbers.

We are so accustomed to seeing and reading frequency distributions that we hardly know how to express a count without using a frequency distribution. What if you had a sheet of paper with the word "Haitian" written on it 205 times as a way of showing the number of people who identified themselves as Haitian? The list below could show the number of people who identified themselves as Haitian in this study.

List of Ethnic Group Members

Haitian, Haitian, Haitian, Haitian, Haitian, Haitian,
Haitian, Haitian, Haitian, Haitian, Haitian, Haitian,
Haitian, Haitian, Haitian, Haitian, Haitian, Haitian,
Haitian, Haitian, Haitian, Haitian, Haitian, Haitian,
Haitian, Haitian, Haitian, Haitian, Haitian, Haitian,
Haitian, Haitian, Haitian, Haitian, Haitian, Haitian . . .

From this list, it would not be clear how many times the word "Haitian" appeared on the list. Nor would this count tell us as much as simply stating, "Among the participants in the study, *Child rearing practices among Haitian and Jamaican immigrants,* 205 people answered the question about their ethnic background by checking the response 'Haitian'."

A frequency distribution is a count of the number of times a specific value of a variable is observed in a population or sample. A frequency distribution gives us the opportunity to view a complete set of scores all at the same time. From the frequency distribution, we can tell if the scores (as a group) are high or low, spread out across the values, or whether the scores cluster around certain values (Rubin & Babbie, 1997).

EXAMPLE OF FREQUENCY DISTRIBUTION TABLES AND GRAPHS

The most accurate and understandable way to present a frequency distribution is by using a table like the one below. However, the most eye-catching way of presenting a frequency distribution is by using a histogram (a line graph), a bar chart, or a pie chart.

In the study *Child rearing practices among Haitian and Jamaican immigrants,* when participants were distributed by group, 205 were Haitian and 151 were Jamaican. The table and charts below tell you the same thing in a quick glance. See Tables 15.1 through 15.4 and Figures 15.1 through 15.2 for a few examples.

Not only is a table of frequency distribution easy to read, but also you can communicate a great deal of information to the readers that could otherwise take a great deal of explaining (Baker, 1994). For illustration purposes, Table 15.2 allows us to add a frequency distribution of gender.

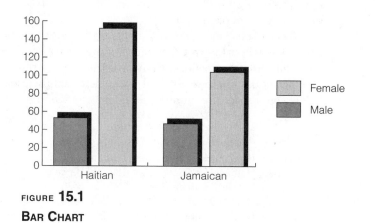

FIGURE **15.1**
BAR CHART

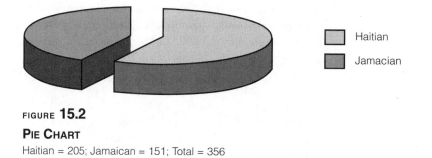

FIGURE **15.2**
PIE CHART
Haitian = 205; Jamaican = 151; Total = 356

TABLE 15.1   FREQUENCY DISTRIBUTION BY ETHNIC GROUP

Group	Haitian	Jamaican	Total
Males	53	47	100
Females	152	104	256
Total	**205**	**151**	**356**

TABLE 15.2   FREQUENCY DISTRIBUTION OF GROUP AND GENDER

Haitians		Jamaicans	
Value Label	Frequency of Value	Value Label	Frequency of Value
Male	53	Male	47
Female	152	Female	104
Total	**205**	**Total**	**151**

TABLE 15.3   LENGTH OF TIME IN UNITED STATES FOR HAITIANS

Value Label	Frequency	Percentage
< 1 yr	3	1
1–3 yrs	21	10
4–6 yrs	51	25
7–9 yrs	55	27
> 9 yrs	75	37
Totals	**205**	**100%**

TABLE 15.4	LENGTH OF TIME IN UNITED STATES FOR JAMAICANS	
Value Label	Frequency	Percentage
<1 yr	2	1
1–3 yrs	8	6
4–6 yrs	20	13
7–9 yrs	26	17
> 9 yrs	95	63
Totals	**151**	**100%**

USING PERCENTAGES TO EXPRESS FREQUENCIES

One of the best ways to communicate the meaning of a frequency distribution is by using *percentages*. Combining frequency of occurrences and the percentages of that frequency is the most effective way to give your readers a picture of the frequency with which the variable occurred.

Frequency percentages are also very "robust." If one reports percentages to represent large numbers, the percentages are likely to be very close to the real numbers that will be found in the population.

QUESTIONS THAT A FREQUENCY DISTRIBUTION CAN ANSWER

Here are a few questions for which a frequency distribution table provides answers.

1. How many people in the study were in the United States for more than 9 years?
    Answer: 170 participants.

2. How many were in the United States for less than 1 year?
    Answer: 5 participants.

3. What percentage of Haitians and Jamaicans were in the United States for more than 9 years?
    Answer: 37% of the Haitians and 63% of the Jamaicans.

4. We could also collapse several of the questions with interval level responses and ask, "What percentage of Haitians and Jamaicans were in the United States for 7 years or more?"
    Answer: 64% of the Haitians and 80% of the Jamaicans.

15.1 *Challenging Your Intuition*

One way to demonstrate the usefulness of a frequency distribution is to challenge your intuition. Would you be willing to bet that the percentage of Haitians (n = 21) who have been in the United States for 1 to 3 years is a smaller percentage than Jamaicans (n = 20) who have been in the United States for 4 to 6 years? You would be right if you guessed "smaller." Luckily, you do not have to guess. The frequency distribution presented in Tables 15.3 and 15.4 will tell you that 21 Haitians is 10% out of a total of 205 Haitians. This is a smaller percentage than the 13% of Jamaicans (20 Jamaicans out of a total of 151).

RESULTS OF THE FREQUENCY DISTRIBUTION ANALYSIS

Using Tables 15.3 and 15.4, you could report the findings to the readers in the following manner:

- Table 15.3 shows that 63% of Haitians who participated in this study have resided in the United States for less than 9 years and, 37% have resided in the United States for more than 9 years.
- Table 15.4 shows that 37% of Jamaicans who participated in this study have resided in the United States for less than 9 years, but 63% have resided in the United States for more than 9 years.

As you can see the two groups are virtually opposite in the number of people and the length of time in the United States. A Haitian participant was as likely to be in the United States less than 9 years as a Jamaican was likely to be in the United States more than 9 years.

The frequency distribution, however, cannot tell us if the differences in the length of time in the United States between the Haitian and Jamaicans reflect reality or if they are simply an accident of the draw. In other words, are the differences real or did we just get an odd ball sample that makes them look different?

To find out if they are different, we must use a bivariate analysis. We test the hypothesis that there is no difference between the groups. A crosstabulation was used to detect any statistically significant differences between the two groups of participants. When "Length of time in the United States" was compared for both groups, a significant difference ($p < .001$) was found to exist between the two groups. In other words, Jamaicans who participated in this study, as a group, had been in the United States statistically significantly longer than Haitian participants

15.1   *The World Population Expressed in Percentages*

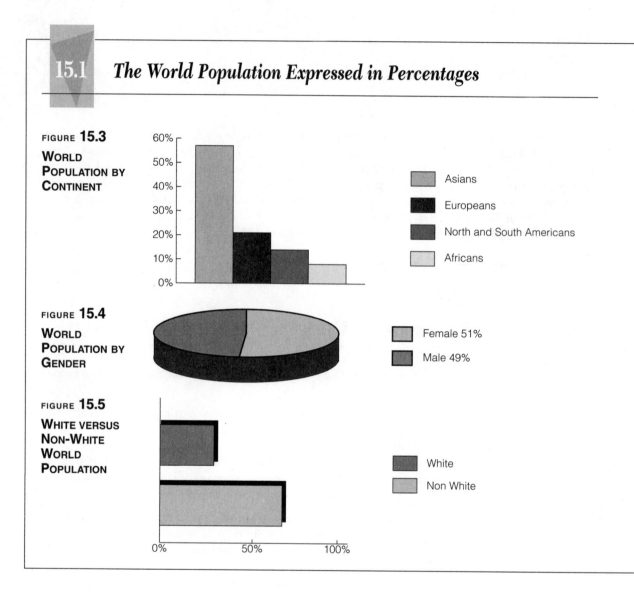

FIGURE 15.3

WORLD POPULATION BY CONTINENT

- Asians
- Europeans
- North and South Americans
- Africans

FIGURE 15.4

WORLD POPULATION BY GENDER

- Female 51%
- Male 49%

FIGURE 15.5

WHITE VERSUS NON-WHITE WORLD POPULATION

- White
- Non White

had been in the United States. How we tested for statistical significance with the chi-square is the subject of Chapter 17.

POSTSCRIPT

Frequency distributions are extremely useful in data analysis. They give us a picture of the people who make up the sample or the population being studied. After you know how many Haitians ($n = 205$) and how many Jamaicans ($n = 151$) participated in the study, it is also informative to know how many Haitians ($n = 27$) and

15.2   *(Continued)*

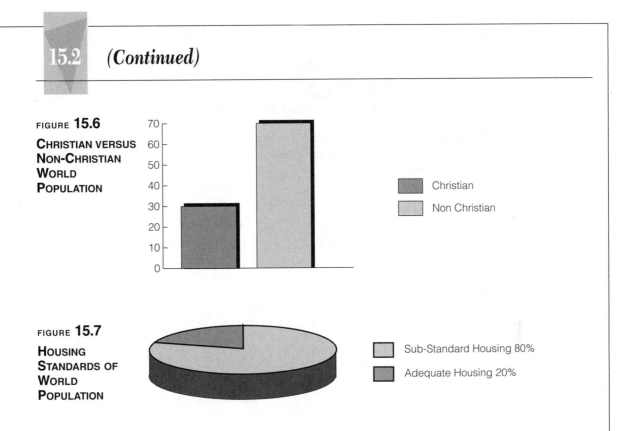

FIGURE **15.6**

CHRISTIAN VERSUS NON-CHRISTIAN WORLD POPULATION

Christian

Non Christian

FIGURE **15.7**

HOUSING STANDARDS OF WORLD POPULATION

Sub-Standard Housing 80%

Adequate Housing 20%

Fifty percent (50%) of the wealth of the world is held by 6% of the world's population. They, who have 50% of the world's wealth, are all citizens of the United States.

Seventy percent (70%) of the world's population cannot read.

Fifty percent (50%) of the world's population suffers from malnutrition.

Only 1% of the world's population has a college education.

Only a fraction of 1% of the world's population owns a computer.

how many Jamaicans ($n = 51$) are naturalized U.S. Citizens (a bivariate analysis). A bivariate comparison such as discussed in Chapters 16 through 19 can provide this information.

In Chapter 16, you will see how to use bivariate analysis with nominal and rank order level data (for example, marital status and gender, religion and political party, home ownership and state of residents). You will also find statistical approaches to use if you have a sample or population that is too small or does not meet the criteria needed to use inferential statistics. These statistical procedures are called *nonparametric* statistical approaches. Chapters 16 through 19 will also present bivariate statistical approaches, but they are called *parametric* or inferential statistical procedures.

REFERENCES

Baker, T. L. (1994). *Doing social research* (2nd ed.). New York: McGraw-Hill.

McPherson-Blake, P. (1991). *Psychosocial factors associated with the immigration of Haitians and Jamaicans to South Florida and changes in their parental role.* Barry University School of Social Work, Miami Shores, Florida. *Dissertation Abstracts International, 52-11A,* page 4092, 00229 pages.

Rubin, A., & Babbie, E. (1997). *Research methods for social work* (3rd ed.). Pacific Grove, CA: Brooks/Cole. Chapter 15 has a good discussion on interpreting descriptive statistics and tables.

NONPARAMETRIC TESTS FOR NOMINAL AND ORDINAL DATA

Group Comparison and Time-Series

WHAT ARE NONPARAMETRIC TESTS?

Nonparametric tests are the opposite of *parametric tests, which have strict assumptions about the data.* These tests for statistical significance require that at least one variable be an interval or ratio level of measure. The sample distribution of the interval or ratio variable(s) must be normally distributed. If you are comparing different groups, the members should be randomly assigned to each group to meet the assumption that group members are independent of one another. The *t*-test, the analysis of variance, and the Pearson product-moment correlation are examples of parametric tests.

Nonparametric tests do not require the strict assumptions about the data that parametric tests require.

This chapter will explain what *nonparametric tests* are, how they work, and how you can use them in your research. The most commonly used nonparametric statistical tests are the *chi-square,* the *Spearman correlation (r^s),* the *Mann-Whitney U test,* the *Wilcoxon sign-ranks test,* and the *Kruskal-Wallis analysis of variance by rank.* In this chapter, examples for most of these nonparametric tests will be presented. Rank order data will be used to demonstrate the hand calculations of the Mann-Whitney U test (Twaite & Monroe, 1979).

Because the chi-square is so useful in research in the helping professions, an entire chapter is devoted to crosstabs and chi-square (Chapter 17). The Spearman correlation is presented in the chapter on correlations (Chapter 19).

The nonparametric tests presented in this chapter are suited for *small samples.* There are restrictions on how small and, in some cases, how large your sample can be when using each test (see Table 16.1 later in this chapter). Although the majority of these nonparametric tests work best with small samples, the chi-square test and the Spearman correlation can handle both small and large samples (Brase & Brase, 1991).

HOW CAN YOU USE NONPARAMETRIC TESTS?

Nonparametric tests are used to analyze nominal and rank order level data. Although nonparametric statistical tests work much like parametric tests, you should use nonparametric tests to analyze nominal and rank order/ordinal level data, typically with small samples.

You can use these tests to analyze nominal and rank order/ordinal data, particularly if your sample is small. Although not as precise as parametric tests, they work in about the same way. You can use nonparametric tests to test your hypothesis in cases where you have nominal and rank order/ordinal data collected from a small sample of people.

If we wish to go beyond frequency analysis with nominal and rank order data so as to identify a relationship between two variables (a bivariate relationship), we must use nonparametric statistical tests. Nonparametric tests must be used with nominal and rank order/ordinal data because nominal data use numbers for names. As such, their numbers have no mathematical value and are assigned arbitrarily. Rank order data numbers do have mathematical value but they do *not* have the precision of *interval* or *ratio level data.* With rank order data, we know how many ranks there are but we do not know the value of each rank level, nor do we know if the difference between the ranks is equal (Burning & Kintz, 1987).

When we use rank order data, we know that rank #1 is better than rank #2, but we do NOT know how much bigger rank #1 is than rank #2. Because the differences are NOT equal between one rank and another rank, rank order data cannot be used to do basic mathematical manipulations, such as adding, finding averages, and squaring of numbers. Nonparametric tests do not require that rank order variables be used to do fundamental math. With interval level data and ratio level data, there are an infinite number of values between intervals. Therefore, interval level data and ratio level data can be used to perform the basic mathematical operations necessary for using the more sophisticated and sensitive statistical parametric tests (Craft, 1992). See Advanced Level 16.1, page 195.

⇨ **Advanced Level**
see page 195

USING A MANN-WHITNEY U Test

The *Mann-Whitney U test* evaluates the differences between 2 groups on 1 rank order measure.

Here is the formula for the Mann-Whitney U test:

$$U_{ob} = n_1 n_2 + \frac{n_i(n_1 + 1)}{2} - R_1{}^* =$$

Here we have used the numbers from the class sample in Box 16.1 to solve the equation:

$$U_{girls} = (9 \times 8) + \frac{9 \times 10}{2} - 100 = 17$$

The computations presented here produced a U statistic of 17 ($U_{girl} = 17$). Once we have the smaller of the two U statistics, which in this case is the U value for girls, we can then go to a table, typically entitled "Critical Values of the Mann-Whitney U Table" found in most statistics texts. Reviewing such a table, the critical value of U with groups of 8 and 9 in each group for a one-tail test at the .05 level of significance is 18 ($U_{critical} = 18$).

To be significant the U_{girl} must be equal or smaller ($\leq$) than the critical value of U ($U_{critical}$). In this case the $U_{girl} = 17$ is in fact smaller ($U_{girl} = 17$) than the critical value of U ($U_{critical} = 18$). This means that there is a significant difference in the ranks on assertive participation for boys and girls at the $p \leq .05$ level of significance.

A visual examination of the ranks held by the boys would suggest that the girls in the class have lower ranks on assertive participation.

---

* R_1 is the sum of the ranks of the girls (see Box 16.1).

16.1 | *An Example Using the Mann-Whitney U Test*

For some years, sociologists have suggested that girls in a math class with boys tend to be less assertive even when they are as knowledgeable about the math being presented. This might explain some of the general differences in math competency between boys and girls. To test the hypothesis that girls are less assertive in math classes than boys, an experimental class was put together by randomly selecting 8 boys and 9 girls.

At the end of the semester, a master teacher who was unaware of the hypothesis (called a "blinded rater") was asked to observe the math class of 17 students and rank order them on assertive participation. Because rank order data are collected on each individual from the master teacher, to analyze this rank order data the Mann-Whitney U test needs to be used to analyze rank order data. This test will allow us to identify differences between the ranking or standing given to girls and boys in relationship to assertive participation in the class. The Mann-Whitney U test will not measure the difference between the boys and girls on assertive participation but it will tell us if more boys than girls are ranked in higher positions in the class.

RANKED SCORES FOR 17 STUDENTS IN THE MATH CLASS

Gender	Rank	Gender	Rank
B	1	G	10
B	2	G	11
G	3	B	12
B	4	B	13
B	5	G	14
G	6	G	15
B	7	G	16
G	8	G	17
B	9		

In this study, the boys appear to rank higher in the class on assertive participation than the girls. However, since the sample is so small, we need to use the Mann-Whitney U test to determine if the difference is large enough to conclude that boys rank significantly higher.

USING A WILCOXON SIGN-RANKS TEST

1. The *Wilcoxon sign-ranks test* evaluates the differences between 1 group of matched cases (for example, people) measured on 1 rank order measure.
2. All pairs of subjects should be matched on one or more control variables such as age, gender, education, experience, position in their agency, etc. Researchers use their best judgment and demographic information to make the matches.
3. Groups A and B become Pre-test and Post-test in the analysis. It works and is interpreted just like the paired sample.

16.2   *An Example of a Wilcoxon Sign-Ranks Test*

It has been suggested that interviewing skills, develop more rapidly when students actually practice the skill rather than study it in a classroom. Professor Gomez, however, believed that students also need basic information on how to interview other people that is best presented in a classroom. Professor Gomez wanted to know more about what combination of classroom instruction and practice produce the best interviewing skills.

To test her hypothesis, she carried out an experiment with 16 randomly selected students in her family practice classes. First, she matched 8 pairs of students who were similar in age, gender, and experience (these are control variables). Second, she randomly assigned the members of each pair to different interviewing skills labs. Members of the same pair were not in the same lab. Lab A was set up to use 3 of 10 lab sessions for classroom instruction that provided basic information, critique of practice interviews and for review. The other 7 days were devoted to practicing interviewing skills using role-play.

Lab B was set up so that no classroom instruction was used, with all 10 lab sessions devoted to the students practicing their interviewing skills using role-play. It was much like a language class where students are forced to speak the language until they master it. In Lab B all basic information, critiques of the student practice interviews, and the reviews were done during the interview practice sessions.

The final assignment in each lab was for each student to videotape a 15-minute role-play interview. The videotaped interviews were then evaluated on a rank order scale that measured levels of interviewing skills by another practice teacher who was unaware of the hypothesis and the lab experiences of the students.

With these rank scores for each matched pair, we can analyze them to see if the students in Lab A ranked significantly higher than students in Lab B on interviewing skills.

A WILCOXON SIGN-RANKS TABLE: RANKED SCORES FOR MATCHED PAIRS OF STUDENTS

Pairs	Lab A	Lab B	Difference	Rank
1	11	4	(−) 7	(−) 3
2	14	22	(+) 8	(+) 4
3	31	48	(+) 17	(+) 7
4	21	20	(−) 1	(−) 1
5	9	14	(+) 5	(+) 2
6	18	40	(+) 22	(+) 8
7	22	32	(+) 10	(+) 5
8	25	38	(+) 13	(+) 6

In this study, the ranks of the matched pairs are clearly different. All but 2 of the 8 students in Lab A did better than the students in Lab B. However, we must use the Wilcoxon sign-ranks Test to determine if the difference is large enough to make the groups statistically significantly different.

COMPUTATIONS FOR THE WILCOXON SIGN-RANKS TEST

The computations are so simple that they are presented in the narrative.

1. Set your table up like the Wilcoxon Sign-Ranks Table above.
2. To find the observed value of the Wilcoxon sign-ranks T, you sum up the rank values of the pairs of students with positive (+) and sum up the values of the negative (-) ranks.
3. In this case, Lab A = 32, and Lab B = 4. The smallest is of course, 4 ($T_{observed}$ = 4).
4. The critical value of T can be found on the table, "Critical Values of T in the Wilcoxon Sign-Ranks Test," found in most traditional statistics texts.
5. In this case the observed T value of 4 must be *equal to or smaller than* ($\leq$) the critical value of T which was 5 at the p $\leq$ .05 level of significance ($T_{critical}$ = 5).
6. Because $T_{observed}$ = 4, which is equal to or smaller than ($\leq$) $T_{critical}$ = 5, the difference is significant at the p $\leq$ .05 level of significance on the variable interview skills.

This finding indicates that the students who experienced 3 days of classroom instruction and 7 days of practice as a group ranked significantly higher on level of interviewing skills than did the students who experienced 10 days practice but received no classroom instruction.

USING A KRUSKAL-WALLIS ANALYSIS OF VARIANCE BY RANK

1. The *Kruskal-Wallis analysis of variance by rank*
   a. evaluates the differences between 3 or more independent groups that are measured on 1 rank order measure, or
   b. evaluates the differences between 3 or more time-series measures of one group that is measured on 1 rank order variable.
2. To find the level of significance for samples fewer than 5 per group, use a table of H values for the Kruskal-Wallis analysis of variance by rank. For samples over 5 per group, use the table for χ^2 distributions. When the group sizes are 6 or more the Kruskal-Wallis H-*Statistic* has the same distribution as the χ^2 distribution.
3. The Kruskal-Wallis analysis of variance by rank is just like the Mann-Whitney U test that analyzes 2 groups, except that the Kruskal-Wallis can analyze 3 or more groups at a time.

The computations are not presented here to save space. When the hand computations were completed, the critical value of H was found on the table typically called "Probabilities Associated with Values of H in the Kruskal-Wallis analysis of variance by rank" found in most statistics texts. In this case, the critical value of H

16.3   *An Example of Kruskal-Wallis Analysis of Variance by Rank Test*

Another test of the assertiveness hypothesis that girls in a math class with boys tend to be less assertive could be done with three groups. In this research study, three groups of randomly selected girls (5 per group) were randomly placed in three different math classes. The hypothesis is that in math classes where there are fewer boys than girls, girls will be more assertive. The three math classes had different gender make up: Class A = 75% boys, Class B = 50% boys, Class C = 25% boys. At the end of the semester, a master teacher was asked to observe the math classes and rank order the students on assertive participation. The rank scores of the girls in the three groups can then be analyzed to see if one group of girls had been significantly more assertive than the other groups of girls.

RANKED SCORE FOR THREE GROUPS OF GIRLS

Group	Rank	Group	Rank
C	1	B	9
C	2	B	10
C	3	A	11
B	4	B	12
A	5	A	13
C	6	A	14
B	7	A	15
C	8		

In this study, the ranks of the 3 groups of girls are clearly different. However, we must use the Kruskal-Wallis analysis of variance by rank to determine if the difference is large enough to make the groups significantly different.

with 2 degrees of freedom (3 groups equals 2 degrees of freedom) was significant at the $p \leq .05$ level of significants on the variable "assertive participation."

This finding indicates that the 3 groups under study are ranked significantly different. However, the significant findings tell us only that the 3 groups are different. The Kruskal-Wallis analysis does not tell us which group is different from the other. A visual examination of the ranks of the groups would suggest the girls in the class with 25% boys were ranked higher than the girls in the other two groups.

OTHER NONPARAMETRIC TESTS FOR UNIVARIATE ANALYSIS

Binomial and Normal Approximation to Binomial Test

This is a statistical test to determine if the responses to a categorical variable with 2 responses (values) is normally distributed.

χ^2 One-Variable Test with Ordered Categories

This is a statistical test to determine if the responses to a categorical variable with 3 responses (values) are normally distributed. This test allows you to compare the distribution of the 3 responses to a known distribution. An example is to compare the number of 3 groups of students by their college major (mental health counseling, family counseling, and social work) over time to the number of students who were in those majors. In this way, we can see if there has been a shift between college majors or if the students in each major remain approximately the same.

Kolmogorov-Smirnov One Variable Test

This test is used with 2 ordinal/rank order variables. For instance, you could study the relationship between a question asking about "satisfaction with service" and a question asking about "satisfaction with the therapist." The rank values for both questions are: 3 = excellent, 2 = good, and 1 = poor. It would be a 3 by 3 crosstabs table (also called crossbreak or crosstabulation table).

OTHER NONPARAMETRIC TESTS FOR BIVARIATE ANALYSIS

Fishers Exact Probability Test

This test compares 2 populations on 1 variable with 2 responses (a dichotomous variable). An example is to compare Haitians and Jamaicans in terms of the percentage of those who are U.S. citizens or non-citizens (a dichotomous variable). We know there is a difference in percentage between the groups, but is the difference large enough to be statistically significant at the $p \leq .05$ level of significance. In other words, is the difference of the cell numbers (cell frequency) an accident within the sample we drew, or is the difference in cell numbers so large that it surely was NOT an accident or a biased sample.

χ^2 Test for Association

This test can be used to study the relationship between 2 categorical or rank order variables. This test will be presented in the next chapter.

χ^2 for Homogeneity

This test is used to compare 2 independent groups (populations) on a categorical variable having 3 or more values. Studying the difference between client satisfaction by gender, the hypothesis could be that "females are more satisfied with the services than males." The categorical variable is "gender." The variable with 3 or more values is "client satisfaction." The values of this variable are: 3 = excellent, 2 = good, and 1 = poor. This would be a 2 by 3 crosstabs table.

McNemar Test

This test is used to compare pre- and post-tests on 1 ordinal/rank order variable that has 3 or more values. We might compare client satisfaction with the therapist, at 2 different times during therapy. The pre-test is given at the 4th session with the posttest administered at the 12th session. The variable "client satisfaction with therapist" has these values: 3 = excellent, 2 = good, and 1 = poor. This would be a 3-by-3 crosstabs table with rank order data.

POSTSCRIPT

Nonparametric statistical tests are helpful in understanding how statistical tests work. They are also very useful in describing the sample or the population you are studying. They are, however, neither as powerful nor as accurate as the statistical procedures presented in the following chapters.

Chapter 17 provides additional bivariate statistical procedures that are used with interval and ratio data. These are the two most powerful levels of measure.

ADVANCED LEVEL MATERIAL

Advanced Level 16.1 Given the simplistic logic of nominal and rank order data, the statistical formulas for nonparametric tests are easy to calculate by hand. This is especially true if the sample is small.

Nonparametric tests are NOT very sensitive to modest or small differences between groups or variables due to the nature of rank order data. *Parametric tests are very sensitive* and very good for picking up small differences between groups and variables. Nonparametric tests are less sensitive than parametric tests because they have less statistical power.

If you have a choice, use parametric tests. If you do not have a choice, if the sample is small, and if you must collect ordinal/rank order data, try to set up the study so that you can use one of the nonparametric tests. Look carefully at the way the groups are set up for the comparison and the minimum and maximum sample sizes needed to do a nonparametric test.

Frequency analysis can give us information only on one variable at a time (univariate analysis). By using nonparametric tests with nominal and rank order data, however, we can describe the relationship between two variables (bivariate analysis) or three or more variables (multivariate). Table 16.1 will help you identify the nonparametric test to use with your sample.

TABLE 16.1   **THREE COMMONLY USED NONPARAMETRIC TESTS**

Name of Test	Used with 1 Rank Order/Ordinal Variable for	Sample Size
Mann-Whitney *U*	Comparison of: • 2 independent groups, OR • 1 experimental and 1 control group.	*Minimum:* Group I = 5 cases Group II = 4 cases *Maximum:* Group I = 20 cases Group II = 40 cases
Wilcoxon Sign-Ranks	Comparison of: • 1 group of matched cases, an experimental with a control case.	*Minimum:* 7 matched cases *Maximum:* 25 matched cases
Kruskal-Wallis Analysis of Variance by Rank	Comparison of: • 3 or more independent groups, OR • 3 or more time-series measures of 1 group.	*Minimum:* Group I = 3 cases Group II = 3 cases Group III = 3 cases OR Group I = 3 cases Group II = 2 cases Group III = 2 cases *Maximum:* Above 5 cases, use χ^2 distribution to determine significance

REFERENCES

Brase, H. B., & Brase, C. O. (1991). *Understandable statistics: Concepts and methods.* Lexington, MA: D. C. Heath.

Burning, J., & Kintz, B. (1987). *Computation handbook of statistics* (3rd ed.). Glenview, IL: HarperCollins.

Craft, J. (1991). *Statistics and data analysis for social work.* Itasca, IL: F. E. Peacock.

Twaite, J.A., & Monroe, J. (1979). *Introductory statistics.* Glenview, IL: Scott, Foresman.

CROSSTABS, THE CHI-SQUARE TEST (χ^2) AND ITS *PHI* COEFFICIENT

What Is a Crosstabs Table and Chi-Square (χ^2) Test?

A crosstabs table (also called a crosstabulation or crossbreak table) can be used to display frequency data that can be separated into groups. Such a graph display can show trends and patterns in the relationship among the variables. The **chi-square** (χ^2) test is a statistical test that allows you to determine the statistical significance of *nominal, rank order/ordinal,* and *interval* level data. You can also analyze *ratio* data with the chi-square (χ^2) test, if you collapse the data into intervals. Finally, understanding how chi-square works can help you understand how other statistical tests work (Gravetter & Wallnau, 1985).

Background on the Crosstabs and Chi-Square Tests

Crosstabs and the chi-square test are two of our oldest forms of data reduction. As a test for statistical significance, the chi-square test is widely used in the helping professions to test research hypotheses. Until the mid-1960s, it was the most commonly reported statistic in social science journals.

This over-reliance on the chi-square test occurred for several reasons. The chi-square statistic is relatively easy to understand. Even more important before the 1990's, the chi-square statistic and the coefficient to determine the strength of the association or independence between two variables (that is, *phi, Cramer's V*) were easy to calculate by hand. At least, they are easy to compute with a hand calculator.

Another reason the chi-square test was used so often is that a great deal of social research was based on survey-type questions that were nominal and categorical. Since the 1970's, however, an ever growing number of social science studies have been using measures, scales, and inventories. These measures produce scores that can be used as interval data. These data (interval data) lend themselves to parametric tests, a more sophisticated form of statistical analysis.

Using the Crosstabulation Table and the Chi-Square Test

The crosstabulation table and the chi-square (χ^2) test are simple to understand and to use. First, the crosstabs table is used to display your data graphically. It is most often seen in the "2 × 2" table format (pronounced "two by two"). This type of table is a square box made up of four cells. Table 17.1 is an example of this type of 2 by 2 table. Second, after you display the data, the chi-square test can be used to statistically analyze the data in the crosstabulation table to test for any significant relationships. See Advanced Level 17.1, page 203.

There are four basic ways to use crosstabulation and chi-square analysis.

Advanced Level
see page 203

1. Crosstabs analysis will allow you to look at the relationship between two variables while controlling for the effects of a third variable. In other words,

TABLE 17.1   ETHNICITY BY RESIDENT STATUS

Immigrant Status	Haitians	Jamaicans	Totals
Naturalized U.S. Citizens	**Cell A** OB = 27/35% EX = 44.9	**Cell B** OB = 51/65% EX = 33.1	78/22%
Not U.S Citizens	**Cell C** OB = 178/64% EX = 160.1	**Cell D** OB = 100/36% EX = 117.9	278/78%
Totals	**205/58%**	**151/42%**	**356**

using the data from the study *Child rearing practices among Haitian and Jamaican immigrants,* you could break out or compare Haitian and Jamaican women who had a high school education or better from the Haitian and Jamaican women who had less than a high school education. This would be a *2 by 2 contingency table.*

After examining the data in Table 17.1 as a 2 × 2 contingency table, you could next compare this relationship in even more detail by comparing Haitian and Jamaican women who were U.S. citizens and non-citizens. This would be a 2 by 2 by 2 contingency table.

Such a table would display what percentage of Haitian or Jamaican women were citizens or non-citizens and what level of education they had achieved. This is very detailed information, giving more detail than the three variables by themselves could tell us. We could then statistically test this relationship between the three variables to determine if the relationships displayed in the crosstabs table were real or an accident in the way the sample was drawn by using the chi-square test.

2. The chi-square test can statistically compare two or more groups that have responded to the same questions that have nominal answers (for example, "yes" or "no"), categorical answers (for example, "Democrat," "Republican," "Other"), and rank/ordinal and interval data. The chi-square test can also test ratio data where the data can be collapsed into groups. For example, using "exact age" and collapsing it into two groups of women, those who were over "30 years of age" and "under 30 years of age," would work with the crosstabs and chi-square χ^2 test.

3. The chi-square can test for the level of statistical significance. You can see if the association or relationship between the above comparisons reach a statistically significant level (at least, p ≤ .05).

4. The chi-square can test for the strength of the association or relationship. You can see how strong the association or relationship is between two categorical questions using the *phi* measure (i.e., *phi* = .72—the closer to 1.00 the stronger the relationship).

THE DIFFERENCE BETWEEN THE χ^2 TEST FOR HOMOGENEITY AND THE χ^2 TEST OF ASSOCIATION

When testing the difference between 2 groups of participants, you use the (χ^2) *test for homogeneity.* The 2 groups are compared on 1 nominal or categorical question. This is a group comparison on a categorical variable. The 2 groups of people in the sample must also be independent of each other. The participants are found in only 1 of the 2 groups.

To test the relationship between 2 nominal or categorical variables you can use the χ^2 *test of association.* In this case, 1 group of people answer the same 2 questions. Both chi-squares are computed in the same way. The difference is that with the χ^2 test of association you can *determine the level of significance and find out how closely they are related* by computing a coefficient called phi or Cramer's V.

FOUR FUNDAMENTAL CONDITIONS FOR USING χ^2

The following four conditions are specific and technical. If your data meet these conditions, then the χ^2 statistical tests can be used to analyze your data, and best of all, the results will be fairly accurate.

Condition 1: All observations must be independent.   The sample should be randomly selected from a larger population. The sample of people should not be picked to reflect one value (for example, citizenship) or the other value (for example, non-citizenship) of the population. Because the sample is randomly picked, the number of citizens and non-citizens in the sample will be similar to the population from which the sample is drawn.

Condition 2: Cells in the crosstabulation table must be mutually exclusive.   This means that each person's citizenship or non-citizenship status (value) is placed in only one cell of the crosstab table. You cannot count a person twice; in other words, a person cannot be counted as both a citizen and a non-citizen. The values of the variable must be treated as if they are, mutually exclusive. Other examples: student or non-student; male or female; below 100 or above 100; married, single, divorced, widower/widow, other.

Condition 3: The expected frequencies of cases for each cell of the crosstabulation table must be at least 5.   This means that if you have a 2 by 2 crosstabulation table, you need a sample of 20 cases (for example, people). If you have a 2 by 3 table, you need a sample of 30. If you have a 3 by 3 table, you will need a sample of at least 45, and so on—in other words, 5 cases per cell in the crosstabulation table.

Condition 4: The distribution of chi-square values is assumed to be continuous. This means that if you were able to plot the values of a variable you wish to use in a chi-square on a graph, the values for each variable would look like a normal curve.

Chi-square χ^2 tests continue to be one of the best ways to look at the relationships between nominal and categorical variables. This is particularly true when working with demographic data to describe the characteristics of the people in your study. See Advanced Level 17.2, page 203.

⇨ **Advanced Level**
see page 203

Statistical Analysis Using the Chi-Square

To demonstrate how the chi-square χ^2 works and to give you a better understanding of how these statistical procedures work, the following will walk you through the steps necessary to hand-calculate a χ^2 analysis. Here is the mathematical formula for chi-square (see Table 17.1, page 199):

$$X^2 = \Sigma \frac{(O - E)^2}{E}$$

O = Observed frequency of occurrence.
E = Expected frequency of occurrence.

This formula is used only with a 2 by 2 chi-square

$$X^2 = \frac{N(AD - BC)^2}{(A+B)\,(C+D)\,(A+C)\,(B+D)}$$

Steps for Computing Chi-Square

Step 1: Enter the appropriate cell frequencies into the computational formula:

$$X^2 = \frac{356\,[(27 \times 100) - (51 \times 178)]^2}{(27+51)\,(178+100)\,(27+178)\,(51+100)}$$

Step 2: Now following the mathematical order of operations, solve the equation. First, perform operations inside the parentheses.

$$X^2 = \frac{356\,(2700 - 9078)^2}{78 \times 278 \times 205 \times 151}$$

Step 3: Now solve the multiplication problems:

$$X^2 = \frac{356 \times 40{,}678{,}884}{78 \times 278 \times 205 \times 151}$$

$$X^2 = \frac{356 \times 40{,}678{,}884}{671{,}228{,}220}$$

$$X^2 = \frac{14{,}481{,}682{,}704}{671{,}228{,}220}$$

Step 4: Finally, divide the denominator (the bottom number in the fraction, 671,228,220) into the numerator (the top number in the fraction, 14,481,682,704). The value of the chi-square test χ^2 is 21.57, which is written in a journal paper as $\chi^2 = 21.57$.

Step 5: We need to do one last bit of math: determine the *degrees of freedom* (df). The degrees of freedom is easy to determine because the number of the degrees of freedom is always one less than the number of categories of the variable of interest (Brase & Brase 1991). In the example presented here, there are four cells. (This is often called a 2 by 2 contingency table.) The formula for finding the degrees of freedom for the chi-square test is:

df = (Number of Rows − 1) × (Number of Columns − 1).

In our example,

df = (2–1) (2–1)

First, perform operations inside the parentheses.

df = (1)(1) OR df = 1 × 1 = 1

Thus: df = 1

⇨ **Advanced Level**
see page 204

See Advanced Level 17.3, page 204.

WEAKNESSES OF THE CHI-SQUARE ANALYSIS

1. A chi-square larger than a 4 by 4 is a bit difficult to interpret visually. If you go beyond a 4 by 4 chi-square, it can be difficult to determine which value of a variable is significantly different.
2. If you wish to analyze ratio data with the chi-square χ^2 test, you will need to collapse the data into intervals. The fewer the intervals, the easier it is to interpret and explain the outcome.
3. Ratio data are best analyzed using statistical procedures based on linear math, such as correlation, regression, and ANOVA.

POSTSCRIPT

Understanding the concept of how chi-square works is helpful in understanding the more sophisticated statistical procedures which all work in a similar way.

In Chapter 18, you will be presented with a procedure to compare 2 groups. This statistical procedure can be used to compare 2 groups or to compare pretest scores with posttest scores.

ADVANCED LEVEL MATERIAL

Advanced Level 17.1 The chi-square test is a statistical test that can determine the existence of an association and/or independence between two nominal or two categorical variables. The test is based on a comparison of the actual observed frequencies of occurrence of the two variables in the population of those who participated in the study. These observations are compared to the expected frequencies of occurrence. If there is NO association between the two variables in the population, the association would not be statistically significant.

Advanced Level 17.2 To make the point, it is interesting and informative to know how many Haitians ($n = 205$) and how many Jamaicans ($n = 151$) participated in the study. Furthermore, it is also important to know how many Haitians ($n = 27$) and how many Jamaicans ($n = 51$) are naturalized U.S. citizens. A crosstabulation comparison quickly shows the difference in the *cell frequencies*. On one hand, there are more Haitians in the study than Jamaicans. On the other hand, more Jamaicans are naturalized U.S. citizens.

Are the differences we see in the crosstabs real differences among the entire population or are they just an accident of the sample we drew? It is important to know if there is a statistically significant difference between the two groups. That the observed frequencies are different does not mean that there is a large enough difference between the two groups to make it a statistically significant difference (Craft, 1992).

Another way of putting it is to ask this: Would you be willing to bet (place a wager of money) that between the two populations there is no real difference in the percentage of people in each group that are naturalized U.S. citizens? If you do want to make that bet and improve your chances of winning the bet, first use the χ^2 test to determine the chances of the groups being the same. Table 17.1 is an example of a "2 by 2 contingency table": 2 groups (Haitians and Jamaicans) tested on 1 variable (citizenship or non-citizenship).

Advanced Level 17.3   *An Example of the Results of a Chi-Square Analysis*

To determine if the difference between the 2 groups is statistically significant, we check for the chances or *odds* of the Haitians and Jamaicans having the same percentage of naturalized U.S. citizens in each group. To do this, we go to a table already compiled for us, typically called, "Critical Values of the Chi-Square Distribution." This table shows that the critical value of chi-square for 1 degree of freedom is 10.8. In our example,(χ^2 = 21.57 indicates that the chi-square is statistically significant at greater than p < .001. (This is written in a journal paper as, (χ^2 = 21.57, df =1, p < .001).)

The *p* stands for *probability.* It (p < .001) indicates that the chance of the two groups having the same percentage of people who are nationalized U.S. citizens is less than 1 in 1000.

Although there might still be a slim chance that the two groups are the same, *the odds are better than 1 to 999 that the groups are different* in the percentages of people in their respective group that are nationalized U.S. citizens. If I were a betting person, I would NOT bet that the two groups are the same.

Determining the Degree of Relation Using Phi (Φ) or Cramer's V

Both the phi (Φ) statistic and the Cramer's V statistic give you an indication of the degree of the strength of relationship between the two variables used in the chi-square procedure. The strength of the relationship varies between 0 and 1. Zero (0) indicates no relationship and 1 indicates a perfect relationship.

The phi statistic is used when both variables in the chi-square procedure are dichotomous; that is each variable has only two options or values. In the example above, we would use the phi statistic to determine the strength of the relationship. The one dichotomous variable is ethnic group, either Haitian or Jamaican. The second variable is status of citizenship, another dichotomous variable.

The Cramer's V statistic is used when at least one of the two variables in the chi-square procedure is NOT dichotomous; that is, at least one (1) variable has more than 2 values or options. An example would be a chi-square with ethnicity (Haitian or Jamaican) as one variable and income as the second variable in the chi-square procedure. In this case, income has more than two options, so we would use the Cramer's V to determine the strength of the relationship between ethnic group and income.

The phi and Cramer's V statistic are typically produced by computer programs that compute chi-square statistics. For this reason, it is important to know which statistic to report as a finding.

The Goodness-of-Fit Test

Goodness of fit is an expression used to describe a statistical procedure for testing the differences between two or more groups. For example, the chi-square test is

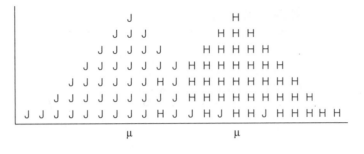

FIGURE **17.1**

H = Haitians and J = Jamaicans

a goodness-of-fit test, as is the ANOVA, because these tests are used to tell if the differences between the two groups are statistically significant.

You can see this goodness of fit in Figure 17.1. If you could plot a normal curve with the data from each of the two groups of Haitians and Jamaicans and overlay the two graphs, as in Figure 17.1, they will not be the same. One does not fit the other very well. This lack of fit indicates that the two groups are different. The question remains, however, are these two groups of people different enough to be statistically significantly different? This is where the chi-square test comes in handy. If the chi-square value is large enough to be statistically significant, this means that the groups are both visually different (the numbers in each cells for each group are different) and statistically different.

The statistical test assures us that the differences did not occur by accident. At least, if the chi-square value is large enough to reach the $p \leq .05$ level of significance, the statistical test assures us that there are only 5 chances out of a 100 that the differences occurred by accident.

To make the point another way, let us say that the two graphs were almost the same but that there was still a difference when you overlaid the two graphs, one on top of the other. In addition, let us say the chi-square test revealed that the differences were not statistically significant. Then, all we can say is that although the two groups look a little different, in reality any differences between the two groups are more than likely accidental. If our sample was perfect, the two groups and our two graphs would be the same.

The goodness of fit test is also a statistical procedure to calculate how well a frequency distribution for your sample fits the distribution of the *null* hypothesis (that is, there is no difference between the groups). For example, if using the data in Table 17.1 produces a good fit, this tells us that there was NO difference between Haitians and Jamaicans in Table 17.1.

REFERENCES

Brase, H. B., & Brase, C. O. (1991). *Understandable statistics: Concepts and methods.* Lexington, MA: D. C. Heath.

Craft, J. (1990). *Statistics and data analysis for social work.* Itasca, IL: F.E. Peacock.

Gravetter, F. J., & Wallnau, L. B. (1985). *Statistics for the behavioral sciences.* New York: West.

THE *t*-TEST

t-test: A statistical test to determine if there is a statistically significant difference between the averages/means of *2* groups on *1* variable (for example, a score on a scale like depression), or to determine if there is a statistically significant difference between scores on a *pretest* and *posttest* taken by the same group.

WHAT IS A *t*-TEST?

The *t*-test is a statistical test used to determine if (1) the means of 2 different groups, or (2) the means of a pretest and posttest are different on an interval or ratio level variable. Interval or ratio level variables are questions like income, age, grade point average (GPA), or the scores on psychosocial scales (considered to be interval-level data). The *t*-test (also called the student's *t* distribution) compares the mean score of 2 groups (not more than 2 groups) or the means of a pretest and posttest to determine if the means are different enough to be statistically significant (at least $p \le .05$).

BACKGROUND ON THE *t*-TEST

Like chi-square (see Chapter 17), the *t*-test is one of the oldest techniques for statistically summarizing data. As a test for statistical significance, it is still widely used in the social sciences to test research hypotheses.

Until the mid 1960s, it was the second most commonly reported statistic in the social science journals behind chi-square. The *t*-test, as a means of testing hypotheses was popular before computers because it was easy to calculate by hand.

Scores from psychosocial measures/scales are interval level data. Although a *Lickert* type scale might be made up of rank order questions, when the answers to the rank order questions are totalled, the summed scores become interval level data.

Another reason the *t*-test was used so often is that a great deal of social research is based on comparing two groups, that is, the experimental group compared to the control group. Since the 1970s, a growing number of studies have been using measures, scales, and inventories. These *scales/measures produce interval level data scores.* Parametric tests of statistical significance can be used with interval level data. The *t*-test, which is a parametric test lets us take advantage of the more precise statistical test when comparing two groups or scores on a pretest and posttest.

USING THE *t*-TEST

1. *The* t-test *can compare two groups of people on one variable or characteristic.* This use of the test is known as the *t*-test for *independent samples.* An example might be comparing the scores of 11-year-old boys and girls on assertiveness. This comparison of the two groups could be based on the Assertiveness Scale for Adolescents (Fisher & Corcoran 1994). The *t*-test would determine if there were a significant difference in assertiveness scores between the two groups of boys and girls.
2. *The second way a* t-test *can be used is by testing the difference between pretest and posttest scores for one group.* This use of the test is known as the *t*-test for dependent samples. For instance, you teach parenting classes to mothers who are at-risk for abusing or neglecting their child(ren). Perhaps the approach you use is different because it includes a new technique for engaging the mothers in the process. To see if the mothers are actually

The statistical tests that are used to compare group means for 3 or more groups are the Analysis of Variance (ANOVA) and Multiple Analysis of Variance (MANOVA); see Chapter 21.

learning parenting skills, the mothers are given a pretest at the beginning of the classes and a posttest when the classes are over to measure knowledge of parenting skills. With the pretest and posttest scores, you can use the *t*-test to see if the mothers made higher or lower scores on the posttest. Statistically significant higher scores on the posttest would suggest increased knowledge.

ASSUMPTIONS NECESSARY BEFORE USING *t*-TESTS

Before we use the *t*-test, the data must meet two criteria: (1) The data must be collected from groups that are representative of the population from which data are drawn. (2) The population must be normally distributed.

For example, if the scores of two groups or the pretest and posttest scores for one group were plotted on a graph, the population scores would look like two bell shaped curves.

We can never know if the population in the sample is normally distributed unless the whole population participates in the study. In this example, such participation would be impossible. One good way to ensure a normal distribution in your sample is to use a relatively large sample, from 100 to 150 participants or more if you can get them. REMEMBER, the more diverse the individuals in the population-at-large, the larger the sample you will need to have a normal distribution in your sample (Craft, 1990).

t-TEST FOR INDEPENDENT SAMPLES

The *t*-test for Independent Samples answers the following question: Is there a statistically significant difference between the averages/means scores of two groups on the same scale or measure?

To use the t-test for independent samples, you need rank/ordinal, internal, or ratio data (scores that can be averaged) obtained from two different groups on the same items or measures. This statistical test will allow you to compare the means/averages of 2 *groups* on 1 *variable* score. The scores can be derived from a single question, but most often they come from a scale or measure.

The groups can be any dissimilar, or even similar, groups: for example, a group of Haitians and a group of Jamaicans, males and females, high school graduates and people who did not graduate from high school.

The other variable (for example, age) must produce a score value having a level of measure that is either: rank order, interval, or ratio. This level of measure is needed in the variable so that the scores can be averaged for each group. The data from the variable could be a single item value or a score from, for example, age, GPA, education level, income, score on the Social Bond Scale, scores on the Cultural Readjustment Scale, or depression scale. All of these scales produce values that can be used to compare two groups using a t-test statistical analysis.

In other words, to use a *t*-test for independent samples, one variable must be composed of two groups' and the second variable must be a rank, interval or ratio level variable.

18.1   *Using the* t-*test for Independent Samples*

The *t*-test can be used to examine the difference between groups and their level of education. If you compare the level of education among people over 25 years of age by race/ethnicity, you will find a statistically significant difference between whites and minority groups (Blacks and Hispanics). In 1991, 21.4% of whites in this age group had finished four or more years of college. In the same year only 10.6% of the minority groups (Blacks and Hispanics) had completed four years of college. A *t*-test would verify our intuition that there is a statistically significant difference (p ≤ .05) between the number of whites and the number of minorities that finish four or more years of college.

The *t*-test could also be used to test the hypothesis that children who were involved in a restorative summer school program with their parents made significantly better grades the following school year. If the children did make better grades in the following year, the *t*-test would tell us if the difference was large enough to be statistically significant or if it was a change that could have happened by chance.

The t-test for Dependent Samples answers the following question: Is there a statistically significant difference between the scores of a group of people who responded to a pretest and posttest (for example on an assertiveness scale)?

t-TEST FOR DEPENDENT SAMPLES

The *t*-test for dependent samples can also be used to compare *1 group* of people on a pretest and a posttest. In other words, you can also use the *t*-test to compare changes people make between taking the pretest and the posttest. For instance, you might want to compare the pretest and posttest scores on a standardized scale on adolescent's socializing skills and assertiveness.

The pretest and posttest questionnaires must produce a rank order, interval, or ratio level score that can be averaged. These scores can be from a single question, but most often they are derived from a scale or measure of some sort.

A ONE-TAIL TEST OR TWO-TAIL TEST?

Do not panic before you finish reading this paragraph, but statistical computer packages will usually ask you to choose a "One-tail test" or "Two-tail test." *It is easy to figure out which one to use.*

- Choose a one-tail test if you think the group could only get a higher score. Suppose you are testing a group of immigrants on cultural readjustment. It is reasonable to assume that this score can move in only one direction— higher—because immigrants cannot make "less adjustment" to the new

18.2   *Using t-test for Dependent Samples*

One way to test the effectiveness of an intervention to improve a withdrawn adolescent's socializing skills is to use a pretest and posttest scale to measure socialization (for example, the Social Avoidance Scale). By using the *t*-test to compare the pretest and posttest scores of the adolescents, you will have evidence that the intervention did or did not work.

If the results of the *t*-test show that the boys' posttest scores are significantly higher (at least at the p ≤ .05 level) than the pretest scores, this is evidence that the intervention worked. Managed care organizations will pay for group interventions that can be shown to be effective.

In contrast, if the statistical results from the *t*-test analysis are NOT statistically significantly improved between the pretest and the posttest,

the intervention did NOT work—that is, the intervention did NOT make a difference on the measure of socialization during the group intervention period.

In another situation, you might need to determine the effectiveness of a therapeutic intervention to reduce aggression in adolescents. The intervention teaches assertiveness. You collect pretest and posttest data using a psychosocial scale on assertiveness. With the data from this scale, you use the *t*-test for dependent samples to test the difference or similarity in scale scores on the pretest and posttest assertiveness scale. The *t*-test for dependent samples is the best *t*-test to use because the pretest and posttest scores are considered related measures.

culture, assuming they were in no position to adjust before migrating to the United States.

- Choose a two-tail test if you think the group could make either higher or lower scores.

The *tails,* as they are called in statistics, refer to the area at either end of the normal curve (see Figure 18.1).

In professional journal articles, the statistical findings from the example would more than likely appear in the text as (t = 5.14; p = .001).

Suppose that, as part of your job you are asked to evaluate an intervention with a teenage, at-risk child. Your goal is to decrease the girl's level of community alienation. The intervention requires participants to take part in a public service program. In a case like this, if you believe that some at-risk children might feel less alienated after participation but that others may feel more alienated, you would use a two-tail test because scores on the alienation scale could go either way. If you believed that the scores could only improve, however, you would use a one-tail test (Twaite & Monroe, 1979).

Most computer software programs such as SPSS use a two-tail test as the default test, but it can be changed to a one-tail test. See Advanced Level 18.1, page 214.

Advanced Level
see page 214

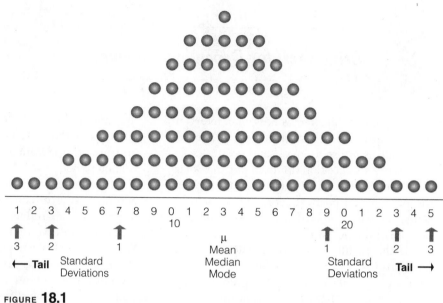

FIGURE **18.1**

A NORMAL POPULATION CURVE

TWO SIMPLE MATHEMATICAL FORMULAS FOR THE *t*-TEST

⇨ **Advanced Level**
  see page 216

The t-test for Independent Samples

$$t = \frac{\bar{X} - \mu_H}{\sqrt{\dfrac{\Sigma X^2 - \dfrac{\Sigma X^2}{N}}{N(N-1)}}}$$

$\bar{X}$ = the sample mean.

μ_H = the value of the hypothesized population mean.

N = the sample size.

The t-test for Dependent Samples

$$t = \frac{\bar{X} - \bar{Y}}{\sqrt{\dfrac{\Sigma D^2 - \dfrac{\Sigma D^2}{N}}{N(N-1)}}}$$

$\bar{X}$ = mean of first group.

$\bar{Y}$ = mean of second group.

D = difference score between each X and Y pair.

N = number of pairs of scores.

Note: The *t*-test will not be computed in this text because of the extensive space needed for the math and the ease of computing the *t*-test with computer programs that do statistical analysis. Many statistics texts give an example of how to do the calculations by hand (Twaite & Monroe, 1979). See references at the end of this chapter.

WHY NOT USE CHI-SQUARE, ANOVA, OR ANCOVA?

Chi-Square

One could ask, "Why not use chi-square to see if the groups are different?" You could, but the *t*-test is a more precise method of testing for the difference in cultural readjustment. Because the scores are an interval level of measure and not nominal, it makes little sense to find a way to change the scale into a nominal variable that can be used with a chi-square statistical test. A nominal question would be, "Do you feel you have made a cultural adjustment to the United States? Please answer 'Yes' or 'No.'"

For variables that ask "yes or no" questions, however, we would use chi-square. The chi-square would be the best statistical procedure to use if the data from both questions were nominal. A "2 by 2" table could be easily constructed to compare Haitians and Jamaicans on the question about cultural adjustment as long as they were asked to answer, "yes" or "no" on that question (see Chapter 17).

The assumptions about the data for using the ANOVA are stricter than the assumptions about the data for using a *t*-test.

ANOVA (Analysis of Variance)

Another statistical procedure that compares two groups is the ANOVA. Conceptually, it is very similar to the *t*-test. The *t*-test tends to be easy to calculate (even by hand) and is easier to understand and explain (see Chapter 21).

ANCOVA (Analysis of Covariance)

If you were going to compare the two groups and wanted to control for education, you would use the *ANCOVA* (analysis of covariance). This procedure can compare two or more groups on one variable, while controlling for the influence of another variable. In the study *Child rearing practices among Haitian and Jamaican immigrants,* there were real differences between the level of education in the two groups. These differences in education could influence the individual's cultural readjustment scores. To get a clearer picture of the true level of cultural readjustment, the ANCOVA is used to control for education. The *ANCOVA* (analysis of covariance) mathematically adjusts the scores so that all participants mathematically have the same level of education. When the two groups are compared, the results are not influenced by differences in education. For more detail, see the chapter on analysis of variance (Chapter 21).

WEAKNESSES OF THE *t*-TEST

The major weakness of the *t*-test is that it can only compare two groups. You will need to use ANOVA if you wish to compare three or more groups. The advantage is that the *t*-test can be hand calculated with relative ease. Given the availability of computer-based statistical programs, however, this is not much of an advantage.

The ANOVA can compare two groups just as accurately as the *t*-test. The difference is that the ANOVA is based on linear math, and the *t*-test compares the means of the two groups. Another advantage of the *t*-test is that many more people understand *t*-test than understand ANOVA.

POSTSCRIPT

The *t*-test is useful in many situations where you wish to compare groups or to compare pretest and posttest scores. What if you wanted to know if two characteristics measured by rank order, interval, or ratio scales occur together? For example, what statistical test would you use to see if there was a statistically significant relationship between education and income? You would use correlations. In Chapter 19, correlational analysis is presented as another type of bivariate statistical test. The *t*-test tells you that a characteristic is significantly shared by two groups of people, but correlation analysis tells you if two characteristics in one group are significantly related and to what degree they occur together in the sample. Researchers in the helping professions have made good use of this bivariate statistical procedure.

ADVANCED LEVEL MATERIAL

Advanced Level 18.1   The *t*-test for independent samples continues to be the best way to examine the relationships between two groups of people on one variable.

For example in the study *Child rearing practices among Haitian and Jamaican immigrants,* we wanted to know if a difference exists between the average/mean cultural readjustment by each group. In this study, there were 205 Haitians ($n = 205$) and 151 Jamaicans ($n = 151$). To measure this perceived adjustment, a psychosocial scale called "Cultural Readjustment" was imbedded in the questionnaire. This psychosocial scale had 16 items, and all questions were answered by each individual in the study.

The research question that a *t*-test for independent samples can answer in this study is, Does one group have a higher average/mean on the scale "Cultural Readjustment" than the other group? Which group members perceive they have made more adjustments to the new culture?

TABLE 18.1   **TABLE OF *t*-TEST RESULTS**

Subscales	Haitians (*n* = 205)		Jamaicans (*n* = 151)		Statistics	
	Mean	SD	Mean	SD	*t* Value	p Value
Cultural Readjustment	2.89	.61	2.59	.49	5.14	.001

To say it in another way: Does a *real* difference exist between the two groups, or is the difference observed in the two groups a result of sampling error or chance?

To answer this research question, we use the *t*-test for independent samples with a one-tail test. The *t*-test is a good test to use because: (1) we want to compare two groups, and (2) because the scale "Cultural Readjustment" produces an interval level score.

The *t*-test will tell us if the difference in the average/mean score on the scale "Cultural Readjustment" is so large that the mean of the two groups is statistically significantly different. To determine if the mean score is statistically significantly different between the 2 groups, we check to see what are the chances or odds that the Haitians and the Jamaicans have a similar mean score on this psychosocial scale.

Results of t-test *Analysis*

The SPSS software program was used to perform a *t*-test on the differences between cultural adjustment scores for this sample of Haitians and Jamaicans. The output is shown in Table 18.1.

In this case, the means/averages are different. Haitians have an average score of 2.89 on the cultural adjustment scale, while the Jamaicans have an average score of 2.59. The standard deviations (sd) also differ, making it difficult to determine if the two groups are really different without using a statistical test such as the *t*-test. What would be your best guess?

Are the two groups really different? To answer this question you can examine the results of the *t*-test. The "*t* value" is 5.14 and the "*p* value," (the probability that the two groups are statistically different) is p = .001. The *p* value indicates that there is only 1 chance in 1,000 that the two groups are identical. In other words, the odds are "1,000 to 1 that the two groups really do differ on the means/averages scored on the cultural adjustment scale. If the scale is reliable and valid, it means that Jamaican immigrants have made more cultural readjustment to life in the United States than the Haitian immigrants have. This is probably true because Jamaican immigrants have lived in the United States, on average, longer than Haitian immigrants.

The *t*-test value has no meaning for us other than it is a coefficient. With the *t*-coefficient and the degrees of freedom, we can find out the level of significance, the "*p* value," by locating it on a "Critical Value of *t*" table. These tables were used extensively before the statistical software was written to do it for us. A "Critical Value of *t*" table can be found in the appendix of most statistics books, however, this table is not needed if you use a computer-based statistical programs (like SPSS) to analyze your data.

Advanced Level 18.2   The two formulas for the *t*-test for independent samples and dependent samples are almost the same. The *t*-test for independent samples (Equation 18.1) is comparing the estimated population mean μ (pronounced "mu") to the sample mean. The *t*-test for dependent samples (Equation 18.2) compares the mean score of the pretest with that of the posttest.

REFERENCES

Brase, H. B., & Brase, C. O. (1991). *Understandable statistics: Concepts and methods.* Lexington, MA: D. C. Heath.

Craft, J. (1990). *Statistics and data analysis for social work.* Itasca, IL: F.E. Peacock.

Twaite, J. A., & Monroe, J. A. (1979). *Introductory Statistics.* Glenville, IL: Scott, Foresman.

CORRELATION

Measure of Association

WHAT IS A CORRELATION?

Many things happen together because of chance when they are not even remotely related. For example, when I take my wife to the dog races, she always bets on dogs with Irish names. Moreover, occasionally she wins. Neither of us really believes there is a relationship between dogs' having an Irish name and winning. A *correlation* can help you determine if two events (that occurred at about the same time) are related to one another, or if it was an accident that the two events happened at about the same time.

USING A CORRELATION

The concept of correlation is the building block for understanding the advanced statistical procedures that can be used in research conducted by helping professionals.

A *correlation analysis* is used when you need to determine the strength of the relationship between 2 *variables* from *1 group*. These are called bivariate relationships. With correlation analysis you can study how a change in one variable (for example, education) is related to change in a second variable (for example, income).

Correlation analysis can be used only to analyze the relationship between 2 variables that have rank/ordinal, interval, or ratio level measures (for example, education and level of income; or age and emotional development).

A correlation analysis is a way of determining the number of times two different events occur together. For example, as one's education increases by one unit of measure (whatever a unit of measure is), one's lifetime earnings increases by one unit of measure (whatever a unit of measure is).

That two variables tend to occur together does not mean they are related. In the 1980s and 1990s there was a major increase in the use of personal computers and a major increase in violent crime. Although a few people might disagree, I would suggest that these two increases are NOT related. One does not logically seem to be associated with the other.

The key to understanding correlation is to remember that the values of the two variables are collected from one group or population and *that the two variables are clearly related to one another*. For example, we can answer a number of questions about the student body at any university. Among this group of students are there correlations between weight and height, GPA. and reading test scores, and parents' education and family income? We would think there would be correlations between these pairs of variables because they are logically related.

A correlation can be used to answer three types of research questions about two related variables (Brase & Brase, 1991).

1. The question of *a relationship between two variables* that are logically associated
2. The question of *the strength of the relationship*
3. The question of *the direction of the relationship* (that is, positive or negative)

TWO TYPES OF CORRELATION TESTS

Only two correlation tests will be used by most of us: the *Pearson product-moment correlation* (r) and the *Spearman rank-order correlation rho* or r^s. If you learn

19.1   *An Easy Way to Understand the Concept of Correlation*

The best way I have found to explain correlation is to use the case of my bank account. When I am paid and put money into my checking account, the account goes up. When I pay bills, money is taken out of my account and it goes down. In this case, the independent variable *being paid* is *positively correlated* with an increase in the dependent variable, my *bank account*.

The independent variable *Paying Bills* is also correlated to the dependent variable, my

bank account. Paying bills and my bank account are *negatively correlated* because as I increase paying bills, my bank account goes down.

The more money I put into my bank account, the more my bank account increases. That is a *positive correlation*. The more money I take out of my account, the more it decreases, a *negative correlation*. It is a very, very strong correlation.

about only one of these correlation tests, the more important and the more powerful of the two is the Pearson product-moment correlation (r). It is the most powerful because it requires variables with values or scores that are either interval or a ratio level of measure. These levels of measure have more precision than rank order/ordinal and nominal variables. The Spearman rank-order correlation (rho) or (r^s) is easy to understand because the name tells us what type of data to use with this test—only rank order/ordinal data.

BACKGROUND ON THE PEARSON r Correlation

The Pearson r was named after Karl Pearson (1857–1936), an English scientist who taught geometry and applied mathematics and mechanics at the University of London. As a student of Francis Galton (the half cousin of Charles Darwin), Pearson applied statistical methods to the study of evolution and heredity, a science he referred to as *biometrics.* In this effort, he developed the Pearson product moment correlation coefficient or the Pearson r (Chernow & Vallasi, 1993).

The Pearson r correlation is the most commonly used inferential statistical test for measuring the degree of association between 2 variables for 1 group.

The Pearson r is important to understand because it is based on linear math and is also the foundation for the more sophisticated statistical procedures of multiple regression (more than 2 variables with 1 group) and analysis of variance (more than 2 variables with 1 or more groups).

WHAT IS A CORRELATION COEFFICIENT?

Usually a *correlation coefficient* is a number between 0 and +1 or −1. The closer the correlation coefficient is to the number +1 or −1, the better it is or as we often say, the stronger the correlation.

A correlation coefficient close to one (+1) or negative one (−1) also means that the two correlated variables are happening in tandem. When one happens and the other happens simultaneously or in close relationship, we say they are correlated. The closer to zero the correlation the less the relationship or correlation existing between the two variables. A zero correlation means that there is NO correlation between the two variables (see Table 19.1).

See Advanced Level, 19.1, page 229.

⇨ **Advanced Level**
see page 229

STRENGTH OF A CORRELATION

We usually refer to correlations as being *weak, moderate,* or *strong.* These terms are loosely connected with ranges of correlation coefficients such as those presented in Table 19.1. These ranges may vary slightly from one text to the next because there is no hard and fast rule about the ranges or degree of strength. When you use a term like weak, moderate, or strong to describe a correlation in a report, always follow the term by presenting the actual correlation you found. This practice allows readers to make up their own minds about the strength of the correlation. An example would look like the following: "There is a weak to moderate correlation between I.Q. at age 2 and I.Q. at age 18 ($r = .31$)."

How good is a good correlation? The strength of a correlation is relative to the seriousness of the situation. If we had never before found a correlation between taking one aspirin a day and a reduction in heart attacks, even a small correlation of $r = .32$ would be a very important correlation. See Advanced Level 19.2, page 230.

⇨ **Advanced Level**
see page 230

FUNDAMENTALS OF CORRELATION ANALYSIS

When we say 2 variables are associated—for example, education and income—we mean that we found a positive association between them. We are saying that when we find individuals with a high school education or less, we typically find individuals whose income is less than average. Moreover, we are saying that when we find individuals with a college education or more, we typically find individuals whose income is above the average. This relationship can be visualized in a scattergram (see Figures 19.1, 19.2, and 19.3).

TABLE 19.1	RANGE OF STRENGTH OF A CORRELATION COEFFICIENT
Range	**Characteristics**
(r = ± .10) to (r = ± .30)	Weak correlations
(r = ± .31) to (r = ± .60)	Moderately strong correlations
(r = ± .61) to (r = ± .99)	Strong correlations
(r = + 1.0) or (r = −1.0)	Perfect correlations
(r = 0.0)	NO correlation

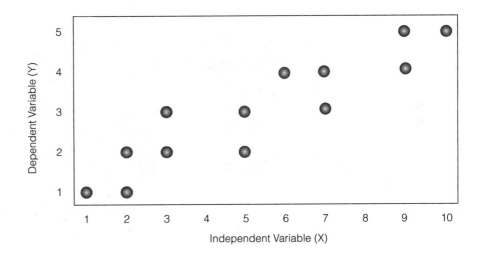

FIGURE **19.1**

POSITIVE CORRELATION

CORRELATION SCATTERGRAMS

For a correlation to exist, there must be 2 variables with the values on one variable (X) paired in some logical way with the values on a second variable (Y), that is, education (X) and Income (Y).

A correlation coefficient indicates the degree to which two interval or ratio level variables can be described by a straight line when plotted on a scattergram.

Figures 19.1, 19.2, and 19.3 show graphs of three correlations: (1) positive correlations, (2) no correlation, and (3) negative correlations.

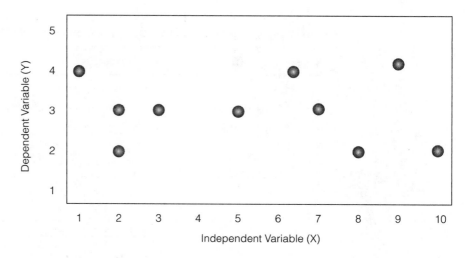

FIGURE **19.2**

ZERO OR NO CORRELATION

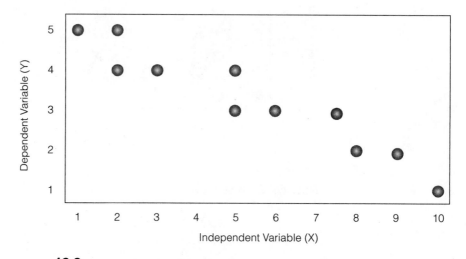

FIGURE **19.3**

NEGATIVE OR INVERSE CORRELATION

As you can see from the scattergram in Figure 19.3, the two variables are represented by the horizontal (Y) and the vertical (X) lines. This method is taken from geometry and it allows us to use linear math to determine the existence of a relationship, its strength, and its direction (that is, positive or negative).

The scattergram is a useful way of representing individual scores on two variables, because you can place any individual person's score on a single point on the scattergram.

THE MATHEMATICAL FORMULA FOR THE PEARSON (r)

The correlation is based on expected variation between the two variables.
The linguistic equation:

$$\text{Correlation } (r) = \frac{\text{the degree to which } X \text{ varies with } Y}{\text{the degree to which } X \,\&\, Y \text{ vary separately}}$$

The mathematical formula (Equation 19.1):

$$r = \frac{N\Sigma\, XY - (\Sigma X)\,(\Sigma Y)}{\sqrt{[N\Sigma\, X^2 - (\Sigma X)^2]\,[N\Sigma\, Y^2 - (\Sigma Y)^2]}}$$

These math symbols stand for

N	=	the number of paired scores
ΣXY	=	the sum of the products of the paired scores
ΣX	=	the sum of scores on the variable X
ΣY	=	the sum of scores on the variable Y
ΣX^2	=	the sum of squares of scores of the X variable
ΣY^2	=	the sum of squares of scores of the Y variable

The Pearson correlation formula can also be expressed as (Equation 19.2)

$$r = \frac{SP}{\sqrt{SS_x \, SS_y}}$$

These math symbols stand for

SP	=	the sum of the products
SS_x	=	the sum of squares for the X variable
SS_y	=	the sum of squares for the Y variable

⇨ **Advanced Level**
see page 230

For an example of a correlation problem, see Advanced Level 19.3, page 230.

AN EXAMPLE OF SPEARMAN CORRELATION (r^s)

Hypothesis: Clients who think their therapist is "above average" to "excellent" perceive themselves as benefiting more from therapy than clients who feel their therapist is "average" or "below average."

Test of the Hypothesis: Use the Spearman correlation to determine if there is a correlation between perception of therapist and perception of benefit from therapy.

Level of Significance: A correlation of .60 (r^s = .60, p ≤ .01) and above would support your hypothesis. The findings would indicate that approximately 36% of the clients who believe their therapist is "good to excellent" will perceive that they are benefiting from therapy. This is better than would be expected with a placebo, which is 33%.

EXAMPLES OF CORRELATIONS FROM A STUDY

Several very interesting Pearson (r) correlations were found among the participants in the study *Child rearing practices among Haitian and Jamaican immigrants.*

Statistical Analysis I

Variable 1   . . .   Cultural Adjustment Scale
Variable 2   . . .   Parental Conflict
Findings: Pearson product-moment correlation
(r = −.42; p ≤ .001)

Finding from Correlation Analysis I

Among these immigrants, there was a moderately strong *inverse correlation* between cultural adjustment scores and parental conflict scores.

(r = −.42; p ≤ .001)

Keep in mind that a correlation does *not* imply *causation.* Thus, all we know from this analysis is that the two variables are related. Consequently, the relationship could be interpreted to indicate that as the scores on the parental conflict scale *decrease,* the scale scores on cultural adjustment *increase.* Because we are working with a correlational relationship, however, the interpretation could be the other way around. In other words, when the scale score on cultural adjustment *increases,* the scores on the parental conflict scale *decrease.*

All we really know from this correlation is that when the cultural adjustment scale score is high we can expect to find a low parental conflict score. We cannot say one variable is causing change in the other variable. See Advanced Level 19.4, page 232.

⇨ **Advanced Level**
see page 232

Statistical Analysis II

Variable 1   . . .   Cultural Adjustment Scale
Variable 2   . . .   Social Support Scale
Findings: Pearson product-moment correlation
(r = −.24; p ≤ .001)

Findings from the Correlation Analysis II

There was a weak *inverse* correlation between the cultural adjustment scale and the social support scale. However, it is interpreted as indicating that when the cultural adjustment scale score is high, the social support scale score will be low, or vice versa. See Advanced Level 19.5, page 232.

⇨ **Advanced Level**
see page 232

OTHER TOPICS RELATED TO CORRELATION ANALYSIS

Several topics, important to the student and the researcher, are related to the use of correlation analysis.

Multiple Correlation

⇨ **Advanced Level**
see page 232

If you have 3 variables and you would like to determine the degree to which 2 of them are related to the third, you would use a multiple correlation technique. The math is an extension of the Pearson *r*.

See Advanced Level 19.6, page 232.

The Correlation Matrix

In many reports and journal articles, correlation matrixes are presented to give the reader the opportunity to see for themselves, at a glance, the degree of association between variables. The coefficients, the level of significance, and the number of people in the sample in Table 19.2 constitute a typical presentation. This table shows the correlations between three variables: parents' education, person's education, and income.

TABLE 19.2   CORRELATION MATRIX (N = 5)

Variables	1. Par ED	2. Per ED	3. Inc
1. Parents' ED	1.00	.48*	.62*
2. Person's ED	.48*	1.00	.72**
3. Income	.62*	.72**	1.00

* Significance at p <.05

** Significance at p <.01

Reading a Correlation Matrix

The key to understanding the correlation matrix is to remember that the variables along the top of the matrix are correlated with the variables along the side of the matrix. In this case, parents' education and income have a correlation coefficient of $r = .62$. The correlation coefficient of person's education and income is $r = .72$. There was also a moderately strong correlation between parents' education and the person's education ($r = .48$). When a variable is correlated with itself, the $r = 1.0$, runs along the diagonal matrix.

You will notice that each side of the diagonal of 1.0 is a mirror reflection of the other side. In most cases, the table would present only the bottom half of the matrix. Nevertheless, if you do see a half matrix you will not be confused by it because you have seen that the other side of the matrix would be just a mirror reflection of the side you can see.

TESTING THE RELIABILITY OF MEASURES AND SCALES

The question answered by the reliability procedure is "How consistent (reliable) are the psychosocial scales that are being used to describe individual behavior or perceptions?" Any time a study uses scales to measure behavior or perception, we must test the reliability of the scales. Scale reliability can be estimated mathematically based on correlations between the items in the individual scales.

Four Approaches to Measuring Reliability Based on Correlation Analysis

High reliability coefficients do not tell us, for example, how well students did on the statistics exam. The reliability coefficients tell us how reliable the exam is for measuring student knowledge. If the test has a high reliability coefficient, we say it has a high level of reliability. As in this case, if the exam has a high reliability coefficient, it tells us how well the exam did in its attempt to measure student knowledge of statistics.

Reliability Tests   A widely used technique is the *split-halves* reliability measure, which splits the items on a scale into two equal groups. Often the odd-numbered items are correlated with the even-numbered items. If they are strongly correlated, it indicates that the individuals who answered the items in both halves did so in a consistent way. If they did poorly on both the odd-numbered and even-numbered questions, this indicates a high level of consistency or reliability. A split-half correlation of .70 or above is considered a good, reliable coefficient. Correlations of less than .70 and above .50 might be usable, but they are weak measures.

The most popular reliability test is the Cornbach's alpha coefficient (α). This is an elaboration of the split-half correlation. The alpha coefficient is an average of the coefficients in split-half procedures where the computer takes the average of the coefficient of every possible split-half until the average or alpha coefficient is stable.

Pretest and Posttest Measures   The *test-retest reliability* measure, also called a *coefficient of stability*, is the product of a correlation between the first test and the second retest. Often a scale or measure is used for a pretest and later as a

19.2 *Test-Retest Reliability*

Students in an undergraduate class in statistics are given a statistics test in the beginning of the semester and at the end of the semester. Before we can make any claim as to how well they did on the test from time 1 to time 2, we must first ask the question about the reliability of the test when used as both the pretest and posttest. We can do that by producing a test-retest reliability correlation.

A strong correlation between the pretest and the posttest would tell us that it was a consistent measure. We would know if the scale was a good pretest/posttest measure even if the students in the class who did poorly on the first statistics test improved on the retest. The scale would still have a high reliability score. In this case, the students' scores varied in a consistent way. Students who did poorly on the first test showed consistent improvement on the retest. Of course, one could have a negative correlation coefficient, which would indicate that students who did well on the pretest did poorly on the retest, and students who did poorly on the pretest did well on the posttest—an outcome we hope to avoid as teachers and students.

posttest. A strong correlation indicates the stability of the items in the scale from the first time it was administered through the second time it was administered. In other words, the people who answered the items in the scale answered them the same way in both the pretest and posttest.

A growing number of psychosocial scales have been developed to be used for pretest and posttest, or as repeated measures. Before using any published scale for a pretest and posttest, study the reported reliability and the circumstances under which the scales were used in previous studies.

Correlation Measures   The *parallel-forms* measure is a correlation between two similar forms. Typically two compatible tests or scales, a pretest and posttest scale, are correlated to produce what is sometimes called a *measure of equivalence and stability.* High correlations, like in the two reliability techniques mentioned above, indicate high levels of consistency in the way the items were answered. This is considered to be an indication of a reliable test. The real problem here is to find or develop good parallel-forms. Many psychosocial scales have been developed for pretest and posttest use, or as time-series measures, but few parallel-forms scales are available. This is due to the difficulty of developing parallel-forms. You need to study parallel-form scales and measures carefully before adopting them for your study. You should ask two questions: What is their reported reliability and under what circumstances they were used in past studies?

19.3   *The Kuder-Richardson Reliability Procedure*

Suppose you and your class of 20 students took a multiple-choice exam on statistical knowledge and marked the answers on a mark-sense form which is graded by a machine.

If the reliability is low, making a good grade on the test depends on "the luck of the draw." Studying for a test with low reliability would not improve your grade on the test. You are just as well off randomly guessing the answers. You have as good a chance or better than a person who studied for the test.

If the test were highly reliable, however, studying would help you get a higher score than a person who randomly guessed at the answers. It is probably better to study for tests, seeing you will not know how reliable the test is until after you have taken it.

Multiple Choice Measures   The procedure to determine the reliability of an item on a multiple choice test like you take in a statistics class is called the *Kuder-Richardson*. This procedure produces a coefficient as a measure of the reliability of the overall test and of each question.

The Kuder-Richardson reliability procedure tests the exam items and answers the question, "How reliable or good is the exam?" How good is it at measuring statistical knowledge in you and your fellow students?

Would you like to see the reliability grade received by your professor on the statistics exam he or she developed to test your knowledge? Of course most of us would like to see how reliable the exams are that we take to earn a grade in a class. What would such a reliability grade (reliability measure) tell us? It would tell us if studying or knowing the subject matter was better than guessing on the test. If reliability was high ($r = .80+$), it would benefit you to study. If the reliability were low ($r = .50$), studying will help some but would be only slightly better than guessing. If the reliability were very low ($r = .25$) the test should be thrown out. If you do take such a test with a reliability of $r = .25$, do not even bother to read the items; flip a coin and guess at the answers.

The Kuder-Richardson coefficient as a measure of reliability does the same thing for each item. Students tend to challenge poorly worded questions on a test. On a test like the above, there is concrete evidence on whether or not each item is fairly homogeneous in terms of how you and your fellow students answered each item. A large coefficient ($r = .70+$) would indicate the item was answered by students in the same way other items were answered. Those who knew the answers to the test items typically got the item correct, while students who tended to guess got the answer incorrect.

An Easy Way to Understand the Concept of Reliability

If students answer questions on a test based on their knowledge of the subject, they will consistently do well or poorly on all the questions depending on whether their knowledge is correct. Either way, doing well or doing poorly would produce a strong correlation ($r = .70+$). If students have no idea and simply guessed at each question, the answers would be random and have little or no correlation with each other. There would be no consistency in the answers to the questions the guessing students got right or wrong. The students who guess are just as likely to answer correctly a question about a "floating beta" (a very difficult question) as they are to miss a question on the term "average" (a very simple question).

WEAKNESSES OF THE CORRELATION ANALYSIS

Like all statistical tests, there are several weaknesses inherent in the correlational analysis. Three of the most important weaknesses are listed here.

1. You cannot use nominal data. You must use rank, interval, or ratio level data in a correlation analysis.
2. The data must meet the strict criteria for all data used in linear math.
3. Correlations do not show causation. They show only association or relationship.

POSTSCRIPT

Bivariate analysis is an important tool when you are doing research in the helping professions. However, human behavior is not often determined by just one cause but rather by multiple causes. To determine which characteristics and to what degree specific characteristics affect behavior we need to use multivariate procedures. Two basic multivariate approaches are used in the helping professions: (1) multiple regression; and (2) multivariate analysis of variance. Chapter 20 will briefly discuss multiple regression, and Chapter 21 will introduce multivariate analysis of variance.

ADVANCED LEVEL MATERIAL

Advanced Level 19.1   A correlation coefficient is a mathematical measure of the extent to which two events or variables occur together. It does not explain why the two variables are related nor does it indicate that change in one variable *causes* change in the other variable. This level of explanation requires the insight/intuition of the researcher.

Correlation coefficients range from 0 to +1.0, which is a positive relationship. In addition, they can range from 0 to –1.0, which indicates a negative relationship (or sometimes referred to as an inverse relationship). Values of +1.0 or –1.0 are both perfect correlations. This means that every time a change occurs in one variable it is accompanied by a change in the second variable. The smaller the correlation the closer the correlation coefficient will be to zero (0). A correlation coefficient of $r = 0.0$ means there is no correlation between the two variables (Twaite & Monroe, 1979).

An example of the importance of the strength of a correlation is the relationship between the I.Q. score of a child at age 2 and his or her I.Q. score at age 18. Although there is a statistically significant correlation, it is a weak correlation of $r = .31$ ($r^2 = .10$). This means that I.Q. scores at 2 years of age explain only 10% of the variance or change in I.Q. at 18 years of age. In other words, what happens between the ages of 2 and 18 explains 90% of your I.Q. score at age 18.

Advanced Level 19.2   Although a correlation of 1.00 means that the value of one variable is associated to changes in the value of the other variable 100% of the time, correlations cannot be interpreted as a percentage of correct prediction. To find out the percentage of predictability of a Pearson's product moment correlation (r), you must square the correlation coefficient (r^2). For instance, if the correlation between variables was $r = .50$, they would actually occur together 25% of the time.

Using the aspirin and heart attack example, if an r of .32 is found, then squared, the r^2 is .10 or 10%. In other words, if 1,000,000 people are going to have at least one heart attack next year, their taking an aspirin a day could prevent 100,000 heart attacks. That is a significant correlation, especially if you are going to be one of the 100,000 people who have a heart attack.

Only *significant correlation coefficients* are said to show that an association exists between two variables. Most computer programs calculate levels of statistical significance when they calculate correlations. If a correlation is NOT significant, this means that any correlation that may exist between two variables is so small that it could have been the result of an accident. You expect to get some small random relationship but not relationships with large correlations unless they are truly occurring together (Lindeman, Merenda, & Gold, 1980).

Advanced Level 19.3   ## An Example of a Correlation Problem

To test the relationship between level of education (X) and income (Y), 5 high school students were selected and interviewed 20 years after graduation. (Note: The population (N=5) is too small to use with the Pearson product moment correlation. For the best results, you need a sample of closer to 100 people [Lindeman, Merenda, & Gold, 1980].) However, to calculate the "r" coefficient so it is understandable, in this example I will use data from 5 people.]

The data collected are presented in the following table:

Scores		Deviations		Products
X	Y	$X - \bar{X}$	$Y - \bar{Y}$	$(X - \bar{X})(Y - \bar{Y})$
1	1	−5	−1	+5
3	8	+2	+1	+2
2	5	−1	0	0
2	7	+1	0	0
2	9	+3	0	0
10	30			+7 = SP
$\bar{X} = 2$	$\bar{Y} = 5$			

The sum of squares for the X values (Education)

X	X^2	$X - \bar{X}$	$(X - \bar{X})^2$
1	1	−1	1
3	9	+1	1
2	4	0	0
2	4	0	0
2	4	0	0
			2 = SS$_x$

The sum of squares for the Y values (Income)

Y	Y^2	$Y - \bar{Y}$	$(Y - \bar{Y})^2$
1	1	−5	25
8	64	+2	4
5	25	−1	1
7	49	+1	1
9	.81	+3	9
			40 = SS$_y$

$$r = \frac{SP}{\sqrt{SS_x \, SS_y}}$$

$$r = \frac{7}{\sqrt{40(2)}} = \frac{7}{8.994} = 0.783$$

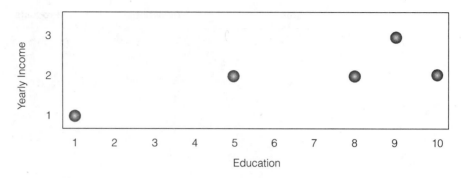

FIGURE **19.4**

EDUCATION BY YEARLY INCOME

The Pearson product-moment correlation (r)

$r = .783$ *or* rounded off $r = .78$

Figure 19.4 is a simple scattergram showing the five cases in the analysis.

There is a strong correlation between level of education and income 20 years after high school for these five people ($r = .78$)

Advanced Level 19.4   As you interpret the meaning of the above correlation, remember that correlational analysis can be used only to determine if there *is* a relationship and *to what degree* the relationship exists between two quantifiable variables. With correlational analysis, no causal relationship is implied, just a relationship (Gay, 1987).

The correlation discussed on page 224 ($r = -.42$) is a moderately strong inverse correlation. It can be interpreted as indicating a moderately strong relationship between their self-reports of adjustment to the culture in the United States and the self-report of parental conflict. This correlation could be interpreted as indicating that the *higher the level* of self-reported adjustment to the culture in the United States, the *less* the self-reports of parental conflict in how they discipline their children. One could also interpret this correlation as suggesting that the *fewer* the self-reports of parental conflict, the *higher the level* of self-reported adjustment to the culture in the United States, or vice versa.

Advanced Level 19.5   Among these immigrants, there was a weak inverse correlation between cultural adjustment scores and social support scores ($r = -.24$; $p \le .001$). However, it is still statistically significant at the .001 level of significance.

Advanced Level 19.6   Again, revisiting the question of the relationship between education and income, you could use a multiple correlation technique to try and get a clearer understanding of how the variables relate: You might decide to use 2 education variables related to income. In addition to the person's education you could add the education level of his or her parents to see if in combination they had a greater influence on the person's income than did just the person's education. It would be interesting to know how 2 variables (the parents' education level and the person's education level) taken together would be related to a person's income 20 years after high school.

What kind of relationship would we expect to see if together the parents' education level and the person's education level affected income? We would find a larger correlation coefficient with the combined two variables on income than for either variable by itself. These two variables *covar* or vary together in this case, because they both contribute to the impact on income. We would find the correlation higher for both ($r = .78$) than for either one, parents' education ($r = .38$) or person's education ($r = .56$), when the other variable was controlled for in the equation.

For instance, if the influence of the parents' education is *removed* or controlled for, the correlation between the two variables, a person's education and income would be lower ($r = .56$). This is a weaker relationship than a correlation between the variables parents' education and person's education taken together and correlated with income ($r = .78$).

Covariance

Covariance is an extremely useful concept for understanding the influence that groups of variables have on a dependent variable, like income in the example above. We realize that many variables influence the level of a person's income. There is no one variable that explains the difference in all people's income. We could think of a few variables that correlate higher with income than most of the other variables. One such variable is education.

Seemingly, the relationship between education and income is a simple bivariate problem—that is, until we realize that we have at least two types of education experiences that may be related to income. They are the impact of the parents' education combined with the impact of the person's education. Logically parents with higher levels of education influence their child's educational efforts and thus affect their children's income as an adult. In this case, the covariance is the degree of influence that the two variables (parents' education and person's education) have in common.

This information on covariance, however, poses another very interesting question. What is the contribution of each variable (parents' education and person's education) to income? To answer this question, we need to use multiple regression, which is explained in the next chapter.

Partial Correlation

This is a technique you can use to remove the influence of a parent's education from a correlation between a person's education and a person's income level. This would tell you what the correlation coefficient is between these two variables when the influence of a parent's education is excluded. In the example used earlier in this chapter, it was $r = .56$ without the influence of the parents' education on income. Of course, this technique cannot tell us the unique contributions of each variable (parents' education and person's education) on income. To answer this question, we need to use multiple regression (see Chapter 20).

REFERENCES

Brase, H. B., & Brase, C. O. (1991). *Understandable statistics: Concepts and methods.* Lexington, MA: D. C. Heath.

Chernow, B. A., & Vallasi, G. A. (Eds.). (1993). *The Columbia encyclopedia* (5th ed.). New York: Columbia University.

Gay, L. R. (1987). *Educational research* (3rd ed.). Columbus, OH: Merrill .

Lindeman, R. H., Merenda, P. F., & Gold, R. Z. (1980). *Introduction to bivariate and multivariate analysis.* Glenville, IL: Scott, Foresman.

Twaite, J. A., & Monroe, J. A. (1979). *Introductory statistics.* Glenview, IL: Scott, Foresman.

REGRESSION AND MULTIPLE REGRESSION

Establishing Causation

Simple regression: A procedure for using the known values on the independent variables (X) to predict an unknown value on a dependent variable (Y).

Multiple regression: A procedure for calculating the weights for each of several (two or more) independent variables (X_1 and X_2). Using their combined weights will give us the highest possible correlation between the predicted Y ($Y_{predicted}$) and observed values of the dependent (also called, criterion) variable Y ($Y_{observed}$).

⇨ **Advanced Level**
see page 254

WHAT IS MULTIPLE REGRESSION?

Multiple regression analysis is *an extension of correlation analysis.* In correlation analysis we can use only one **independent** and one **dependent variable,** but in multiple regression, we can use one or several independent variables and one dependent variable.

In correlation analysis, the r stands for the correlation between the independent variable and the dependent variable. In multiple regression, the R stands for the correlation of all the independent variables simultaneously in the analysis of the variance found in the dependent variable.

USING REGRESSION AND MULTIPLE REGRESSION

Simple regression analysis allows us to use the values of an independent variable (X) to make an educated guess about the value of the dependent variable (Y). **Multiple regression analysis** allows us to use information about the values of many (two or more) independent variables (Xi) to make an educated guess about the value of one dependent variable (Y). The i represents the number of independent variables used in the analysis.

You can use a regression analysis to show *causation,* that is, to show that a change in an independent variable (X) causes a change in a dependent variable (Y). See Advanced Level 20.1, page 245.

BACKGROUND ON REGRESSION

Along with his pioneer work developing correlation statistics, Sir Francis Galton (1889) developed the regression procedure. He observed that children typically regressed toward the mean/average for characteristics such as height and weight. Galton called this phenomena "regression to mediocrity." Later, in conjunction with Karl Pearson, he devised a number of regression and multiple regression techniques (Cherry, 1994).

THREE CRITERIA FOR CAUSATION TO EXIST

Although the regression procedure can establish mathematical support for claiming causation, three important conditions must be met before causation can be declared.

1. The independent variable must come before the dependent variable in *time of occurrence.*

2. There must be a *logical reason* for the independent variables *to be related* to the dependent variable. The relationship cannot be spurious.
3. There must be a *statistically significant* amount of correlation among the independent and dependent variables. This is determined by using regression or multiple regression analysis (Rubin & Babbie, 1997).

Time of Occurrence

For the independent variable (X) to cause any change in the dependent variable (Y), logically the independent variable (X), must come before the dependent variable (Y). For instance, education precedes income (education usually comes before the big bucks).

A Logical Reason to Be Related

For the independent variable (X) to cause any change in the dependent variable (Y), logically, the two variables also must be related; that is, there must be some reason to believe that the independent variable (X) will cause a change in the dependent variable (Y). For instance, there is good reason to believe that income depends, in large part, on the education one has obtained. The relationship between the two variables cannot be spurious or coincidental. For example, although the rooster crows before the sun peeks over the horizon, the crowing does not call the sun to rise. .

Must Be Statistically Significant

The independent variable (X) must correlate with the dependent variable (Y) at an acceptable level of significance. The correlation between the two must reach at least $p = .05$ (read: probability equals point zero five).

HOW DOES SIMPLE REGRESSION WORK?

To understand simple regression, let us use the problem of trying to predict how much per month it will cost us to use a cellular telephone.

Given that we would rather die than call a cellular telephone representative and ask what would be the monthly fee and cost per minute, we try to find another way. For data, we have a friend's cellular telephone bills over several years, however, the monthly statement gives only the total amount of the monthly bill and the number of minutes of airtime used that month.

Although this is very limited information to work from, regression analysis can be used to fill in the gaps. Using this limited information, regression analysis will tell us that there is a monthly fee and what it is, as well as telling us what it will cost us per minute of airtime. With these two values (monthly fee and cost per minute), we can do simple math to figure out what it would cost us to use a cellular telephone.

To use a regression analysis for this problem, first enter the monthly statement information on the two variables into a data file.

In this case the equation symbols are as follows:

X = Minutes of airtime (the values of the independent variable)

Y = The monthly cost from two years of monthly statements (values of the dependent variable)

a = The membership fee (a value that is constant for Y when X is valued at zero)

b = The cost per minute of airtime (a value that is constant and represents the slope of the linear line)

Now we use the following formula to find $b_{predicted}$ and $a_{predicted}$. We already have the collected values of Y and X.

$$Y = b_{predicted} X + a_{predicted}$$

Using simple math and the data on the two variables over two years, we can determine both the *monthly membership fee (a)*, and the *cost per minute for airtime (b)*. With these two values (a and b), we can then predict exactly how much it will cost us to use our cellular telephone given the minutes we plan to use it per month. We would simply plug in the number of minutes we plan to use it (X) into the formula. The mathematical amount derived for Y is our best prediction.

Suppose that when we used regression analysis we found that a (the monthly membership fee) was $20 and b (the cost per minute of airtime) was 31 cents ($00.31). With these two values we plug them into the regression equation to predict Y (the monthly bill), based on the number of minutes we intend to use our new cellular telephone.

To demonstrate how we can use this information to predict the future, let us take two plans for using the cellular telephone. One plan allows us to use only 30 minutes of airtime a month. The second plan allows us to use it 60 minutes a month.

What would it cost if we use the cellular telephone for 30 minutes a month?

$Y = bX + a$
$Y = \$ .31(30) + \$20$
$Y = \$ 9.30 + \$20$
$Y = \$29.30$

What would it cost, if we use the cellular telephone 60 minutes a month?

$Y = bX + a$
$Y = .31(60) + \$20$
$Y = \$18.60 + \$20$
$Y = \$38.60$

As you can see, first we used the old monthly statements (data) and regression analysis to find the constants a and b. When we found these values, we plugged them into the formula with the value of a possible independent (X) variable and produced a predicted value for the dependent variable (Y), the predicted monthly bill.

With this precise information, we can test our predictions. In the case above, we can use the cellular telephone for 30 minutes for one month and then use it for 60 minutes in the next month to test our predictions. Of course, it might be easier to break down and call the cellular telephone representative to ask for the information. See Advanced Level 20.2, page 246.

⇨ **Advanced Level**
see page 246

HOW DOES MULTIPLE REGRESSION WORK?

Let us continue to use the cellular telephone example we used in explaining the simple regression analysis. What we found is that our friend only uses her cellular telephone in peak hours but never uses it during off hours. We want to know how much the monthly bill will cost if we use it during both peak hours and off hours.

First, we have to find new data. We need monthly statements that give us the monthly cost broken down into the number of peak hours (7 A.M. to 7 P.M.) and the number of off hours (7 P.M. to 7 A.M.). We go to another friend and get her monthly statements. She uses both peak hours and off hours. Of course, it would have been smart to go to her in the beginning, but we did not know that the breakdown of time was important when we collected our data the first time. This lack of knowledge about an important variable is a typical problem in the world of social research. What we have now is data on three variables:

X_1 = Minutes of peak-hours airtime (the values of the independent variable number 1)

X_2 = Minutes of off-hours airtime (the values of the independent variable number 2)

Y = The monthly cost from two years of monthly statements that include the cost for both peak-hour and off-hour airtime (values of the dependent variable)

Using multiple regression analysis, we can find the values of the missing constant values, which are as follows:

a = The monthly fee (a value that is constant for Y when X is valued at zero)

b_1 = The cost per minute for peak-hours airtime (this value is constant and represents the slope of the linear line for variable number 1)

b_2 = The cost per minute of off-hours airtime (this third value is constant and represents the slope of the linear line for variable number 2)

To demonstrate how we can use this information in a multiple regression analysis to predict the future, let us take the same two plans for using the cellular telephone. One plan allows us to use 30 minutes of peak-hour airtime a month and 30 minutes of off-hour airtime a month. The second plan allows us to use 60 minutes of peak-hour airtime a month and 60 minutes of off-hour airtime a month.

What would it cost, if we use the cellular telephone for 30 minutes of peak-hour airtime a month and 30 minutes of off-hour airtime a month?

$$Y = b_1X + b_1X + a$$
$$Y = \$.31(30) + \$.22(30) + \$20$$
$$Y = \$9.30 + \$6.30 + \$20$$
$$Y = \$35.60 \text{ a month}$$

What would it cost for 60 minutes of peak-hour airtime a month and 60 minutes of off-hour airtime a month?

$$Y = b_1X + b_2X + a$$
$$Y = \$.31(60) + \$.22(60) + \$20$$
$$Y = \$18.60 + \$13.20 + \$20$$
$$Y = \$51.80 \text{ a month}$$

As you can see, first we used a new data set from additional monthly statements. These statements gave us data on the monthly bills (Y) and the number of minutes used during the peak hours and the number of minutes used during the off hours to find the constants (the monthly membership fee). Given this information, we can find the b values (the weight or slope of each independent variable (X) in the multiple regression equation). When we found these values, we plugged them into the formula with the values for each possible independent variable ($X_{1,2...n}$) and produced a predicted value for the dependent variable (Y), the predicted monthly bill using both variables.

⇨ **Advanced Level**
see page 246

See Advanced Level 20.3, page 246.

SCATTERGRAMS OF MULTIPLE REGRESSIONS

The following two scattergrams (Figures 20.1 and 20.2) will help you to visualize the relationships that exist between 2 independent variables and 1 dependent variable.

The scattergram in Figure 20.1 shows the relationship between the independent variable (peak rates) and monthly bill. As you can see, they are highly correlated.

The scattergram in Figure 20.2 shows the relationship between the independent variable (off-hour rates) and the dependent variable (monthly bill). As you can see, they also are highly correlated.

These scattergrams tell us that each independent variable contributes to the final monthly cellular telephone bill. To find out what a monthly bill would be for any month, we can add the constant and the contribution of each independent variable for a specific month:

1. Multiply the minutes used for a specific month during peak hours times the cost at peak rate.
2. Multiply the minutes used for the same month during off-hours times the cost at off rate.
3. Add the peak-rate cost to the off-rate cost and the monthly membership fee (the constant), and you will have the cellular telephone bill for that specific month.

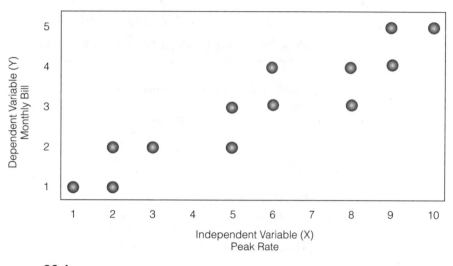

FIGURE **20.1**

REGRESSION OF PEAK-HOUR RATES (*X*) and Monthly Bill (*Y*)

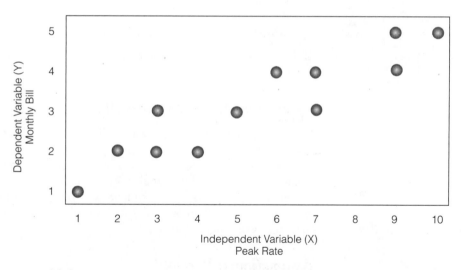

FIGURE **20.2**

REGRESSION OF OFF-HOUR RATES (*X*) and Monthly Bill (*Y*)

⇨ **Advanced Level**
see page 246

Of course, for most of us it is easier to wait for the cellular telephone bill. With multiple regression techniques we do not have to wait, however, we can predict the upcoming bill. See Advanced Level 20.4, page 246.

Assumptions about Data Used in a Multiple Regression Analysis

The following are assumptions that data are expected to meet before they can be used for a multiple regression analysis. Many of the assumptions are assumed to be met if the data is collected randomly (Norušis, 1990).

Assumption 1: Value Determination

The values of the dependent variable (Y) must be determined by the values of the independent variable(s) (X).

In the data, for each fixed value of the independent variable (X), the dependent variable (Y) must be a random variable, which has a specific probability distribution. The mean and variance of the random variable Y depends on the value of X.

Assumption 2: Independence

The Y values are statistically independent of each other. If the Y values were *not* independent of each, some Y values would cause other Y values to change.

Assumption 3: The Straight Line Assumption

If the average values of Y for each fixed value of X are connected by a line, you will have a straight line.

Assumption 4: Homoscedasticity

The homogeneity of variance is a condition of the data where the variance for Y is the same for any given X.

Each independent variable in a multiple regression equation must be linearly related to the dependent variable. If one independent variable in an equation is not linearly related to the dependent variable, it will provide misleading information. If the word, "homoscedasticity" is broken down, "homo" means "the same" and "scedastic" means "scatter."

Assumption 5: Normality

⇨ **Advanced Level**
see page 252

For any fixed value of the independent variable(s) (X), the values of Y are normally distributed. See Advanced Level 20.5, page 252.

Residuals and Outliers

Like multicollinearity issues, *residuals* and *outliers* found in your data are also a problem when using multiple regression, MANOVA, discriminate analysis, or any of the multivariate statistical procedures based on linear algebra. Residuals and outliers are the data points that fall on either side of the linear regression line that is plotted from the statistical analysis of the data. If all the data points fall on or near the predicted linear line, there are no residuals. This suggests that the assumptions that the data are expected to meet before being used for a multiple regression analysis are being met. If enough data points are not on or near the predicted linear line, however, this indicates that your data may *not* be meeting the assumptions that are required for analyzing your data with multiple regression. Although measurement error is a problem, once it has been identified there are statistical procedures to help correct it.

Officially, outliers are residuals that are 3 or more standard deviations from the mean. These residuals are very different from the typical residual, which is routinely just slightly off center of the mean, but always within 3 standard deviations of the mean.

RANDOM AND SYSTEMATIC ERROR

Random error: The term "error in measurement" describes how far away the observed scores of a data set are from the predicted scores of the data set. Random error, unlike systematic error, has no consistent pattern; it varies from score to score. Therefore, random error decreases the reliability of the scale.

Systematic error: A type of error in measurement that has a uniform effect on the results. This error is derived from systematic bias. Unlike random error, the degree of systematic error does not vary from person to person. It is a constant and steady influence. Systematic error decreases the validity of measurement but does not necessarily decrease the measure's reliability.

⇨ **Advanced Level**
see page 253

There are two general classes of residuals. They are customarily referred to as **random error** and **systematic error.** A question on a scale that is confusing or difficult for the participant to understand and answer will produce inconsistent answers or random error. A question that asked, "What is your income?" would yield widely different answers. How would a respondent define "income?" Without more specificity, the answers would be widely different from those to a more specific question that asked, "What is your individual yearly earned income from all sources?"

As an illustration of systematic error, in 1983 when conducting the study for my dissertation about alcohol and drug use among graduating college seniors in 1983, I discovered that the scale asking questions about current, illegal drug use had an unacceptably high rate of systematic error. The seniors had systematically underreported their illegal drug use. They feared that the information might get into the wrong hands. If they would be discovered (they reasoned), it would harm their future careers. Although there was no chance that individuals could be identified by their answers on their questionnaires, why should graduating seniors take any chance? Although I asked the questions because I was an inexperienced researcher, I knew the individuals who answered the questions would be anonymous. However, I am glad they protected themselves. At any rate, the fear of the students induced systematic measurement error into the scores on the scale to measure illegal drug use.

In the scattergram in Figure 20.3, the residuals are represented by the 2 bold data points on the scattergram. One residual data point has a value of 5 on the independent variable and 1 on the dependent variable. The other data point has a value of 1 on the independent variable and 9 on the dependent variable.

From the scattergram, it is clear that the predicted values of the data points do not fit the observed values of the data points. The observed data points that do not fit the predicted linear line are residuals—left over after the fit of the best linear model. See Advanced Level 20.6, page 253.

20.1   *A Joke*

Speaking of measurement error, it seems a young researcher who asked a
question about gender of the participants did not quite get the results he
had expected. On the questionnaire, he used a fill-in-the-blank question
that appeared on the questionnaire as, "SEX _____." When he collected
the questionnaire, he found to his amazement that about half of those who
responded to the question answered "Yes," while the remainder answered,
"Not sure" or "I've got a headache."

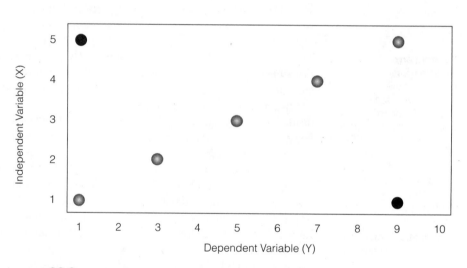

FIGURE 20.3

REGRESSION EQUATION

WEAKNESS OF REGRESSION ANALYSIS

The primary weakness of regression analysis is a result of its statistical strength.
Although regression is one of the most powerful statistical data analysis procedures we have, it demands that the data meet strict requirements. If the data are
flawed, the result of a regression analysis is similar to the old phrase associated
with computers: Garbage in, garbage out!

POSTSCRIPT

Multiple regression is very useful for predicting relationships and for showing to what degree characteristics are related in one group. At times, however, we need to know the same information about several groups. We need to see how groups differ or are the same on several characteristics. In these cases we use multivariate analysis of variance. Chapter 21 introduces you to analysis of variances (ANOVA). This statistical procedure allows you to compare 3 or more groups. Once you have seen this procedure, the more complex procedures of MANOVA and MANCOVA are presented.

ADVANCED LEVEL MATERIAL

Advanced Level 20.1   A regression analysis is used when you need to predict the change that occurs in a dependent variable (Y) that is caused by one or more independent variables (Xi). With regression analysis, you can show how a change in each independent variable *predicts* a change in the dependent variable (Y), controlling for the influence of the other independent variables.

Although you could use a number of advanced statistical multivariate approaches to analyze your data, you will probably be able to use at least one of two advanced statistical tests in almost all of your quantitative research projects.

The two most versatile and most often use approaches are the following:

1. **Multiple Regression.** You would use multiple regression to analyze the data you collected from one group, on the same variables, at one time.
2. **Analysis of Variance.** You would use analysis of variance to analyze the data you collected from two or more groups, on the same variables, either at one time or at time intervals.

Regression is used when the researcher needs to determine the weight (β or beta weight) for each independent variable (X) that will have the highest correlation between the predicted values of the dependent variable (Y) and the observed values of Y.

You would use regression analysis with a problem if you have collected your data (for example, level of education and gross income) from one group or population (for example, a group of 150 high school students 10 years after graduation). You would be analyzing how the independent variable (that is, education) affects the dependent variable (Y) (that is, income) for this population.

Regression analysis can be used to analyze the relationship only between 2 or more variables that are interval or ratio level measures (for example, education and level of income).

The research question you can answer with regression analysis: Does level of education for this group affect income some 10 years after graduating from high school?

Advanced Level 20.2   The regression equation, also called a *straight-line regression equation* is the same as the linear equation and can be expressed in the following way:

$$Y_{predicted} = bX + a$$

This is what the symbols stand for:

> X = The value of the independent variables
> Y = The predicted value of the dependent variable
> a = A value that is constant for Y when X is valued at zero
> b = A value that is constant and represents the slope of the linear line (often called a *beta weight*)

Advanced Level 20.3   The multiple regression equation can be expressed in the following way:

$$Y_{predicted} = b_1X_1 + b_2X_1 + \ldots + b_nX_n + a$$

This is what the symbols stand for:

> X_1 = The values of independent variable number 1
> X_2 = The values of independent variable number 2
> X_n = The values of other additional independent variables . . . the n indicates it could be any number of additional variables, three or more
> Y = The predicted value of the dependent variable
> a = A constant value based on the combined value for Y when the Xs have values of zero, often called the "residual"
> b_1 = A value that is constant and represents the slope of the linear line for variable number 1
> b_2 = A value that is constant and represents the slope of the linear line for variable number 2
> b_n = A value that is constant and represents the slope of the linear line for the additional variable added to the equation

Advanced Level 20.4   ## *Why Is Variance of the Data Important?*

When we say, as we did in the cell phone example, "For data, we have a friend's cellular telephone bills over several years," we are saying that we think we have enough different amounts of airtime minutes and different monthly bills to be able to identify the deviations in the dependent variable caused by the independent variable. Using this data with its different values, we will be able to find averages (means) and then the missing values with which to predict the monthly bills based on the minutes we plan to use the cellular telephone.

What we are looking for in the data are monthly statements that will give us enough variation around the mean (average monthly minute cost and average monthly bill) to find cost of membership and the cost per minute. If all the monthly bills were the same (no variance in the data), we could not hope to find the missing values, because we would not have anything to go on. We would, for

TABLE 20.1 **DEPENDENT VARIABLE: SUBJECTIVE BURDEN**

Step No.	Independent Variable	Multiple-R	R-Sq. Value*	F Level	Sig.
1	Marital Intimacy	.406	.165	6.126	.019
2	Community Bond	.524	.274	5.664	.008

* In addition to the R-Sq. being reported, in some papers you may see an adjusted R-Sq. The adjusted R-Sq. is typically a smaller coefficient. The adjusted R-Sq. is reported in your paper if your study sample is under 100 participants.

TABLE 20.2 **DEPENDENT VARIABLE: DESIRE TO INSTITUTIONALIZE**

Step No.	Independent Variable	Multiple-R	R-Sq. Value	F Level	Sig.
1	Family Bond	.418	.148	6.547	.016
2	ADL Level	.573	.283	7.326	.003

all intent and purposes have only two bits of information: (1) the monthly bill is always the same, and (2) the minutes used each month are always the same.

When the data file is big enough to account for the majority of the *deviation* from the mean, we can use what is called the *least-squares solution* to find the linear-line that is the *best-fit* for the data on the scattergram. This deviation from the mean is referred to as measurement error (Lindeman, Merenda, & Gold, 1980).

In Figures 20.1 and 20.2, for there to be a perfect regression, all the points of data would need to be in a straight line. As you can see, they are not in a straight line; however, they are linearly related.

Examples of Regression Tables and Their Interpretations as Found in Professional Journals

Tables 20.1 and 20.2 represent the findings of a study of 152 caregivers of the frail elderly. First, the hypothesis is presented. Second, Table 20.1 is presented. Third, an explanation is given based on how the findings presented in Table 20.1 support or do not support the hypothesis (Raju, 1992).

Hypothesis I

The higher the levels of individual, family, and community bond, and prior marital relationship, the lower the level of subjective burden.

In this study, Hypothesis I was partly supported. A statistically significant relationship was found between the subjective burden (dependent variable), and marital intimacy and community bond (independent variables). As shown in Table 20.1, step 1 of the multiple regression analysis reveals that marital intimacy (an independent variable) accounted for 16.5% of the variance in subjective burden (the dependent variable) ($F = 6.125$, $p < .019$). In step 2, marital intimacy and community bond (the independent variables) combined accounted for 27.4% of the variance in subjective burden (the dependent variable) ($F = 5.664$; $p < .008$). It was evident that the higher the levels of prior marital intimacy between the caregiver and the care receiver, and the higher the community bond among the caregivers, the lower the subjective burden.

Hypothesis II

The desire to institutionalize the person being cared for will be significantly influenced by levels of objective burden, subjective burden, social bond, use of formal services, religiosity, prior marital intimacy, and activity limitations of the care receiver.

Hypothesis II was partially supported. There was a significant relationship found between the dependent variable (desire to institutionalize) and two of the seven independent variables (family bond and the activity limitations of the care receiver). In step 1 of the multiple regression analysis, family bond explained 14.8% of the variance in desire to institutionalize ($F = 6.547$; $p < .016$). In step 2, the activity limitations of the care receiver and the family bond accounted for 28.3% of the variance in the desire to institutionalize ($F = 7.326$; $p < . 003$). These findings indicated that there was less chance of the elderly care receivers being institutionalized when they had a lower level of functional disability and when higher levels of family bond were present among the caregivers.

Curvilinear Regression

When you read of a curvilinear relationship between two variables in a journal article, what it means is that the relationship between two variables is not a straight linear line, a straight-line regression, but instead the regression line is a curve. This type of data does not lend itself to a multiple regression interpretation. Using a straight-line regression to fit curvilinear data will provide misleading information about the relationship between the variables, as demonstrated in the scattergram (Figure 20.4).

Independent Variable (X)	Dependent Variable (Y)
1	1
2	2
3	3
4	4
4	6
3	7
2	8
1	9

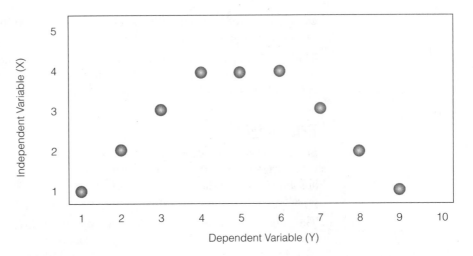

FIGURE **20.4**

CURVILINEAR REGRESSION

See Chapter 26 for the statistical procedure for analyzing curvilinear data using the regression.

Stepwise Regression

Four approaches are generally used to select the best-fit hierarchical order of variables in a regression equation: backward elimination, forward selection, all-possible-regression, and stepwise regression approach. These approaches are needed because the first variables entered into a regression equation might appear to be more important than they are in reality.

Most helping professional researchers today use the *stepwise regression* approach. It is generally a feature of most computer programs that provide regression procedures. This approach combines the features of both the forward selection and the backward elimination approach. The first variable selected to enter the equation is the variable with the highest significant correlation with the dependent variable. The second variable selected for the equation has the highest significant partial correlation with the dependent variable. To this point, the step-wise procedure is the same as the forward selection, but at this point it becomes different. When the second variable is selected, the contribution of each variable to the model is reexamined. The procedure now compares the partial F value of the first variable in light of the second variable entering the equation to see if the first variable should be removed. As a result, it is not unusual for a variable selected early in the process to be rejected or dropped in the hierarchical order of variables in the regression equation after it has been evaluated in light of the variables entered later in the stepwise process. The first variable entered into the equation can reflect a superfluous relationship between the first independent variable and the dependent variable.

The backward elimination procedure is carried out in much the same way as the forward approach except that it eliminates the weak useless variables that do not contribute to the explanation of the variance in the dependent variable.

Beta Weights

Stepwise regression is the regression procedure we use when a computer statistical package is doing the statistics for us. This regression approach uses the absolute weight of the *beta (β) coefficient,* associated with each variable in the equation, to determine the order of importance among the independent variables.

The beta (β) coefficient, also called the *standardized regression coefficient,* estimates the magnitude of change in the Y (dependent variable) that is associated with 1 unit change in an X variable (one of the independent variables). These beta (β) coefficients are the regression coefficients when the variables in the model are expressed as standard scores (z-scores). When variable scores are transformed into z-scores, the coefficients are more compatible since they are all in the same unit of measure.

The beta (β) coefficient is an estimate of change that will occur in the dependent variable as a result of 1 unit change in a specific independent variable. This is the beta (β) coefficient for a given independent variable when you control for the effect of all other independent variables in your regression model.

Dummy Variables

In regression analysis you can use variables with nominal levels of measurement, provided you make them into what is called *dummy variables.* Aside from all the jokes one could make about a variable being a dummy, making a nominal variable into a dummy variable means that you set up your data file so that the nominal variable is treated like an interval level measure. Using a dummy variable as an independent variable in a regression equation allows us to identify different categories of the nominal variable that might influence the dependent variable.

Making a nominal variable into a dummy variable is easy. For example, with the variable "gender," females are assigned the number 1 and males are assigned the number 0 (or vice versa). These numbers have no value other than representing the *presence* or *absence* of a category in the original variable. In this case, gender forms what could be called the female influence (females = 1, males = 0). The closer to 1, the more the influence is female.

Interpreting the Statistical Output on a Dummy Variable

If the gender variable has a high β coefficient that is close to the value of 1.0, we would say the change in the dependent variable is caused by femaleness. If the gender variable has a low coefficient that is close to the value of 0.0, we would say that any change in the dependent variable is NOT caused by femaleness (Lindeman, Merenda, & Gold, 1980).

Examples of Dummy Variables

Gender   = 1 for Females

                          0 for Males

Marital Status = 1 Married

                       = 0 Single

Additionally, you can convert a variable with five categories (like the marital status variable): married, single, divorced, widowed, and other.

Marital Status dummy variable #1, Married

=   1 Married

=   0 Not Married

Marital Status dummy variable #2, Single

=   1 Single

=   0 Not Single

Marital Status dummy variable #3, Divorced

=   1 Divorced

=   0 Not Divorced

Marital Status dummy variable #4, Widowed

=   1 Widowed

=   0 not Widowed

Of course, you noticed that although we had five categories for this nominal variable, we created only four dummy variables. The category "'Other" was left out.

If there are five categories for a nominal variable, you break the nominal variable into four new dummy variables. You leave out one of the categories that serves as the *reference category* against which all other dummy categories are compared. Therefore, if you have a nominal variable with four categories you can only make three new dummy variables. If you have a nominal variable with two categories, you can only make one new dummy variable, and so on.

The nominal variable "marital status," can be used as an example. The problem with entering all five categories into a regression equation is that the first four categories entered as independent variables (married, single, divorced, and widowed) will be perfectly correlated to the fifth independent variable, the dummy variable, "other." This correlation among independent variables violates the assumption of the data that the independent variables in a regression equation are not strongly correlated and that they contribute unique information about the dependent variable.

Advanced Level 20.5   *Multicollinearity*

The issue of multicollinearity is relevant when using multiple regression, MANOVA, discriminate analysis, or any of the multivariate statistical procedures based on linear algebra. Multicollinearity must be considered when you make a statement about the relationship among variables. The question is, How do two independent variables affect each other and the dependent variable? The two independent variables must NOT account for the same variance. In other words, the two independent variables should not be measuring the same thing about the dependent variable at the same time in your regression equation (Cohen & Cohen, 1975).

For example, let us say you are interested in the effect of self-esteem and self-concept on grade point average (GPA) of junior high school students. Both of these concepts, self-esteem and self-concept, tend to measure the same thing in junior high students. If the self-esteem scale can help predict GPA, then the self-concept will predict GPA with about the same accuracy because they both measure the same *one* dimension, feelings about self.

If you put the values of the two scales measuring self-esteem and self-concept into one multivariate analysis, however, you will induce multicollinearity into the statistical results. In this case, if you did not know that the two scales measured virtually the same dimension, as a result of reading the inflated regression results, you would be led to conclude that together these two variables explain a great deal more about GPA than they really do.

Perfect collinearity is a condition in which one of the independent variables (X) has a perfect linear relationship with one or more of the other independent variables (X).

Near-collinearity means that there is a linear relationship between two or more of the independent variables (X), but it is *not a perfect linear relationship*.

Multicollinearity is a problem in non-experimental or quasi-experimental research because it is difficult to control all the influences that effect the independent variables or to be precise as to what a scale is measuring in any particular group of people. We hope we are measuring what we think we are measuring (internal validity), but we have no empirical way of completely testing this assumption.

Consequently, you might be measuring the same dimension with what seems to be two different scales (for example, self-esteem and self-concept).

Although there are a number of indicators of multicollinearity, some of the most obvious are the following:

1. In your statistical results, the F-test for all of the independent variables in the regression equation is significant; however, none of the individual independent variable regression coefficients are significant.
2. In your statistical results, the standardized betas "blow up." You will see betas with coefficients that are greater than the value of 1, and these coefficients will have the opposite, positive or negative, sign from betas of similar values.

3. In your statistical results, the correlation matrix of the estimates of the independent variables will contain large correlations.
4. You use the same variables with two different samples, and you get very different regression coefficients.

There are several ways to prevent or manage multicollinearity:

1. Increase the size of your sample.
2. Eliminate from the equation one of the independent variables or scales that tend to be measuring the same domain.
3. Combine independent variables that are suspected of being redundant, making them into one independent variable.
4. You can use principal component regression to reduce the effect of multicollinearity on the results of the data analysis.

Advanced Level 20.6   Residual analysis can help you determine if your data violate any of the assumptions that data are expected to meet before they can be analyzed using one of the multiple variate statistical procedures based on linear math.

To test for any violation of these assumptions, statistical computer programs such as SAS and SPSS can produce scattergrams and coefficients that will help you decide how to adjust for the violations.

To correct for the violation of an assumption(s), we use data transformations and weighted-least-squares procedures (Kleinbaum & Kupper, 1978).

REFERENCES

Cherry, A. L. (1994). *The socializing instinct: Individual, family, and social bonds.* Westport, CT: Praeger, Greenwood.

Cohen, J., & Cohen, P. (1975). *Applied multiple regression/correlation analysis for the behavioral sciences.* Hillsdale, NJ: Erlbaum.

Kleinbaum, D. G., & Kupper, L. L. (1978). *Applied regression analysis and other multivariable methods.* Belmont, CA: Duxbury.

Lindeman, R. H., Merenda, P. F., & Gold, R. Z. (1980). *Introduction to bivariate and multivariate analysis.* Glenville, IL: Scott, Foresman.

Norušis, M. J. (1990). *SPSS Advanced statistics student guide.* Chicago: SPSS, Inc.

Raju, Kariavanon-M. (1992). *Psychosocial adjustment of caregivers to the frail elderly.* Barry University School of Social Work, MiamiShores, Florida. Available from *Dissertation Abstracts International*, 52-11-A. Page 4093, 00171 pages.

Rubin, A., & Babbie, E. (1997). *Research methods for social work* (3rd ed.). Pacific Grove, CA: Brooks/Cole.

ANALYSIS OF VARIANCE (ANOVA, MANOVA, ANCOVA, AND MANCOVA)

Group Comparisons

WHAT IS THE ANOVA?

The **ANalysis Of VAriance (ANOVA)** and its sister tests are the most versatile and useful of all the statistical tests available to us. *The ANOVA can detect differences between and within two, three or more GROUPS, on one or more variables.* ANOVA considers groups to be two or more groups in a population, a pretest and posttest, or two or more time periods in time-series data. This is a major advantage over any statistical test we have described to this point.

The number of groups we can analyze using the *t*-test (see Chapter 18) is limited to only two groups. However, even the simple ANOVA, often called the *one-way* ANOVA, can analyze any number of groups on one variable. The more sophisticated variations of the ANOVA can do much more.

These truly sophisticated variations on the ANOVA test are identified by the following commonly used abbreviations.

ANOVA	=	ANalysis Of VAriance
MANOVA	=	Multiple ANalysis Of VAriance
ANCOVA	=	ANalysis of COVAriance
MANCOVA	=	Multiple ANalysis of COVAriance

⇨ **Advanced Level**
see page 259

See Advanced Level 21.1, page 259.

USING ANOVA, ANOCOVA, MANOVA, AND MANCOVA

You can use the ANOVA procedure to test for differences between two or more groups, two or more groups in a population, or two or more conditions related to clinical treatment. Your data must have at least 1 independent variable and 1 dependent variable. The independent variable must be a *nominal* variable with *two or more categories* that represent different groups (for example, Haitians and Jamaicans). The dependent variable must have scores that are interval or ratio level measures such as the psychosocial scale called "family bond."

For example, we would use ANOVA to compare the two immigrant groups Haitian and Jamaican on their scores on a measure of family bonds. The groups of Haitians and Jamaicans (identified on a nominal variable) can be compared on their scores on the family bond scale (an interval level measure).

This ANOVA problem could be solved using the simplest form of an ANOVA, the one-way ANOVA. At this level, it is little more than the equivalent of the *t*-test. Furthermore, the one-way ANOVA is a bivariate analysis.

By extending the ANOVA equation, you can also use one or more (interval and ratio) variables both as the characteristics (variables) you are comparing the groups on and you can use other (interval or ratio) variables as *control variables*. This procedure is called *Analysis of Covariance* (ANCOVA). Using the ANCOVA, we are able to control for the differences in the groups that we are not interested in studying.

Take the case where we were interested in the attitude of immigrants related to childcare. We suspected that the longer most immigrants were in the United

States, the more they tended to change their ideas about child rearing practices. We were not judging their attitudes, but trying to observe how they changed. Using ANCOVA, we could control for time in the U.S. and find the differences in the degree or speed the two groups change attitudes related to childcare. There are many other unique ways to use variations of the ANOVA procedure.

BACKGROUND ON ANOVA

Whereas regression analysis was developed to study humans, the ANOVA was developed as a research tool in agriculture. Like regression, ANOVA is widely used and respected in the helping professions. It is accepted as one of the best ways to statistically determine group differences. It has three research problem areas it can help solve: (1) group comparisons using survey data, (2) experimental group comparisons, and (3) time-series analysis (using the scores from two or more points in time as the groups). The ANOVA is very flexible and it is excellent for testing hypotheses in the helping professions. You need to try to get at least a conceptual understanding of the ANOVA and what it does.

UNDERSTANDING HOW THE ANOVA WORKS: SCATTERGRAMS OF THREE GROUPS

On the graph in Figure 21.1, the three (3) groups are different.

On the graph in Figure 21.2, groups 1 and 2 appear to be almost the same, but they are different from group 3.

The two scattergrams in Figure 21.1 and 21.2 represent only two possible combinations of how groups may differ. These differences are what the ANOVA procedure is able to help us understand. In Figure 21.1, the 3 groups differ significantly with regard to the variables being measured in this study. In Figure 21.2, two of the groups are similar but significantly different from the third group.

This situation is often expressed in journal articles as follows: "Participants in groups 1 and 2 were not as affected by the experience as the participants in group 3."

REGRESSION VERSUS ANOVA

When we use regression analysis, we are looking at how variables affect variables. When we use the ANOVA, we are looking to see if several groups are different on specific variables.

Another way of describing the difference between regression analysis and ANOVA is to remember that with regression analysis you use only 1 dependent variable, and you use 1 or more independent variables, collected from 1 group.

```
            1                  2                 3
         1  1  1          2  2  2          3  3  3
      1  1  1  1  1    2  2  2  2  2    3  3  3  3  3
   1  1  1  1  1  1  2  1  2  2  2  2  2  3  2  3  3  3  3  3  3  3
1  1  1  1  1  1  1  2  1  2  2  2  2  2  3  2  3  3  3  3  3  3  3  3  3
1  1  1  1  1  1  1  2  1  2  2  2  3  2  3  2  3  3  3  3  3  3  3  3
1  1  1  1  1  1  2  2  2  1  2  2  2  2  2  2  2  3  3  3  3  3  3
```

FIGURE **21.1**

SCATTERGRAM OF THREE GROUPS

```
            1     2                              3
         1  1  1  2  2                        3  3  3
      1  1  2  1  2  2  2                   3  3  3  3  3
   1  1  1  2  1  2  2  1  2             3  3  3  3  3  3  3
1  1  1  2  1  2  2  1  2  2  2       3  3  3  3  3  3  3  3  3
1  1  2  1  2  1  2  1  1  2  2  2  3  2  3  3  3  3  3  3  3  3
1  2  1  2  1  1  2  2  2  1  2  3  2  2  2  3  3  3  3  3  3  3
```

FIGURE **21.2**

SCATTERGRAM OF THREE GROUPS

It is the opposite with the ANOVA. When using the ANOVA, you use 2 or more groups in the form of 1 independent variable (it must be nominal), and you use one or more dependent variables.

ANOVA   = 2 or more groups (1 nominal, independent variable)
              1 or more dependent variables

Regression = 1 group only
              1 or more independent variables

but only,   1 dependent variable

Scattergrams of the regression and ANOVA will also help you see the difference in the jobs they do and how they do it. (See Figures 21.3 and 21.4.)

The ANOVA looks for difference between 2 or more groups. The regression looks for a linear relationship between 2 or more variables in 1 group.

Remember—as in regression analysis—in ANOVA, you can use rank/ordinal data if you have a sample over 100, if your data is normally distributed, and if the interval variable has at least 4 levels. You can also use dummy variables to handle nominal variables that you wish to study. See Advanced Level 21.2, page 260.

⇨ **Advanced Level**
see page 260

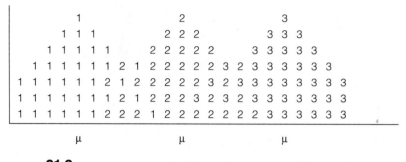

FIGURE **21.3**

A **THREE-GROUP** ANOVA

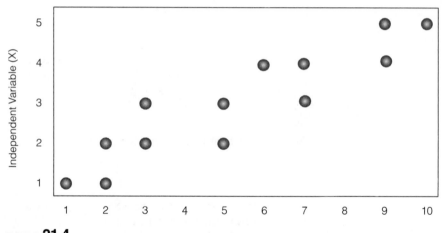

FIGURE **21.4**

THE REGRESSION RELATIONSHIP

A GOOD SAMPLE SIZE FOR ANOVA

Usually the suggested sample sizes are between 25 and 50 cases per group; however, the more cases the better. For best results, the total number in the study (total population size) should be over 100 participants or 25 per group, whichever is the largest. If you have two groups, select two samples of 50+ in each group. If you have three groups, select three samples of, say, 35+ in each group. If you have 5 groups in your ANOVA study, the total sample size should be over 125 participants. The group sizes should be as equal as possible, but this is not always possible. See Advanced Level 21.3, page 260.

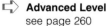

Advanced Level
see page 260

STATISTICAL ASSUMPTIONS ABOUT DATA USED IN AN ANOVA

The assumptions about the data that you will use to do an analysis of variance (ANOVA) are the same assumptions necessary to use regression analysis (see Chapter 20). In addition to starting with a random sample for the experiment, the participants are randomly assigned to either the experimental group or the control group (Norušis, 1990).

WEAKNESSES OF THE ANOVA

The weaknesses for the different types of ANOVA are the same as the weaknesses for regression analysis. The ANOVA requires that the data meet the strict requirements regarding distribution and representativeness.

POSTSCRIPT

The two most often used sophisticated statistical procedures in research in the helping professions are regression and analysis of variance. These two procedures can do a great deal for us in our research. The next five chapters will introduce you to other statistical procedures that you might want to use or that you will find in journal articles. Chapter 22 presents factor analysis, which is a variation on correlation analysis.

ADVANCED LEVEL MATERIAL

Advanced Level 21.1

The real charm of the ANOVA is that the one-way ANOVA, which compares two or more groups on one variable, can still be done with a hand calculator. It is a bit drawn out, but it does help one's understanding of what is happening to the data and how it is being manipulated.

Another way of conceptualizing the ANOVA is to think of it as determining the extent of the differences in the group means. It mathematically compares the observed differences in their means with the hypothetical mean (for example, a mean for the groups if they were the same). We would say that the two groups are statistically significantly different if the variance of the observed distribution is large enough (approximately 3 standard deviations from the hypothetical mean). If this occurs, we can state that there would be only 5 chances in 100 that the observed difference between the two groups occurred by accident, that it was a random event (Brase, & Brase, 1991).

Another way of visualizing the ANOVA: If the groups are statistically different, the scores for the two groups will cluster around two signficantly different values along a linear regression line.

You can build on what you already know to conceptualize the ANOVA. First, picture two regression graphs, one for each group. The ANOVA procedure is based on linear math. You already have a good idea of how a linear relation looks on a graph from Chapter 20. Now picture two linear graphs, representing two regression analyses done at the same time (see Figure 21.1).

Advanced Level 21.2   ## Dummy Variables

The only way to use nominal variables in regression analysis is to make them into dummy variables (see the chapter on regression). With ANOVA, you must use a nominal variable; it is your one and only independent variable. You can also use dummy variables as dependent variables in an ANOVA, however, based on the same logic for using them in regression analysis. You could NOT use a dummy variable in your ANOVA equation as your independent variable if the nominal variable (the dummy variable) has to be broken down into several dummy variables.

Advanced Level 21.3   ## A Caution

Just a reminder, it is NOT a good idea to separate people into different groups based on the *mean* of a variable such as age, income or I.Q. (rank, interval, or ratio data for your grouping variables). This is because the majority of the people (68%) are the same or at least within one standard deviation of the mean. Using the mean to differentiate the two groups will result in a serious problem. The groups will be too similar to tell us anything, or the differences found will result from the skewness created when the groups were formed by separating them per the mean of the entire group. Think of a normal curve, and you will realize that one group will be the mirror image of the other.

Multi-Nomial Distribution

If you have collected data from a large group of people and find that there is a clear bimodal or tri-modal distribution you can use the ANOVA to analyze the data. The data must be ratio, interval, or rank order level data, like income (see the scattergram in Figure 21.5) to use the ANOVA. You could not use the data in Figure 21.5 in a regression analysis because the data are not linearly related or in one normally distributed group; it is made up of two groups. However, the data in Figure 21.5 will make a very good grouping variable (the independent variable) in an ANOVA.

Fundamentals of the MANOVA Problem

A research problem that would benefit from a MANOVA analysis would be to compare two or more groups on two characteristics, such as "family bond" and "alienation." Much like the *t*-test, the MANOVA would tell us which groups had higher scores on the scales to measure family bond and alienation.

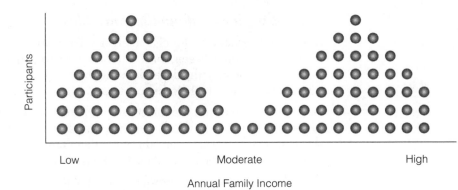

FIGURE **21.5**

A BIMODAL DISTRIBUTION OF INCOME

The Interaction Effect

In addition, the MANOVA analysis will tell us if the two dependent variables had an interaction effect. Interaction among the dependent variables in the MANOVA means that each dependent variable explains a specific effect on the groups you are comparing. As well, there is a combined effect of the two dependent variables on the groups, called the interaction effect.

In this case, the interaction of high family bond and low alienation result in more interest in U.S. citizenship. Not only would the groups of Haitians and Jamaicans differ on each variable, family bond and alienation, but the two groups would also differ on a positive or negative interest in citizenship.

The advantage is that together with their interaction the two dependent variables explain more of the difference between the two groups than the two dependent variables do separately. This occurs because their separate contributions are added together, accounting for their interaction effect. For instance, gasoline by itself does not cause a lot of concern. A lighted match is not much to worry about either. However, the interaction of the two combined (a lighted match and gasoline) is something much more than the whole of the two parts.

The ANCOVA Problem: Control Variables and Covariance

Although we can learn a great deal from a multivariate analysis, we also can learn a great deal if we can control for the influences of one or more additional variables when we do a multivariate analysis. Using the ANCOVA (ANalysis of COVAriance) approach, you can find group differences on the dependent variable and at the same time control the influence of another variable (a control variable). You would use a variable as a control variable if you thought it might distort the relationships between your independent and dependent variables.

Controlling for Confounding Variables

A confounding variable—or characteristics like a father's education—can change the causal relation between, for illustration purposes, education (the independent variable) and income (the dependent variable). In this case, the father's education can distort the causal relationship between a person's education and income.

One way it could distort the relationship would be if the person's income is helped by the father's level of education. In other words, if a person's father is well educated, given an equal education, that person might earn more income than a person with the same education whose father has a poor education.

ANCOVA will allow us to control the effect of the help given the child's income. Once the effect of the father's education is controlled, we will better be able to see the results of education on income. At least the relationship will not be distorted by the contributions made by the father's education (Lindeman, Merenda & Gold, 1980).

Using ANOVA for Analyzing Survey Data

Most of the data from survey questionnaires are suitable for using the ANOVA procedures. Items on survey questionnaires that ask about gender, political party affiliation, marital status, religion, grade level are examples of nominal level variables with categories such as male or female; Democrats, Republican, Other; and so on. These make excellent independent grouping variables for an ANOVA procedure.

Once you have identified the item with the groups on it (for example, gender), that is your independent variable; you then select another item from the questionnaire as your dependent variable (for example, income). Remember, you can also use dummy variables to represent your nominal variables as your dependent variables (items) that you are not using as your independent variable (gender). You might decide to use political party as a dependent variable (by making it into a dummy variable) to see if there is a difference in political affiliation by gender. In the ANOVA, nominal variables, such as gender and political party, can be used as grouping variables (the independent variable), and in a second analysis they could be used as dummy variables, which allows them to be used as dependent variables. It can get confusing, and it is not a good idea to use many dummy variables.

If you have data from a survey where the majority of the items collected are nominal data, you would be better off using one of the log-linear approaches rather than ANOVA or regression analysis. For a description of how this test works, see Chapter 26.

Using ANOVA for Analyzing Experimental Data

The best way to understand this application of the ANOVA is with an example of the setup of an experimental design where you would use ANOVA to do the analysis.

One experimental approach for using the analysis of variance (ANOVA) would be the pretest-posttest research situation. A typical situation in the field of education is the procedure for testing a new teaching method.

To compare teaching methods—a new teaching method against an old teaching method—the experiment would be set up so the new teaching method class was the experimental group and the old method class was the control group (Lindeman, Merenda, & Gold, 1980).

In an experiment of this nature, the random assignment of the participants to the control and experimental group must be used to ensure equality between the control and experimental group. Random assignment is a must if you plan to use the ANOVA to analyze the data.

The ANOVA can be used to compare the groups on how much they learned between the pretest and the posttest. The ANOVA will tell us if the experimental group did significantly better than the control group.

In addition, with ANCOVA when we are comparing the groups on how much they learned, at the same time we can control for such differences in the group participants as GPA, pass experience, major, or grade level. These differences might not be equalized by the random assignment process.

Using ANOVA for Analyzing Time-Series Data

In a time-series research situation using a pretest and posttest method you might give the two classes 3 tests. At the beginning of the course, the two classes take a pretest (Test #1). After 6 weeks, the two groups are given a second pretest (Test #2). Then, when the course ends, the two classes are given a posttest (Test #3). What we hope is that over time the students continue to learn content. They have very little knowledge of the content at the pretest. They have learned a great deal by mid-semester and have learned even more by the end of the course. This is a time series analysis. The MANOVA allows us to use two or more tests or points in time.

Time-series really shows off its potential with data collected at different intervals in time. Take for example, an opinion poll used to track positive and negative attitudes on the Vietnam War since 1970. With these data, we can set up a data file where the opinion of different groups, say male and female, are represented. Using this type of time-series data and ANOVA, we can see how the difference between male and female attitudes about Vietnam changed or did not change over time (Norušis, 1990).

Examples of a MANOVA Table and Its Interpretation

In the following table, we have two groups (Haitians and Jamaicans), and we want to test the hypothesis that the two groups differ on the characteristics of cultural readjustment and social support.

TABLE 21.1   **MANOVA FOR TWO GROUPS AND TWO VARIABLES**

Source of Variation	Sum of Squares	DF	F Value	Sig. Level
Main Effects (between)	27.72	2	35.58	.001
Social Sup.	16.91	1	7.74	.002
Cultural Adj.	11.67	1	1.93	.04
Two-way Interaction	xx	2	0.73	
Residual (within)	xxx	356		
Total	xxx			

In Table 21.1, MANOVA, the output tells us that the two groups differ on both social support and cultural adjustment. It also tells us that the two groups differ more on social supports than on cultural adjustment. Additionally, Table 21.1 tells us a very important fact: these two variables combined to have an interaction effect. This is to say that each variable explains a unique amount of the difference between the two groups, and that the combination of the two variables explains an additional amount of the difference between the two groups. This amount is in addition to what the two variables as individuals explain about the difference between the two groups.

The MANOVA table tells us that Haitians and Jamaicans are statistically significantly different on both variables. The combination effect (the interaction effect) also creates a third characteristic, and it is statistically significantly different.

The MANOVA table can also help us better conceptualize how the ANOVA procedure works. If you view Figure 21.1 in this chapter, it will help you understand the concept of between group and within group variance. If you look at the scattergram in Figure 21.1, you will see there is an overlap between the three groups on the scattergram. The ANOVA makes adjustments for the within group variance (overlap) and then determines if the groups are still different enough to reach a $p \leq .05$ level of significants. In this way, the MANOVA tells us if there is significant difference between the groups.

MANCOVA Explained

Building on the explanation for the MANOVA, the MANCOVA gives us a truer (more genuine) statistical difference between the two groups by *controlling for covariance*. It will be a more accurate difference because the possible influence of a third variable (that is, income) can be controlled. In this way, you can keep it from influencing the relationship between the two variables of interest (social supports and cultural adjustment) and the groups.

With the MANCOVA procedure, we have statistical coefficients of group differences on each of the two variables of interest (social supports and cultural adjustment). Furthermore, we know that the coefficients of the variables (social supports and cultural adjustment) are not artificially increased or decreased because of the difference in group income.

For example, let us go back to the difference between the Haitians and Jamaicans on social supports and cultural adjustment. The reason the Jamaicans might have made more cultural adjustments is that the Jamaicans had both a larger support system and, on average, a higher income with which to make cultural changes.

If we use the MANCOVA procedure for controlling the differences in income, any differences found by the variables social supports and cultural adjustment will not be mixed with differences caused by differences in the levels of income between the two groups.

REFERENCES

Brase, H. B., & Brase, C. O. (1991). *Understandable statistics: Concepts and methods.* Lexington, MA: D. C. Heath. Pages 556–566 provide an understandable presentation of the ANOVA procedure.

Lindeman, R. H., Merenda, P. F., & Gold, R. Z. (1980). *Introduction to bivariate and multivariate analysis.* Glenville, IL: Scott, Foresman.

Norušis, M. J. (1990). *SPSS Advanced statistics student guide.* Chicago: SPSS, Inc.

FACTOR ANALYSIS

What Is Factor Analysis?

Factor analysis is a flexible statistical procedure that can be used in a wide range of research designs, such as hypothesis testing, concept mapping, and case studies. It can handle several types of data, such as survey and time-series data. Factor analysis is not a new method. It has been widely studied by statisticians and methodologists and has wide applications. It produces a set of equations that can be used to describe and predict behavior (Norušis, 1990). See Advanced Level 22.1, on page 270.

▷ **Advanced Level**
see page 270

Using Factor Analysis

Factor analysis, which is based on the product moment correlation procedure, can be used to discover the underlying patterns among a larger group of variables (questions and/or scales) used in your study. Most questions on a questionnaire are not independent of each other, even if we think they are. They can be grouped into *subsets of the questions* that are related to each other in one way or another. These subsets of the questions at first may not be obvious. This is where factor analysis can be helpful. The underlying patterns among the questions become apparent when they are examined utilizing factor analysis.

In factor analysis, these subsets are called factors. The factors are identified by generating correlation coefficients between all of the variables in the study. The factors are subsets of variables that tend to correlate with each other in the factor better than they do with other variables and other factors. The best factor is the simplest factor structure with the clearest, most understandable meaning. As you will see below, it is a great deal easier to explain what five factors tell us than it is to explain the meaning in data on 54 items.

Factor analysis can be used *to explore* and *detect patterns* in large data sets. It can be used *to test hypotheses* about the structure of the data. We can hypothesize about the number of statistically significant factors in the data and their factorial loadings. It also can be used to *construct indices* (for example, measures and scales). The factor procedure will also identify the number of important factors in your data, or it will allow you to specify the number of factors you want to look for in the data (Lindeman, Merenda, & Gold, 1980).

The most distinguishing feature of factor analysis is its data reduction ability. It has the capability to organize a larger number of variables in a study into a smaller set of components (factors) made up of sets of related variables. Based on an array of correlation coefficients between the variables in the study, factor analysis can be used to extract the subsets of the related variables. The factors themselves represent overarching components of behavior, for example, classroom management. The variables in this factor represent only a portion of possible questions that could tap into this larger component of behavior.

The purpose of the factorial analysis is to identify the simplest factorial structure with the clearest, most understandable interpretation of the items forming the factors.

267

BACKGROUND ON FACTOR ANALYSIS

Factor analysis: The resolution of a set of variables linearly in terms of a small number of categories or "factors." This resolution can be accomplished by the analysis of the correlation among the variables. A satisfactory solution will yield factors, which convey all the essential information of the original set of variables. The chief aim is to attain scientific parsimony or economy of description—data reduction.

Factor analysis was developed as a means of analyzing data obtained from psychological testing by extracting several factors from a matrix of correlations among the tests. The two main conceptual contributors to the development of factor analysis are Charles Spearman and Karl Pearson. In 1901, Karl Pearson set forth "the method of principal axes" that was the first conceptualization of the rotation matrix of grouped characteristics of variance.

In 1904, Charles Spearman published his two-factor theory. This was the beginning of 40 years of work on factor analysis. His method was limited to 10 variables because prior to computers, the calculations for more than 10 variables were too difficult to do manually.

Other contributors include L.L. Thurstone, who is credited with first using the term factor analysis, and who developed multiple factor analysis, and Raymond Cattell, who used factor analysis to develop a "theory of personality." Cattell (1957) identified 171 trait-words that we most often use to describe human characteristics. He then asked judges to rate individual subjects on the descriptive words. The 171 trait-words formed subgroups of words, which constituted 15 to 20 primary factors of personality.

FUNDAMENTALS OF FACTOR ANALYSIS

Factor analysis first constructs a correlation matrix using the values of the variables in the study. In the next step, it extracts the initial factors. The procedure identifies and combines similar variables into these basic, unrefined factors. These initial factors are generally called *principal components*. The first factors produced are constructed from the linear combinations of the original variables. Finally, the procedure allows you to rearrange the variables in the factors by rotating the factors through any of 360 degrees until you find the clearest and most interpretable factor solution.

Two types of rotations may be employed during this step: the orthogonal (that is, varimax rotation) or the oblique (that is, oblimin). The rotations can be between pairs of factors at 90 degrees (orthogonal) or at some oblique angle (less than or more than 90 degrees). This process changes the position of the factor's vectors in relation to the correlation matrix. Rotation helps to find which variables load the strongest on which factor. The key is to find a solution is which each variable loads heavily only on one factor. If it is a weak factor solution, you will notice that any number of variables may load equally on several factors. In a poor factor solution, the factor loadings—for example for the variable in Table 22.2 named "Attends relevant meetings"—may be equally distributed or split between two factors. In other words, unlike the factor loading of .87, if it were a poor factor solution this variable could have a factor loading of .50 in factor 1 and .50 in factor 2. If this were the case, the shared loading would indicate that this was not the best factor solution.

In fact, when we tried the varimax rotation (which I always try before an oblique rotation), there were many variables with near equal loadings on two or more factors. Consequently, we had to try the oblique rotation to find a better factorial solution. With the oblique rotation, we found what we were hoping to find: high variable loadings that were isolated to single factors. Using the oblique rotation, the structure of the variables made sense from our perspective. It was the clearest and most explainable set of factors we found.

When using factor analysis, I try the orthogonal factor solution first because it is mathematically easier to compute and explain. An orthogonal factor solution indicates that each factor is independent of the other factors. In the real world, however, most factors are not totally independent of each other. The best empirical solutions are most often found using an oblique rotation, which can handle this interrelationship and lack of independence.

For instance, in the study of student teacher supervisors, Bing and Cherry (1987), "Assessment of Student Teachers by College Supervisors," in the journal *Psychological Reports*—(Bing and I found humor in the way our names appeared in the journal)—the five factor solution was derived by employing an oblique rotation. The varimax solution did not provide the simplicity and clarity that the oblique solution did—parsimony. For an example of the use of factor analysis, see Advanced Level 22.2, page 271.

⇨ **Advanced Level**
see page 271

WEAKNESSES OF FACTOR ANALYSIS

When factor analysis is used to analyze a number of variables, this statistical procedure will generate one or more factors whether they make sense or not.

For example, in the first statistical output when we used factor analysis to analyze the data for the Bing and Cherry (1987) paper, we discovered that all of the variables in one factor had large numbers of missing answers. True, the variables in this factor had something in common, missing data, but that was not what we were looking for from the factor. We made the connection because the variables did not pass our validity tests based on content and context validity. Our revelation: What if the variables with missing data had been, per chance, interpreted as an important finding? Then we asked ourselves, "How many times in professional papers that we have read have these types of error been made?" It is easy enough to do.

Naming the Factors Is a Creative Process

Nothing in the statistical output tells you what the factor means except for the variable loadings. Granted this is a great deal of information, but then you are on your own. You use professional judgment and a good bit of intuition. I do it by writing down the names of the variables in the factor, per their loadings, which indicated how important they are to the factor. A variable's importance is determined by its factorial loadings. Then, I ponder the variables in the factor until I come up with a dimension that incorporates all of the variables and their hierarchical values as characteristics.

In reality, for the Bing and Cherry (1987) study, we had no idea what dimension these variables might represent. On the face of it and after subjecting the factor to questions about content and context validity, it came down to our agreeing that the names we picked to represent the five factors seemed better than the other choices we came up with during this process.

Factors Tend to Be Unstable

Factor analysis is problematic as a procedure for hypothesis testing. Factors are so unstable that the slightest change in variables or their values can totally rearrange the variables that make up a factor.

In another study on college student alcohol and drug use (Cherry, 1987), I used factorial analysis to test the hypothesis that the 85 items composing 18 scales used in the study would constitute 18 varimax factors. Although a difficult test to pass for most scales, only one scale did poorly, and it was dropped. This use of factor analysis demonstrated that there was a great deal of stability and consistency among the variables/items in each scale that formed a factor. In the journal article, I referred to this procedure as "factorial validity."

▷ **Advanced Level**
see page 273

See Advanced Level 22.3, page 273.

POSTSCRIPT

Factor analysis is extremely useful in many situations. It is most often used to test the dimensions of a scale or measure. Working with the reliability procedures presented in Chapter 19, factor analysis can be used to help produce reliable and stable scales and measures.

In the next chapter, an extension of regression analysis, discriminant analysis, will be presented. This procedure can be used to develop typologies among people you might study or might have as clients at your social service agency. It is very useful in the helping professions for verifying subgroups in a large population.

ADVANCED LEVEL MATERIAL

Advanced Level 22.1   Factor analysis in the helping professions permits the study of behavioral phenomena of great complexity and diversity. It is able to untangle complex interrelationships among the data and organize it into patterns that reveal independent influences or causes at work. It offers both a technique of analysis and a theoretical structure that can help mold the findings into scientific theory. It deals with a wide assortment of social phenomena and allows for both inductive and deductive manipulation of quantitative data.

OBLIQUE FACTOR 1:
TABLE 22.1   MANAGEMENT OF THE INSTRUCTIONAL ENVIRONMENT

Items in Factor 1	Factor 1 Loadings	b²
1. Structured physical environment to facilitate learning.	.81	.67
2. Uses positive, fair, consistent measures to manage disruptive behavior.	.72	.80
3. Establishes and/or maintains clear standards for classroom routines.	.72	.75
4. Uses groups to facilitate learning.	.61	.60
5. Is alert to the actions of all students in the room.	.58	.68
6. Uses varying teaching strategies to support individual learning styles.	.54	.72
7. Prepares and adapts materials as needed for students of all ability levels.	.54	.68

* Commonalties: This indicates the percentage of unique variance that can be attributed to the variable. The remainder of the variance is shared with the other variables in the equation (Rummel, 1970).

OBLIQUE FACTOR 2:
TABLE 22.2   PROFESSIONAL RESPONSIBILITY

Items in Factor 2	Factor 2 Loadings	b²
1. Supports and adheres to the policies of the Board of Education and the school.	.98	.87
2. Is punctual.	.89	.77
3. Attends relevant meetings.	.88	.77
4. Uses the NEA Code of Ethics of the Education Profession as a guide to professional behavior.	.83	.69
5. Maintains a clean and safe classroom.	.80	.72
6. Maintains acceptable attendance.	.72	.67
7. Uses a grading system consistent with school policy.	.56	.68

* Commonalties: This indicates the percentage of unique variance that can be attributed to the variable. The remainder of the variance is shared with the other variables in the equation (Rummel, 1970).

Advanced Level 22.2   *An Example of Factor Analysis Output*

The output of the factor analysis is organized into columns of variables with their factor loadings (called coefficients) that form the factors. Tables 22.1 and 22.2 present the variable names and the loadings of factors 1 and 2 from the Bing and Cherry (1987) paper cited above. Factors 3, 4, and 5 are also discussed.

Interpretation of Output   The two factors above seem to meet the chief aim of factor analysis—that is, "attaining scientific parsimony or economy of description—data reduction," as per the definition of factor analysis presented earlier in this chapter. The two factors have seven variables each, which appear to be a subset of more encompassing dimensions. Factor 1 is made up of variables that tend to be related to the broader issue of management of the instructional environment. The second seemed related to professional responsibility. Of course, the names of the dimensions to which these variables belong were not identified by the factor analysis program. As statisticians, we came up with the name of the dimensions and agreed between ourselves that each of these seven individual variables probably represented a large set of behaviors important to classroom management and professional responsibility. This is the creative process that gives us so much trouble when using factor analysis. Why these names? Why not others?

To be able to appreciate the conceptual elegance of factor analysis, think of taking 482 student evaluations done by 33 college student teacher supervisors. Now think of trying to make sense of them. Although it may seem nearly impossible, in fact, these evaluations are no different from a collection of statements that describe what college supervisors expect to see in student teachers to which they will give a passing grade. This is their subjective grading criteria, based on an order of importance that, in this case, the college supervisors did not even know they were using.

The characteristic these college supervisors valued the most was the ability of the student teacher to control the students in the classroom. The second most important characteristic was the students' compliance with what the local board of education perceived as a teacher's professional responsibility. Factor 3 or the third characteristic was "human relations." Factor 4 seemed to tap a dimension we called "planning of instruction." Factor 5 represented the skills of "communication."

Supported by the way an oblique factor analysis organized the variables in the study, for Bing and me, these broader dimensions seemed to sum up the major characteristics that the college supervisors were looking for in student teachers. You, like all who read the journal article, will have to decide if our interpretation of the set of variables in each factor is congruent with your knowledge of the subject and your deductive conclusions.

Your deductions of the meaning of these factors (sets of variables) are as legitimate as ours. For instance, you might think that a major influence on the supervisors' opinion should be knowledge of the academic subject being taught. Perhaps it is or should be, but it was apparently not very important to these supervisors, as "knowledge of subject" was not one of the five factors identified by this factor analysis.

You may even deduce that the views of the supervisors are really affected by the appearance of the classroom. If the physical environment is pleasing to the supervisor and the teacher is a pleasant person, the student teacher will be graded highly, despite being nearly ignorant about the subject being taught. It is interesting that the most important variable in the most important factor is "structured physical environment to facilitate learning."

Assumptions about Data Used in a Factor Analysis

The data you collect for your study should be checked to see if it meets the mathematical assumptions necessary to perform a factor analysis. To check the adequacy of the data:

1. You would run a Bartlett's test for sphericity (test for normal distribution) on the variables you intend to use in the factor analysis. If the coefficient is *not* statistically significant (p ≤ .05), you should *not* use those variables in a factor analysis.
2. You would run a Kaiser-Meyer-Olkin (KMO) measure of sampling adequacy. The KMO value ranges from 0 to 1. In this case, the smaller the value (say, .035) the less basis you have to use factor analysis with the variables you subjected to the KMO test. The closer to 1—for example, .65 or higher—the more support you have for analyzing the variables with factor analysis.

Advanced Level 22.3 ## Additional Terms in Factor Analysis

Several terms have unique meaning with regard to factor analysis.

R-type and Q-type factor analysis: R-type factor analysis, the most common type, is used when you examine variables for underlying patterns and relationships. When using Q-type factor analysis, you are analyzing the relationships between individuals rather than between variables. In Q-type, your respondents (subjects) are used for the analysis. In R-type, your variables are used for the analysis.

Iteration: A process that improves the estimate of commonality. The first iteration begins with the R^2 commonality estimate as the main diagonal element of the correlation matrix. After each iteration, the diagonals are replaced with the new commonality estimates until additional estimates do not change, but are stable. In the Bing and Cherry (1987) study, it took 34 iterations to find the best estimates of commonality.

Eigenvalue: The total sum of the variance that each factor accounts for in the factor analysis. Typically, to be identified as a factor, a set of variables must have an eigenvalue of 1. This is the convention and generally the default setting in most computer programs that perform factor analysis; however, the value can be lowered or increased in most computer programs.

REFERENCES

Bing J. R., & Cherry, A. L. (1987). Assessment of student teachers by college supervisors. *Psychological Reports, 61*, 275–283.

Cattell, R. B. (1957). *Personality and motivation structure and measurement.* New York: Harcourt, Brace, & World.

Cherry, A. L. (1987). Social bond theory and alcohol use among college students. *Journal of College Student Personnel, 28*(2), 128–135.

Lindeman, R. H., Merenda, P. F., & Gold, R. Z. (1980). *Introduction to bivariate and multivariate analysis.* Glenville, IL: Scott, Foresman.

Norušis, M. J. (1990). *SPSS advanced statistics student guide.* Chicago: SPSS, Inc.

Rummel, R. J. (1970). *Applied factor analysis.* Evanston, IL: Northwestern University Press.

DISCRIMINANT ANALYSIS

WHAT IS DISCRIMINANT ANALYSIS?

Whereas factor analysis is an extension of correlational analysis, *discriminant analysis* is an extension of regression analysis. The objective of discriminant analysis is to analyze the difference between two or more groups and to use the difference in variables to classify the members. First, it statistically analyzes which variables are important for distinguishing group membership. Second, using scores obtained by each participant in the study, the discriminant procedure evaluates how well the selected discriminant variables are able to classify group members (Lindeman, Merenda, & Gold, 1980).

USING DISCRIMINANT ANALYSIS

➪ **Advanced Level**
see page 279

If you need to develop a way of classifying members of two or more groups (for example, male or female, or Democrat, Republican, other) based on the independent variables in your study, you should consider using discriminant analysis. This statistical procedure uses a subset of the independent variables to differentiate between two or more groups that are identified on a dependent variable (for example, graduated, nongraduated, or heavy users; light to moderate users; abstainers) (Norušis, 1990). See Advanced Level 23.1, page 279.

BACKGROUND ON DISCRIMINANT ANALYSIS

Discriminant analysis is another way of employing regression techniques to analyze data. This variation on regression takes your independent variables and uses them as discriminating variables. It then selects one or more subsets of independent variables that distinguish between two or more groups that are identified on a nominal, dependent variable.

   Discriminant analysis is one of the analytic methods in the family of multivariate methods. It can analyze multiple independent and dependent variables simultaneously.

DIFFERENCES BETWEEN *t*-TEST, ANOVA, FACTOR ANALYSIS, AND DISCRIMINANT ANALYSIS

The *t*-test tells us how two groups differ on one variable. The ANOVA and MANOVA describe how two or more groups differ on one or more variables. Factor analysis uses no groups but organizes the variables into subsets of related

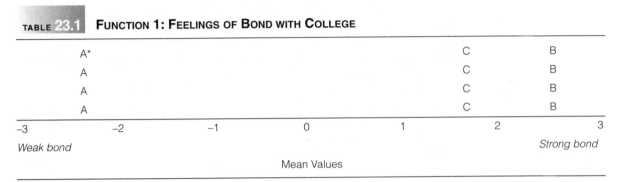

TABLE 23.1   **FUNCTION 1: FEELINGS OF BOND WITH COLLEGE**

A*						C	B
A						C	B
A						C	B
A						C	B

-3	-2	-1	0	1	2	3
Weak bond						Strong bond

Mean Values

* The stacks of letters depict the mean position of the group represented by the letters:
A = Heavy Drinkers, B = Moderate to Light Users, C = Abstainers.

variables called factors or dimensions. Discriminant analysis identifies subsets of independent variables as discriminant functions. These discriminant functions describe the groups that make up the dependent variable.

The discriminant procedure produces one less discriminant function than you have groups in the equation. For example, a three group analysis would produce two discriminant functions. These discriminant functions tell us in what ways the groups differ. Although the discriminant functions are much like factors in factor analysis, discriminant functions are not generally rotated to find the best solution. When discriminant functions are rotated, the procedure is no longer able to determine what percentage of the variance the discriminant functions explain.

FUNDAMENTALS OF DISCRIMINANT ANALYSIS

The best way to conceptualize a discriminant analysis is to visualize the participants forming several groups along a continuum that is represented by the discriminant function. This function or dimension that forms a continuum is a linearly related set of independent variables. In Table 23.1, the discriminant function "feelings of bond with college" forms a continuum from a weak bond to a strong bond. Along this continuum, the three groups formed around three different group means. This is a good discriminant function because it was able to classify the membership in 74% of the cases.

Table 23.1 illustrates the findings of Discriminant Function 1. Among these college seniors, those who identify themselves as heavy drinkers scored low on the variables related to a bond with college. Interestingly, the light to moderate users felt a stronger bond to college than the abstainers. This is because the abstainers have a stronger bond to another organization, such as a religious group. In this situation, the light to moderate users had a strong bond to the college community. They were college students who either increased their consumption of alcohol or reduced their drinking to a range in-line with what they perceived as acceptable drinking levels among students on that college campus. The abstainers, by and large, were students who did not drink because of a strong bond with a religious organization that did not use alcohol or a bond to a family who abstained.

The above explanation is not necessarily easy to understand. However, it is easier to understand and explain than the eight different variables that made up the discriminant function. For an example of the use of discriminant analysis, see Advanced Level 23.2, page 279.

⇨ **Advanced Level**
see page 279

Stepwise Selection

A model to determine the best order for the variables to be entered into the regression equation is the same as is used in regression analysis, "stepwise regression" (see Chapter 21).

WEAKNESSES OF DISCRIMINANT ANALYSIS

As you would expect because it is based on regression analysis, discriminant analysis has the same inherent weaknesses as all of these elaborate statistical procedures. It requires that the data meet strict requirements because if the data are flawed, the results of analysis will be flawed.

Furthermore, we use discriminant analysis because it is easier to explain one dimension than it is to explain the relationship between eight variables. When you have four or more groups, the discriminant analysis procedure becomes very complicated. In the case of four groups you will have to explain how they differ on three dimensions. The more groups, the more complicated and the less comprehensible for the researcher and the anticipated audience.

POSTSCRIPT

Discriminant analysis can be used in many research situations in the helping professions. Whereas discriminant analysis tells us about the variables that make up subgroups in a sample or population, another procedure, path analysis, can help us ascertain how one event affects events that follow it in time. For example, it would be helpful if we had an idea of how much influence peer pressure and parents have on a college student's alcohol drinking behavior. As you will see in Chapter 24, path analysis can help us determine the degree of influence that is exerted by both peer pressure and parents on college student drinking.

ADVANCED LEVEL MATERIAL

Advanced Level 23.1   For example, in a 1987 paper, "Social Bond Theory and Alcohol Use Among College Students," in the *Journal of College Student Personnel,* I reported using discriminant analysis to identify several sets of independent variables that would predict whether a student belonged to one of three groups who consume alcohol: (1) Heavy Users, (2) Light to Moderate Users, and (3) Abstainers. The 14 independent variables used in the discriminant analysis covered the students perspectives on alcohol use and social bonds. The dependent variable was a single question that asked the students to indicate how much alcohol they typically drank. Their self-reported level of alcohol consumption was used to identify to which category on the dependent variable they belonged.

In this study, the dimension that distinguished abstainers from light to moderate users and from heavy users was the student's Level of Attachment and Commitment to the college community. This attachment and commitment in turn controlled the level of alcohol consumption of the students. The higher the level of attachment and commitment to either a religious organization or the college community, the more the student tended to comply with the perceived acceptable level of drinking in the college community.

Discriminant analysis allowed me to go beyond the description provided by 8 variables in a single dimension. This makes it a great deal easier to interpret. Describing one dimension rather than the meaning of 8 variables is more comprehensible for both the researcher and the anticipated audience.

Advanced Level 23.2   ## *An Example of Discriminant Analysis Output*

Tables 23.2 and 23.3 consist of statistics reported in the study, "Social Bond Theory and Alcohol Use Among College Students."

When you examine Tables 23.2 and 23.3, the first thing to check is the level of significance. If the two functions are not statistically significant, there is no need to go on. Seeing that both functions are significant, now look to see how well the discriminant function classified the group members. A note at the bottom of Table 23.2 indicates that the two discriminant functions were able to classify group membership in 74% of the cases. This is far better than chance or classifying randomly, which would be 33% for three groups.

You would next notice that eight variables compose Discriminant Function 1 and six variables make up Function 2. Read the description of each variable and make your own decision as to whether or not you agree with the summary of the meaning of the variables proposed by the author.

Now that you know the variables that make up these two functions, you can differentiate membership a great deal better than by guessing. The dimensions probably relate to the summary meaning provided by the author. To check the

STEPWISE DISCRIMINANT ANALYSIS USING
TABLE 23.2 **PSYCHOSOCIAL SCALES**

Psychosocial Scales and Variables	Structure Coeff.*	
	Function 1	Function 2
1. Perception of responsible drinking	.68	
2. Intolerance of minor deviance	−.45	
3. Religious commitment	−.42	
4. Drinking standards	−.38	
5. Friends as models for drinking	.32	
6. GPA	.32	
7. Perceived parental approval of teenage drinking	−.25	
8. Marital status	−.22	
9. Negative reasons for drinking		−.53
10. Parents as models for drinking		.31
11. Positive reasons for drinking (related to reducing tension)		.28
12. Age		.26
13. Positive reasons for drinking (related to self- esteem)		.24
14. Homework involvement		−.20

* The coefficients above are from the structured matrix and are the calculations of the pooled-within-group correlations between canonical discriminant functions and discriminant variables. Group membership was predicted correctly in 74% of the cases.

CANONICAL DISCRIMINANT FUNCTION
TABLE 23.3 **FROM THE STEPWISE ANALYSIS**

Functions	1	2
Eigenvalue	0.564	0.268
Cumulative % of explained variance	67.79	32.21
Canonical correlations squared	.60	.46
Wilk's lambda	.504	.789
X_2	129	45
df	28	13
Significance	.000	.000

author's interpretation, however, you would look at the eigenvalue for each discriminant function to determine how much variance each function was able to explain. In this case, Function 1 explained over half of the variance between the three groups (eigenvalue = .564), and Function 2 explained slightly over a quarter of the variance among the groups (eigenvalue = .268). This indicates that the two functions were unable to explain approximately 18% of the variance between the three groups. Explaining 82% of the variance in anything is substantial.

Now you might want to see how much variance each function could explain of the 82%. The "cumulative percentage of explained variance" row in Table 23.3 is the place to find out. The cumulative percentage figures will always add up to 100%. Considering the variance that the two functions explain (82% explained variance), Function 1 accounts for 67.79% of that percentage of explained variance and Function 2 accounts for the remaining 32.21%. Function 1 appears to be a solid dimension.

The "squared canonical correlations" is much like the eigenvalues in that it also indicates the relative capability of the two functions to classify the groups. These correlations are fairly good, as are the eigenvalues.

The next statistic to check, and a very important one, is the Wilk's Lambda. This statistic gives us yet another view of the discriminating power of these functions. The larger the Wilk's Lambda the less discriminating power left in the set of discriminating variables. After Function 1 was removed, the Wilk's Lambda was .504. This indicates that a substantial amount of discriminating power still exists in the variables. After Function 2 was removed, however, the remaining power to discriminant group differences had dropped considerably (Wilk's Lambda =.789).

Finally, if you really wanted to check out the author, you would make a note of the chi-square (χ^2) coefficients and their related degrees of freedom (df). Then, to check the level of significance you use a chi-square table of significant values (Table of Critical Values of the Chi-Square Distribution).

This discriminant statistic tells us that the variables in the discriminant analysis form two powerful functions that can do a very good job of classifying three groups of students by their attitudes toward the college community, peers, and family.

One of the prevention program strategies this finding suggests is that programs for college students, particularly first year students, that help them develop bonds and support systems at the university will help them on many levels. Specifically, however, such programs will help reduce the risk of long-term heavy drinking while in college. For all college students, but particularly for sophomores, who have few positive bonds with the college community or religious organization, or who have lost or let go of existing bonds without replacing them with other equally as strong and positive bonds, the chances are that these students are or will have psychosocial problems. This situation could very likely lead to extended heavy drinking behavior. Interventions need to be made available before such behaviors harm the student and his or her future.

TABLE 23.4   CALCULATING THE DISCRIMINANT FUNCTION SCORE

Psychosocial scales and variables in Factor 1	Discriminant Function Coefficient	Person #1 value for variable	Totals
1. Perception of responsible drinking	.68	5	3.4
2. Intolerance of minor deviance	−.45	3	−1.35
3. Religious commitment	−.42	6	−2.52
4. Drinking standards	−.38	2	−0.76
5. Friends as models for drinking	.32	4	1.28
6. GPA	.32	4	1.28
7. Perceived parental approval of teenage drinking	−.25	3	−0.75
8. Marital status	−.22	2	−0.44
(Constant)			−0.23
TOTAL Individual Discriminant score			−0.09

In discriminant analysis, the first task of the procedure is to produce the discriminant function(s). Discriminant analysis uses all the variables in the equation to form the discriminant function. Procedurally, even if a seemingly superfluous variable contribution is small, it contributes to the function coefficients. The second task, the classification of an individual participant to one group or another is based on the values of the linear combination of variables for that particular individual.

To compute the value of an individual's function score, you multiply the individual's score on a variable by the function coefficient for that variable. After you have a value for each variable, you add the values together and the sum is the function 1 score for that individual. The individual score determines group membership.

An example of how to calculate the individual factor score for person #1, using the Discriminant Function 1 is presented in Table 23.4. See Chapter 25, page 293, for additional advanced level material (25.1 on discriminant analysis).

REFERENCES

Cherry, A. L. (1987). Social bond theory and alcohol use among college students. *Journal of College Student Personnel,* 28(2), 128–135.

Lindeman, R. H., Merenda, P. F., & Gold, R. Z. (1980). *Introduction to bivariate and multivariate analysis.* Glenville, IL: Scott, Foresman.

Norušis, M. J. (1990). *SPSS Advanced statistics student guide.* Chicago: SPSS, Inc.

PATH ANALYSIS

WHAT IS PATH ANALYSIS?

Path analysis is a way to use regression procedures to help determine how one event affects events that follow it in time. For instance, it would be very helpful if we had an idea of how much influence factors like peer pressure and parents have on a college student's alcohol drinking behavior. If we knew what kind of experiences leave college students more at-risk of experiencing alcohol and drug problems in college, we could do a great deal to prevent it. Fortunately, there is a statistical procedure that can help us make this type of determination, called path analysis. See Advanced Level 24.1, page 286.

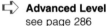
Advanced Level
see page 286

USING PATH ANALYSIS

Path analysis shows how events or experiences that occurred in the past influence behavior in the present. In terms of alcohol and drug risk among college students, we have used path analysis to examine the influences in a teenager's life that influences his or her alcohol use and abuse in college. Path analysis can provide a pictorial graph of the relationships among variables that occur at different points in time (see Figure 24.1).

FUNDAMENTALS OF PATH ANALYSIS

The major constraint for using path analysis is that the variables in the path diagram must be related, and the variables must have occurred at different points in time. This is also one of the assumptions about the relationship between all independent and dependent variables in a regression equation. As you may remember, the independent variable must precede the dependent variable in time to meet one of the assumptions of causation. With path analysis, however, it is necessary for a time interval to exist among the independent variables, as well as between the independent variables and the dependent variable. See Advanced Level 24.2, page 286.

Advanced Level
see page 286

WEAKNESSES OF PATH ANALYSIS

It is easier to explain the time-order relationship between the variables with a path diagram (see Figure 24.1) than without it. The problem with path analysis is that the procedure is still done by hand. There is no computer program to establish the causal order of the variables for you; that is determined by you, the researcher. Nor is there a computer program to create the path diagram, which is also done by hand.

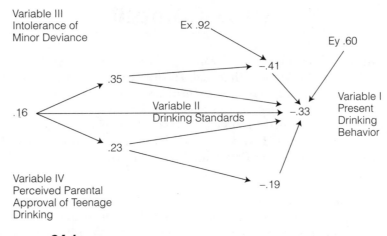

Variable III
Intolerance of
Minor Deviance

Ex .92

Ey .60

Variable I
Present
Drinking
Behavior

Variable II
Drinking Standards

Variable IV
Perceived Parental
Approval of Teenage
Drinking

.35

.16

.23

−.41

−.33

−.19

FIGURE **24.1**

PATH DIAGRAM OF INFLUENCES ON COLLEGE SENIOR DRINKING

As the primary researcher, you decide the structure of the relationship among the variables. You also use the computer regression program to calculate the partial betas, which are the path coefficients that show the causal impact one variable has on another.

Another weakness is that the diagram becomes very confusing if too many variables are represented on the diagram. Duncan (1966), who did a great deal of the early work on path analysis, used four variables to explain this analytical approach. More than six or seven variables make the diagram very complicated. The purpose for using path analysis is to explain a group of complicated correlations between several independent variables and a dependent variable. The objective of path analysis is simplifying and clarifying the relationships among the variables. If there are four or five time periods with several variables at each time period, however, the explanation becomes lost in a complicated web of connecting lines and coefficients. Such path diagrams defeat the purpose of path analysis. The intent is to clarify relationships, not confuse them.

POSTSCRIPT

So far we have discussed several statistical procedures that explain and clarify group membership. In Chapter 25, you will find a procedure to help you identify subgroups in a larger sample or population. Cluster analysis is a very valuable tool when you look for subgroups in an agency population to better tailor services and interventions to meet their needs.

ADVANCED LEVEL MATERIAL

Advanced Level 24.1   A path analysis is made up of a series of regression equations between each variable in the path model. The *beta* from the regression analysis is used as the path coefficient or the degree of strength of the impact of one variable on the variable that follows. In this model, each variable except for the last one will be used as an independent variable and then as a dependent variable as the variables move through time. A review of the chapters on correlation and regression will help you better understand the path analysis concept.

Advanced Level 24.2   The best way to understand path analysis is to visualize a diagram like that in Figure 24.1. This path diagram that illustrates how one variable influences another variable later in time can be very useful in explaining causal relations. The path analysis diagram (Figure 24.1) was used to demonstrate the long-term effect of parental influence on college student drinking behavior. This paper, published in the *Journal of Alcohol and Drug Education,* is called "A Social Bond: An Application of Control Theory in the Study of Alcohol Use Among College Seniors" (Cherry, 1987).

Explanation of a Path Diagram

Path analysis assumes that because of a network of relationships, changes/variations in Variable I (in this case, present drinking behavior) are influenced by the attitude expressed in Variable II (drinking standards) and that changes in Variable II and probably changes in Variable I are caused by Variable III (intolerance of minor deviance) and Variable IV (perceived parental approval of teenage drinking). A graph of the path that connects the variables gives a distinctive and clearer picture of their relationship. The graph clearly depicts a causal model. The degree to which a student tolerates minor deviance in others (Variable III), a gauge developed over the life of the student, and the student's perception of their parents' approval of teenage drinking (Variable IV), a standard that they accepted or rejected, influenced the drinking standards they established for themselves as college students (Variable I).

Moreover, although tolerance of minor deviance in others (Variable III) and the student's perception of their parents' approval of teenage drinking (Variable IV), have a strong direct effect on the development of drinking standards, they also have a weak effect on present drinking behavior.

Interestingly, Variable III, student tolerance of minor deviance, exerts the most direct influence (−.41) on present alcohol use and a strong direct influence on drinking standards (.35). Thus, the variable student tolerance of minor deviance is, in turn, indirectly contributing to the impact of the individual student's drinking standards on the student's present alcohol use.

TABLE 24.1 MULTIPLE REGRESSION ANALYSIS PREDICTING PRESENT ALCOHOL USE AMONG SENIORS (N=466)

Psychosocial Measures	R*	R SQ.	R SQ. Change	Adjusted R SQ.
Intolerance of minor deviance	.70	.49		.45
Drinking standards	.84	.72	.23	.67
Perceived parental approval of teenage drinking	.90	.81	.09	.76

* Multiple Rs are from a stepwise regression with overall Fs significant at the .001 level or beyond.

TABLE 24.2 CORRELATION MATRIX FOR PSYCHOSOCIAL MEASURES IN REGRESSION ANALYSIS

Psychosocial Variables	Var. 1.	Var. 2.	Var. 3.	Var. 4.
1. Intolerance of minor deviance	1.00			
2. Drinking standards	.40	1.00		
3. Perceived parental approval of teenage drinking	.23	.20	1.00	
4. Present alcohol use (dependent variable)	−.41	−.43	−.19	1.00

The variables in this example have two important qualities that make path analysis possible: They have a weak but natural causal order, and they are causally closed (Blalock, 1971; Heise, 1975; Pedhazur, 1982). The scale, perceived parental approval of teenage drinking, reflects the respondents' perception of their parents' attitudes about teenage drinking when the seniors were teenagers. This is clearly a distal variable. Of the other two, the development of intolerance to minor deviant behavior would logically begin earlier than the development of drinking standards. In Figure 24.1, it is assumed that drinking standards are weakly determined both by intolerance of minor deviant behavior and by perceived parental approval of teenage drinking. Additionally, it is assumed that all three of these variables in turn have a direct effect in determining present alcohol use. By following the relationships among these variables (perceived parental approval of teenage drinking, intolerance of minor deviant behavior and drinking standards, a mediating variable), we can identify both direct and indirect effects of perceived parental approval of teenage drinking and intolerance of minor deviant behavior or present alcohol use.

Two variables, tolerance of minor deviant behavior and retrospective data on the level of perceived parental approval of teenage drinking, have a bivariate relationship that is partly causal and partly spurious. Regarding this relationship, a case could be made for proposing that perceived parental approval of teenage drinking is merely a reflection of the parents' perceived attitudes about deviant behavior in general. Whatever the larger dimensional basis for this exogenous variable, the path model suggests that parents' attitudes toward teenage alcohol use has a direct influence on the seniors' standards for drinking and has both a direct and an indirect influence on the seniors' present level of alcohol use.

Intolerance of minor deviant behavior also has a direct influence on the seniors' standards for drinking and has both a direct and an indirect influence on the seniors' present level of alcohol use.

The "independent errors" by Ey and Ex (see Figure 24.1) suggest that residual factors or variables not among the independent variables used influenced drinking standards and present alcohol use. Little of the variance in the variable drinking standards was accounted for by either of the variables perceived parental approval of teenage drinking or intolerance of minor deviance, which resulted in a rather large estimate of residual covariation (Ex = .92). The magnitude of this independent error (the influence of variables not in the model) suggests that the variable drinking standards was tapping a dimension that the other two independent variables were not. The residual factors affecting present drinking behavior, on the other hand, were substantially smaller (Ey = .60), indicating that the three variables are tapping almost half the factors that influence present drinking. Nevertheless, a residual of this size suggests that additional independent variables measuring residual factors would improve the model.

The effect of the independent variable intolerance of minor deviance on the variable drinking standards and the dependent variable present alcohol use was greater than the effect of perceived parental approval of teenage drinking on attitudes. It is very important that perceived parental approval of teenage drinking could shape the teenager to such an extent that it was reflected in the behavior of the college senior. The impact is of interest, raising such questions as what approach to disapproval of teen drinking was important in shaping the drinking behavior of the college seniors.

Intolerance of minor deviant behavior was the most robust variable in the multiple regression and in the path model. The total direct and indirect effects of this variable accounted for over half (−.53) of the variance in present alcohol use. The total direct and indirect effects of perceived parental approval of teenage drinking (−.27) is not very large, but it is only slightly smaller than the genuine effect of drinking standards (−.33), and this scale is the most proximal independent variable to the dependent variable in the model. This means that it is the closest variable to the final dependent variable present drinking behavior.

REFERENCES

Blalock, H. M. (1971). *Causal models in the social sciences.* Chicago: Aldine.

Cherry, A. L. (1987). Undergraduate alcohol misuse: Suggested strategies for prevention and early detection. *Journal of Alcohol and Drug Education,*32(3): 1–6.

Duncan, O. D. (1966). Path analysis: Sociological examples. *American Journal of Sociology,* 72, 1–16.

Heise, D. (1975). *Causal analysis.* New York: Wiley.

Pedhazur, E. (1982). *Multiple regression in behavior research* (2nd ed.). New York: Holt, Rinehart, & Winston.

CLUSTER ANALYSIS

What Is Cluster Analysis?

Cluster analysis is a way to classify "birds of a feather"; that is, it examines the data collected on the variables for each person or case and then classifies the cases that are similar on the same variables. The beauty of this approach is that you do not need to know beforehand which case belongs in which group. Cluster analysis finds the natural groups of cases that are similar on the variables used in the study.

Using Cluster Analysis

You can use cluster analysis when you believe that subgroups exist within a larger population. If you wish to classify, let us say, people into subgroups but you do not know to which subgroup each individual belongs, you would use cluster analysis to find out. It is assumed that you are using the best available scales and measures to examine the individual characteristics of interest. Given reasonably good data, you might be able to identify relatively homogeneous subgroups in your population without knowing beforehand 1) what group(s) the individuals belonged to, or for that matter 2) how many subgroups exist in the total population.

The problem with cluster analysis is that when used alone, it has limited explanatory and predictive value. It will tell you about group membership and even help you find out how many groups exist in the population under study, but it will not tell you what variables it used to identify group membership. As a result of using cluster analysis, you know to which group each case belongs, but you do not know the difference in characteristics. You would need to employ other statistical procedures to describe the groups. In Advanced Level 25.1, page 294, the research study presented initially uses cluster analysis to identify four hypothesized groups. Then discriminant analysis is used to help describe the characteristics of the groups identified by the cluster analysis.

▷ **Advanced Level**
see page 294

Background on Cluster Analysis

Cluster analysis was first used in biology to classify animals and plants, and it is also used in medicine to identify diseases and their stages. In marketing, it is used to identify people with the same buying habits. In the field of adolescent research, it has been used to identify subgroups of runaways by their background and characteristics.

Discriminant Analysis versus Cluster Analysis

Both discriminant analysis and cluster analysis classify cases into subgroups or categories based on the variables under study. When you use discriminant analysis, however, you must know to which group each member belongs. Discriminant analysis then provides you with a combination of variables and variable weights that can be used to develop a classification rule.

For example, if you are interested in distinguishing among several groups of runaway juveniles, based on cases whose group membership is known, discriminant analysis is one of the best statistical tests. Discriminant analysis will produce sets of variables called discriminant functions. These sets of variables can then be used to describe the groups of runaway juveniles—that is, typologies or profiles. These descriptions can also be used to classify future cases by group when group membership is unknown. They can be classified because they fit the profile.

With cluster analysis you do not need to know to what group the cases belong because it shows the natural clusters that exist in the population. Your only control is to determine the number of clusters you want the analysis to find. You can request computer programs that do cluster analysis to find two or more clusters in the data. However, cluster analysis will not give us any help identifying the characteristics of group members. For this information we need to use another approach, like discriminant analysis.

Factor Analysis versus Cluster Analysis

Although cluster analysis might sound similar to factor analysis, the difference is that factor analysis organizes the variables into related groups called factors, but cluster analysis organizes the cases or participants into related groups. In more technical terms, in factor analysis each variable is expressed as a linear combination and assigned to a unique factor that is specific to that variable. The factors made up of similar variables are estimated as linear combinations of the original variables (Norušis, 1990). The product of cluster analysis is the identity of homogeneous cases that it assigns to groups or clusters.

FUNDAMENTALS OF CLUSTER ANALYSIS

As stated earlier, one of the assumptions of cluster analysis is that group membership for all cases is unknown. Furthermore, you do not even need to know the number of groups that exist in the population. Cluster analysis can both identify group membership for each case and determine the number of groups in the population under study. Cluster analysis can identify (1) homogeneous groups or clusters, and (2) group membership for each individual.

For example, by asking juveniles who identified themselves as runaways a number of questions about their social, family, and individual bonds, we were able to identify several distinct subgroups of juveniles with similar reasons for leaving home. In the past, a number of different categories for juveniles who run away had been suggested in the literature. These categories, however, had been derived intuitively by practitioners and qualitative researchers but had not been verified quantitatively. If the intuitive groupings, the categories of juveniles with similar characteristics, did exist in the real world, we hypothesized that by using psychosocial scales and statistical tests we could show it quantitatively.

Using the data on the variables we collected from the juveniles and using cluster analysis, we were able to verify that four subgroups did exist in the population of juveniles we were studying. (This study, "Combining Cluster and Discriminant Analysis to Develop a Social Bond Typology of Runaway Youth," was reported in the journal, *Research on Social Work Practice,* 1993, Vol. 3 No. 2, pages 175–190.) In this study, the cluster analysis supported the general intuitive categories suggested in the literature before this study. These findings were validated using a separate discriminant analysis of the same data. The four groups that classified by the characteristics using cluster analysis were named Running To, Running From, Thrown Out, and Forsaken.

WEAKNESS OF CLUSTER ANALYSIS

In addition to being unable to identify the characteristics of the groups it identifies, cluster analysis has a weakness similar to factor analysis: it will produce a mathematical solution and identify subgroups in the population data, even if no meaningful subgroups exist. In other words, this analysis has no way of telling you that the cluster solution arrived at is meaningful or useful in the real world. Like factor analysis, cluster analysis will reach a solution even when there is not one.

This is not so much a disadvantage as it is an extra step you must take during the analysis. Once you have your data in a final data file, before beginning the cluster analysis, you will need to use a statistical procedure to convert your data into "Z scores." Z scores are also called "standard scores" because the value of the raw score obtained by each participant is expressed as a percentage of 100. For instance, a score of 20 on a scale having 50 points is 40%, so the Z score is 40. Z scores are often used to avoid the inappropriate influence of variables with large scale scores as compared to variables with small scale scores.

POSTSCRIPT

Cluster analysis is not used a great deal because it is complicated, and the data must meet the strict assumptions of linear math. In Chapter 26, you will find a number of other advanced statistical tests: Canonical Correlational Analysis, Log-Linear, and Time-Series Models. These statistical procedures are useful when the data meets the strict assumptions of linear math. You will also see them again in research articles in journals produced by organizations in the helping professions.

Advanced Level Material

Advanced Level 25.1 ## *An Example of Cluster Analysis*

In cluster analysis, as in other statistical procedures, the types of subgroups you identify depend on your choice of variables. In the example presented here, the runaway groups were identified using psychosocial scales that measured social bonding behavior. However, other subgroups existed in this population of juveniles. For example, if we had used educational variables, we would have identified groups that had educational themes.

Using the data collected from the variables of interest, the clusters are represented by the distance between them. To find this distance, you can use several approaches. In the SPSS statistical program, agglomerate hierarchical clustering is used to identify clusters. In this procedure, the squared Euclidean distance is used to measure "nearness."

The agglomerative hierarchical cluster begins by considering all cases to be individual clusters. If you have 180 participants, you will have 180 clusters in the beginning of the cluster analysis. In the second step, two cases are combined to form one cluster of two cases and 178 other clusters of individual cases. In the third step, one of two things might happen: Another case might be added to the existing cluster, or two cases might be clustered together to make a second or new cluster. This third step is a repeat of step two and is performed with each case until all cases are grouped in a cluster that best fits the characteristic of the individual case.

In this type of cluster analysis, the distance between the clusters is an average of the distances of all possible pairs of cases between the clusters. To understand how this works, it is easier to demonstrate it with two clusters. Let us assume that the two clusters we are working with are made up of four cases. Cases 1 and 2 fall into Cluster A and cases 3 and 4 make up Cluster B. The distance between clusters A and B is the average distance between all possible combinations of the cases in each cluster (that is, 1 & 3, 1 & 4, 2 & 3, 2 & 4).

The output presented here is from the data gathered for the study of juvenile runaways. For this analysis, the predictor variables were first tested and were found to meet the basic assumptions for linear modeling. Next, we use the quick cluster analysis procedure found in the SPSS statistical program. This procedure classifies large numbers of cases efficiently into clusters. This procedure, however, requires the researcher to specify the number of clusters or groups in the sample. In this case, because of the previous analysis (Zide & Cherry, 1992), four groups were hypothesized to exist in the sample.

Before the cluster analysis was carried out, all values were converted to Z scores or standard values to avoid the inappropriate influence of variables with large-scale scores as compared to variables with small-scale scores.

TABLE **25.1**   ANALYSIS OF VARIANCE

Variables	Cluster Mean Sq.	DF	Error Mean Sq.	DF	F	Prob.
ZRELBOND	33.84	3	.593	242	59.06	.000
ZSCHBOND	36.01	3	.516	217	69.77	.000
ZASEBOND	21.50	3	.668	185	32.20	.000
ZINDBOND	27.04	3	.660	230	40.96	.000
ZMOBOND	22.69	3	.721	233	31.49	.000
ZFABOND	15.59	3	.787	205	19.82	.000

The first cluster analysis for this study produced four very unequal groups in which the first group had only nine cases. This was far from what was expected. After examining the nine cases, it was decided that these youths, characterized by high scores on all scales, made up a small subgroup of youths that should be dropped.

After dropping these nine cases, believed to be outliers, from the analysis, we continued the search for the best groups in the sample. The second cluster analysis produced four groups that seemed more consistent with previous findings: Thrown Out youths (n = 52); Running From youths (n = 71) youths; Running To youths (n = 63); and, Forsaken youths (n = 63). Table 25.1 contains the mean squares for examining differences between the clusters. As explained earlier, cluster analysis, much like factor analysis, is somewhat exploratory; in other words, it will provide any number of clusters the researcher requests. The researcher's knowledge of the population should not be discounted, and it is, in fact, necessary in this and all statistical analyses.

Checking the Clusters

To check these clusters for accuracy, we used a four by four chi-square analysis to crosstabulate the youths identified by the cluster analysis. This classification was compared to youths identified by the scales developed to categorize these youths. The chi-square value of 26.45, p < .0017, indicates that although there are slight differences in group membership, the two sets of groups are statistically significant. The Cramer's V (V = .19, p < .0017) suggests an association between the two sets of groups (Table 25.2). Although there are differences, the self-classified groups are not significantly different from the groups derived using cluster analysis. This helps confirm that the groups identified by cluster analysis are similar to the criterion provided by self-classification. More important, the cluster classification variable is not a biased reflection of the individual's response to a univariate question.

CHI SQUARE TABLE *:
TABLE 25.2   **SELF-IDENTIFIED GROUPS BY CLUSTER GROUPS ****

Cluster Groups	Self Classified Groups				
	A	**B**	**C**	**D**	**Raw Score**
A	24	17	17	12	70/29%
B	4	15	23	7	49/20%
C	17	12	23	11	63/26%
D	15	12	11	21	59/25%
Column/Row	60/25%	56/23%	74/31%	51/21%	241/100%

* Chi square = 26.45; p < .0017 Cramer's V = .19; p < .0017. Of the 258 total cases, nine were dropped as a sub cluster. Additionally, eight other cases were dropped because the respondents did not identify themselves by a category.

** The groups are represented by letters: A = Thrown Out; B = Running From; C = Running To; D = Forsaken

Determining the Usefulness of the Clusters

There is no way of knowing if the cluster solution is meaningful or useful in the real world. You can, however, apply several criteria to the cluster solution to see if it is practical.

1. Are the clusters greatly different from what you expected to find?
2. Is the cluster solution reliable? Do you get the same or similar solution from sample to sample?
3. Do the variables used to identify the clusters make sense as descriptions of the groups?
4. Are the clusters practical and useful?

Using Discriminant Analysis to Define Clustered Groups

Discriminant analysis, like regression analysis, allows the researcher to determine and rank important variables that can distinguish these youths by group membership. Because the cluster analysis gives no information on the linear organization of the variables used in the development of the clusters, a discriminant analysis was performed. The results of the analysis—the discrimination functions, the group means, and the discriminant classification results tables—are presented for examination (Tables 25.3, 25.4, and 25.5).

This discriminant function information is useful because it demonstrates how the variables were used to find the clusters leading to the development of the four groups. It also is critical for describing the characteristics of the four types of runaway and homeless youth that were hypothesized. Table 25.4 shows the three discriminant functions derived from the discriminant analysis. The asterisks identify the variables that most influence the function. These functions

TABLE 25.3 THE STANDARDIZED DISCRIMINANT COEFFICIENTS (N = 249)

Scales	Function 1	Function 2	Function 3
School Bonds	.659*	.028	−.204
Religious Bonds	.475*	−.457	.119
Assertiveness	.207	.591*	.276
Mother Bond	.278	.368*	.301
Individual Bond	.108	.471	−.712*
Father Bond	.134	.299	.411*

* Variables that best represent the function.

TABLE 25.4 GROUP MEANS (N = 249)

Groups	Function 1	Function 2	Function 3
A. Thrown Out (n=31)	−3.487	−.211	.044
B. Running From (n=75)	1.064	−1.592	.015
C. Running To (n=70)	.778	1.148	1.909
D. Forsaken (n=73)	.678	1.079	−1.116

TABLE 25.5 DISCRIMINANT CLASSIFICATION RESULTS

Actual Groups	No. of Cases	Predicted Group Membership A	B	C	D
Group A	63	58 92.1%	3 4.8%	0 0%	2 3%
Group B	63	4 6.3%	52 82.5%	2 3.2%	5 7.9%
Group C	52	4 7.7%	2 3.8%	46 88.5%	0 0%
Group D	71	2 2.8%	0 0%	1 1.4%	68 95.8%

Percent of "grouped" cases correctly classified: 89.96%; 249 cases were processed. No cases were excluded. Of the 258 total cases, 9 were dropped as a sub cluster.

TABLE 25.6	RELATIONSHIP OF GROUPS BY GROUP MEANS FUNCTION 1, COMMUNITY BONDS

Groups A through D*						
A				DC B		
A				DC B		
A				DC B		
A				DC B		
−3	−2	−1	0	+1	+2	+3
			Mean Values			

* The stacks of letters depict the mean position of the group represented by the letters:
A = Thrown Out; B = Running From; C = Running To; D = Forsaken

provide an estimate of the probability that a youth with a given set of measures will be from one of the four identified groups. Table 25.5 presents the number of youths in each discriminant group and the grand means for each group for each function in relationship to the scales used in the analysis. Table 25.5 also presents discriminant classification results of predicted group membership. This shows that using these measures in this discriminant equation can identify group membership in 90% of the cases.

Typologies

Unfortunately, describing the characteristics and differences among the groups using discriminant function is again a creative process. Because the discriminant function coefficients are standard scores, the three functions and the group means can be presented visually (Tables 25.6 through 25.9) (Lindeman, Merenda, & Gold, 1980).

Function 1 (Table 25.6), combines variables that can be defined as a "community bond" function because it is made up of bond scales that relate to social institutions (religion and school). This function clearly separates the Running To and the Forsaken group from the other two groups. The group means simply that the Running To group had good community bonds when they left home. It also distinguishes the Forsaken group from the other three groups, implying that these youths had very few community bonds when they left.

Function 2 (Table 25.7) is suggested to represent the assertive behavior of the youth. This function is made up of the assertiveness and mother bond variables. This function distinguishes the Running From group as being the least assertive and the Running To group as the most assertive. This might indicate that a

| | | | | | **RELATIONSHIP OF GROUPS BY GROUP MEANS** | | | |
| | | | | | **FUNCTION 2, ASSERTIVENESS/MOTHER BOND** | | | |

TABLE 25.7

			Groups A through D*				
B		A		DC			
B		A		DC			
B		A		DC			
B		A		DC			
−3	−2	−1	0	+1	+2	+3	
			Mean Values				

* The stacks of letters depict the mean position of the group represented by the letters:
A = Thrown Out; B = Running From;
C = Running To; D = Forsaken

Running To group is emotionally healthier, its members better able to protect themselves on the street.

Function 3 is presented in two tables, 25.8 and 25.9. This is done because individual bond is represented by a negative coefficient in this function and the father bond as a positive coefficient. To understand their meaning in relationship to each other, it is necessary to invert the individual bond coefficient. For this reason, the group means are presented in separate tables.

Table 25.8 shows how individual bond in relationship to father bond distinguishes the Thrown Out group from the other three groups. It indicates that the Thrown Out group has few bonds with other people as compared to the other groups.

Table 25.9 shows how the father bond characterizes the Thrown Out group. Apparently, this group had fairly good relationships with their fathers before they were 13 years old as compared to the other groups.

These discriminant functions separate the Thrown Out group from the other three groups in terms of a lack of bonds with friends and other non-family acquaintances. They had good relationships with their fathers or father figures before turning 13 years old. This break or loss of father bond could be one of the reasons their behavior became so disruptive to the family that they were thrown out.

The Running From group differs from the other three groups in their lack of assertiveness and an apparently poor bonding experience with their mother. This group typically reported both physical and/or sexual abuse as the reason they left home. They also reported more involvement in exploitative sexual behaviors on the street.

The Running To group is unique because of their positive community bonds, assertiveness, and apparent good bonding experience with their mother.

RELATIONSHIP OF GROUPS BY GROUP MEANS
TABLE FUNCTION 3A*, INDIVIDUAL BOND

Groups A through D**

-3	-2	-1	0	+1	+2	+3
		D	B A		C	
		D	B A		C	
		D	B A		C	
		D	B A		C	

Mean Values

* Because individual bond is represented by a negative coefficient and father bond by a positive coefficient,
their meaning in relationship to each other is inverted. For this reason, each variable is presented in a separate table.

** The stacks of letters depict the mean position of the group represented by the following letters:
A = Thrown Out; B = Running From; C = Running To; D = Forsaken

RELATIONSHIP OF GROUPS BY GROUP MEANS
TABLE 25.9 FUNCTION 3B*, FATHER BOND

Groups A through D**

-3	-2	-1	0	+1	+2	+3
	C	A B		D		
	C	A B		D		
	C	A B		D		
	C	A B		D		

Mean Values

* Because individual bond is represented by a negative coefficient and father bond by a positive coefficient,
their meaning in relationship to each other is inverted. For this reason, each variable is presented in a separate table.

** The stacks of letters depict the mean position of the group represented by the following letters:
A = Thrown Out; B = Running From; C = Running To; D = Forsaken

These youths typically report that they ran away from home looking for a more exciting life.

The Forsaken juveniles are distinctive for their lack of community bonds. Bonds to institutions in their community could be valuable sources of support to these youths whose families are unable to continue to provide for them.

REFERENCES

Cherry, A. L. (1993). Combining cluster and discriminant analysis to develop a social bond typology of runaway youth. *Research on Social Work Practice, 3*(2), 175–190.

Lindeman, R. H., Merenda, P. F., & Gold, R. Z. (1980). *Introduction to bivariate and multivariate analysis.* Glenville, IL: Scott, Foresman.

Norušis, M. J. (1990). *SPSS Advanced statistics student guide.* Chicago: SPSS, Inc.

Zide M., & Cherry, A. L. (1992). A typology of runaway youth: An empirically based definition. *Child & Adolescent Social Work Journal, 8*(2): 155–168.

OTHER ADVANCED STATISTICAL TESTS

Canonical Correlational Analysis, Log-Linear, and Time-Series Models

CANONICAL CORRELATIONAL ANALYSIS

Canonical correlational analysis is an extension of multiple regression analysis. Multiple regression is used when you wish to determine the effect of **more than one** independent variable on **only one** dependent variable. Canonical correlational analysis is a way of determining the effect of **more than one** independent variable on **more than one** dependent variable.

USING CANONICAL ANALYSIS

In the helping professions, it is unrealistic to believe that an intervention (an independent variable) affects only one area of a person's life (affects one dependent variable). In fact, the hope of helping professionals who develop interventions for one problem or another is that the intervention will affect several aspects of a person's life (affect several dependent variables). To find out if it has affected several aspects of a person's life, the helping professional will need to use canonical correlational analysis to measure several components of an intervention on several dependent variables at one time. See Advanced Level 26.1, page 307.

⇨ **Advanced Level**
see page 307

LOGISTIC REGRESSION ANALYSIS

Logistic regression analysis is much like linear regression. Whereas linear regression requires a dependent variable that is a continuous measure (a rank order, interval, or ratio level of measure), logistic regression allows you to use a dichotomous variable (such as a "yes" or "no" answer) as a dependent variable. It is a multivariate technique for estimating the probability that several independent variables can predict a change in a nominal/dichotomous dependent variable. It was designed to use nominal data as a dependent variable with nominal, categorical, and continuous independent variables.

USING LOGISTIC REGRESSION ANALYSIS

One of the problems with data collected in the human services field is that it is collected without considering how it will be analyzed. Far too often the data consist of a "yes" or "no" response to a question asked by a counselor or social service worker. Are you receiving food stamps? Are you receiving aid from another agency? Have you received treatment for a mental disorder in the past? These are very important questions, and case records are replete with nominal (or dichotomous) data.

It is important in the human services to be able to use this type of question as a dependent variable to find out, for example, what social characteristics can predict a person's being hospitalized for a mental disorder. In this case, we need a statistical procedure that will allow us to use a nominal question (like the "yes" or "no" questions already mentioned) as the dependent variable with quantitative independent variables. Logistic regression is designed for such a case.

If you want to know why one treatment approach works or does not work with agency clients, logistic regression analysis can help you estimate the probability that the treatment will or will not work with your clients. It can provide a solution from a set of independent variables (at least one should be continuous) that can predict the occurrence of a nominal dependent variable. See Advanced Level 26.2, page 307.

⇨ **Advanced Level**
see page 307

LOG-LINEAR ANALYSIS

Log-linear analysis, often referred to as "hierarchical log-linear analysis," is a multivariate procedure that allows you to describe the relationships between the categorical variables in a crosstabulation table where a multivariate explanation is important.

USING LOG-LINEAR ANALYSIS

For example, you have a 3 by 3 crosstabs table where you are examining data on juvenile crime. Data are available on whether the adolescent is attending school (school attendance), has failed a grade in the past (school failure), has been arrested in the past (previous arrest), lives in an intact family (family support), lives in a high crime neighborhood (living environment), and is a teenager or not (age category). With log-linear analysis, you can obtain an odds ratio to determine if there is statistically significant evidence that a relationship exists among the variables in the crosstabulation table. This approach is more precise than using the chi-square statistic. See Advanced Level 26.3, page 308.

⇨ **Advanced Level**
see page 308

LOGIT LOG-LINEAR ANALYSIS

Logit analysis is a special type of log-linear model used in SPSS that allows you to use categorical data as the dependent and independent variables in a multivariate analysis. Whereas logistic regression is designed to use nominal data as a dependent variable with nominal, categorical and continuous independent variables, the logit procedure is designed to use a dependent variable with two or more categories and independent variables that are nominal or categorical.

USING LOGIT LOG-LINEAR ANALYSIS

In many cases in human service research, our data are not nominal (binary— "present" or "not present"); they are categorical. Several different categories (more than two) can be used to identify an individual characteristic. These data are often presented in a crosstabulation table. The relationship between the variables is difficult to explain if one of the variables is considered a dependent variable. For example, it could be helpful to use drug of choice as a dependent variable to see how several independent variables affected the choice of drugs used by people in a substance abuse treatment program. Independent variables such as previous treatment, presence of pathology, gender, and educational category could possibly help explain the choice of drugs used. A multiway table showing these categorical independent and dependent variables would be interesting. Still, it would not help explain the relationship between the dependent variable drug of choice and the independent variables (previous treatment, presence of pathology, gender, and educational category). To get a clearer picture of the relationship, you will need to use a logit analytical approach. Another advantage of this approach is that the data do not have to meet all the assumptions necessary to perform a linear model analysis. See Advanced Level 26.4, page 309.

⇨ **Advanced Level**
see page 309

TIME-SERIES ANALYSIS: REGRESSION AND MANOVA

There are two basic approaches for analyzing data that are collected over time. One approach is to use a regression analysis in which the independent variable is time, and the analysis tests the effect of time on the dependent variable. The other approach is the MANOVA, in which the repeated measures over time are viewed as a set of multiple dependent variables. The difference lies in how the data are set up in the data file.

With regression analysis, the data collected over time are organized in the rows, and the dependent variables are in columns.

For a time-series analysis using MANOVA, both the grouping variable and the data collected at each time period are placed in the columns of the data file. In this data file, the data are collected on the same variable over several periods in time. This setup is often referred to as a statistical analysis of "repeated measures." The analysis is a comparison of how the groups differ on the repeated measures or how they differ on the measures taken over time.

Both procedures provide information of the statistical significance of changes over time. Both procedures provide information on the variance accounted for by the passing of time.

There is another important difference between the two approaches. Regression analysis can do a curve estimation of the data but cannot handle covariance. MANOVA can handle covariance but does not provide a curve estimate.

Time-Series Using Regression Analysis

Let us say you have collected data over a period of time, perhaps every other month for a year on a characteristic that changes. One way to test the hypothesis that there has been a statistically significant change in the variable or characteristic over time

---

26.1 | *Example of Time-Series Using Regression Analysis*

In an effort to help group leaders develop the most effective drug prevention workshops with children, I collected pretest and posttest data from the participants in each group. At the end of each year, I analyzed the data from the workshops that had been conducted and gave feedback to the workshop leaders about ways they could improve their presentations.

After six years of collecting data on the pretest and posttest, I wanted to see if the feedback had resulted in significant changes in the learning that took place over that period of time.

The question was, Did the yearly feedback improve the presentations of the workshop leaders enough to increase the posttest scores of the children? I hypothesized that the pretest would remain the same over the six years, but that the posttest would show a significant increase in learning over time. The output provided by the linear analysis over time was an R^2 of .915 at a significant level of .0007 (R^2 =.915, p < .0007). Because the beta was positive (.956743), we can conclude that there was a great deal of positive change over time (Cherry, Cherry, & Sainz, 1998).

➡️ **Advanced Level**
see page 309

is to use regression analysis to do a time-series analysis. The regression procedure will tell you if there has been a statistically significant change over time. It will also tell you how much variance time accounts for in the dependent variable (Pedhazur, 1982). See Advanced Level 26.5, page 309. See Box 26.1 for an example of time series using regression analysis.

Time-Series Using MANOVA

You would use the MANOVA to do a time-series analysis if you needed to control for another variable so that time was not affected by, let us say, age of the participants. The example in Box 26.2 shows how the MANOVA is used in a time-series analysis.

➡️ **Advanced Level**
see page 310

See Advanced Level 26.6, page 310.

POSTSCRIPT

Now that you have finished analyzing your data, you are ready to write up your analysis. The next chapter will assist you in that process. Chapter 27 provides you with a standard outline for writing a research paper for a research class, a dissertation, or for writing an article for a professional journal in the helping professions.

Example of Time-Series Using MANOVA

After an intensive summer school program with 40 children who had failed elementary school and their parents who attended three workshops on how to help tutor their children, the report card grades were collected over four grading periods. Because we did not want the children's age to affect their grades, we used the MANOVA and age as a covariate.

The four grading periods were analyzed using gender as the grouping variable. The hypotheses that were tested proposed (1) that there would be a significant change in grades over the four time periods even when age was controlled and (2) that there would be no difference in grades between males and females.

The analysis found that the difference between gender was not significant ($F = .821$, df $= 3$, $p < .486$) but that there was a significant increase in grades over the four reporting periods ($F = 45.18$, df $= 3$, $p < .000$). This indicated not only that the summer school program helped the children move into the next grade, but also that they developed the tools to continue to improve their grades after summer school (Warren, 1998).

ADVANCED LEVEL MATERIAL

Advanced Level 26.1   Canonical correlational analysis can help you determine the degree of linear relationship between **more than one** independent variable and **more than one** dependent variable. Canonical correlational analysis is different from multiple regression, which measures the degree of the linear relationship between **more than one** independent variable and **only one** dependent variable. Canonical correlational analysis helps determine the effect of **more than one** treatment variable on the independent side with **more than one** outcome variable on the dependent side (Lindeman, Merenda, & Gold, 1980).

Advanced Level 26.2   An advantage of the logistic regression approach is that your data does not have to meet all the assumptions necessary to perform linear model analysis. If a dependent variable has only two values, the distribution of errors cannot be assumed to be normal. Logistic regression does not require normal distribution of error. It does not require that there be normality of the independent variables, nor equal variance-covariance matrices in the two groups.

In a logistics regression analysis, the statistics that reveal the relationship between the independent variables and the nominal dependent variable are the "Wald coefficient," the "significant level," and the "logistic coefficient." In the SPSS program the logistic coefficient is identified as the "Exp(B)." The Exp(B) reports the odds of an event occurring; it is defined as the ratio of the probability that it will occur to the probability that it will not occur. If the logistic coefficient, the Exp(B), has a value of 3.5, this means that with any one unit of change in the independent variable, the value of the other dependent variables remaining the same, the odds are increased by a factor of 3.5. In other words, if there is a one-unit change in the independent variable and the other dependent variables remain the same, there will be a 3.5 unit change in the nominal dependent variable.

The logistic regression procedure also produces a classification table to assess the goodness-of-fit of the model. The classification procedure is similar to the one produced by a two group discriminant analysis procedure. The procedure classifies the cases as occurring or not occurring. The classification table produced will display the number of cases correctly and incorrectly classified as, for example, passing or failing the examination from the predictor variables.

The following will illustrate how the findings from a logistic regression analysis would be reported in a research paper or article. Let us say you were reporting on a study that tested a family intervention with students failing in school. You would report the results as follows: 42 (70%) of the passing students were correctly classified by the model and 63 (84%) of the failing students were classified correctly. To estimate the improvement of this solution over chance, we can use the *tau* statistic that is used in the discriminant analysis procedure. In this case, the standardized measure of improvement beyond chance, the model would correctly classify 66% of the passing and failing candidates. This classification is a 16% increase over what would be expected by chance, which would classify 50% in each group (Norušis, 1990).

Advanced Level 26.3   The log-linear analysis estimates maximum-likelihood parameters of variables in a crosstabulation table. Observed and estimated cell frequencies and goodness-of-fit statistics are used along with log-odds ratios to analyze the frequency counts of observations appearing in each cell of the crosstabulation table. The odds ratio indicates whether or not there is statistically significant proof that there is a relation between the variables in the crosstabulation table.

The log-linear model views the expected cell frequency of the crosstabulation table as a linear function. This is similar to the way the ANOVA treats categorical data. The log-linear analysis is not concerned with the main affect, which is the primary focus of the ANOVA; with log-linear analysis you are more interested in the interaction between the variables in terms of how many interactions are needed to estimate the cell frequencies. In other words, log-linear analysis can help you determine if there are interactions among the variables or if the variables are independent of each other. The goal is to find the most parsimonious model for the data, as well as to consider, in an orderly way, any relationships that could exist among the variables under study.

Like logistic regression, log-linear analysis does not require normal distribution of error. It does not require that there be normality of the variables, nor equal variance-covariance matrices in the groups (Norušis, 1990).

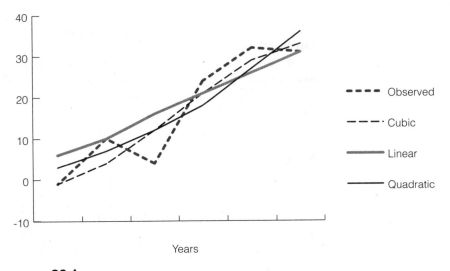

FIGURE **26.1**

POSTTEST

Advanced Level 26.4

Like log-linear analysis, logit analysis estimates maximum-likelihood parameters of variables in a crosstabulation table. For example in the case discussed on page 305, you can investigate the relationship between drug of choice and the independent variables: previous treatment, presence of pathology, gender, and educational category. The odds ratio statistic will tell you if the chances are statistically important. In other words, the independent variables predict the drug of choice. Like log-linear analysis, although the overall goodness-of-fit test indicates that the model fits the data, it does not tell us if there are individual cells that lack a "goodness-of fit" (Heise, 1975).

Advanced Level 26.5

You can also use regression analysis to test for curvilinear changes in data over time if a scatter plot of your data suggests there may be a curve in the data. In other words, the data are not linear but tend to curve over time. In the example, discussed in Box 26.1, the scatter plot (the observed line in Figure 26.1) suggested that the data did curve. In fact, the observed line in Figure 26.1 showed that the posttest scores were fairly high to begin with and that they dropped in the third year and then picked up again over the next three years.

In Figure 26.1 the data over six years is plotted and tested using three different time-series analytical approaches: linear, quadratic and cubic. Whereas the linear analysis explained 91.5% (R^2 =.915, p < .0007) of the variance of posttest scores over six years, the quadratic curve which plotted one inverse curve was able to explain 93.8% (R^2 =.938, p < .0038) of the variance of posttest scores over six years. This is a better fit of the data to reality, but the cubic is even better. The data in Figure 26.1 is not just a single curve; rather, it curves two times. The curve first goes up and then goes down. Therefore, the cubic analysis is able to explain 95.3% (R^2 =.953, p < .0169) of the variance of the posttest score over six years. The cubic time-series analysis not only explains more of the variance, but also it is obvious to the eye; it is a better fit and a better reflection of reality. Of course, the data must meet the assumptions required for regression analysis. Most modern statistical analytical packages do a variety of tests to help determine if your data meets the required assumptions.

Advanced Level 26.6

In the example in Box 26.2, the control variable age was not a significant influence on grades or gender (F = .428, df = 3, p < .733); however, we would not have known that if we had not controlled for age. Although the confounding variables must be continuous (rank, interval, or ratio level measures), it is possible to control for a number of confounding variables using MANOVA to test repeated measures. Of course, the data must meet the assumptions required for this statistical approach. Again, most modern statistical analytical packages do a variety of tests to determine if your data meets the required assumptions.

REFERENCES

Cherry, A. L., Cherry, M. E., & Sainz, A. (Jan. 1998). *A six-year longitudinal study of a substance abuse prevention program: Instrument construction and measuring effectiveness.* A conference presentation at the Research for Social Work Practice International Conference, Miami, FL.

Heise, D. R. (1975). *Causal analysis.* New York: Wiley.

Lindeman, R. H., Merenda, P. F., & Gold, R. Z. (1980). *Introduction to bivariate and multivariate analysis.* Glenville, IL: Scott, Foresman.

Norušis, M. J. (1990). *SPSS Advanced statistics student guide.* Chicago: SPSS, Inc.

Pedhazur, E. (1982). *Multiple regression in behavior research* (2nd ed.). New York: Holt, Rinehart, & Winston.

Warren, M. (1998, Spring). *Resiliency and at-risk children: An analysis of factors impacting on the development of resiliency.* Barry University School of Social Work, Miami Shores, FL. Available from University Microfilm International, Michigan. DAI, Vol. 58-12A, Page 4815, 00181 pages.

Writing Research Papers and Journal Articles

Chapter 27

A MODEL FOR WRITING A RESEARCH PAPER FOR CLASS, A DISSERTATION, OR AN ARTICLE FOR A PROFESSIONAL JOURNAL

WRITING FOR YOUR AUDIENCE

If your writing skills are weak (punctuation, spelling, or organization), GET HELP!

If you write a paper on a study for a research class, for submission to a professional journal, or for your dissertation, you might want to use some version of this format. This is only one outline; other outlines are available. For your own edification, however, consider consulting one of the formats for writing your paper. It will be useful to you, especially in your first few efforts.

The length of your research paper depends on the requirements of the situation. You might need to cut back on the number of pages suggested here to meet the page requirements of your class assignment. The best approach is to cut the length of each section. The best policy is to follow closely the page requirements for the class assignment or the page requirements for the journal. Even so, you can apply the principles of the following format, which relays the message to the professor or editor that you think logically and can present your findings in an orderly and convincing way.

If you are writing a dissertation or a book on a study, the same general headings can be used as chapters instead of headings. In a book or dissertation, you will be covering the same type of material and areas, but in more detail and with more precision.

This section will also help you better understand and comprehend the link between a research project and writing a research paper. When you finish analyzing your data, much of the work will have been done. This is true especially if you do not intend to write about your research study. Writing it down in an organized and presentable way is usually the last step in the research process.

Writing about your findings also fulfills the responsibility of a professional researcher in the helping professions. We are obliged to disseminate the findings of our work. As you prepare your manuscript, ask several colleagues to critique it.

If you have not already reviewed Chapters 4 and 5, on qualitative and quantitative studies, depending on the type of study you did, review Chapter 4 for a qualitative study or Chapter 5 for a quantitative study. Reviewing these chapters will enhance your understanding of the processes involved in conducting a research study in the helping professions.

STYLE REQUIREMENTS

Obtain the journal's information for authors or dissertation instructions from your university before you begin the writing process. Study them, follow directions, and call the editor, your dissertation chair, or your teacher with questions on format, if you need to.

This format for writing a professional paper is *not* a substitute for a *style manual*. Journals and your professor will require that you write your research paper using one of several style manuals, such as the *Publication Manual of the American Psychological Association* (APA) (1994). Today in the helping professions, the APA style manual is the most widely used by professional journals.

The format that follows is based on a length of 20 pages for a paper or 100–150 pages for a dissertation. Both are assumed to be double-spaced and written in APA style.

NINE PARTS OF A QUANTITATIVE RESEARCH PAPER

The number of double-spaced pages per part *are only suggestions* and will vary from research paper to research paper.

Part 1: The Title	10–15 words
Part 2: The Abstract	25–50 words
Part 3: The Introduction	2 pages research paper 10 to 15 pages dissertation
Part 4: The Literature Review and Theoretical Proposal	7 pages (+or–) research paper 40 to 45 pages dissertation
Part 5: The Hypothesis Statement	1 page research paper 3 to 5 pages dissertation
Part 6: The Methodology Section	
A. The Population	2 pages research paper 10 to 15 pages dissertation
B. The Design	1 page research paper 5 to 15 pages dissertation
C. Instrumentation, Reliability, and Validity	1 page research paper 5 to 10 pages dissertation
Part 7: The Findings	3 pages (+or–) research paper 15 to 20 pages dissertation
Part 8: Conclusion and Discussion	3 pages (+or–) research paper 15 to 20 pages dissertation
Part 9: The References	No page limits

> Always make sure the final copy of the paper you submit to a journal is as perfect as it can possibly be; that is, it should be polished.

First impressions are important. What credence would you give an empirical study that was presented in a careless way: poorly written, hard to understand, not presenting the literature in a logical way, and so forth? I imagine you would have the same response I have had on many occasions. Above everything else, I wonder if the research was done with more care than the paper was written.

PART 1: THE TITLE (10 TO 15 WORDS)

Although coming up with a title for your paper may seem like an easy job, it can be rather difficult. I spent years trying to come up with the title of my book *The Socializing Instincts: Individual, Family and Social Bonds.* I wanted a title that in the fewest words possible would summarize my theories and conclusions and would let the reader know I would be delineating social bond theory.

The *purpose of the title* is to inform the reader about the study. So as much as possible, the title of your paper should be able to stand alone in terms of expressing what the reader can expect to find.

Remember, your title, the one you dreamed up, will be the first thing that readers see. It will either convince them to read your abstract or to skip your paper altogether.

If you are lucky enough to get your paper accepted for publication, your title is also important for *publication indexing.* Your title is likely to appear in indexes of publications such as the Psychological, Sociological, or Social Work Research Abstracts, to mention just a few.

One Approach for Developing a Title

One approach for picking a title is to try to use some form of the names of the variables or questions your research addresses.

Here are some examples of titles:

Social Bonds: Running To, Running From, Thrown Out, and Forsaken Youth

The Psychosocial Adjustment of Caregivers to the Frail Elderly

African-American Extended Families and Kin Help Networks in the 1990s

A Comparative Study of Women in Three Cultures Who Have Been Raped

Factors Affecting the Extent of Computerization in Human Service Agencies

Child Rearing Practices among Haitian and Jamaican Immigrants [The paper by this title, which was first a dissertation, will be used as an organizing example of how the parts of a professional, a research paper, and a dissertation are written and organized.]

Common Errors in Paper Titles

1. The title begins with references to the method or findings: "This Is a Report on the . . ." or "An ABAB Single Subject Design Was Employed . . . "
2. The title uses abbreviations: "ADD, ADHD, and CP Are Compared on Several Factors"
3. The title is too long: "Method Choice in Social Work Education: The Influence of Cognitive Style Dimensions, Perception of Relevance of Field Dependence-Interdependence and Cognitive Complexity-Simplicity Characteristics, and Acknowledged Reasons for Method Track Membership."

Your title should reflect the main idea of the paper with style and flair.

PART 2: THE ABSTRACT (25 TO 50 WORDS)

The length of the abstract will vary from journal to journal, but it typically ranges from 25 to 50 words. It is important to keep the abstract within the word limits specified by the journal.

The three parts of the abstract are the following:

1. A brief statement of the problem.
2. A brief explanation of the data-gathering method and procedures.
3. A brief summary of the findings.

These brief but extremely important statements that compose the abstract are succinct summaries based on the three general parts of your paper. Remember, the first thing the reader sees after the title and the author's name is the abstract. It also is the part the reader is most likely to read. Try to make the abstract interesting, easy to comprehend, and informative. A good abstract will increase the audience of your paper.

The best time to write your final title and abstract is when you have finished writing your paper.

PART 3: THE INTRODUCTION (1 TO 2 DOUBLE-SPACED PAGES)

The introduction is to inform the reader of the specific problem or issue you have studied and the research strategy you used.

Address the following questions in the introduction:

1. *What was the purpose of your study?* This should be a paragraph stating the reason you did your research study. In the paper "Child rearing practices among Haitian and Jamaican immigrants," the purpose was stated in a straightforward way:

   The purpose of this study was to examine the cultural transition of parental roles of Haitian and Jamaican immigrants in South Florida.

2. *What previous research or articles in the literature support the need for the research you did? How does your study fit into previous research in the area?* Cite several supporting references. Use one to three paragraphs to describe and cite other research or authors who call for a study like you have done. How does it fit into the larger picture? This is a brief statement because you will go into more detail in the literature review.

   Use logical arguments and references to the literature to verify that the problem exists and that additional research is needed. In other words, tell us why it is a problem worth our interest and thus our time to read your paper.

   During the 1980s, about 30% of the United States population growth of 19 million was due to immigration (Bureau of the Census, 1991). Furthermore, immigrants from around the world continue to come to the United States in large numbers. These immigrant groups, although seeking to fulfill various dreams, have to make many adjustments to our culture (Dyal & Dyal, 1981). Past and present research on immigrant groups suggest they experience major role stressors and conflicts (Lambert, Knight, & Weisz, 1989). One sphere of this adjustment is in the area of child care.

3. *What are the theoretical implications of your study?*

   Immigrant parents experience various role conflicts and role ambiguities, alienation and loneliness, because they are caught between the perceived demands of the old and new cultures (Dyal & Dyal, 1981).

Do NOT expect the editor of a journal to edit your paper. They do NOT do that. If the manuscript needs work, they might give you an option to rewrite it. Don't count on it!

PART 4: THE LITERATURE REVIEW (6 TO 10 DOUBLE-SPACED PAGES)

In this section *you report on the literature you studied before you stated your hypothesis and conducted the research study.* Here you must build a convincing link between the literature you report in your literature review and the rest of your paper. The statements made in the introduction and the hypothesis you plan to test must support each other in a logical way.

Literature reviews are organized and orderly presentations of what we know about some specific topic.

They can be organized in different ways:

1. *Chronologically by fields, problem area, and/or by school of theory.* Suppose you want to write a literature review for a paper entitled "The Changes in the Behavioral Management for the Severely Mentally Retarded in Public Facilities." To organize your literature review using a chronological approach you would use journals that publish professional papers related to mental retardation and look for articles that describe issues related to your topic over the last 10 to 20 years. Then find a book that gives a historical summary for your topic to fill in the questions about earlier events in this area. The literature review would end with a summation in support of your hypothesis that will follow.

2. *Across fields on a problem issue or topic.* If you focus on a problem that cuts across professional fields, such as teen drug use, your literature review could report the research and theoretical conclusions in each field (Anthropological, Sociological, Psychological, and so forth). It would end with a summation in support of your hypothesis that will follow.

The literature should cover the areas important to your study.

Using the Outline

Use the following outline for the literature review

I. Introduction to the background of the problem you have studied
   A. Historical background and development of the problem
   B. Literature that succinctly reviews the historical assumptions related to the reasons for the problem
   C. Literature on current reasons and causes for the problem

II. Theoretical explanations for the problem
   A. Background and the development over time of the theory or theories that are relevant to the study of the problem
   B. The current theory or theories that are relevant to the study of the problem in this research report or paper

III. Measures/scales used to study the problem
   A. General literature related to measures/scales that have been used to study the problem

    B.   Literature on the measures/scales that have been used to study the problem for this research report or paper

IV. Conclusion of the literature review
    A.   Briefly summarize the literature relevant to your study
    B.   Finally, briefly summarize the literature relevant to the hypothesis you will present next

Using the Diamond-Shaped Pattern

This diamond-shaped pattern is offered as a sample format to help you present the material you collected to do your literature review. Other formats might be used, but this approach is fairly generic. This format has three patterns. Section 1 of the review focuses on the research problem. Section 2 expands to a broad overview of the information the reader needs to have an understanding of the research problem. Section 3 ends by refocusing on the current issues related to the research problem; particularly those issues related to and supporting the hypothesis you present following the literature review.

Section I.   The opening section *focuses on the background* related to the research question.

    For example, in the paper on child-rearing practices among Haitian and Jamaican immigrants, the literature review began with a discussion of the effect on immigration of the 1965 change in immigration policy in the United States. It was brief and informative but not exhaustive. It began,

> Haitians and Jamaicans have been steadily increasing in numbers in the U.S. since the early 1970s (U.S. Census). [The opening paragraph went on to cover relevant supporting literature for this statement and the consequences of this change.]

    After you have introduced the problem, you are ready to develop the background literature.

Section II.   The mid-section expands into *a broader, general background* on the history and theoretical bases related to your research problem.

    Often, simply following the historical development of knowledge about the research question is a good way to organize this part of the review. This chronology of information uncovered about your area of research interest gives the literature review a great deal of structure.

    In this mid-section of the literature review, you would *cover sub-categories of importance* to the research question and theoretical framework. These may include reviews of theoretical explanations, reviews of the measures and/or instruments you intend to use, and other related questions.

    The journal paper presented earlier offers this example:

Sub Heading: Immigration to the United States

This part would begin with a short history of immigration to the U.S. It would end with a short historical review of immigration as it relates to both Haitians and Jamaicans.

Sub Heading: Cultural Norms and Child Care

This subheading would cover the theoretical explanation of the problems of cultural adjustment and its effect on child-rearing practices. For example, a statement describing the problem might read:

> Haitian parents bring to this culture the practice of using corporal punishment as a means of disciplining their children (Charles, 1981). The Jamaicans also have a similar method of child discipline. As a result, Haitian and Jamaican parents face conflicts in the way they customarily discipline their children and the general norm of non-corporal punishment in the United States. Changing this behavior is often difficult.

At this point the reader should have sufficient background information to understand the next section that will focus on current issues related to your research interest.

Section III.   The literature review concludes by *refocusing on the current issues* related to the research problem. This section summarizes the important literature and theory as the material presented relates to the research question and the hypothesis you will present at the end of the section.

Typically, the literature review concludes in several clear, scientifically supported statements. These concluding statements emerge from the literature and will support the research questions or hypothesis.

Some Do's and Don'ts

1. *Cite only relevant studies, papers, and books* in your literature review. They should be essential for building your case. Make sure the references used are linked to specific issues and theory related to your research. Do not pack material from studies and articles that might be loosely related to increase the size of your literature review. Furthermore, do not use studies that are interesting but do not contribute anything important to your research review.
2. *To summarize previous research and literature,* emphasize major conclusions, findings, and relevant methodological issues presented in the literature. Again, avoid nonessential details.
3. *Show the logical continuity* between previous and present work reported in the literature.
4. *Controversial issues* in the literature related to your study should be dealt with equitably. An uncomplicated statement that says "some studies support one conclusion and others support another conclusion" is sufficient. This is much better than a broad or all-encompassing discussion that distracts the reader's attention from your topic.

5. Despite your personal opinion, *avoid animosity and ad hominem arguments* (attacking other people personally rather than questioning their ideas) in developing your research proposal.

6. *Do not plagiarize the work of others.* Copying almost verbatim from articles and abstracts is plagiarism. When writing the literature review section on a report or professional research paper be sure to carefully follow the conventions that avoid plagiarism.

   When using a direct quote from another's material, quote marks are used to set it off and the specific reference is given. In the *Publication Manual of the American Psychological Association,* 4th edition, if the direct quote is more than forty words, the quote is set off in an indented block, and the reference and page number are given.

   The main point is that you do not present the work of others as if it were your work. This includes ideas in addition to written work. If you use a model for a study conducted by someone else, you need to give the original author credit. If you use an idea in the discussion section of a paper to develop a study question, you must give attribution to the author from whom you took the idea. (*Publication Manual of the American Psychological Association,* 1994).

Plagiarism: Presenting the work of another in your study without citing the source.

Paragraph Topics

From the paper presented earlier, the following are examples of paragraph topics in a literature review.

Background on the Problem . . .

	Topics
Paragraph 1:	Changes in immigration patterns
Paragraphs 2-3:	Reasons for changes
Paragraphs 4-5:	Effect on the social service system
Paragraphs 6-8:	Specific effect on child welfare
Paragraphs 9-10:	The issues as they relate to child care
Paragraph 11:	Cultural conflicts in childcare expectations
Paragraph 12:	Description of traditional childcare in Haiti and Jamaica

Subheading:	**Theoretical Framework**
	Topics
Paragraph 13:	Culture as it shapes human behavior
Paragraph 14:	Overview of theory
Paragraph 15:	Chronological review of the theory and how it has been used to explain behavior
Paragraph 16:	Early chronology of theory
Paragraph 17:	Later chronology of theory
Paragraph 18-19:	The link to role theory (This theory tends to explain how social and cultural expectations are activated in the individual.)

Paragraph 20: Summary of the relevant theoretical propositions that are proposed to explain child-care problems among Haitian and Jamaican immigrant parents

Now you are ready to present the reader with the statement of the research problem or hypothesis.

PART 5: STATING THE HYPOTHESIS (1 PARAGRAPH TO ONE DOUBLE-SPACED PAGE)

The hypothesis logically follows the topics presented in the literature review. After we have completed a comprehensive literature review, we are as familiar and knowledgeable about, for example, culture and child-rearing practices as we can get without doing our planned research project. The hypothesis is the summation of your knowledge, training, and intuition.

For help composing a research question or hypothesis, see the section in Chapter 5 on formulating the hypothesis or testable research question.

> NOTE: Check your literature review to make sure that it has literature that covers all areas mentioned in the hypothesis. It is easy to leave a body of knowledge out of the literature review. For example, if we were to propose that high self-esteem was related to fewer pregnancies, I would need to have a review of the literature on self-esteem, teen pregnancy, and self-esteem and teen pregnancy.

The hypothesis you report at this time is the one you proposed before you did the study, NOT the hypothesis or research question you wish you had asked before you started the research study. In most papers, hypotheses or research questions are stated in a single paragraph.

The following are a few examples of lead-in sentences for research questions or hypotheses.

> *Lead-in sentence for stating a research question:* The next logical question to ask is . . .
> *For multiple questions:* Among the research questions that have been left unanswered, this study will address: (1) . . .
> *Lead-in sentence for stating the hypothesis:* The general hypothesis tested by this research study was . . .
> *Perhaps followed by:* This general hypothesis was broken down into four, more specific hypotheses: (1) . . .

For example, in the paper on child-rearing practices among Haitian and Jamaican immigrants, the research questions could be stated in the following way:

> This study sought to answer the following questions about Haitian and Jamaican parents as caregivers:
>
> 1. Is there a difference in parental conflict between Haitian and Jamaican immigrant caregivers that have low levels of cultural adjustment?

2. Do Haitian and Jamaican caregivers that experience more difficult life events experience higher levels of parental conflict?
3. Will Haitian immigrant caregivers as a group, experience lower levels of contentment with their life situation than Jamaican immigrant caregivers?
4. Do the Haitian and Jamaican immigrant caregivers with support systems adjust to the United States culture with less difficulties than those Haitian and Jamaican immigrant caregivers without support systems?

Now you are ready to tell us how you tested your hypothesis.

PART 6: THE METHODOLOGY SECTION (6 TO 8 DOUBLE-SPACED PAGES)

The heading "Methodology" is the most commonly used heading found in professional journal articles and research papers.

In the *methodology section* you report exactly what you did and how you did it. This section tells how the study was conducted, and the report should be detailed enough to permit an experienced researcher to replicate the study. It also allows us to evaluate the methods used to do the study.

The methodology section is made up of three subsections. These subsections, discussed in more depth in Chapters 8 through 11 are:

1. The population or sample (1 to 2 pages)
2. The procedure (design and data collection) (1 to 2 pages)
3. Instrumentation and reliability/validity (1 to 2 pages)

> Although professional journal writing is different from literary writing, you do not have to throw out style or make your paper dull.

The Population Subsection (1 to 2 double-spaced pages)

This subsection should address several major issues related to your population or sample:

1. Who participated in your study?
2. How many participants were there? A simple statement is all that is needed: The total sample size was 356 immigrants: 205 Haitians and 151 Jamaicans.
3. How were they selected?
4. Describe the major demographic characteristics and other relevant information on the participants in your study. Characterize the participants in your research study in terms of the information collected on the demographic items on the questionnaire. Use the actual numbers, frequencies, averages, standard deviations, or range to describe participants' ages, gender, race/ethnicity, education, and other important characteristics that will help the reader get a good picture of the people who participated in your research study.

Tables and figures are useful tools for presenting the participants' demographics, as shown by the following example from the Haitian/Jamaican study:

A frequency table was employed to describe similarities and differences among the two groups. There were no significant differences in the distribution of sex or age among the two groups. However, there was a significant difference (p < .001) in the ethnic distribution between the two groups. Some 97% (198) of the Haitians were Black while 86% (130) of the Jamaicans were Black.

There was a significant difference (p < .001) in the length of time they had resided in the United States. Figure I shows that 63% of the Jamaicans and 37% of the Haitians had resided in the United States for over 9 years.

FIGURE I: TIME IN UNITED STATES

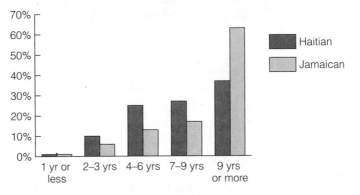

5. How do the participants who took part in your study differ from those in your sample that refused to take part in your study?
6. Tell us why your participants are appropriate to test your hypothesis.

   Haitians and Jamaicans were chosen for this study because of the lack of information available on child rearing practices among these two recent immigrant groups, and because of the problems many experience at the hands of child protection workers who do not take into consideration the cultural conflict these new immigrants face.

7. Tell the reader how your participants were able to handle the tasks required of your measures (questionnaire, tests, scales, and so forth). For example, could the immigrants read and understand the questions? In this case two questionnaires were used, one in English for the Jamaican participants and one in Creole for the Haitian participants.

The Procedure Subsection (1 to 2 double-spaced pages)

This subsection should summarize each step in the execution of your research study. In doing so, it should at least answer the following questions:

1. Where and how did you collect your data?
2. What were the instructions to the participants?

3. If you used groups in your study, how were the groups formed or members selected and differentiated?
4. What other important factors or events might have affected the study or participants?

Instrumentation and Reliability/Validity Subsection (2 to 3 double-spaced pages)

This subsection should summarize information on how well the measures and scales did when measuring the characteristics of the participants in your study. Reliability and validity issues are addressed in this part of your paper.

1. Summarize how well your measures/scales worked with the participants in your study. This is particularly important if the scales were not tested with people like your participants, or if the scales were not intended to be used in the way you employed them in your study.
2. List any scale items dropped. How does this affect the scale in terms of reliability?
3. List any scale items changed for this study. How does this affect the scale?

The Cultural Readjustment Scale (Spradley & Phillips, 1972) was used to determine ". . . how people feel when they live in another culture or anticipate living in one." The original Cultural Readjustment Scale had 33 items. This study utilized only 16 of these items. These items were composed of a short-version of the scale being tested for the first time. This revised scale, used with these two groups had an acceptable level of reliability (Cornbach's Alpha = .86). It is believed to have similar validity to the longer version of the scale.

4. Specify the reliability coefficients obtained for the measures/scales used with these participants. If you used a number of different scales, this is a good place to use a table with Reliability Coefficients.

Multiple Table Construction

A few tables and figures can be helpful in summarizing your analysis and findings. Too many tables and figures are as bad as too few.

Although you do not want to overdo it, each table should be constructed to present several types of information. This means combining information. Be careful, though, because it is easy to make tables very confusing. I suggest that you look for examples of tables and figures in the journal to which you plan to submit your paper. We use tables and figures to help clarify our findings.

You can construct a table that displays the following, as the example shows:

1. The name of the scale.
2. The number of items in each scale.
3. The number of people who answered all the items in each scale.
4. The mean and standard deviation of each scale.
5. The reliability coefficients obtained by the participants for each scale.

Table 1: The N, Mean, Standard Deviation, Scale Items, and Cornbach's Alpha for Scales

(Haitians' & Jamaicans' responses are combined in this table)

Psychosocial Scales	N	Mean	SD	No. of Items	Alpha
Cultural Readjustment	355	44.3	9.31	16	.86
Child Rearing H/J	354	56.7	7.40	24	.68
Child Rearing US	352	52.1	5.53	24	.73
Life Events	354	124.7	83.63	20	.53
Contentment	354	34.8	6.96	10	.83
Social Support	351	39.1	12.63	15	.91
Isolation	352	28.2	5.1	9	.58

PART 7: THE FINDINGS SECTION (3 [+ OR –] DOUBLE-SPACED PAGES)

The *purpose of the findings section* is to summarize the analytical procedures utilized with the data and the results of the statistical tests related to the hypotheses or the research questions of your study.

The findings section typically has 2 subsections:

1. A brief description of the statistical procedures employed to analyze your data
2. A report of the results of the hypothesis tests

Describing Your Statistical Procedures

1. To begin, tell us what statistical package was utilized to analyze your data, such as SPSS or SAS. It may be as simple as the sentence below.

   The correlations between each pair of scales and their level of significance were calculated using SPSS, the Statistical Package for the Social Sciences.

2. Now, summarize the statistical procedures you employed to statistically analyze your data and test your hypothesis.

   Two-tail *t*-tests were performed between the two immigrant groups on each of the six scales (see Table II). Table II shows the means, standard deviations, *t*-values, and p-values for each test. Pearson correlations also were used to examine the relationship between the variables under study.

Reporting the Results of Each Test of the Hypotheses

In this subsection you summarize the results of the statistical analysis of the variables (the measures or scales used in the questionnaire) that are related to your research questions or hypotheses.

1. Use one paragraph per research question or hypothesis and
   a. Briefly rephrase or restate the hypotheses
   b. Report the results of the statistical test

   When considering the cultural adjustment made in the U.S. and comparing this to child rearing practices in Haiti and Jamaica, there was a small but significant difference ($t = 5.14$, $p < .001$). There were higher levels of cultural adjustment (Mean = 2.89, SD= .61) among Haitians than among Jamaicans (mean = 2.59, SD = .49). However, there were greater reported differences in child rearing practices in Haiti (mean = .131, SD = .22) than in Jamaica (mean = .033, SD = .20) when compared to parenting in the U.S. ($t = 4.42$, $p < .001$).

2. This is *not* the place to try *to interpret or discuss the implications of the results* of the statistical analysis. The discussion of the findings takes place in the last part of your paper, not here.
3. Report all statistical results relevant to your hypotheses, both those that support your hypothesis and those that run counter to your hypothesis.
4. When writing about the statistical procedures employed to analyze your data, be brief, but give sufficient detail to support the findings you report.
5. When you report tests of significance (chi-square, *t*-test, correlations, analysis of variance, etc.) related to your hypotheses, include the values or coefficients with the level of significance obtained by the analysis of the data.

   There was a small but significant difference ($t = 5.14$, $p < .001$). [The "t" stands for "*t*-test" and the "p" stands for "probability" or, as it is more often referred to, "the level of significance."]

   a. If it is a group analysis, report the degrees of freedom (chi square = 26.45; df = 3; $p < .001$)
   b. Often the direction of the effect on the relationship between two variables that results from the statistical test is important to report. It may be a positive or a negative relationship.

   There were no significant differences in the number of negative life experiences between the two groups. Furthermore, negative life experiences did not increase the chances that a parent would use a harsher approach to child rearing. Although it was a very small correlation ($r = -.10$, $p < .025$), it still suggests that negative life experiences are not predictive of harsh child rearing practices among these immigrants.

6. Do *not* report as significant relationships that are really close to being significant but are not. Unless the p value falls between p = .050 and p = .000, social science research convention says the relationship is not considered statistically significant. Using the cut off p = .05, *statistical results such as p < .051, p < .052, or p < .053 are best interpreted as occurring by pure chance.*

   Now you get to tell us what you think you found.

PART 8: CONCLUSION AND DISCUSSION SECTION (3 [+ OR −] DOUBLE-SPACED PAGES)

The *purpose of the conclusion and discussion section* is to evaluate and interpret the statistical findings. This is the place for you to draw conclusions and discuss the implications of the results of your study.

Questions to Guide the Conclusion Section

1. What has your research endeavor contributed to our understanding of the problem or issue you studied?
2. How has your study helped better explain the problem or the issue?
3. What conclusions and theoretical ramifications can you support with the findings from your study?

Do's and Don'ts for the Conclusion Section

1. Typically, this section begins with a clear statement about the support or lack of support for your original hypothesis.
2. Given the results of the tests of the hypothesis, explain your findings in terms of how you see them playing out in the real world.
3. Compare the similarities and differences between your analysis and other relevant research studies you found in the literature. The literature should help clarify the conclusions you draw.

   In addition to the psychosocial variables employed in this study, the demographic variables that influenced changes in child rearing practices were: Length of Stay in the U.S., Education, Income, and Number of Children in the Household. People would normally expect that the longer the person stays in the culture, the more they change. However, these changes and the rate of change are dependent upon Income and Educational level of the immigrant (Dyal & Dyal, 1981; O'Guinn, Imperia, & MacAdams, 1987). In this context, income does not necessarily imply the income in relationship to other U.S. citizens but income in relationship to their reference group.

4. Do *not* just restate what you say earlier in the paper.
5. Each statement in this section should add to the reader's understanding of the problems or issues you researched.

   In terms of support systems, if Haitians are having child rearing problems and are isolated from their community, an intervention would be to help them connect or reconnect with community support systems. If Jamaicans are experiencing difficulties in their child rearing practices and are isolated from their extended family, the intervention would be to help them reestablish the family bonds and/or community support systems.

6. Report the shortcomings of the study, but do not disorient the reader with minutia or try to explain away nonsupport. Several areas are particularly problematic: The sample may be inadequate or not what we would like it to be; the return rate may have been inadequate or less than desirable; scale reliability may have been poor; and/or the validity of the measures may be questionable. We would report these problems in the limitations section of our report or research paper.

Among the limitations of this study is the paucity of literature and research on child rearing practices among Haitians and Jamaicans. In addition, there has been very little written in the last 20-25 years that addresses the changes in child rearing practices that have to be made when a person moves from one culture to another. Furthermore, the sample of participants was somewhat older than was expected. The variables used in this study are only a small number of the variables that influences child rearing practices and the measures were not developed to be used in cross cultural research. Finally, more research in this area is needed, especially today, when the U.S. has immigrants coming from areas as culturally diverse as Asia, South America, and the Caribbean.

7. Very briefly, state any suggestions for future research.
8. Finally, conclude with a summary statement that wraps up your research findings.

In summary, the process that changes the child rearing practices of immigrant Haitian and Jamaican parents are not well understood by most helping professionals. Moreover, there is a need for helping professionals who work with families to identify and discern parenting problems from problems related to cultural adjustment. This research suggests that psychosocial influences must be taken into consideration and are important in helping Haitian and Jamaican parents modulate child-rearing practices not culturally appropriate in their new country, the United States.

> In most cases, the more you attempt to write professional quality papers, the better you will get at writing professional quality papers.

PART 9: THE REFERENCE SECTION (NO PAGE LIMIT; DOUBLE-SPACED)

The *purpose of the reference section* is to cite all references mentioned in the text of your paper.

1. When citing references obtain and follow the "Information for Authors" that is provided by each journal editor.
2. Make careful note of the different ways that various types of literature are to be cited in the journal to which you intend to submit your article. The American Psychological Association Manual (1994) is specific on the way you cite different types of material using APA style.

HELPFUL HINTS FOR SUBMITTING A PAPER FOR PUBLICATION

1. If you are NOT familiar with the journal, you need to find out if they publish the kind of research you have done. The easiest way to determine this is to go to the library and review the publications over the last several years.
2. Select several journals that might be interested in your research. Pick the one you would most likely be published in and send in your paper. If your paper is rejected, send it out as soon as possible to an alternative journal.
3. *Never submit your paper to more than one journal at a time.* All professional journals have a policy against reviewing articles that are simultaneously being reviewed by another journal. If it is rejected by a journal, you can then submit it to another journal.
4. On average, about 1 in 5 papers submitted for peer review are accepted for publication. The best writers have had papers rejected by professional journals. Do not give up; send it off again.
5. Before being published, the average professional paper will have been submitted to three previous journals.
6. All journal articles have gone through several rewrites before they are finally published.
7. If your paper is rejected, correct the errors that were identified by the journal reviewers and resubmit it. You might consider trying journals in a different field with a focus compatible with your research.
8. Do not be discouraged; keep trying. Publishing professional papers can be difficult even for the best researchers and writers.

Most journals use the "blind review process" to determine if a paper is acceptable for publication in their journal. A blind review means that those reviewing the paper do not know who wrote it. The reviewers judge the paper solely on merit and preferences of the reviewers.

Take heart! No one is born to write professional journal articles; each of us has learned the hard way—by doing.

POSTSCRIPT

Good luck in your research and writing endeavors. I hope you found this book helpful in your effort.

REFERENCES

Charles, C. (1981). *A panorama of Haitian culture.* Project Maise.

Dyal, J. A., & Dyal, R. Y. (1981). Acculturation, stress and coping: Some implications for research and education. *International Journal of Intercultural Relations, 5,* 301–328.

Government Publications: *Bureau of the Census* (1991). United States Department of Commerce. Washington, D.C. 20233.

Lambert, M. C., Knight, F., & Weisz, J. R. (1989). Over- and under-controlled clinic referral problems of Jamaican and American children and adolescents: The culture general and the culture specific. *Journal of Consulting and Clinical Psychology, 54*(4), 467–472.

O'Guinn, T. C., Imperia, G., & MacAdams, E. A. (1987). Acculturation and perceived family decision-making input among Mexican-American wives. *Journal of Cross-Cultural Psychology, 18*(1), 73–93.

Publication manual of the American psychological association (4th ed.). (1994) Washington, DC: American Psychological Association.

Spradley, J. P., & Phillips, M. (1972). Culture and stress: A quantitative analysis. *American Anthropology, 74,* 518–519.

Glossary

Alternate Hypothesis A substitute explanation for a phenomenon if the originally stated hypothesis is not supported by the data when the hypothesis is tested.

Analysis of Variance (ANOVA) An inferential statistical method of data analysis that compares the means of two or more groups to determine if the means are statistically different.

Applied Research Research conducted to provide information or techniques that can be applied to the problems or needs of individuals, groups, or agencies; the opposite of pure research.

Average The mean, median and mode are examples of mathematical averages used in the helping professions.

Binomial Variable A variable that only has 2 attributes. For example, gender only has two attributes: male and female.

Bivariate Analysis The analysis of two variables at the same time to determine the empirical relationship between the two variables. Statistical procedures such as crosstabs table (also called crosstabulation or crossbreak table), t-test and the Pearson's correlation (r^2) are examples of statistical procedures that are used to do bivariate analyses.

Causal Relationship A relationship existing between at least two elements in which one element is causing change in the other element—for example, the causal relationship between the independent variable (level of education) and the dependent variable (personal income).

Central Categories The final categories constructed. "The ultimate goal of this process is the identification of core categories that explains the phenomenon" (Heppner, Kivlighan & Wampold, 1992).

Chi-Square Test A statistical test that can determine the existence of an association and/or independence between two nominal or two categorical variables. The test is based on a comparison of the actual observed frequencies of the two variables occurring in the population in the study and the expected frequencies of the variables if there were NO association between the two variables in the population.

Cluster Sample   A multistage sample in which natural groups are sampled initially, with the members of each selected group being sub-sampled afterward. For example, you might select a sample of U.S. colleges and universities from a directory, get lists of the students at all the selected schools, and then draw samples of the students from each. This procedure is discussed in Chapter 8.

Codebook   A book or list that identifies the codes used to represent each variable and their values. For example, the codebook might list Question 2 as a gender question. Male is coded as (1) and female is coded as (2). A codebook is very important, especially after time has elapsed, and you must go back to the raw data file.

Coding   The process whereby you assign codes (typically in the form of numbers) to variables and their values used in a study. Coding is done so that the values can be entered into a computer and analyzed.

Concept   Describes some commonality or relationship within a group of facts; a general idea about some phenomena, typically based on a number of observations.

Confidence Interval   The estimated probability that a population parameter lies within a given confidence interval (the range of values within which a population parameter is estimated to lie). For example, we might want to answer the question, "What percentage of registered voters would vote (today) for Candidate A?" Given appropriate survey results and the statistical analysis, we will be able to say with 95% confidence that between 35% and 45% of all registered voters would vote (today) for Candidate A.

Constant Comparison   A method of qualitative data analysis consisting of a systematic method for deductive data analysis (Glaser & Strauss, 1967). Using this approach, , the researcher begins to develop concepts and working hypotheses based on patterns emerging from inductive observations. Next the researcher conducts more interviews or collects more observations. This new data are compare to the concepts and tentative hypotheses developed from earlier interviews and observations. This approach continues until the researcher reaches "theoretical saturation"(Glaser & Strauss, 1967; Rubin & Babbie, 1997).

Construct Categories   A cluster of items organized together to characterize or measure aspects of a broader concept. These categories are made up of "analyst-constructed typologies." Construct categories are formed out of the *descriptive categories;* construct categories "should explain the descriptive categorizing and their interrelations" (Heppner, Kivlighan & Wampold, 1992).

Construct Validity   The degree to which a measuring devise (scale, inventory, etc.) measures the range of meanings of the hypothetical concept.

Control Group   In an experimental design, the group that receives either no treatment or a different treatment from that of the experimental group.

Control Variable   A variable that is not manipulated but held constant in an attempt to explain the relationship between the variables under study. Control variables are usually physical or mental characteristics of the subjects.

Criterion-Related Validity   Validity that is determined by performance on a test as compared to performance on another criteria. For example, you develop a scale to determine a student's success in graduate school. To establish criterion-related validity, you do a follow up study to determine if the students who did well on your test succeed in graduate school.

Cross Sectional Study   A study based on observations representing a single point in time. Thus, the study gathers the data for the analysis at one point in time. This differs from a longitudinal study, which gathers data over a long period of time.

Data (plural)   Data are measures of variables made under specific and known conditions that are gathered and analyzed. Datum is singular.

Deductive Reasoning   A reasoning process in which one moves from the general to the specific. Quantitative researchers use deductive reasoning when they combine several independent variables to predict change in a dependent variable. For example, we know that in the general population there is a strong correlation between level of education and life satisfaction. Accordingly, one might deduct and hypothesize that helping mothers with children living in housing projects) obtain a basic education and marketable job skills would result in their moving out of poverty. Testing this hypothesis would require a large, quantitative study of an intervention to provide education and marketable job skills to a large, stratified random sample of mothers with children living in public housing (see **inductive reasoning**).

Dependent Variable   The variable affected or changed by the *independent variable*. For example, if the average student's level of education is dependent in part on family income, then family income is an independent variable, and of course, the average student's level of education is the dependent variable.

Descriptive Categories   Categories made up of sets of participant remarks that are similar and that come directly from the language used by the participants. These are also referred to as "indigenous typologies" (Marshall & Rossman, 1989; Patton, 1990).

Descriptive Statistics   Statistical computations describing either the characteristics of a sample or the relationship among variables in a sample. Descriptive statistics merely summarize a set of sample observations.

Dichotomous Variable   A variable, like gender, that has only two characteristics or values.

Ecological Fallacy   Inferring attributes to individuals based on the observation collected about groups.

Experiment   A research technique or method that attempts to isolate the impact of an *independent* variable on a *dependent* variable under fixed and controlled conditions.

Face Validity   A judgement by the researcher that a scale or other instrument of measure seems to be a measure of a characteristic or trait. For example, because the frequency of good grades in school is an indication of a student's academic ability, it has face validity.

Factor Analysis   The resolution of a set of variables linearly in terms of a small number of categories or "factors." This resolution can be accomplished by the analysis of the correlation among the variables. A satisfactory solution will yield factors, which convey all the essential information of the original set of variables. The chief aim is to attain scientific parsimony or economy of description—data reduction.

Field Study   The process of collecting and analyzing detailed and descriptive observations of individuals and groups in a given setting.

Generalizability   The degree to which a research finding can be assumed to exist in a broader population than the sample from which the finding was obtained. As an example, would you generalize the findings about students in a southern university to all the college students in the United States?

Hawthorne Effect   A change in behavior among people who are being studied because they are being studied. The term comes from the experience of researchers who were involved in productivity studies at the Hawthorne plant of the Western Electric Company in Chicago, Illinois. The researchers found that the act of studying the workers affected the behavior of the workers. Today, the term refers to the impact of the research process on the people in the study.

Heterogeneous   Consisting of dissimilar elements or parts; not homogeneous.

Historical Research   A technique that uses previous observations and records (archival data) to address questions about events and the meaning of events in the past.

Homogeneous   Of the same or similar nature or kind.

Hypothesis   A statement about the nature of things typically based on theory. It is a testable statement about the relationship between two or more variables.

Hypothesis Testing   The procedure of determining whether the stated relationship between two or more variables is indeed found to exist in the real world.

Independent Variables   Cause or determine change in the characteristics of a *dependent variable*. For example, when you pay your bills (an independent variable), the money you have in the bank (the dependent variable) goes down.

Inductive Reasoning   A reasoning process where one uses specific observations to propose generalizations that apply to the whole. Qualitative researchers often use inductive reasoning. Based on the information gathered from a few mothers with children who were living in a housing project, one might suggest that a lack of education, and of marketable job skills was the reason these families were living in poverty.

Inferential Statistics   The assortment of statistical computations appropriate for making inferences from findings based on sample data to the larger population from which the sample data were collected. See also descriptive statistics.

Inverse Relationship   A relationship between two variables in which one variable increases in value as the other variable decreases in value. For example, when you pay your bills (an independent variable), the money you have in the bank (the dependent variable) goes down. There is an inverse relationship between the money in your bank account and the bills you pay.

Inferential Statistics   The ability to make inferences about the larger population based on a representative sample drawn from that population. Inferential statistics use an assortment of statistical computations for making inferences to the larger population from which the sample data were collected from findings based on the sample data.

Internal Validity   In experimental research, the issues as to whether or not the independent variable caused the effect observed in the dependent variable.

Interrater Reliability   The consistency among two or more independent observers who are scoring the same characteristic or behavior. The consistency of their scores is reflected in the degree of correlation among the observations made by the observers.

Interval Measure   A collapsed ratio variable that is based on predetermined equal intervals.

Intervening Variable   A variable (B) that exists between an independent variable (A) and a dependent variable (C). Consequently, the independent variable (A) affects the dependent variable (C) only by affecting the intervening variable (B), and the intervening variable (B) affects the dependent variable (C).

Judgmental Sample   A nonprobability sample where researchers use their own judgement about the individuals that best represent a larger population under study.

Key Informant   A person who has unique information about a situation you wish to study. For example, to begin a study of the success of a program to help families move from welfare to work, you contact several counselors who have been working on such a program in a housing project. After interviewing the key informants, you would interview individuals who were successful or unsuccessful in moving from welfare to work.

Law   In social research, like all science, a law is considered to be a universal generalization about classes of facts.

Level of Significance   The proportion of chance that an observed, empirical relationship can be attributed to sampling error. If a relationship is significant at the .05 level (p = .05), it means that there is only 5 chances in a 100 that the relationship is occurring by accident or because of sampling error.

Likert Scale   A scale with items using standardized response categories such as *strongly agree, agree, disagree,* and *strongly disagree.* This type of composite measure was developed by Rensis Likert to improve measurement in social research.

Longitudinal Research   Research involving the collection of data over an extended period of time, often over several years.

Matching   In experimental research, a technique for making sure individuals in both the experimental group and the control group are similar on specific characteristics that could affect the outcome of the intervention.

Mean   The arithmetic average of a set of scores; computed by summing a set of scores and dividing the sum by the number of scores in the set.

Median   Another type of average; the point in a distribution where 50% of the scores are above it and 50% of the scores are below it.

Mode   Another type of average; the score attained by more individuals than any other score on a specific variable.

Multivariate Analysis   The analysis of three or more variables at the same time so as to determine the empirical relationship between the three or more variables. Statistical procedures such as multiple regression, and analysis of variance are typically used for multivariate analyses.

Multiple Regression   A procedure for calculating the weights for each of several (two or more) independent variables (X_1 and X_2). Using their combined weights will give us the highest possible correlation between the predicted Y ($Y_{predicted}$) and observed values of the dependent (also called, criterion) variable Y ($Y_{observed}$).

Nonparametric Statistics   Statistics from variables that you assume are not normally distributed. The chi-square test is the most often used non-parametric test.

Nonprobability Sample   A sample in which the probability used to select each is unknown. For example, judgmental (purposive) and quota samples are nonprobability samples.

Null Hypothesis   A proposal based on theory, stating that there will be NO relationship between characteristics. The *null hypothesis* is the reverse of the hypothesis. For example, if we hypothesize that there is a relationship between poor family/social bonds and whether a child participates in juvenile behavior, the null hypothesis is that there is no relationship between poor family/social bonds and a child's participating in juvenile behavior.

Operational Definition   An empirical measure of a concept—for example, the operational definition of intelligence is an IQ test.

Paradigm   A fundamental model or conception that organizes our view of what we are studying.

Parameter   A specific value of a population that is used as a reference to determine the value of other population variables.

Parametric Test   Hypotheses tests (in the form of tests of significance) based on assumptions about the parameter values of the population. These tests of statistical significance require that at least one variable is an interval or ratio level of measure. The sample distribution of the interval or ratio variable(s) must be normally distributed. If you are comparing different groups, the members should be randomly assigned to each group. This will help meet the assumption that group members are independent of one another. The t-test, analysis of variance, and the Pearson product-moment correlation are examples of parametric tests.

Placebo   In medical research, often a harmless "sugar pill" or unmedicated preparation given to a person instead of a medicine. The person taking the medication would be a member of a control group for a medication study of the efficacy of an experimental medication. The effects of the placebo on each participant will be compared to the effect of the medication on members in the experimental group. Typically, 33.3% of the placebo group will have some positive improvement simply because they think the pill will help them. Consequently, the medication or intervention must have a positive affect on more than 33.3% of the experimental group members.

In the helping professions, a similar model is used to compare the affects of social and psychological interventions on experimental and control group members. See Box 2.5 in Chapter 2 for and example of using placebos in medical research. See the section "An Example of Spearman Correlation (r^s) in Chapter 19 for an example of how the placebo effect relates to statistics.

Plagiarism   Presenting the work of another in your study without citing the source.

Positive Relationship   A relationship between two variables where one variable increases or decreases in value as the other variable increases or decreases in value. For example, when you put your pay check into the bank (an independent variable), the amount of money you have in the bank (the dependent variable) goes up. There is a positive relationship between banking your pay check and the money in your bank account.

Posttest   In an experimental study, a measure of the dependent variable after the experimental intervention has been applied.

Pretest   In an experimental study, a measure of the dependent variable before the experimental intervention has been applied.

Probability Sample   A sample where the probability of being selected to be in the sample is known. A sample selected using probability theory and some type of random-sampling technique.

Qualitative Research   Qualitative methodology is based on the direct observation of behavior as it occurs. Its roots are in *field research*. Today it is most often referred to as *naturalistic research*. Qualitative (naturalistic) research is based on the phenomenological research traditions. "Phenomenological researchers attempt to understand how participants make meaning of and through their interaction" (Heppner, Kivlighan & Wampold, 1992).

The nonnumerical approach for collecting, analyzing and interpretation of observational data for the purpose of discovering underlying meanings and patterns of relationships. Field research and historical research are two examples.

Quantitative Research   The arithmetic measurement and analysis of independent and dependent variables used to represent characteristics such as behaviors, attitudes, and skills. It is the numerical expression of observations so that the observations can be described and used to explain the phenomena under study (see Chapter 5).

Quasi-Experimental Design   An experimental design in which some condition required to be a true experiment is not met. Most often, this condition is the inability to randomize group assignments.

Quota Sample   A type of nonprobability sampling where the researcher first identifies specific desired characteristics in the population (strata); then the sample is selected based on those specified characteristics. In this way, the sample will have the same distribution of characteristics as are found in the population being studied.

Random Error   The term "error in measurement" describes how far away the observed scores of a data set are from the predicted scores of the data set. Random error, unlike systematic error, has no consistent pattern; it varies from score to score. Consequently, random error decreases the reliability of the scale. Random error can be caused by questions on a scale that the participants do not understand.

Regression Toward the Mean   (also referred to as statistical regression). The phenomenon of expecting extremely high test scores on a measurement will be followed by test scores closer to the mean. For example, a person who typically receives averages grades (78%) on math tests obtains an extremely high score on a math test (100%). The principle known as regression toward the mean would suggest that on the next math test the person's test score would be lower. On the next math test, the person's score is 80%. The reason for this change in math test scores might not be a lack of studying, but might be the result of the phenomenon regression toward the mean. Extreme scores above or below the mean tend to be followed by scores closer to the mean score. In this case, a score of 80% is closer to the mean of 78% than 100%.

Reliable and Valid Measures   In Quantitative (statistical) Research in the helping professions, these measures tend to be psychosocial scales that measure such things as *self-image, locus of control, depression,* and *motivation to study.* These scales give us the level of intensity and direction. For the *depression* and *motivation* scales, we are given a level of intensity of feelings. For the *self-image* and *locus of control* scales, we are given the direction to which the participants lean.

Reliability   That quality of a measurement method suggesting that the same data would have been collected each time in repeated observations of the same phenomenon. In other words, the reliability of a measure or a scale depends on its ability to produce consistent results each time it is used.

Replicating a Previous Study   Trying to reproduce a study in every way to see if you get the same results.

Representativeness   The degree of representativeness tells us to what degree the sample is like the population as a whole. In terms of developing a specific therapeutic intervention, if a psychotherapeutic group to increase family bonds was effective with a *representative* experimental group, it it very likely to work with many similar families.

Representative Sample   A sample that is much the same as or that has the distribution of characteristics found in the larger population from which the sample was selected. Because of this relationship between the sample and the larger population, descriptions and explanations obtained from an analysis of the sample may be assumed to adequately the population from which the sample was selected. The likelihood of representativeness is enhanced using probability sampling techniques. An extremely important point: A probability sample meets one of the assumptions necessary to use inferential statistics to analyze the data collected from the sample. These procedures allow the findings to be generalized to the larger population.

Research Design   A detailed plan outlining how the research hypothesis will be tested or the method that will be used to test the hypothesis. It is composed of the concepts and techniques that are employed in the research study.

Research Question   A question about a problem or condition that is not based on any theoretical framework, such as asking young women without college plans who score in the upper quartile on the SAT why they do not plan to attend college.

Sample   A group of subjects, selected according to accepted standards of sampling theory, that will participate in a scientific study.

Sampling Frame   A list of all of the elements of a population from which the sample is selected. All or almost all members of the population under study must be included in the sampling frame.

Sampling Interval   The equal distance between units from a population for a sample, selecting every kth person.

Scale   A set of items (typically more than one item) used for measuring a property or characteristic such as depression. The measure is composed of items that have logical or empirical structure. A quantitative score is usually derived from the measure.

Simple Random Sample   The simplest probability sampling approach. It is a sample where each unit (for example, people) found in a population of interest had an equal chance of being selected to be members of the sample for the study.

Simple Regression   A procedure for using the known value on an independent variable (X) to predict an unknown value on the dependent variable (Y).

Single-Subject Design   A quasi-experimental design featuring continuous or near continuous measurement of the dependent variable on a single research subject over a time interval that is divided into a baseline phase and one or more phases during which the independent variable is manipulated. The experimental effects are inferred by comparisons of the subject's responses between the baseline and intervention phases.

Statistic   A summarization of data; a numerical statement about a group of observations. It utilizes numbers to describe the results, for example, of testing a hypothesis. The Pearson's r correlation between level of education and level of income is a statistic.

Statistical Significance   A term used to indicate that a finding in a social research study did not likely occur by chance. For example, I have consistently found a statistically significant relationship between age and income among full-time employees.

Stratified Random Sampling   A probability sampling procedure. The population is first divided into strata (for example, education level: high school, undergraduate, master level and doctoral level). Then random sampling procedures are used to obtain a sample of participants from each stratum. This approach tends to improve the representativeness of a sample.

Survey A data-collecting technique used to gather information from individuals who respond to specific questions related to the focus of the study.

Systematic Error A type of error in measurement that has a uniform effect on the results. This error is derived from systematic bias. Unlike random error, the degree of systematic error does not vary from person to person. It is a constant and steady influence. Systematic error decreases the validity of measurement but does not necessarily decrease the measure's reliability. Systematic error can be caused by asking questions of participants who might systematically lie about the answer (for example, asking police officers, "Have you ever used an illegal drug?")

Systematic sample A type of probability sample where after a random starting number is selected, every kth unit on a list is selected for inclusion in the sample. kth in research jargon stands for an equal interval used to select the sample. For example, if we choose every 100th person on a list of students, kth = 100. If we choose every 25th person on a list of students, kth = 25.

t-Test A statistical test to determine if there is a statistically significant difference between the averages/means of 2 groups on 1 variable (for example, a score on a scale like depression), or to determine if there is a statistically significant difference between scores on a *pretest* and *posttest* taken by the same group.

Test-Retest Reliability An approach used to test the consistency, or stability, of a measure used at two or more points in time.

Triangulation The use of more than one imperfect data collection alternative in which each option is vulnerable to different potential sources of error. For example, instead of relying exclusively on a client's self-report of how often a particular target behavior occurred during a specified period, a significant other (teacher, cottage parent, and so on) is asked to monitor the behavior as well.

Type I Error A Type I error (level of significance), is based on the statistical probability of the relationship occurring by chance. The Greek letter alpha (α) symbolizes Type I error.

Type II Error A Type II error is called power. This suggests there is power in the ability to reject the null hypothesis when it should be rejected. In statistical jargon we say, a Type II error is taking the risk of rejecting a null hypothesis.

Typology A typology is a systematic classification of characteristics and traits that the participants or groups of participants have in common.

Units of Analysis The individual units in your sample are the units of analysis. The basic unit to be measured: the individual, a group, an agency, a department, a community, etc.

Univariate Analysis This is the analysis of one variable at a time. It describes one characteristic of a population or sample at a time.

Unobtrusive Observation A situation in which the observer's discretion prevents those being observed from knowing it. An example is gathering data about the educational level of health care clients from their case records.

Validity A descriptive term used for a measure that accurately reflects the concept it is intended to measure. For example, your IQ would seem a more valid measure of your intelligence than would the number of hours you spend in the library.

Variable The logical grouping of characteristics such as gender. For example, gender is made up the attributes of female and male.

References

Aaron, H. J. (1975). Cautionary notes on the experiment. In Pechman, J. A., & Timpane, P. M. (Eds.). *Work incentives and income guarantees* (pp. 168–189). Washington, D.C.: Brookings Institution.

Alba, R. D. (1985). *Italian-Americans: Into the twilight of ethnicity.* Englewood Cliffs, NJ: Prentice Hall.

Anthony, J. C., & Helzer, J. E. (1991). Syndromes of drug abuse and dependence. In L. N. Robin & D. A. Regier (Eds.) *Psychiatric disorders in America: The epidemiologic catchment area study.* New York: Free Press (116–154).

Ashford, J. B., Lecroy, C. W., & Lortie, K. L. (1997). *Human behavior in the social environment: A multidimensional perspective.* Pacific Grove, CA: Brooks/Cole.

Baker, T. L. (1994). *Doing social research* (2nd ed.). New York: McGraw-Hill.

Barlow, D. H., & Hersen, M. (1984). *Single case experimental design: Strategies for studying behavioral change.* New York: Pergamon.

Blalock, H. M. (1971). *Causal models in the social sciences.* Chicago: Aldine.

Block, J. H., Block, J., & Roberts, G. (1984). Continuity and change in parents' child rearing practices. (Rev., McPherson and Cherry, 1991). *Child Development, 55*(2), 586–597.

Blythe, B. J., & Tripodi, T. (1989). *Measurement in direct practice.* Newbury Park, CA: Sage.

Bhaskar, R. (1989). *Reclaiming reality: A critical introduction to contemporary philosophy.* London: Verso.

Bing J. R., & Cherry, A. L. (1987). Assessment of student teachers by college supervisors. *Psychological Reports, 61,* 275–283.

Boom, M., Fischer, J., & Orme, J. (1995). Evaluating practice: Guidelines for the accountable professional (2nd ed.) Boston: Allyn & Bacon.

Brase, H. B., & Brase, C. O. (1991). *Understandable statistics: Concepts and methods.* Lexington, MA: D. C. Heath.

Brecher, E. M. (1972). *Licit & illicit drugs.* Boston: Little, Brown.

Bromley, D. B. (1986). *The case-study method in psychology and related disciplines.* New York: Wiley.

Brookins, G. K. (1993). Culture, ethnicity and bicultural competence: Implications for children with chronic illness and disability. *Pediatrics, 91,* 1056–1062.

Buechier, S. (1990). *Women's movement in the United States.* New Brunswick, NJ: Rutgers University.

Burning, J., & Kintz, B. (1987). *Computation handbook of statistics* (3rd ed.). Glenview, IL: HarperCollins.

Buss, A. H., & Perry, M. (1992). The aggression questionnaire. *Journal of personality and social psychology, 63,* 452–459.

Campbell, D. P., & Stanley, J. C. (1963). *Experimental and quasi experimental designs for research.* Boston: Houghton Mifflin.

Carlton-Laney, I. (1997). Elizabeth Ross Haynes: An African American reformer of womanist consciousness. *Social work, 42*(6), 573–583.

Cary, M. P., Gordon, C. M., Morrison-Beedy, D & Mclean, D. A. (1997). Low-income women and HIV risk reduction: Elaborations from qualitative research. *AIDS and behavior, 1*(3), 163–168.

Cattell, R. B. (1957). *Personality and motivation structure and measurement.* New York: Harcourt, Brace & World.

Chambers, D. E. (1995). Economic analysis. In L. R. Edwards (Ed.), *Encyclopedia of social work* (19th ed., pp. 829–831). Washington, D.C.: NASW

Chambers, D. E., Wedel, K. R., & Rodwell, M. K. (1992). *Evaluating social programs.* Boston: Allyn & Bacon.

Charles, C. (1981). *A panorama of Haitian culture.* Project Maise.

Chernow, B. A., & Vallasi, G. A. (Eds.). (1993). *The Columbia encyclopedia*(5th ed.). New York: Columbia University.

Cherry, A. L. (1987). Social bond theory and alcohol use among college students. *Journal of College Student Personnel, 28*(2), 128–135.

Cherry, A. L. (1987). Undergraduate alcohol misuse: Suggested strategies for prevention and early detection. *Journal of Alcohol and Drug Education, 32*(3), 1–6.

Cherry, A. L. (1992). Separation anxiety and school phobia: An intervention to revive the school bond. *Case Analysis: In Social Science and Social Therapy, 3,* 3–10.

Cherry, A. L. (1993). Combining cluster and discriminant analysis to develop a social bond typology of runaway youth. *Research on Social Work Practice, 3*(2), 175–190.

Cherry, A. L. (1994). *The socializing instinct: Individual, family, and social bonds.*Westport, CT: Praeger, Greenwood.

Cherry, A. L., Cherry, M. E., & Sainz, A. (Jan. 1998). *A six-year longitudinal study of a substance abuse prevention program: Instrument construction and measuring effectiveness.* A conference presentation at the Research for Social Work Practice International Conference, Miami, FL.

Cherry, A. L., & Dillon, M. E. (unpublished manuscript, 1999). *Moving from welfare to work: Six years later in two housing projects.*

Cohen, J. (1969). *Statistical power analysis for the behavioral sciences.* New York: Academic.

Cohen, J., & Cohen, P. (1975). *Applied multiple regression/correlation analysis for the behavioral sciences.* Hillsdale, NJ: Lawrence Erlbaum.

Cote, J. E. (1992). Was Mead wrong about coming of age in Samoa? An analysis of the Mead/Freeman controversy for scholars of adolescence and human development. *Journal of Youth and Adolescence, 21*(5), 499–528.

Craft, John. (1990). *Statistics and data analysis for social work.* Itasca, IL: F. E. Peacock.

Croskey, L. (Spring 1999). *An analysis of personal psychological and cognitive factors between pregnant and/or parenting and never pregnant black adolescent females.* Barry University School of Social Work, Miami Shores, FL. Available from University Microfilm Inter, Mich.

DeParle, J (1996, October 20). Slamming the door: The low-wage jobs of the new economy cannot pay the rent. *New York Times* [Sunday Edition], p. 6–52.

Devore, W., & Schlesinger, E. G. (1991). *Ethnic-sensitive social work practice* (3rd ed.). New York: Macmillan.

Duncan, O. D. (1966). Path analysis: Sociological examples. *American Journal of Sociology, 72,* 1–16.

Dunlap, K. (1996). Supporting and empowering families through cooperative preschool education. *Social Work in Education, 18*(4), 210–221.

Dyal, J. A., & Dyal, R. Y. (1981). Acculturation, stress and coping: Some implications for research and education. *International Journal of Intercultural Relations, 5,* 301–328.

Ewalt, P. L.& Mulroy, E. A. (1997). Locked out: Welfare reform, housing reform, and the fate of affordable housing. (Editorial) *Social Work, 42*(1), 5–6.

Faden, R. R., & Beauchamp, T. L. (1986). *A history and theory of informed consent.* New York: Oxford University Press.

Fisher J., & Corcoran, K. J. (1994). *Measures for clinical practice: A sourcebook* (2nd ed.). New York: Free Press.

Gay, L. R. (1987). *Educational research* (3rd ed.,).Columbus, OH: Merrill.

Gilgun, J. F. (1990). Steps in the development of theory using a grounded theory approach. *Qualitative Family Research Newsletter, 42*(2), 11–12.

Gillespie, D. (1995). Ethical issues in research. In L. R. Edwards (Ed.), *Encyclopedia of social work* (19th ed., p. 884). Washington, D.C.: NASW.

Glaser, B., & Strauss, A. (1967). *The discovery of grounded theory.* Chicago: Aldine.

Goldberg, G. S., & Kremen, E. (1990). *The feminization of poverty: Only in America?* New York: Praeger.

Government Publications: Bureau of the Census (1991). United States Department of Commerce. Washington, D.C. 20233

Gravetter, F. J., & Wallnau, L. B. (1985). *Statistics for the behavioral sciences.* New York: West.

Gustavsson, N. S., & Segal, E. A. (1994). *Critical issues in child welfare.* Thousand Oaks, CA: Sage.

Gyarfas, M., 1983. The scientific imperative again. *Social service review, 57,* 149–150.

Heatherington, L., Friedlander, M. L., & Johnson, W. F. (1989). Informed consent in family therapy research: Ethical dilemmas and practical problems. *Journal of Family Psychology, 2,* 373–385.

Heise, D. (1975). *Causal analysis.* New York: Wiley.

Heppner, P.P., Kivlighan, D. M., & Wampold, B. E. (1992). *Research design in counseling.* Pacific Grove, CA: Brooks/Cole.

Ho, M. K. (1987). *Family therapy with ethnic minorities.* Newbury Park, CA: Sage.

Hooyman, N. R. (1994). Diversity and population at risk: Women. In F. Reamer (Ed.), *The foundations of social work knowledge.* New York: Columbia University Press.

Hoshmand, L. L. (1989). Alternative research paradigms: A review and teaching proposal. *The counseling psychologist, 17,* 3–79.

Isaac, S. (1978). *Handbook on social research and evaluation.* San Diego, CA: Edits.

Jayaratne, S. (1977). Single-subject and group designs in treatment evaluation. *Social Work Research and Abstracts, 13*(3), 35-44.

Jones, J. (1981). *Bad blood: The Tuskegee syphilis experiment.* New York: Free Press.

Kamerman, S. (1995). Gender role and family structure changes in the advanced industrialized west: Implications for social policy. In K. McFate, R. Laeson, & W. J. Wilson (Eds.), *Poverty Inequality and the future of social policy: Western states in the new world order* (pp. 231–256). New York: Russell Sage Foundation.

Karis, J. M., & Wandrei, K. E. (1995). Person-in-environment. In L. R. Edwards (Ed.), *Encyclopedia of social work* (19th ed. pp. 1818–1827). Washington, D.C.: NASW.

Katzer, J., Cook, K. H., & Crouch, W. W. (1991). Evaluation information: A guide for users of social science research (3rd ed.). New York: McGraw-Hill.

Kleinbaum, D. G., & Kupper, L. L. (1978). *Applied regression analysis and other multivariable methods.* Belmont, CA: Duxbury.

Kuhn, T. S. (1970). *The structure of scientific revolutions.* Chicago: University of Chicago Press.

Lambert, M. C., Knight, F., & Weisz, J. R. (1989). Over- and under-controlled clinic referral problems of Jamaican and American children and adolescents: The culture general and the culture specific. *Journal of Consulting and Clinical Psychology, 54*(4), 467–472.

Leary, W. E. (1993). Black hypertension may reflect other ills. *New York Times* (Oct. 22), B6.

Levy, R. L., & Olson, D. G. (1979). The single-subject methodology in clinical practice: An overview. *Journal of Social Service Research, 3,* 25–49.

Liebow, Elliot (1967). *Tally's corner.* Boston: Little Brown.

Lindeman, R. H., Merenda, P. F., & Gold, R. Z. (1980). *Introduction to bivariate and multivariate analysis.* Glenville, IL: Scott, Foresman.

Lindsey, E. (1997). Feminist issues in qualitative research with formerly homeless mothers. *AFFILIA Journal of Women & Social Work 12*(1), 57–75.

Lofland, J., & Lofland, L. H. (1995). *Analyzing social settings* (3rd ed.). Belmont, CA: Wadsworth.

Maas, H. S. (1966). *Five fields of social service: Review of research.* New York: National Association of Social Work.

Manning, S. S. (1997). The social worker as a moral citizen. *Social Work, 42*(3), 223–230.

Marlow, C. (1993). *Research methods for generalist social work.* Pacific Grove, CA: Brooks/Cole.

Marshall, C., & Rossman, G. (1989). *Designing qualitative research.* Newbury Park, CA: Sage.

Matocha, L. K. (1992). Case study interviews: Caring for persons with AIDS. In J. F. Gilgun, K. Daly, & G. Handel (Eds.), *Qualitative Methods in Family Research* (66–84). Newbury Park, CA: Sage.

Matyas, T. A., & Greenwood, K. M. (1991). Problems in the estimation of autocorrelation in brief time series and some implications for behavioral data. *Behavioral Assessment, 13,* 137–157.

McCracken, G. (1988). The long interview. *Qualitative research methods series No. 13.* Newbury Park, CA: Sage.

McFate, K. (1995). Trampolines, safety nets, or free fall. In K. McFate, R. Laeson, & W. J. Wilson (Eds.) *Poverty Inequality and the future of social policy: Western states in the new world order* (pp. 631–663). New York: Russell Sage Foundation.

McPherson-Blake, P. (1991). *Psychosocial factors associated with the immigration of Haitians and Jamaicans to South Florida and changes in their parental role.* Barry University School of Social Work, Miami Shores, Florida. Available from *Dissertation Abstracts International, 52-11A,* page 4092, 00229 pages.

McRoy, R. (1995). Qualitative research. In L. R. Edwards (Ed.), *Encyclopedia of social work* (19th ed., pp. 2009–2015). Washington, D.C.: NASW.

McGee, C. (1997). Children's experiences of domestic violence. *Child and Family Social Work, 2*(1), 13–23.

Mead, M. (1933), *Coming of age in Samoa.* New York: Morrow

Miller, M. C. (1992). Political ads: Decoding hidden messages. *Columbia Journalism Review, 30*(5), 36–39

Miller, R. S., & Lefcourt, H. M. (1982). The assessment of social intimacy. *Journal of Personality Assessment, 46,* 514–518.

Monette, D. R. (1986). *Applied social research: Tools for the social services.* New York: Holt, Rinehart and Winston.

Montgomery, R. V., Gonyea, J. G., & Hooyman, N. R. (1985). Caregiving and the experience of subjective and objective burden. *Family Relations, 34*(1), 19–26.

Montgomery, R. V.; Stull, D. E., & Borgatta, E. F. (1985). Measurement and the analysis of burden. *Research on Aging, 7*(1), 137–152.

Munir, K., & Earls, F (1992). Ethical principals governing research in child and adolescent psychiatry. *Journal of the American Academy of Child and Adolescent Psychiatry, 31*(3), 408–414.

Myers, L. L., & Thyer, B. A. (1997). Should social work clients have the right to effective treatment? *Social work, 42*(3), 288–298.

Nachmias, D., & Nachmias, C. (1987). *Research methods in the social sciences.* New York: St. Martin's.

Newman, B. S. (1994). Diversity and populations at risk: ays and lesbians. In F. Reamer (Ed.), *The foundations of social work knowledge.* New York: Columbia University Press.

Norušis, M. J. (1990). *SPSS Advanced statistics student guide.* Chicago: SPSS, Inc.

O'Guinn, T. C., Imperia G., & MacAdams, E. A. (1987). Acculturation and perceived family decision-making input among Mexican-American wives. *Journal of Cross-Cultural Psychology, 18*(1), 73–93.

Patton, M. (1990). *Qualitative evaluation methods.* Newbury Park, CA: Sage.

Payton, O. D. (1988). *Research: The validation of clinical practice* (2nd ed.). Philadelphia, PA: F. A. Davis.

Pedhazur, E. (1982). *Multiple regression in behavior research* (2nd ed.). New York: Holt, Rinehart, & Winston.

Piven, F. F., & Cloward, R. A.(1971). *Regulating the poor: The function of public welfare.* New York: Vintage.

Plake, B. S., & Parker, C. S. (1982). Mathematics anxiety rating scale-revised (MARS-R). *Education and psychological, 42,* 551–557.

Polansky, N. A. (1975). *Social work research* (2nd ed.). Chicago: University of Chicago Press.

Popple, P. R., & Leighninger, L. (1996). *Social work, social welfare, and American society.* Boston: Allyn & Bacon.

Publication manual of the American psychological association. (1994) 4th ed., Washington, DC: American Psychological Association.

Raju, Kariavanon-M. (1992). *Psychosocial adjustment of caregivers to the frail elderly.* Barry University School of Social Work, MiamiShores, Florida. Available from *Dissertation Abstracts International,* 52-11-A. Page 4093, 00171 pages.

Regehr, C.& Antle, B. (1997). Coercive influences: Informed consent in court-mandated social work practice. *Social Work, 42*(3), 300–306.

Reid, W. (1987). Research in social work. In A. Minahan (Ed.), *Encyclopedia of social work* (18th ed., Vol 2, pp. 474–487). Spring, MD: National Association of Social Work.

Rennie, D. L., Phillips, J. R., & Quartaro, G. K. (1988). Grounded theory: A promising approach into conceptualization in psychology? *Canadian Psychology/Psychologie Canadienne, 29,* 139–150.

Robinson, J. P., Shaver, P. R., & Wrightsman, L. S. (1991). *Measure of personality and social psychological attitudes.* New York: Academic.

Rubin, A., & Babbie, E. (1997). *Research methods for social work* (3rd ed.) Pacific Grove, CA: Brooks/Cole.

Rummel, R. J. (1970). *Applied factor analysis.* Evanston, IL: Northwestern University Press.

Scalise, J.J., Ginter E. J., & Gerstein, L. H. (1984). A multidimensional loneliness measure: The loneliness rating Scale (LSR). *Journal of Personality Assessment, 48,* 525–530.

Schuerman, J. (1982). The obsolete scientific imperative in social work research. *Social Service Review, 56,* 144–127.

Sedlack, R. G. and Stanley, J. (1992). *Social research: Theory and method.* Boston: Allyn & Bacon.

Segal, M. (1988). Should you take aspirin to help prevent a heart attack. *FDA Consumer, 22,* June.

Selltiz, C., Wrightsman, L. S., & Cook, S. W. (1976). *Research methods in social relationships* (3rd ed.). New York: Holt, Rinehart, & Winston.

Singleton, R. A., Straits, B. C., & Straits, M. M. (1993). *Approaches to social research* (2nd ed.). New York: Oxford University Press.

Skidmore, F. (1975) Operational design of the experiment. In Pechman, J. A., & Timpane, P. M. (Eds.). *Work incentives and income guarantees* (pp. 168–189). Washington, D.C.: Brookings Institution.

Soukhanov, A. H. (ed.) (1992). *The American heritage dictionary of the English language* (3rd ed.). New York: Houghton Mifflin.

Spradley, J. P., & Phillips, M. (1972). Culture and stress: A quantitative analysis. *American Anthropology, 74,* 518–519.

Theodoratus, R. J. (1997). Not even wrong: Margaret Mead, Derek Freeman, and the Samoans. *The Social Science Journal, 34*(1), 344–443.

Thomas, E. J., & Rothman, J. (1994). An integrative perspective on intervention research. In J. Rothman & E. J. Thomas (Eds.), *Intervention Research* (pp. 1–15). New York: Haworth.

Thyer, B. (1992). Clinical anxiety scale (CAS). In Hudson, W. W. (1992). *The WALMYR assessment scales scoring manual.* Tempe, AZ: WALMYR.

Twaite, J. A., Monroe, J. A. (1979). *Introductory statistics.* Glenville, IL: Scott, Foresman.

Tyson, K. (1995). *New foundations for scientific social and behavioral research: The heuristic paradigm.* Boston: Allyn & Bacon.

Warren, M. (1998, Spring). *Resiliency and at-risk children: An analysis of factors impacting on the development of resiliency.* Barry University School of Social Work, Miami Shores, FL. Available from University Microfilm International, Michigan. DAI, Vol. 58-12A, Page 4815, 00181 pages.

Wilkinson, W. K., & McNeil, K. (1996). *Research for the helping professions.* Pacific Grove, CA: Brooks/Cole.

Wolpe, J. (1990). *Practice of behavior therapy* (4th ed.). New York: Pergamon.

York, R. O. (1997). *Building competencies in social work research: An experiential approach.* Boston: Allyn & Bacon.

Index

TO THE OWNER OF THIS BOOK:

I hope that you have found *A Research Primer for the Helping Professions* useful. So that this book can be improved in a future edition, would you take the time to complete this sheet and return it? Thank you.

School and address: _____

_____

Department: _____

Instructor's name: _____

1. What I like most about this book is: _____

_____

_____

2. What I like least about this book is: _____

_____

_____

3. My general reaction to this book is: _____

_____

_____

4. The name of the course in which I used this book is: _____

_____

5. Were all of the chapters of the book assigned for you to read? _____

   If not, which ones weren't? _____

6. In the space below, or on a separate sheet of paper, please write specific suggestions for improving this book and anything else you'd care to share about your experience in using this book.

_____

_____

OPTIONAL:

Your name: _____ Date: _____

May we quote you, either in promotion for *A Research Primer for the Helping Professions*, or in future publishing ventures?

Yes: _____ No: _____

Sincerely yours,

Andrew L. Cherry, Jr.